Shipping Interdiction and the Law of the Sea

In this comparative study of shipping interdiction, Douglas Guilfoyle considers the state action of stopping, searching and arresting foreign flag vessels and crew on the high seas in cases such as piracy, slavery, drug smuggling, fisheries management, migrant smuggling, the proliferation of weapons of mass destruction and maritime terrorism. Interdiction raises important questions of jurisdiction, including how permission to board a foreign vessel is obtained, whether boarding-state or flag-state law applies during the interdiction (or whether both apply), and which state has jurisdiction to prosecute any crimes discovered. Rules on the use of force and protection of human rights, compensation for wrongful interdiction and the status of boarding-state officers under flag-state law are also examined. A unified and practical view is taken of the law applicable across existing interdiction regimes based on an extensive survey of state practice.

Douglas Guilfoyle is a Lecturer at University College London, where he teaches public law and public international law.

CAMBRIDGE STUDIES IN INTERNATIONAL AND COMPARATIVE LAW

Established in 1946, this series produces high quality scholarship in the fields of public and private international law and comparative law. Although these are distinct legal sub-disciplines, developments since 1946 confirm their interrelation.

Comparative law is increasingly used as a tool in the making of law at national, regional and international levels. Private international law is now often affected by international conventions, and the issues faced by classical conflicts rules are frequently dealt with by substantive harmonisation of law under international auspices. Mixed international arbitrations, especially those involving state economic activity, raise mixed questions of public and private international law, while in many fields (such as the protection of human rights and democratic standards, investment guarantees and international criminal law) international and national systems interact. National constitutional arrangements relating to 'foreign affairs', and to the implementation of international norms, are a focus of attention.

The Board welcomes works of a theoretical or interdisciplinary character, and those focusing on the new approaches to international or comparative law or conflicts of law. Studies of particular institutions or problems are equally welcome, as are translations of the best work published in other languages.

A list of books in the series can be found at the end of this volume.

Shipping Interdiction and the Law of the Sea

Douglas Guilfoyle

CAMBRIDGE
UNIVERSITY PRESS

CAMBRIDGE UNIVERSITY PRESS
Cambridge, New York, Melbourne, Madrid, Cape Town, Singapore, São Paulo, Delhi

Cambridge University Press
The Edinburgh Building, Cambridge CB2 8RU, UK

Published in the United States of America by Cambridge University Press, New York

www.cambridge.org
Information on this title: www.cambridge.org/9780521760195

First published 2009

Printed in the United Kingdom at the University Press, Cambridge

A catalogue record for this publication is available from the British Library

Library of Congress Cataloguing in Publication data
Guilfoyle, Douglas.
　Shipping interdiction and the law of the sea / Douglas Guilfoyle.
　　p.　cm. – (Cambridge studies in international and comparative law)
　Includes bibliographical references and index.
　ISBN 978-0-521-76019-5 (hardback)　1. Seizure of vessels and cargoes.
　2. Jurisdiction over ships at sea.　3. Maritime law–Criminal provisions.
　4. Law enforcement.　I. Title.　II. Series.
　KZ6580.G85 2009
　341.4′5–dc22　　　2009018066

ISBN 978-0-521-76019-5 hardback

Contents

Foreword

Part of the fascination of the law of the sea is the way in which – despite major technological change – similar problems are faced, and familiar legal concepts deployed, over generations and even centuries. This is true of many of the issues addressed so adeptly by Douglas Guilfoyle in his work on interdiction of foreign ships at sea. We have piracy still with us, a subject dealt with in more detail by the 1982 Law of the Sea Convention than maritime delimitation. We have the old law of hot pursuit adapted to expanded maritime zones. We have *The Lotus*, which concerned jurisdiction to prescribe not to enforce, but which stipulated, *a fortiori*, a flag-state monopoly of high seas enforcement which constitutes the main challenge for those concerned to interdict suspect ships or cargos at sea.

At the same time, facing the relatively simple and well-known jurisdictional rules for high seas interdiction in time of 'peace' we have a range of old and new challenges to international and national law – people smuggling as well as drug smuggling, illicit fisheries, the suspected transport of weapons of mass destruction or of strategically interdicted cargos, and so on. Some of these problems may be transient – like the 'pirate radio stations' of the 1960s. Others are perennial.

As Guilfoyle shows, underlying every lawful interdiction there must be jurisdiction not only to enforce by the very act of boarding and inspection but also to enforce through prosecution and confiscation, disposal or return. That jurisdiction may be distributed among different states. It is more sustainable, and usually simpler from an operational point of view, to use existing recognized jurisdictions (especially that of the flag state) than to assert or invent new ones, via Chapter VII of the United Nations Charter or otherwise. This search for sustainable solutions helps to explain the quite high levels of co-operation revealed in state practice, for example in the various ship-rider schemes and the conclusion of a range of bilateral and regional treaties and arrangements on such matters as drug trafficking (supplementing the UN Narcotics Convention of 1988) and interdiction of weapons of mass destruction and precursor material.

This book both assembles and organises the now extensive legal materials but explains them in a balanced and informed way. Douglas Guilfoyle's grasp not only of the law but also the practice (and the underlying practicalities) is most impressive. His will become the standard work in its field.

James Crawford
Lauterpacht Centre for International Law

Preface

This work reflects the law as it stood, to the best of the author's knowledge, on 14 August 2008, unless otherwise indicated. The discussion of piracy off Somalia, however, was updated to cover the numerous developments to 31 December 2008. In quoted material some spellings may have been regularised for consistency with the general text. On occasion, the author's translation of certain material is presented as a quotation. In such cases the original text is presented in the footnote.

An earlier draft of Chapters 2 and 9 was published as 'Maritime interdiction of weapons of mass destruction' (2007) 12 *Journal of Conflict and Security Law* 1. The case study on Somali piracy in section 4.1.8 was first published as 'Piracy off Somalia: UN Security Council Resolution 1816 and IMO regional counter-piracy efforts' (2008) 57 *International and Comparative Law Quarterly* 690. Earlier versions of the author's arguments relating to the law of countermeasures in Chapter 6, section 6, and Chapter 10, section 3.2, appeared as 'Interdicting vessels to enforce the common interest: maritime countermeasures and the use of force' (2007) 56 *International and Comparative Law Quarterly* 69.

All website addresses were accurate as at 14 August 2008.

Acknowledgements

While writing may be a solitary activity, it does not occur in isolation. This book began as a doctoral dissertation at Cambridge, where I was enormously fortunate in the support I received over three years of study. First and particular thanks are due to my supervisor, Professor James Crawford, whose commitment to students is exemplary. I benefited greatly from his extraordinarily prompt and detailed comments on drafts; this work would have been very much the poorer without his influence.

I must also thank those practitioners and academics who were kind enough to speak to me about my research, some several times, or to offer comments on earlier drafts of certain chapters. I am especially grateful to Dr Rosalie Balkin, Annabelle Bolt, Professor Jane Dalton, Amos Donoghue, Ricardo Federizon, Vladimir Fedorenko, Dame Hazel Fox, Dr John Kalish, Lt Commander Brad Kieserman, Holly Koehler, Professor Dennis Mandsager, Peter McColl, Joao Neves, Wayne Raabe, Dr Rosemary Rayfuse, Captain J. Ashley Roach (Ret.), Abda Sharif, Leo Strowbridge, Chris Trelawny, Deirdre Warner-Kramer and Mark Zanker, among many others. Nothing in this book should be taken, however, as representing the views of others or the organisations for which they work.

The topic of this work was suggested in the course of writing a master's thesis under the supervision of Professor Christine Gray. I was lucky to have the benefit of her early influence and continued support. I was fortunate also in having Professor Bill Gilmore and Dr Roger O'Keefe as my doctoral examiners. Their thorough, challenging and helpful comments greatly improved the present work. Ultimate responsibility for the present text and any errors in it, of course, remains with me.

I gratefully acknowledge the generous financial support of the Gates Cambridge Trust throughout my doctoral study, as well as funding provided by the UK government's Overseas Research Students Award Scheme. Trinity Hall and the Faculty of Law's Yorke Fund provided vital grants for travel.

A researcher also benefits from a supportive environment. I owe the Trinity Hall community a great debt: individual friends will excuse my not singling them out. Similarly, among law research students, the Cherry Blossoms were (and continue to be) fabulously generous colleagues and friends. Particular thanks must go to those who read parts of this work in draft, especially Isabelle Van Damme, Kimberley Trapp and Alex Mills. Kerry Tetzlaff checked my Italian translations and Efthymios Papastavridis helped me to find a number of treaties. The final text of this book was prepared during a month spent at the Lauterpacht Centre for International Law, where I had the benefit, among many others, of sharing a desk with Natalie Klein and the proof-reading of John Morss. I would also like to thank Finola O'Sullivan, Jodie Barnes and Richard Woodham at Cambridge University Press, as well as the copy-editor Philippa Youngman, for all their assistance.

Final and heartfelt thanks are due for the support of my family throughout: my mother Pamela, my father Adrian, my sister Blythe, and especially Zoë, who was good enough to marry me the month after this work was submitted.

University College London

Abbreviations

AFDI	*Annuaire Français de Droit International*
AJIL	*American Journal of International Law*
ALJ	*Australian Law Journal*
Annotated Commander's Handbook	A. Thomas and J. Duncan (eds.), *Annotated Supplement to the Commander's Handbook on the Law of Naval Operations* (Newport, Rhode Island: Naval War College, 1999)
Arrest Warrant Case	*Arrest Warrant of 11 April 2000 (Democratic Republic of the Congo v. Belgium)*, Judgment, [2002] ICJ Rep. 3.
AYBIL	*Australian Yearbook of International Law*
BCICLR	*Boston College International and Comparative Law Review*
Brownlie	Ian Brownlie, *Principles of Public International Law*, 6th edn (Oxford University Press, 2003)
BYIL	*British Yearbook of International Law*
CAMLR Convention	Convention for the Conservation of Antarctic Marine Living Resources 1980, (1980) 19 ILM 841
Caribbean Area Agreement	Agreement concerning Cooperation in Suppressing Illicit Maritime and Air Trafficking in Narcotic Drugs and Psychotropic Substances in the Caribbean Area 2003 (see W. Gilmore (ed.), *Agreement Concerning Co-operation in Suppressing Illicit Maritime and Air Trafficking in Narcotic Drugs and Psychotropic Substances in the Caribbean Area* (London: The Stationery Office, 2005))

CCAMLR	The Commission for the Conservation of Antarctic Marine Living Resources
Churchill and Lowe	R. Churchill and A. Lowe, *The Law of the Sea*, 3rd edn (Manchester University Press, 1999)
CJIL	*Chicago Journal of International Law*
CJTL	*Columbia Journal of Transnational Law*
CWILJ	*California Western International Law Journal*
CYBIL	*Canadian Yearbook of International Law*
DLR	*Deakin Law Review*
DJILP	*Denver Journal of International Law and Policy*
EJIL	*European Journal of International Law*
FSA	The United Nations Agreement for the Implementation of the Provisions of the United Nations Convention on the Law of the Sea of 10 December 1982 relating to the Conservation and Management of Straddling Fish Stocks and Highly Migratory Fish Stocks 1995, 2167 UNTS 88
GGULR	*Golden Gate University Law Review*
Gidel	G. Gidel, *Le Droit International Public de la Mer: Le Temps de Paix*, 3 vols. (Paris: Sirey, 1932)
GILJ	*Georgetown Immigration Law Journal*
GWILR	*George Washington International Law Review*
Harvard Research	J. Bingham *et al.*, *Harvard Research in International Law: Draft Convention on Piracy*, (1932) 26 AJIL Supp. 739
High Seas Convention	Geneva Convention on the High Seas 1958, 450 UNTS 82
HILJ	*Harvard International Law Journal*
ICCPR	International Covenant on Civil and Political Rights
ICJ	International Court of Justice
ICLQ	*International and Comparative Law Quarterly*
ICTY	International Criminal Tribunal for the former Yugoslavia
IJMCL	*International Journal of Marine and Coastal Law*
IJRL	*International Journal of Refugee Law*
ILC	International Law Commission
ILC Articles on State Responsibility	The Articles on Responsibility of States for Internationally Wrongful Acts, annexed to UNGA Res. 56/83 (28 January 2002)

ILM	*International Legal Materials*
ILR	*International Law Reports*
IMO	International Maritime Organization
ITLOS	International Tribunal for the Law of the Sea
IYBHR	*Israel Yearbook on Human Rights*
IYBIL	*Italian Yearbook of International Law*
JALC	*Journal of Air Law and Commerce*
JCSL	*Journal of Conflict and Security Law*
JICJ	*Journal of International Criminal Justice*
JIML	*Journal of International Maritime Law*
JMLC	*Journal of Maritime Law and Commerce*
LJIL	*Leiden Journal of International Law*
Lotus Case	Lotus Case, [1927] PCIJ Ser. A No. 104
McDougal and Burke	M. McDougal and W. Burke, *The Public Order of the Oceans*, reissue of 1962 edn (New Haven: New Haven Press, 1987)
Meyers	Herman Meyers, *The Nationality of Ships* (The Hague: Martinus Nijhoff, 1967)
Migrant Smuggling Protocol	The Protocol against the Smuggling of Migrants by Land, Sea and Air, Supplementing the United Nations Convention against Transnational Organized Crime 2000, (2001) 40 ILM 384
MJIL	*Melbourne Journal of International Law*
MULR	*Melbourne University Law Review*
NAFO	North Atlantic Fisheries Organization
NAFO Scheme	NAFO Conservation and Enforcement Measures
NATO *Travaux Préparatoires*	J. Snee (ed.), *NATO Agreements on Status: Travaux Préparatoires*, International Law Studies 1961 (Newport, Rhode Island: Naval War College, 1966)
NEAFC	The North-East Atlantic Fisheries Commission
NEAFC Scheme	NEAFC Scheme of Control and Enforcement
NILR	*Netherlands International Law Review*
NJIL	*Nordic Journal of International Law*
n.m.	nautical miles
NPAFC	North Pacific Anadromous Fish Commission
O'Connell	D. O'Connell, *The International Law of the Sea*, I. Shearer, ed. 2 vols. (Oxford: Clarendon Press, 1984)
ODIL	*Ocean Development and International Law*

Official Records: *Narcotics* *Convention* *Conference*	UN Economic and Social Council, *Official Records of the United Nations Conference for the Adoption of a Convention against Illicit Traffic in Narcotic Drugs and Psychotropic Substances, Vienna, 25 November–20 December 1988*, vol. II, Summary Records of Meetings of the Committees of the Whole, Committee II
Oppenheim, 8th edn	H. Lauterpacht, *Oppenheim's International Law: A Treatise: Volume I, Peace*, 8th edn (London: Longman, 1958)
Oppenheim, 9th edn	R. Jennings and A. Watts, *Oppenheim's International Law: Volume I, Peace*, 9th edn (Harlow: Longman, 1992)
PSI	Proliferation Security Initiative
RDI	*Rivista di Diritto Internazionale*
ReCAAP	Regional Cooperation Agreement on Combating Piracy and Armed Robbery against Ships in Asia 2005, (2005) 44 ILM 829
Recueil des Cours	*Recueil des Cours de l'Academie de Droit International de la Haye*
RFMO	Regional Fisheries Management Organization
RGDIP	*Revue Générale de Droit International Public*
SCLR	*Southern California Law Review*
SDILJ	*San Diego International Law Journal*
SDLR	*San Diego Law Review*
SEAFO	South East Atlantic Fisheries Organization
Shaw	M. Shaw, *International Law*, 5th edn (Cambridge University Press, 2003)
SJICL	*Singapore Journal of International and Comparative Law*
SOFA	Status of Forces Agreement
SUA Convention	Convention for the Suppression of Unlawful Acts Against the Safety of Maritime Navigation 1988, (1992) 1678 UNTS 201
SUA Protocol 2005	Protocol to the Convention for the Suppression of Unlawful Acts against the Safety of Maritime Navigation, IMO Doc. LEG/CONF.15/21, 1 November 2005
SYBIL	*Spanish Yearbook of International Law*

Third Restatement of Foreign Relations Law	American Law Institute, *Restatement of the Law Third: The Foreign Relations Law of the United States* (St. Paul, Minn.: American Law Institute, 1987)
TLCP	*Transnational Law & Contemporary Problems*
TMLJ	*Tulane Maritime Law Journal*
UMIALR	*University of Miami Inter-American Law Review*
UNCLOS	United Nations Convention on the Law of the Sea 1982, 1833 UNTS 3
UNCLOS Commentary	M. Nordquist et al. (eds.), *United Nations Convention on the Law of the Sea 1982: A Commentary*, 5 vols. (The Hague, Martinus Nijhoff, 1985–95).
UNHCR	(Office of the) United Nations High Commissioner for Refugees
UN Narcotics Convention	United Nations Convention against Illicit Traffic in Narcotic Drugs and Psychotropic Substances 1988, (1989) 28 ILM 497
UN Practical Guide	UN Office on Drugs and Crime, *Practical Guide for Competent National Authorities under Article 17 of the United Nations Convention against Illicit Traffic in Narcotic Drugs and Psychotropic Substances of 1988* (New York: United Nations, 2003)
UQLJ	*University of Queensland Law Journal*
VJTL	*Vanderbilt Journal of Transnational Law*
WCPFC	Western and Central Pacific Fisheries Commission
YBILC	*Yearbook of the International Law Commission*; references to pages are given in the format [1955] I YBILC, 10
YJIL	*Yale Journal of International Law*
ZaöRV	*Zeitschrift für Auslandisches Offentliches Recht und Volkerrecht*

Table of treaties and other international agreements

Table of cases

NATIONAL DECISIONS

PART I
General principles

1   Introduction: policing the oceans

The oceans are critical both to states' interests and to human prosperity, being a highway for commerce, a shared resource and a vector for threats to security. Ninety per cent of legal international trade moves by sea.[1] The oceans are also used by smugglers transporting prohibited substances or irregular migrants. Certain trade by sea, not previously unlawful, is now prohibited as threatening international security, for example supplying a non-state actor with weapons of mass destruction (WMD), or transferring such materiel to North Korea or Iran.[2] States may also have strategic concerns regarding the possibility of certain states covertly acquiring WMD and seek to prevent such transfers by sea.[3]

The oceans also feed humanity. Forty per cent of the protein consumed in the developing world is supplied by seafood.[4] The vast resource represented by world fish stocks is difficult to govern. Illegal, unreported or unregulated fishing threatens coastal state economies and human food security. To reduce such activity some states have implemented at-sea boarding and inspection measures to monitor fishing practices.

Vessels at sea are also vulnerable to violence. Ships are robbed or hijacked with alarming frequency, raising concerns that such attacks could finance terrorism or result in seized vessels being used as 'floating

---

[1] United Nations Division for Ocean Affairs and the Law of the Sea, *Oceans: The Source of Life* (New York: United Nations, 2002), p. 13, www.un.org/Depts/los/convention_agreements/convention_20years/oceanssourceoflife.pdf.

[2] SC Res. 1696 (31 July 2006), para. 4; SC Res. 1718 (14 October 2006), paras. 8(a) and (b); SC Res. 1737 (27 December 2006), paras. 3, 4 and 7; SC Res. 1803 (3 March 2008), para. 8. See also SC Res. 1747 (24 March 2007), para 5; and SC Res. 1540 (28 April 2004), para. 2.

[3] M. Byers, 'Policing the high seas: the Proliferation Security Initiative' (2004) 98 AJIL 526.

[4] Jared Diamond, *Collapse: How Societies Choose to Fail or Succeed* (London: Penguin, 2006), p. 479.

bombs' to attack major ports.[5] Individuals have also taken to the seas to circumvent state regulation, for example, the 'pirate radio' stations of 1960s Europe.

The law of the sea must harmonise states' competing interests in exploiting and regulating maritime activities; as part of this enterprise it should provide for the orderly allocation of jurisdiction to suppress unlawful or undesirable activities. This book examines interdiction at sea, using the term 'interdiction' to describe a two-step process:[6] first, the boarding, inspection and search of a ship at sea suspected of prohibited conduct; second, where such suspicions prove justified, taking measures including any combination of arresting the vessel, arresting persons aboard or seizing cargo. Throughout, the first exercise of enforcement jurisdiction will be referred to as 'boarding' or 'search' and the second as 'seizure'. Some authors distinguish between a 'right of approach' ('droit d'approche') and a 'right of enquiry' ('droit d'enquête du pavillon')[7] and may distinguish both from 'interdiction'. The 'right of approach' is based on the view that it is not unlawful for a government vessel (including warships) on the high seas to draw near a foreign vessel to observe its flag or other marks of nationality.[8] Given the doctrine of the freedom of the high seas, this 'right' seems redundant, possibly reflecting only a presumption that such actions by warships are not inherently hostile.[9] The distinct 'right of enquiry' may allow a government vessel to board a vessel, inspect its papers, question those aboard and possibly search it.[10] Interdiction might then be thought of as the further act of arresting the vessel. There is no real difference between distinguishing between a 'right of inquiry' and 'interdiction' and talking of the boarding and seizure phases of

---

[5] E. Barrios, 'Casting a wider net: addressing the maritime piracy problem in southeast Asia' (2005) BCICLR 149 at 153; 'Malacca Strait: no immediate threat from terrorists', *Lloyd's List*, 22 February 2008, p. 5.

[6] 'Interdiction' was first used in this sense by the US military in the 1940s and 1950s; see *Oxford English Dictionary* online http://dictionary.oed.com, interdict *v.*, Add: 4, and cf. interdiction *n.*, n. 4; although it probably entered English from French legal usage, e.g. [1950] II YBILC 67 at 69.

[7] Gidel, I, 289–300.

[8] This right may include the power to *require* a merchant ship to show its flag. See the comments of J. P. A. François, [1955] I YBILC, 26. This proposition was not codified. Note, however, that François also used 'droit d'approche' to describe what is called here the right of inquiry: [1954] II YBILC, 8 at para. 7.

[9] But see O'Connell, pp. 802–3.

[10] UNCLOS, Article 110; High Seas Convention, Article 22.

interdiction. Both acts may be considered as part of 'interdiction', since seizure is always conditioned upon and preceded by boarding.

Interdictions may be conducted by coastal states, flag states or third states. A coastal state may be able to interdict vessels in various regulatory zones adjacent its coasts. A flag state has jurisdiction to interdict vessels granted its nationality on the high seas (i.e., that ocean area not subject to coastal state jurisdiction). Other states may only conduct an interdiction under a permissive rule of international law or with permission from the flag state or the coastal state in whose regulatory zone the vessel is present. The present study is especially concerned with high seas interdictions conducted by non-flag state vessels and interdictions in waters subject to coastal state jurisdiction conducted by foreign vessels. Such interdictions involve the jurisdictions of two states. This raises questions of general international law, the simultaneous validity of two national laws of police procedure and substantive criminal law aboard a vessel, state immunity and state responsibility. Interdictions which, if properly conducted, implicate only one national legal order are only briefly discussed.

The present discussion is accordingly divided into three parts. Part I introduces general principles of maritime jurisdiction. Part II considers the application of these jurisdictional principles in particular law enforcement contexts, as well as their interaction with other applicable international law rules which may affect the conduct of interdictions, such as obligations regarding the safety of life at sea or the protection of refugees. Part II considers fields of maritime policing practice in roughly the historical order in which the law has emerged. Chapters in Part II thus deal with piracy and the slave trade, drug trafficking, high seas fisheries management, unauthorised broadcasting, the transnational crimes of migrant smuggling and human trafficking, and maritime counter-proliferation of WMD. The analysis is historically situated, but focuses on modern state practice. While the law on piracy, slaving, drug trafficking, fisheries management and unauthorised broadcasting, respectively, represent different responses to different problems, they also represent a range of possible legal regimes that could be adapted to emerging concerns such as transnational criminal activity and WMD proliferation. What will be shown is that the approach founded on state consent to interdiction, adopted in drug smuggling and fisheries regulation, has prevailed over allocating universal and unilateral interdiction rights, as in the cases of piracy, slaving and unauthorised broadcasting.

Part III deals with the positive law applicable to interdiction that can be deduced from existing interdiction practice and general rules of international law. The evidence in Part II reveals that there is no general international law of interdiction in the sense that general interdiction rights will arise if one proves that a certain activity is sufficiently damaging to the interests of an individual state or the wider international community. However, insofar as interdiction is a common tool of law enforcement applied in different contexts, useful observations may be made about the rules applicable in the course of any legally permitted interdiction. While a range of principles can be deduced, by far the most important relate to the use of force by a boarding party. Use of force is thus the principal concern of Chapter 10. Chapter 11 deals with the consequences of the simultaneous validity of two national legal orders during the conduct of an interdiction and considers three questions: the application of the boarding state's law to conduct discovered aboard a vessel; the boarding state's obligations under flag or coastal state law; and the immunity, if any, enjoyed by boarding state officials before flag or coastal state courts for their conduct. Chapter 12 deals with the consequences of wrongfully conducted boardings and issues of state responsibility.

Finally, it should be noted that this book is only concerned with the laws of peace and does not consider the laws of blockade, contraband or other belligerent rights, or Security Council-mandated interdiction regimes.[11] These provide a completely autonomous foundation for the exercise of boarding state jurisdiction, and do not implicate concurrent jurisdiction in the same manner as peacetime interdiction.

[11] See generally *Annotated Commander's Handbook*, ch. 7; Louise Doswald-Beck (ed.), *San Remo Manual on International Law Applicable to Armed Conflicts at Sea* (Cambridge University Press, 1995), pp. 176–80, 214–21; G. Politakis, *Modern Aspects of the Laws of Naval Warfare and Maritime Neutrality* (London: Kegan Paul, 1998), Part II; Wolff Heintschel von Heinegg, 'The law of armed conflict at sea', and M. Bothe, 'The law of neutrality' in Dieter Fleck (ed.), *The Handbook of Humanitarian Law in Armed Conflicts* 2nd edn (Oxford University Press, 2008), pp. 475–569, 571–604; N. Ronzitti, 'The crisis of the traditional law regulating international armed conflicts at sea and the need for its revision' in Natalino Ronzitti (ed.), *The Law of Naval Warfare: A Collection of Agreements and Documents with Commentaries* (Dordrecht: Martinus Nijhoff, 1988), pp. 1–58; D. Guilfoyle, 'The Proliferation Security Initiative: interdicting vessels in international waters to prevent the spread of weapons of mass destruction?' (2005) 29 MULR 733, 744–7. On Security Council-authorised interdiction regimes see R. McLaughlin, 'United Nations mandated naval interdiction operations in the territorial sea?' (2002) 51 ICLQ 249; Alfred. H. A. Soons, 'A "new" exception to the freedom of the high seas: the authority of the UN Security Council' in Terry D. Gill and Wybo P. Heere (eds.), *Reflections on Principles and Practice of International Law: Essays in Honour of Leo J. Bouchez* (The Hague: Nijhoff, 2000), pp. 205–21.

2 Basic principles of maritime jurisdiction

1 State jurisdiction over vessels at sea

This book principally examines situations where one state exercises jurisdiction over a vessel otherwise subject to the exclusive jurisdiction of a flag or coastal state. 'Jurisdiction' refers to a state's power 'under international law to govern persons and property by its [national] law' and to 'make, apply, and enforce rules of conduct' to that end.[1] It is commonly held that

> the first and foremost restriction imposed by international law upon a State is that – failing the existence of a permissive rule to the contrary – it may not exercise its power ... in the territory of another State. ... [Jurisdiction] cannot be exercised by a State outside its territory except by virtue of a permissive rule derived from international custom or from a convention.[2]

State power applied beyond territorial limits seems exceptional, justifiable only by permissive rules or exceptions. The extraterritorial exercise of state jurisdiction over maritime areas and vessels at sea thus requires explanation. International law distinguishes between the scope of prescriptive and enforcement jurisdiction of national criminal law; ordinarily the latter is regarded as absolutely territorially constrained, while the former may extend extraterritorially in

---

[1] David Harris, *Cases and Materials on International Law*, 6th edn (London: Sweet & Maxwell, 2004), p. 265, and Vaughan Lowe, 'Jurisdiction', in M. Evans (ed.), *International Law*, 2nd edn (Oxford University Press, 2006), p. 335; cf. Meyers, pp. 33–40.

[2] *Lotus Case*, 18–19; cf. Brownlie, p. 297; Michael Byers, *Custom, Power and the Power of Rules: International Relations and Customary International Law* (Cambridge University Press, 1999), p. 53; Roger O'Keefe, 'Universal jurisdiction: clarifying the basic concept' (2004) 2 JICJ 735 at 740.

certain cases.[3] A state may prohibit or regulate at least certain classes of extraterritorial conduct ('prescriptive jurisdiction') even where it has no authority to enforce that law outside its territory ('enforcement jurisdiction'), such prescription being logically independent of enforcement.[4] This may result in states having concurrent jurisdiction over the same conduct, but this is a more desirable outcome than no state having jurisdiction. The exercise of concurrent jurisdictions with respect to the same acts may be regulated by rules of priority, as discussed in subsequent chapters. In addition to prescriptive and enforcement jurisdiction, some authors refer to 'curial' or 'adjudicative' jurisdiction to describe the power of local courts to hear a case and impose penalties. Although this will normally be coextensive with prescriptive jurisdiction, the term remains useful in certain situations, especially those involving some procedural immunity from the application of a substantive law (which will apply if the immunity is waived).

States may assert prescriptive jurisdiction over the extraterritorial conduct of their nationals and potentially over extraterritorial criminal conduct affecting their nationals ('active' and 'passive' nationality jurisdiction). Thus where a citizen of state A murders a citizen of state B in the territory of state B, both states may have prescriptive jurisdiction over the offender's conduct, but only state B may arrest him while he remains in state B's territory. As the Permanent Court of International Justice (PCIJ) said in the *Lotus Case*,

[f]ar from laying down a general prohibition to the effect that states may not extend the application of their laws and the jurisdiction of their courts to persons, property and acts outside their territory, ... [international law] leaves them ... a wide measure of discretion which is only limited in certain cases by prohibitive rules.[5]

It has helpfully been said of this passage:

A distinction must be made between prescriptive jurisdiction and enforcement jurisdiction. The above-mentioned *dictum* concerns *prescriptive jurisdiction*: it is about what a State may do *on its own territory* when investigating and prosecuting crimes committed abroad, not about what a State may do on the territory of other states... Obviously, a State has no *enforcement jurisdiction* outside its territory: a State may, failing permission to the contrary, not

---

[3] Lowe, 'Jurisdiction', pp. 337 ff.
[4] O'Keefe, 'Universal jurisdiction', esp. at 755.
[5] *Lotus Case*, 19. On the contested meaning and correctness of this dictum, see Lowe, 'Jurisdiction', p. 341; O'Keefe, 'Universal jurisdiction', 738 n. 12; Meyers, pp. 52–3.

exercise its power on the territory of another State. ... In other words, the permissive rule only applies to prescriptive jurisdiction, not to enforcement jurisdiction: failing a prohibition, State A *may,* on its own territory, prosecute offences committed in State B *(permissive rule)*; failing a permission, State A *may not* act on the territory of State B.[6]

However, the rule that enforcement jurisdiction is ordinarily territorial is qualified in maritime cases. As exceptions to the general rule, flag states may exercise criminal enforcement jurisdiction over acts committed aboard their flag vessels in international waters ('the high seas'), and under certain circumstances so can non-flag states.

Interdiction concerns the extraterritorial exercise of enforcement jurisdiction, and in any given case one must first ascertain the permissible extent of that jurisdiction. An interdiction has two potential steps. The first is stopping, boarding and searching the vessel for evidence of the prohibited conduct ('boarding'). Where boarding reveals evidence of such conduct the arrest of persons aboard and/or seizure of the vessel or cargo may follow ('seizure', although some treaties refer to 'disposition').

Boarding and seizure involve different exercises of enforcement jurisdiction. Coastal states may have jurisdiction over a vessel present within certain regulatory zones adjacent their coasts. When it is in international waters a vessel is subject to the exclusive jurisdiction of its flag state, therefore government vessels generally may not board foreign vessels in international waters without flag state consent.[7] Flag state consent will also be required for some interdictions by coastal states, where a vessel is interdicted in a regulatory zone in respect of acts which the coastal state lacks express jurisdiction to regulate.

Where a flag state grants consent to a state seeking to interdict its vessel ('the boarding state'), such permission usually constitutes only a partial waiver of flag state jurisdiction. Permission to board seldom automatically includes permission to seize. Such situations are sometimes inaccurately said to create 'concurrent' jurisdiction. Jurisdiction will be concurrent as to rights of boarding, but not seizure.

---

[6] *Arrest Warrant Case*, 169 at para. 49 per Judge ad hoc Van Den Wyngaert (Dissenting Opinion), footnote omitted (emphasis in original). Many would dispute, however, any suggestion that prescriptive jurisdiction is generally unconstrained: Lowe, 'Jurisdiction', p. 341.

[7] *Lotus Case*, 25; High Seas Convention, Article 6(1); UNCLOS, Article 92(1). On exceptions, see *Oppenheim*, 9th edn, p. 736.

Concurrent jurisdiction might properly arise where, as under some drug interdiction treaties, the boarding state is granted enforcement permission both as to boarding and seizure, but the flag state reserves a right to withdraw its consent and resume exclusive control over any detention and subsequent prosecution. This is called 'primary' or 'preferential' jurisdiction, but such terms are strictly a misnomer: the phenomenon derives from the fact that permission may be given subject to conditions, including conditions subsequent.

It is probably more accurate to describe most interdictions as creating a parallel jurisdiction in the boarding state. Both flag and boarding state jurisdictions will apply aboard the vessel. The question is, first, the extent of the boarding state's authority (granted by the flag state or by treaty or customary rules) and, second, which jurisdiction takes precedence if a search proceeds to seizure and then prosecution. Such rules of priority are usually provided for, sometimes in a less than satisfactory way, in relevant treaties.[8]

2 Zones of maritime jurisdiction

2.1 Introduction

Jurisdiction to interdict a vessel without flag-state permission depends upon its location. It is thus necessary to sketch the basic principles of maritime jurisdiction and discuss several points about enforcement jurisdiction that are sometimes poorly understood. Under the 1982 United Nations Law of the Sea Convention ('UNCLOS'),[9] three forms of coastal state jurisdiction are acknowledged over adjacent waters: a territorial sea, a contiguous zone and an exclusive economic zone (EEZ). Each of these will be discussed in turn before considering the specific issues of hot pursuit, flag-state jurisdiction and stateless vessels.

2.2 Territorial sea

Generally a coastal state's zones of maritime jurisdiction are elective: they do not exist unless declared by the coastal state.[10] International

---

[8] See especially Chapter 5.

[9] 1833 UNTS 3, entered into force 16 November 1994, 157 parties at 16 July 2008, www.un.org/Depts/los/reference_files/status2008.pdf.

[10] A state has, however, inherent rights over seabed and subsoil resources of its continental shelf: *North Sea Continental Shelf Cases*, [1969] ICJ Rep. 3 at 22; O'Connell, ch. 13; Churchill and Lowe, ch. 8; cf. [1950] II YBILC 67 at 87–113.

law, however, imposes at least a 3-n.m. territorial sea upon coastal states.[11] The permissible maximum breadth of the territorial sea is uncertain as a matter of customary law. Arguably, such a variety of claims existed prior to UNCLOS that there was no single historically established rule, although such claims seldom extended beyond 12 n.m.[12] Under UNCLOS, a state's territorial sea may extend up to 12 n.m. from its 'baselines' (Art. 3). In theory, as UNCLOS is not a universal convention, non-party states could assert various lesser limits and demand their reciprocal acknowledgement. Although a few states briefly attempted this, experience suggests that state practice has gravitated towards the treaty rule.[13]

Under UNCLOS, a coastal state's sovereignty extends throughout its territorial sea, although its exercise is subject to the Convention and 'other rules of international law'.[14] The main constraint upon state enforcement jurisdiction within territorial waters is the 'innocent passage' immunity accorded merchant ships in UNCLOS Articles 17–28. Under UNCLOS, a coastal state can enforce its criminal law against ships bound for, or leaving, its internal waters. Article 27 specifies that a coastal state generally 'should not' exercise criminal enforcement jurisdiction over foreign flag vessels (and those aboard) simply passing through territorial waters. Exceptions include crimes committed aboard affecting the coastal state, the master requesting assistance or suppressing drug trafficking. However, the phrase 'should not' is 'hortatory only' and does not clearly prohibit criminal law enforcement in other cases.[15] Churchill and Lowe explain the provision as codifying usage. Although all states ordinarily restricted their exercise of enforcement jurisdiction within territorial waters to the circumstances described above, views differed on that practice's significance. Some states believed their enforcement jurisdiction was restricted to those subject matters, others, that their jurisdiction was plenary, but that they restrained its exercise out of comity. The latter

---

[11] *Anglo-Norwegian Fisheries Case*, [1951] ICJ Rep. 116 at 160, per Judge McNair (Dissenting Opinion); Churchill and Lowe, pp. 80–1.

[12] Byers, *Custom, Power and the Power of Rules*, pp. 114–18; Churchill and Lowe, pp. 77–81.

[13] Byers, *Custom, Power and the Power of Rules*, pp. 104–5; cf. US Department of Defense, *Maritime Claims Reference Manual* (June 2005), www.dtic.mil/whs/directives/corres/html/20051m.htm.

[14] UNCLOS, Article 2(3).

[15] I. Shearer, 'Problems of jurisdiction and law enforcement against delinquent vessels' (1986) 35 ICLQ 320 at 327; contra Meyers, pp. 77–80; cf. Evans, 'Law of the sea', pp. 630–1, 633.

view appears to have prevailed under UNCLOS; without imposing binding limitations, Article 27 represents the accepted bases of jurisdiction to which states should generally conform.[16] This conclusion is confirmed by the drafting history. Article 27 replicates the language ('should not') of the Territorial Sea Convention,[17] which was deliberately chosen over the proposed words 'may not' in order to preserve a coastal state's plenary jurisdiction, including enforcement jurisdiction, over territorial waters.[18] The law has, then, historically rejected a general prohibition over criminal enforcement jurisdiction subject to exceptions, and has deliberately adopted permissive language exhorting restraint. The only absolute exclusion of enforcement jurisdiction is in the case of a crime 'committed before the ship entered the territorial sea' where that merchant vessel is simply passing through territorial waters without entering port.[19] Public vessels on non-commercial service are generally immune from such enforcement jurisdiction, but must comply voluntarily with certain coastal state regulations and may be required to leave the territorial sea if they do not.[20]

2.3 The contiguous zone

The contiguous zone extends a further 12 n.m. seaward from the territorial sea.[21] Within it 'states have limited powers' under UNCLOS Article 33 to enforce 'customs, fiscal, sanitary and immigration laws'.[22] UNCLOS allows coastal states only to 'exercise "control" (not sovereignty or jurisdiction)' in order either to *prevent* infringement of the specified laws within the state's territory or territorial sea, or to *punish* acts already committed within its territory or territorial sea.[23] Shearer, following Fitzmaurice, argues that the connotations of 'control' limit *preventive* state action to 'inspections and warnings' rather than

---

[16] Churchill and Lowe, pp. 95–9; contra, *Third Restatement of Foreign Relations Law*, II, pp. 46–8.

[17] Convention on the Territorial Sea and the Contiguous Zone 1958, 516 UNTS 205, Article 19.

[18] Shearer, 'Problems of jurisdiction', 327; Churchill and Lowe, p. 97; cf. [1956] II YBILC, 274–5.

[19] UNCLOS, Article 27(5).   [20] *Ibid.*, Articles 31–33.

[21] *Ibid.*, Article 33(2).   [22] *Ibid.*, Article 33(1). Churchill and Lowe, p. 132.

[23] Shearer, 'Problems of jurisdiction', 330; cf. G. Fitzmaurice, 'Some results of the Geneva Conference on the Law of the Sea' (1959) 8 ICLQ 73, 113; contra, S. Oda, 'The concept of the contiguous zone' (1962) 11 ICLQ 131 at 152–3; [1956] II YBILC, 6 (J. P. A. François, special rapporteur on the regime of the high seas).

arresting vessels.[24] Some treat Article 33 as allowing plenary criminal law enforcement, respecting the specified subject matters, up to the 24-n.m. limit.[25] This fails to give separate meanings to 'prevent' and 'punish'. The power to 'punish' is conditioned upon criminal acts having occurred *within* a state's territory or territorial sea. By analogy with the doctrine of hot pursuit, this appears an express extension of an otherwise impermissible jurisdiction. This condition limiting the exercise of jurisdiction to 'punish' would be redundant if relevant criminal laws were continuously enforceable up to the 24-n.m. limit. The scope of enforcement jurisdiction within the contiguous zone is thus more limited than sometimes thought.

However, the view that Article 33 limits coastal state enforcement to punishing acts committed in its jurisdiction by vessels leaving its territorial waters also goes too far.[26] So long as the acts of a vessel situated within the contiguous zone produce an infringement of a coastal state's customs or fiscal, sanitary or immigration laws in the territorial sea, 'control' could be asserted to punish those acts.[27] Classically, under the doctrine of 'constructive presence', this includes 'hovering' mother-ships transferring illicit cargoes to smaller boats to complete smuggling offences within state territory.[28] The same approach is taken in UNCLOS provisions on hot pursuit. These allow a coastal state to commence pursuing a vessel outside its territorial waters (or contiguous zone or EEZ) following offences completed within an area of its jurisdiction by the vessel's small boats or other craft 'working as a team' with it.[29]

There has been some debate between 'simple' and 'extensive' views of constructive presence.[30] The 'simple' or narrow view held that constructive presence was only made out where the mother ship's own boats were used to make contact with the shore. The extensive view, that other vessels may come out from shore to make contact with a mother ship on the high seas, certainly seems to be contemplated by

---

[24] Shearer, 'Problems of jurisdiction', 330.

[25] See *Annotated Commander's Handbook*, pp. 20, 244; *Third Restatement of Foreign Relations Law*, II, pp. 30, 49; J. Ashley Roach and Robert W. Smith, *United States Responses to Excessive Maritime Claims*, 2nd edn (London: Martinus Nijhoff, 1996), p. 481.

[26] Shearer, 'Problems of jurisdiction', 330; Fitzmaurice, 'Some results', 113; O'Connell, pp. 1057–9.

[27] M/V 'Saiga' (No. 2), (1999) 38 ILM 1323 at 1408, per Judge Laing (Separate Opinion).

[28] O'Connell, pp. 1093–4.

[29] UNCLOS, Article 111(1) and (4); and see Chapter 5, sections 1 and 2.

[30] O'Connell, pp. 1092–3.

the broad drafting of UNCLOS, adopted in turn from the 1958 Geneva Convention.[31] In 1958 this may have been more progressive development of the law than codification of custom and was contrary to much of the case law.[32] However, its re-enactment in UNCLOS and subsequent state practice suggest that it is now the generally applicable rule.[33]

2.4 The Exclusive Economic Zone

The EEZ's outer limit is 200 n.m. seaward of the coastal state's baselines.[34] UNCLOS Article 56 allocates certain rights within the EEZ to the coastal state, principally 'sovereign rights' over economic resources including fisheries, and 'jurisdiction' over marine research, artificial islands and environmental protection. Article 58 reserves certain rights to other states, including freedom of navigation. Clearly, a coastal state has power to exercise enforcement jurisdiction in the EEZ regarding those subject matters over which it has sovereign rights.[35] Enforcement rights over matters of 'jurisdiction' only, such as environmental protection, are beyond the scope of this work.[36]

2.5 The continental shelf

The continental shelf is both a legal and geological concept. It is defined in UNCLOS Article 76(1) as 'the seabed and subsoil of the submarine areas that extend beyond … [a state's] territorial sea … to the outer edge of the continental margin, or to a distance of 200 nautical miles', whichever is greater.[37] Within this area, under Article 77, a coastal state exercises inherent 'sovereign rights for the purpose of exploring it and exploiting its natural [seabed and subsoil] resources' to the exclusion of other states.[38] This might lead one to conclude

---

[31] High Seas Convention, Article 23.

[32] W. Gilmore, 'Hot pursuit and constructive presence in Canadian law enforcement', (1988) 12 *Marine Policy* 105 at 110; *Grace and Ruby* [1922] 283 Fed. 475; *Marjorie E. Bachman* [1925] 4 Fed. (2nd) 405; *Frances Louise* [1924] 1 Fed. (2nd) 1004; contra, *Henry L. Marshall* [1923] 292 Fed. 486.

[33] *R v. Sunila and Soleyman* (1986) 28 DLR (4th) 450; *Re Pulos* (Tribunal of Naples, Italy), (1976) 77 ILR 587; W. Gilmore, 'Hot pursuit: the case of *R v Mills and Others*', (1995) 44 ICLQ 949 at 954–5.

[34] UNCLOS, Article 57.

[35] See Chapter 6, section 2.1 on EEZ fisheries law.

[36] See Shearer, 'Problems of jurisdiction', 328; UNCLOS, Articles 211 and 220.

[37] Space prevents discussion of claims over an extended continental shelf under UNCLOS, Articles 76(2)–(8). See generally Ted L. McDorman, 'The role of the Commission on the Limits of the Continental Shelf: a technical body in a political world' (2002) 17 IJMCL 301.

[38] See n. 10, above.

that a coastal state could thus interdict vessels engaged in unlicensed exploitation of seabed resources or surveys of the continental shelf. The legal questions involved are, however, more complex.[39]

As regards the coastal state's exclusive rights of 'exploration' over the continental shelf, it must be noted that other states are still permitted to engage in 'scientific research' in 'the water column' beyond the EEZ.[40] Even if a coastal state has jurisdiction to prevent foreign *exploration* of its continental shelf, the distinction between impermissible exploration of the continental shelf and permissible scientific research in the water column above it has 'never [been] made explicit'.[41] Under UNCLOS Article 246 coastal states '*in the exercise of their jurisdiction*, have the right to regulate, authorize and conduct marine scientific research in their exclusive economic zone and on their continental shelf' (emphasis added). As a result, 'all research in the EEZ and on the continental shelf requires the consent of the coastal state'.[42] This combination of an express reference to jurisdiction and the requirement of consent might be thought to support a right to interdict unlicensed scientific exploration. However, apart from possible distinctions between scientific exploration *on* the continental shelf and *in* the water column over it,[43] several commentators argue that such restrictions should not apply to hydrographic surveys. The argument made is that such surveys are a matter of the safety of navigation and thus fall within the freedoms of navigation on the high seas and not regulated 'scientific exploration'.[44]

The coastal state enjoys exclusive jurisdiction over fixed structures on the continental shelf. While this jurisdiction would grant authority to regulate the exploitation of continental shelf resources by unlicensed fixed structures, a further problem may arise. Much drilling is now conducted using mobile offshore drilling units (MODUs), which may move under their own power. Neither the Continental Shelf Convention 1958 nor UNCLOS 'deals specifically with [this] issue'.[45] Nonetheless, there is only limited state practice involving assertions

[39] Indeed, the separate provision in the EEZ regime for 'sovereign rights for the purpose of exploring and exploiting' and jurisdiction over such activities might imply the latter does not always follow from the former: UNCLOS, Article 56.

[40] UNCLOS, Article 257.

[41] O'Connell, p. 1031, referring to Geneva Convention on the Continental Shelf 1958, 499 UNTS 311, Articles 5(1) and (8). The observation is equally true of UNCLOS.

[42] Churchill and Lowe, p. 405.   [43] *Ibid.*, pp. 407 ff.

[44] *Ibid.*, p. 405 n. 3.   [45] *Ibid.*, p. 154.

of law-enforcement jurisdiction against foreign vessels, MODUs or unlicensed structures for their activities on the continental shelf, and the issue will not be considered in great detail here.[46]

3 Jurisdiction upon the high seas: flag and stateless vessels and hot pursuit

3.1 A flag state's exclusive jurisdiction

International waters, still commonly referred to as 'the high seas', constitute that remainder of the world's oceans not claimed as territorial or contiguous waters or as EEZs. While in international waters a vessel is subject to its flag state's exclusive jurisdiction, absent the exceptions discussed in subsequent chapters. The same holds true in areas of limited jurisdiction (the contiguous zone and EEZ) in respect of subject matters where international law does not allocate jurisdiction to the coastal state. This exclusive jurisdiction principle is codified under treaty.[47] The paramount value accorded this principle is not surprising. All states have a common economic interest in maintaining respect for rules protecting their shipping and trade through affording all others the same protections.

Under UNCLOS Article 91, ships 'have the nationality of the State whose flag they are entitled to fly'. UNCLOS does not require the formal registration of ships in order for them to enjoy nationality. Indeed, many states' national legal systems allow smaller vessels to fly their flag if owned by a national and only require vessels of a certain size to be formally registered.[48]

3.2 Stateless vessels

Stateless vessels are those lacking any claim to nationality under UNCLOS Article 91 on the basis either of state registration or some other right to fly a state's flag.[49] Vessels flying two or more flags according

---

[46] See the discussion of Dutch action against Radio Nordzee in Chapter 7, section 2, and *Guyana v. Suriname* (2008) 47 ILM 164 at paras. 151 and 263 ff.

[47] High Seas Convention, Article 6(1); UNCLOS, Article 92(1); contra, *Lotus Case*, 22.

[48] O'Connell, p. 753; V. Lowe and R. Churchill, 'The International Tribunal for the Law of the Sea: Survey for 2001' (2002) 17 IJMCL 463 at 474–5; Meyers, pp. 149–50; cf. [1956] I YBILC, 67 ff. and A. D. Watts, 'The protection of merchant ships' (1957) 33 BYIL 52, 60 ff.

[49] As discussed in Chapter 5, section 7; cf. N. Hunnings, 'Pirate broadcasting in European waters' (1965) 14 ICLQ 410, 427–8.

to convenience may also be 'assimilated' to stateless vessels.[50] Under UNCLOS Article 110 (although not under the High Seas Convention Article 21), any state may board and inspect a vessel suspected of being stateless. Not directly addressed by UNCLOS is the further question whether, if indeed stateless, a vessel can then be seized. There are two opposing views on this question. The first, taken in practice by the United States and on occasion the United Kingdom, is that a stateless vessel may be seized by any state as it enjoys the protection of none.[51] The second is that some further jurisdictional nexus or permissive rule is required to justify seizure.[52] This second view seems more consonant with treaty practice. Not only is the issue of seizure not addressed in UNCLOS, it remains ambiguous in the 1988 UN Narcotics Convention, a treaty directly concerned with law enforcement proclaiming the interest of all states in suppressing drug trafficking.[53] While the UN Narcotics Convention clearly contemplates action against stateless vessels extending to 'suppressing' the vessel's 'use' for illicit purposes,[54] there may not be a corresponding grant of permissive jurisdiction to prescribe and prosecute offences committed aboard. The jurisdictional provisions of the Convention only apply to events aboard vessels boarded pursuant to agreements with flag states.[55] While the Convention does provide that '[t]his Convention does not exclude the exercise of any criminal jurisdiction established by a Party in accordance with its domestic law',[56] this could not allow the assertion of a jurisdiction prohibited at general international law. This lack of any clear statement

---

[50] Article 92(2), UNCLOS.

[51] Shaw, p. 547; *Annotated Commander's Handbook*, p. 239; Evans, 'Law of the sea', p. 636; *United States v. Cortes*, 588 F.2d 106, 110 (1979); *United States v. Marino-Garcia*, 679 F.2d 1373, 1383 (1982); Criminal Justice (International Co-operation) Act 1990 (c. 5), ss. 19(1) and 20; *Molvan v. Attorney General for Palestine* [1948] AC 351 at 369; (Privy Council) (1948) 15 ILR 115 at 124. One might also cite older US cases such as *US v. Klintock* 18 US 144 (1820) and *US v. Holmes* 18 US 412 (1820); however, it is not always clear in these cases if vessels were presumed to be without nationality because they had been held pirate vessels. On the 'denationalisation' theory of piracy see Chapter 4, section 1.2.

[52] Churchill and Lowe, p. 214; Hunnings, 'Pirate broadcasting', 427. Australian legislation permits the search of certain stateless fishing vessels on the high seas but not their seizure or the arrest of persons aboard: Fisheries Management Act (Cth) (No. 162 of 1991), s. 87H.

[53] UN Convention against Illicit Traffic in Narcotic Drugs and Psychotropic Substances 1988, (1989) 28 ILM 497 (UN Narcotics Convention), entered into force 11 November 1990, 183 parties at 14 March 2008.

[54] UN Narcotics Convention, Article 17(2).   [55] *Ibid.*, Article 4(1)(b)(ii).

[56] *Ibid.*, Article 4(3).

of a right to seize stateless vessels may be thought significant. If the right was uncontroversial, its omission from both UNCLOS and the UN Narcotics Convention would be difficult to understand. The choice is one between states being free to prescribe the conduct of stateless vessels and take enforcement action to that end, or their only having such jurisdiction in limited cases such as constructive presence, active or passive nationality or universal jurisdiction over certain crimes.[57]

If one state seizes a stateless vessel in international waters, then by definition no other state will be able to assert diplomatic protection over it.[58] However, persons aboard will ordinarily be nationals of some State capable of making claims on their behalf.[59] Of course, if the crew has the nationality of the interdicting vessel, they might well be subject to the interdicting state's jurisdiction on the same nationality principle said to justify high seas jurisdiction over flag vessels.[60] Firm conclusions about the position of stateless vessels must be deferred pending an examination of state practice.[61]

3.3 Hot pursuit

A government vessel or aircraft may pursue a vessel into international waters where it has 'good reason' to believe that vessel has broken coastal state law.[62] Hot pursuit may commence in territorial, contiguous or EEZ waters according to the kind of law implicated.[63] While there is some limited discussion of hot pursuit in this book,[64] it is not generally relevant to interdiction as presently defined. If properly commenced, hot pursuit results in the unequivocal right of the

---

[57] See *Lotus Case*, 20; Meyers, pp. 318–21 contra the approach in Lowe, 'Jurisdiction', pp. 341 ff., and B. Stern, 'L'extraterritorialité revisitée' (1992) 38 AFDI 239, 251–6. Extensions of territorial jurisdiction, including objective territoriality/effects jurisdiction are discussed further at Chapter 5, section 2 and Chapter 7, section 2.

[58] *Molvan v. Attorney General for Palestine* [1948] AC 351 at 369; (Privy Council, 1948) 15 ILR 115 at 124.

[59] Churchill and Lowe, p. 214; Louis Sohn, 'International law of the sea and human rights issues' in T. Clingan (ed.), *The Law of the Sea: What Lies Ahead?* (Honolulu: Law of the Sea Institute, 1988), p. 51 at p. 59. Practitioners the author has spoken to are unaware of this ever actually happening.

[60] C. Colombos, *The International Law of the Sea*, 6th edn (London: Longman, 1967), p. 285; Hunnings, 'Pirate broadcasting', 481.

[61] See discussion in Chapter 5, section 2; Chapter 6, sections 3.2, 5.2, 5.3 and 6.2; Chapter 7, section 2; Chapter 8, sections 2.3 and 2.4; Chapter 9, section 5; and Chapter 11, section 2.

[62] UNCLOS, Article 111.   [63] Shearer, 'Problems of jurisdiction', 328.

[64] See Chapter 6, section 5.5.

coastal state to seize a vessel pursued onto the high seas.[65] This is an extension of existing coastal state enforcement jurisdiction which entirely ousts the jurisdiction of the flag state.[66] It therefore does not give rise to the issues of concurrent jurisdiction that are the focus of this study.

4 Conclusion

It has been suggested that coastal states have a strong enforcement power near the shore, a power 'slowly diminishing [over distance] to practically zero when reaching the high seas'.[67] The position is, however, more complex. If UNCLOS Article 27 is merely hortatory, only comity restrains coastal states from enforcing national criminal law against vessels in their territorial waters. Enforcement jurisdiction over certain subject matters is also allowed in the contiguous zone to the extent that the activity took place, or had effect, on shore or within territorial waters. Limited 'control' may also be exercised in the contiguous zone to prevent such infringements.

The EEZ constitutes a patchwork of 'sovereign power' (including enforcement jurisdiction) over some subject matters and mere 'jurisdiction' (not necessarily extending to enforcement) over others. Interdiction to manage EEZ fisheries will thus be allowed while unilateral action against vessels suspected of transporting WMD materiel through the EEZ, for example, will not.

Upon the high seas, and in respect of many activities in the EEZ and contiguous zone, a vessel is generally subject only to its flag state's exclusive jurisdiction. Maritime enforcement thus requires flag state action or consent if the vessel is not in a location, or engaged in an activity, subject to coastal state enforcement jurisdiction. A variety of treaty arrangements have thus been established to facilitate consensual interdiction of foreign-flagged vessels. These treaties, dealing with drug interdiction, fisheries management, suppression of certain

---

[65] See generally Nicholas M. Poulantzas, *The Right of Hot Pursuit in International Law*, 2nd edn (The Hague: Martinus Nijhoff, 2002); Churchill and Lowe, pp. 214–16; O'Connell, pp. 1075–93; Gilmore, 'Hot pursuit and constructive presence'; Gilmore, 'Hot pursuit: the case of *R v. Mills and Others*'; *R v. Sunila and Soleyman* (1986) 28 DLR (4th) 450; *MV 'Saiga' (No. 2)*, 1352 ff. (at paras. 139–152), and 1395–6 per Judge Anderson (Separate Opinion).

[66] Subject to prompt release proceedings under UNCLOS, Article 292.

[67] Sohn, 'International law of the sea', 59; cf. Meyers, p. 41.

transnational crimes and the proliferation of WMD, are discussed in subsequent chapters. However, one must first examine those cases where general international law has allocated unilateral, high seas rights of interdiction to all states principally as regards the suppression of piracy and, in a more limited way, the slave trade.

PART II

Interdiction and maritime policing

3 General introduction to Part II

UNCLOS says much about maritime jurisdiction but little about substantive criminal law. UNCLOS parties are obliged to cooperate in suppressing only three particular offences in international waters: piracy,[1] illicit narcotics traffic[2] and unauthorized broadcasting.[3] Of these, high seas jurisdiction to *enforce* is only generally granted over piracy and unauthorized broadcasting,[4] and the latter only in a qualified form.[5] All UNCLOS parties are also obliged *individually* to 'prevent and punish' the use of their flag vessels in the slave trade, but there is no general duty of cooperation to this end, let alone universal high seas enforcement jurisdiction.[6]

These are significant preliminary distinctions to make. Discussion of non-flag-state interdictions on the high seas usually begins with UNCLOS Article 110. Article 110 provides for visit and inspection upon suspicion of:

- piracy;
- slave trading;
- unauthorised radio broadcasting;
- statelessness; and
- a vessel being of the same nationality as the interdicting vessel, despite 'flying a foreign flag or refusing to show its flag'.

In respect of each of the grounds listed in Article 110 a duly authorised State vessel 'clearly marked and identifiable as being on government service' may exercise a 'right of visit' to board the vessel and inspect

---

[1] UNCLOS, Article 100.   [2] *Ibid.*, Article 108.   [3] *Ibid.*, Article 109.
[4] *Ibid.*, Articles 105 and 109.   [5] See Chapter 7.
[6] Contrast Articles 99 and 110(1)(b), UNCLOS, with Articles 100, 105 and 110(1)(a), UNCLOS.

23

its papers and, where suspicion remains, may proceed to 'further examine' the vessel.[7] This list may be apt to mislead; as discussed above, not all such suspect vessels are necessarily subject to seizure. The grant of enforcement jurisdiction may be limited. That fact does not reflect a presumption that piracy and unauthorised broadcasting are more serious crimes than slavery, for example. Viewed in anything but an historical light the law of the sea appears inconsistent – if not morally incoherent – in allocating boarding rights and enforcement jurisdiction.

What we can observe is a long accretive history of experiments in designing jurisdictional regimes to deal with given problems. It has been noted that the law of the sea's 'long-held emphasis on the freedom of navigation and the concomitant respect for the flag State's exclusive jurisdiction' reflects states' preference 'to permit encroachment on their exclusive jurisdiction to the minimum extent possible'.[8] McDougal and Burke conceived the law of the sea as representing a balance between the exclusive interests of coastal or flag states, in matters such as the regulation of coastal fisheries or a flag vessel's internal economy, and the inclusive (or general) interests of all states in matters such as freedom of navigation or high seas fishing.[9] This present study is concerned with matters of state security interests, broadly conceived: violence against shipping, smuggling, counter-proliferation, human food security. In this realm of maritime security Klein has suggested that

[w]hen account is taken of the inclusive interest in promoting maritime security, there is less motivation to uphold exclusive flag State authority tenaciously. Rather it appears that the counterbalance of exclusive interests in flag States has become overly burdensome.[10]

Viewed in a certain light, however, all interests are inclusive.[11] Freedom of navigation, for example, is not simply the reconciliation of

---

[7] UNCLOS, Article 110; [1950] II YBILC, 41. The ILC view was that where a boarding party proceeded to an examination, such a search 'must in no circumstances be used for purposes other than those which warranted stopping the vessel', [1956] II YBILC, 284.

[8] N. Klein, 'Legal limitations on ensuring Australia's maritime security' (2006) 7 MJIL 306 at 334.

[9] McDougal and Burke, ch. 1.   [10] Klein, 'Legal limitations', 335–6.

[11] A point appreciated by Klein: N. Klein, 'The right of visit and the 2005 Protocol on the Suppression of Unlawful Acts Against the Safety of Maritime Navigation' (2007) 35 DJILP 287 at 329–32 (arguing that claims for greater enforcement jurisdiction to protect states' security interests may involve reconceptualising such claims as 'inclusive in nature, rather than exclusive').

the divergent interests of coastal states and flag states. The supposed conflict of interests between flag states and coastal states in the territorial sea is the artificial opposition of two complementary ideas; coastal states may have as much interest in freedom of navigation in other states' territorial waters as flag states have in theirs.[12] Coastal states are also flag states, and many flag states have coasts. Reciprocity alone may account for the strength of the innocent passage regime without needing to presume that a balance between competing interests dictates strict limits upon coastal state sovereignty over territorial waters.[13]

The same observation may be made of the high seas regime. While, as Klein suggests, a different view of the interests involved might have brought about a radically different law of the high seas, it has not. The international community has not followed the piracy model of granting universal enforcement rights to suppress other threats to the general interest on the high seas. Part of the reason, undoubtedly, has been distrust about who might do the enforcing and against whom. Many states have flagged merchant vessels; few have the resources to conduct at-sea interdictions. The model that has won acceptance over time, and shows little likelihood of being displaced by a sudden change in states' perspective or policy preferences, is consensual interdiction. Its rise, and the slow growth of secondary rules regarding the conduct and consequences of such interdictions, can only be assessed historically. It is therefore best to begin with piracy and the slave trade, before turning to the great drivers of modern interdiction practice, treaties dealing with drug interdiction and fisheries inspection. Such consensual interdiction arrangements are contemplated in UNCLOS Article 110(1), which refers to 'acts of interference' regarding foreign flagged vessels in the exercise of 'other powers conferred by treaty'.[14] The development and application of these models to later prohibited activities such as migrant smuggling and WMD proliferation can then be considered. Unauthorised broadcasting may be considered a transitional experiment, peculiar to its subject matter. It is included both for completeness and because the balance struck in its allocation of enforcement jurisdiction illustrates broader concerns.

---

[12] Gidel, III (i), pp. 168–9, 169 n. 1; Churchill and Lowe, p. 81.

[13] Colombos, *International Law of the Sea*, p. 316; cf. Churchill and Lowe, pp. 94–8.

[14] Cf. High Seas Convention, Article 6. Treaty, however, should not be taken to be the only valid means of giving such consent: ad hoc consent is frequently relied on in practice.

4   Piracy and the slave trade

1 Piracy

1.1 Introduction

Although once thought to be principally of historical interest,[1] piracy is once again a field of scholarly contention, not all of it productive. The upsurge in academic interest coincides with renewed concern in maritime safety bodies and amidst fears that contemporary terrorist organisations may use hijacked vessels as weapons against ports or international commerce. This chapter addresses several long-standing misconceptions about piracy as defined under UNCLOS, including criticisms that this definition is narrower than the customary rule; excludes politically motivated violence (e.g. terrorist attacks); and that it wrongly excludes unlawful attacks made by state vessels. Whatever commentators might wish, the UNCLOS rule is the only generally applicable one and the only clear candidate for having customary status.

The academic debate has several principal causes. First, the term 'piracy' only acquired some settled legal meaning relatively recently. In historical discussion pirates are usually contrasted with state-licensed 'privateers'. However, the term 'pirate' was also used to describe a range of activities in the Renaissance, many of which were either lawful or seen as self-help, such as exacting taxes on vessels using disputed sea lanes.[2] It was thus common for sixteenth- and seventeenth-century

---

[1] *Harvard Research*, 765–6.

[2] A. Rubin, 'The law of piracy' (1986–7) 15 DJILP 173 at 189–90, 213. Similarly, some Somalian fishermen turned pirates now seize and ransom foreign fishing vessels and fishermen to 'levy a kind of privatised tax or toll' on the extensive, often unlicensed, foreign trawling in Somali waters: N. Rankin, 'A Basque encounter with pirates',

sovereigns to refer to political allies as 'privateers' and to enemies as 'pirates'.[3] Second, confusion often resulted from failing to distinguish between piracy at international law and various national offences, more widely or narrowly drawn, called piracy.[4] This problem is compounded by international law's reliance on national authorities to prosecute and punish the offence. Third, recent writings on whether terrorism can constitute piracy tend to ignore elements of the conventional crime or become overly concerned with 'universal jurisdiction' over piracy, an unfortunately misleading label, given the separate meaning that term has since acquired in international criminal law.

For present purposes the international law of piracy has three relevant aspects:

(1) piracy is a crime of individual liability under general (or customary) international law;
(2) all states have a common jurisdiction to suppress and punish piracy; and
(3) piracy constitutes an *automatic* exception to the rule of exclusive flag-state jurisdiction allowing boarding and seizure regardless of flag-state consent or whether the boarding state is affected by the vessel's activities.

Discussing piracy thus involves discussing a crime, a head of jurisdiction and an exception to exclusive flag-state jurisdiction. Most commentary on the law, especially calls for its expansion to cover terrorist offences, tend to discuss only one or two of these aspects.

Assuming that one can treat the High Seas Convention and UNCLOS as having codified the law (a debate addressed below), the elements of the crime are:

(1) an act of violence, detention or depredation;
(2) committed for private ends;
(3) on the high seas or in a place outside the jurisdiction of any state; and
(4) by the crew or passengers of a private ship or aircraft, against another vessel or persons or property aboard.

BBC News, 10 May 2008, http://news.bbc.co.uk/1/hi/programmes/from_our_own_correspondent/7392623.stm. See further below, at Chapter 4, section 1.8.

[3] *Ibid.*, 198.

[4] O'Connell, pp. 966 ff.; *Harvard Research*, 764; cf. *Re Piracy Jure Gentium* [1934] AC 586; E. Dickinson, 'Is the crime of piracy obsolete?' (1924–5) 38 *Harvard Law Review* 334 at 340–4. Such confusion remains common; see, e.g., *US v. Shi*, 525 F.3d 709 (2008) at 723.

Obviously, without all four elements being present conduct cannot be characterised as piracy. Discussion nonetheless often overlooks some elements (especially the fourth 'two vessels' requirement) and concentrates too much on others (especially the 'private ends' requirement).

1.2 The prohibition on piracy: theoretical justifications

Piracy is a very different law enforcement subject matter from trafficking in drugs, weapons of mass destruction or migrants, each of which concerns at-sea activities ancillary to unlawful activities on-shore. More closely analogous to fisheries management, piracy involves at-sea boardings in consequence of at-sea activities. Unlike almost all other offences, piracy does away with the requirement of flag-state consent prior to the boarding and seizure. All states thus have a common extraterritorial enforcement jurisdiction over piracy. The necessary corollary, common prescriptive jurisdiction over piracy on the high seas, is recognised as a matter of customary[5] and conventional law.[6]

One theory held that this followed from the presumptive 'denationalisation' of the pirate and pirate vessel.[7] As *hostis humani generis*, an enemy of all mankind, the pirate may romantically be presumed to have 'disclaimed all state allegiance';[8] or the pirate may be thought to be a self-made outlaw, having repudiated all superior authority.[9] The theory has been widely rejected. 'Denationalisation' is clearly not the rationale under UNCLOS, Article 104 of which provides that a pirate vessel 'may retain its nationality', although such 'retention or loss of nationality' is left solely to the flag state's national law. International law is indifferent to the vessel's nationality and interdiction rights exist regardless.

The better rationale is that, as piracy endangers a common interest of all states (high-seas freedom of navigation), the exclusive jurisdiction of flag states does not obtain.[10] The consequences of this proposition have seldom been fully explored. If correct, piracy is not merely a head of jurisdiction, nor strictly an exception to the rule of exclusive

---

[5] *Re Piracy Jure Gentium*, 588–9; *US v. Klintock*, 18 US (5 Wheaton) 144 (1820) at 152; *Harvard Research*, 764.

[6] UNCLOS, Article 105.

[7] Gidel, I, pp. 331–2; *Oppenheim*, 9th edn, 746; *Harvard Research*, 825 ff., and authorities quoted at 758; [1950] II YBILC 67, 70.

[8] *Harvard Research*, 781, 823, cf. 817–18.   [9] O'Connell, p. 970.

[10] Antonio Cassese, *International Criminal Law* (Oxford University Press, 2003), p. 24; McDougal and Burke, p. 808; C. Crockett, 'Toward a revision of the international law of piracy' (1976) 26 *DePaul Law Review* 78 at 81.

flag-state jurisdiction. Such exceptions usually concern only a right of visit, not of seizure or law enforcement. Piracy may be thought of as a case where states, through a customary or conventional rule, have given comprehensive permission in advance to foreign states' assertion of law enforcement jurisdiction over their vessels resulting in the *absence* of any flag state immunity from boarding.

The 'common interest' rationale also squares pragmatically with the primacy generally accorded to coastal states' territorial jurisdiction and management of territorial waters. The law of piracy only applies to events on the high seas; factually piratical acts committed in territorial waters are not, at international law, piracy, and the special common jurisdiction does not apply. A theory predicated on pirates as '*hostes humani generis*' would surely not draw such arbitrary geographical distinctions.[11] Being an 'enemy of all mankind' is thus not a substantive element or consequence of the offence, but purely a rhetorical phrase reflecting its seriousness.[12]

1.3 Current legal definitions: conventional and customary law

1.3.1 UNCLOS

It has long been acknowledged that piracy is a crime which all states may punish; however, there has been significant disagreement over what actually constitutes piracy.[13] It is convenient to start from the modern definition of piracy and then consider its historical defensibility. The most authoritative statement of the modern law of piracy is found in UNCLOS, Articles 100–107. Article 100 provides that all parties have a duty to co-operate 'to the fullest possible extent in the repression of piracy'. Article 101 defines piracy as

(a) any illegal acts of violence or detention, or any act of depredation, committed for private ends by the crew or the passengers of a private ship or a private aircraft, and directed:
  (i) on the high seas, against another ship or aircraft, or against persons or property on board such ship or aircraft;

---

[11] See Lowe, 'Jurisdiction', pp. 348–9, making the point that the best rationale for the jurisdiction over piracy may be the difficulty of apprehending such criminals otherwise.

[12] *Harvard Research*, 796, 806–7; cf. Dickinson, 'Is the crime of piracy obsolete?', 351 ff.

[13] *Oppenheim*, 8th edn, p. 609; *Harvard Research*, 739; cf. *US v. Smith*, 18 US (5 Wheaton) 153 (1820) at 161, and the eighteen-page footnote at 163–80. On *animo furandi* as an element, see Alfred Rubin, *The Law of Piracy* (Newport: Naval War College Press, 1988), pp. 116 n. 49, 324.

    (ii) against a ship, aircraft, persons or property in a place outside the jurisdiction of any State;

  (b) … voluntary participation in the operation of a ship or of an aircraft with knowledge of facts making it a pirate ship or aircraft; [or]

  (c) … inciting or … intentionally facilitating an act described in subparagraph (a) or (b).

This is now generally regarded as codifying custom.[14] The relevance of piracy to the present book is the boarding provisions contained in UNCLOS. Under Article 110 a foreign-flagged vessel can be visited by the public vessel of any state on suspicion of piracy, and under Article 105 a pirate vessel may be seized and its crew prosecuted under the seizing vessel's national law. These provisions reproduce the relevant articles of the High Seas Convention,[15] and have their origin in the work of the Harvard Research Committee's codification project of the 1930s. Given its influence on subsequent treaty-drafting,[16] especially through its impact upon the ILC draft articles on the law of the sea,[17] the Harvard Draft Convention remains an appropriate starting point.

1.3.2 The Harvard Draft Convention

Piracy was conceived under the Harvard Draft Convention as 'a special common basis of jurisdiction'; an exception to the rule that a state's ordinary jurisdiction 'is limited … to its territory and ships and persons or things therein, to its nationals abroad and … injuries to interests under its protection'.[18] The principal reason for taking this approach was the presumption that if piracy was a crime it would place a positive duty upon states to punish it, which seemed inconsistent with several states lacking relevant national laws.[19] Strictly, this approach is correct. While the relevant ILC draft, the High Seas Convention and UNCLOS all reflect a positive duty for states to co-operate in suppressing piracy they do not actually oblige states to punish it.[20] Under Article 105 of UNCLOS, any state *may* seize a pirate vessel and its courts *may* 'decide upon the penalties to be imposed'. This implies a permissive,

---

[14] Brownlie, p. 229.   [15] High Seas Convention, Articles 13–21.
[16] McDougal and Burke, pp. 810–11.
[17] See [1955] I YBILC at 40 ff., [1956] II YBILC 253 at 282–4.
[18] *Harvard Research*, 757, 768.   [19] *Harvard Research*, 755–6, 760.
[20] The consequences of the difference between a duty to co-operate in or with enforcement activity and actually to enforce certain rules is explored in the fisheries context in Chapter 6, sections 3.1 and 6.2.

not mandatory, grant of universal jurisdiction and a choice of means as to how to co-operate to suppress piracy.

It is sufficient to quote the Harvard Draft's definition for comparison with the UNCLOS definition set out above.

Piracy is any of the following acts, committed in a place not within the territorial jurisdiction of any state:

(1) Any act of violence or of depredation, committed with intent to rob, rape, wound, enslave, imprison or kill a person or with intent to steal or destroy property, for private ends without bona fide purpose of asserting a claim of right …

(2) Any act of voluntary participation in the operation of a ship with knowledge of facts making it a pirate ship.

(3) Any act of instigation or of intentional facilitation of an act described in paragraph 1 or paragraph 2 of this Article.[21]

Evidently, much of this language was retained verbatim in what has become UNCLOS Article 101.

While some would argue that the High Seas Convention did not succeed in codifying the original customary rule,[22] the subsequent treaty practice indicates the contrary. The provisions were re-enacted in UNCLOS without debate[23] and with little more than stylistic changes,[24] and the UNCLOS definition of the crime has now also been reproduced in a regional treaty.[25] Given that there are now 153 state parties to UNCLOS,[26] the continued existence of a different customary crime (even assuming that the original treaty provision was not codifying) seems unlikely. There is no articulated opposition to the UNCLOS formulation, including from states in regions where piracy occurs. Indeed, it is precisely such states which have turned to the UNCLOS definition in drafting new regional arrangements.

The argument that the UNCLOS definition diverges from the historical definition fails to consider the effect the successively re-enacted treaty rule may have had on international law[27] and assumes

---

[21] Harvard Draft Convention, Article 3; see *Harvard Research*, 743, 768.

[22] Rubin, *Law of Piracy*, p. 344; O'Connell, p. 970; Barrios, 'Casting a wider net', 161.

[23] M. Halberstam, 'Terrorism on the high seas: the *Achille Lauro*, piracy and the IMO Convention on Maritime Safety' (1988) 82 AJIL 269 at 284.

[24] Rubin, *Law of Piracy*, p. 337.

[25] Regional Cooperation Agreement on Combating Piracy and Armed Robbery against Ships in Asia 2005, (2005) 44 ILM 829 (ReCAAP), Article 1(1).

[26] See www.un.org/Depts/los/reference_files/status2007.pdf (current to 4 April 2007).

[27] *North Sea Continental Shelf Cases*, [1969] ICJ Rep. 1969, 3 at 41; Brownlie, p. 6.

that any underlying customary rule has not changed in fifty years. Further, it treats the historical diversity of opinion as supporting a *broader* rule than the UNCLOS definition. While that conclusion is not impossible, neither is it necessary. If the rule that states can generally agree upon is a 'lowest common denominator' narrower than that expounded by some commentators, it seems more likely that this represents the rule's settled core than an arbitrary departure from it. The critical issues to address under any of the slightly varying definitions are:

(1) whether the requirement that piracy be committed for 'private ends' excludes politically motivated offences;
(2) the consequences of the limitation upon jurisdiction that the crime must occur 'on the high seas' or 'outside the jurisdiction of any state'; and
(3) the meaning of 'universal' jurisdiction over piracy.

The analysis here will be given practical content by reference to contemporary piracy, particularly state practice in the region surrounding the Malacca Strait and off Somalia. These are among the regions most specially affected by piracy and are also at the centre of the first regional and international counter-piracy arrangements.

1.4 The exclusion of political offences?

The words 'for private ends' in the conventional definitions of piracy have engendered controversy. Some have assumed that they restrict the offence to acts motivated by personal gain; thus holding any other motivation, especially a political one, precludes piracy being committed. This was not the drafters' intention in either the Harvard Draft or the High Seas Convention.[28] While many writers historically referred to piracy as 'robbery on the high seas', the intent to rob was not necessarily part of the offence. When one contends that

armed men, sailing the seas on board a vessel without any commission from any state, could attack and kill everybody on board another vessel … without committing the crime of piracy unless they stole, say, an article worth sixpence, … [one is] almost tempted to say that a little common sense is a valuable quality in the interpretation of international law.[29]

---

[28] Halberstam, 'Terrorism on the high seas', 277.
[29] *Re Piracy Jure Gentium* [1934] AC 586 at 594.

The common interest of all states served by the rule against piracy is the safety of navigation upon the high seas. Acts of violence, revenge or rape are as much a hazard to a vessel's safety, crew and passengers as mere robbery.

A similar approach is required in assessing claims that the 'private ends' requirement excludes politically motivated acts. The Harvard Draft included the words 'for private ends' with the express intent of excluding civil-war insurgents.[30] However, that intention must be read against references to the limited belligerent rights of 'recognised insurgents'.[31] That is, it had sometimes been said that insurgents whose actions on the high seas were limited to attacking vessels of the government they were attempting to overthrow enjoyed a limited exception from being classed as pirates.[32] The exemption could be understood as not being about motive but the class of vessel attacked, being those that are legitimate targets for insurgents in the course of a civil conflict.

Rather than focus on objective criteria such as the status of the vessels involved, academic debate has focused on whether the exemption relies on subjective intent. This has raised for discussion whether various acts committed on the high seas by groups engaged in self-determination struggles can be distinguished from those of pirates or terrorists on the basis of motive alone. While this debate will be canvassed more extensively below, at the outset it should be said that many such arguments are based on examples which, regardless of motive, would not constitute piracy. It is enough to consider several scenarios:

(a) passengers or crew of a vessel in territorial or international waters mutiny, seize the vessel and take others aboard hostage in an attempt either to negotiate with a particular government or governments or to intimidate them into taking certain actions (the *Santa Maria* and *Achille Lauro*);

(b) aboard such a hijacked vessel, in territorial or international waters, the insurgents kill a hostage (*Achille Lauro*);

---

[30] *Harvard Research*, 798.

[31] *Ibid.*, 857. The importance of this does not appear to have been fully appreciated in the report of ILC rapporteur J. P. A. François when he quotes the *Harvard Research* at 786; see [1955] I YBILC, 40. The Harvard Draft only excluded acts committed for 'private ends without *bona fide* purpose of asserting a claim of right'. Insurgents were thus excluded as persons prosecuting a claim of belligerent rights.

[32] *Harvard Research*, 798 ff., 857 ff.; Halberstam, 'Terrorism on the high seas', 275, 278–9, 288; *Oppenheim*, 9th edn, 748 ff.; *US v. Klintock* 18 US 144 (1820).

(c) hijackers board a vessel from their own craft (such as a speedboat),
     take control of the vessel by force and take the passengers hostage
     in territorial or international waters (as occurs off Somalia);
(d) the hijackers in (c) kill one of the hostages;
(e) insurgents engaged in a struggle to overthrow a recognised state
     government attack ships indiscriminately in that state's territorial
     waters to finance their actions;
(f) insurgents engaged in a struggle to overthrow a recognised
     government attack its warships or government vessels in
     international waters; and
(g) the same insurgents attack foreign-flagged private vessels in
     international waters.

Many of these cases are excluded under any definition of piracy before
one could arrive at questions of political motive. To return to the definition: piracy is violence committed from one vessel against another
in international waters and excludes 'offences committed in a place
subject to the ordinary jurisdiction of a State'.[33] Cases (a) and (b) are
not piracy because only one vessel is involved. The vessel remains subject to the exclusive jurisdiction of the flag state and its criminal law
applies to events aboard. Cases occurring entirely within territorial
waters are similarly matters solely for the criminal jurisdiction of the
coastal state. Thus, the cases considered in (c) and (d) regarding territorial waters, and also (e), cannot be piracy.

The case in (f) is arguably first a matter for the international law
applicable to internal conflicts, regardless of what flag the insurgents are
flying. One might thus presume the governing law to be the customary
law and minimum convention law (such as Common Article 3 of the
Geneva Conventions) applicable to a non-international armed conflict.
However, this helps us little as the law of naval warfare applicable to
a non-international armed conflict has received little scholarly attention.[34] There was, prior to the High Seas Convention, a further conflict
over whether any exception to the law of piracy applied only to *recognised* insurgencies (i.e. recognised by states not a party to the conflict).
While the Harvard Draft took this restrictive approach,[35] Lauterpacht
considered that 'in general, the attitude of governments consists of
refusing to treat as pirates the vessels of *unrecognised* insurgents, so

---

[33] [1955] I YBILC, 42; quoting *Harvard Research*, 809–10.
[34] See, however, H. Lauterpacht, 'Insurrection et piraterie' (1939) 46 RGDIP 513;
     O'Connell, pp. 975–7; Ronzitti, 'Crisis of the traditional law', pp. 10–13.
[35] See references above, at n. 30.

long as their depredations are limited to the [vessels] of their state of origin'.[36]

The exception for insurgents (recognised or not) would be easiest to justify if it could be claimed that *inherently* insurgents cannot meet the definition of piracy so long as they attack only the ships of their own government. Such a claim can be made if one accepts that insurgents attacking legitimate targets in an internal conflict are exercising a limited form of public power. This follows logically from the proposition that a state's form of government may be internally reconstituted by civil war; thus an insurgency may represent, in embryonic form, a future effective government. Insurgents can thus be distinguished from both pirates and terrorists on the basis that they have the recognised capacity at international law to become a lawful government.[37] This limited public power or status has nothing to do with the subjective intent of the insurgency per se, but rather the qualified form of international personality it holds as a potential future government and the fact that the exception is predicated on an objective condition, the choice of targets. Again, this can be understood on the basis that any other class of vessel (foreign-flagged or not) would not be legitimate targets in a civil war.

The law applicable to the insurgents in (g) is obviously that of piracy. This follows not only from the plain words of the modern definition, but also from the proposition that direct attacks upon civilians are generally prohibited by international humanitarian law. Further, the laws of armed conflict make it quite clear that an insurgency may not exercise belligerent rights such as stopping and searching neutral or third-party ships for contraband and seizing cargoes.[38] If such activity is not recognised as a belligerent right, the only applicable law must be piracy. No further immunity arises. While a victorious insurgency is liable as a matter of state responsibility for 'illegal acts or omissions by their forces occurring during an armed conflict',[39] this does not

---

[36] My emphasis and translation: 'En général, l'attitude des gouvernements consiste à refuser de traiter comme pirates des navires d'insurgés *non reconnus*, tant que leurs déprédations se limitent à leur Etat d'origine.' Lauterpacht, 'Insurrection et piraterie', 518, cf. 515, 516, 521, 523; contra, *The Ambrose Light* 25 Fed. 408 (SDNY 1885) at 412. A broader rule can be discerned in inter-American treaty practice: Rubin, *Law of Piracy*, p. 297.

[37] ILC Articles on State Responsibility, Article 10.

[38] *Harvard Research*, 857; Lauterpacht, 'Insurrection et piraterie', 518; Ronzitti, 'Crisis of the traditional law', p. 11.

[39] Brownlie, p. 438; cf. [2001] II(2) YBILC, 50–2.

necessarily mean that such illegalities are retroactively protected by state immunity. The rule of state responsibility applying to insurgencies is already something of an anomalous exception. Besides, in cases where a state organ acts in excess of its powers, nothing precludes there being a simultaneous finding of individual criminal liability and state responsibility (for failure to prevent the illegality). Piratical acts against private vessels are clearly beyond the limited 'powers' of an insurgency and cannot subsequently be clothed in state immunity merely because, if the insurgency succeeds, they may also attract state responsibility.

This leaves us with one scenario only where, if political intent may constitute an exception to piracy, it would be relevant: case (c), where insurgents acting in international waters board a vessel from their own craft, seize it and take the passengers hostage. Some debate along these lines was prompted by the 1961 *Santa Maria* and the 1985 *Achille Lauro* incidents, despite the first being a case of the mutiny of passengers and the latter a case of members of the Palestine Liberation Front (PLF) boarding the vessel while in port.[40] The argument commonly made is that the 'private ends' requirement means 'any hijacking … for political reasons is automatically excluded from the definition of piracy'.[41] Indeed, the lack of express reference to piracy committed for political motives in the ILC's draft articles was criticised by Czechoslovakia during the High Seas Convention negotiations.[42] It is, nevertheless, a view fundamentally mistaking the rule's purpose and the interests involved.

The test of piracy lies not in the pirate's subjective motivation, but in the lack of public sanction for his or her acts. This is why vessels on military or government service, absent the revolt of the crew, cannot, by definition, be pirate vessels.[43] To claim that a 'political' motive can exclude an act from the definition of piracy is to mistake the applicable

---

[40] McDougal and Burke, pp. 821–3; Halberstam, 'Terrorism on the high seas', 269.

[41] Shaw, p. 549; cf. *Annotated Commander's Handbook*, p. 224; *Third Restatement of Foreign Relations Law*, II, p. 85 n. 2; McDougal and Burke, p. 822; Barrios, 'Casting a wider net', 153; Crockett, 'Toward a revision of the international law of piracy', 80; T. Garmon, 'International law of the sea: reconciling the law of piracy and terrorism in the wake of September 11th' (2002) 27 TMLJ 257 at 258 and 274; E. Stiles, 'Reforming current international law to combat modern sea piracy' (2004) 27 *Suffolk Transnational Law Review* 299 at 324–5; *Harvard Research*, 786.

[42] United Nations Conference on the Law of the Sea, *Official Records, Vol. IV: Second Committee (High Seas: General Régime)*, UN Doc. A/CONF.13/40, 78, para. 33.

[43] UNCLOS, Article 103.

concept of 'public' and 'private' acts. The essence of a piratical act is that it neither raises 'the immunity which pertains to state or governmental acts'[44] nor engages state responsibility.[45] Public acts are tested not by reference to the political or subjective motives of an actor, but by reference to state sanction or authority;[46] or in the case of the historical exemption sometimes accorded insurgents prior to the law's codification, by whether the attacked vessel was a legitimate target for an insurgency.

It is not merely that pirates sail without 'sanction from any public authority or sovereign power'[47] that renders them liable to prosecution; it is that their acts impinge upon the monopoly of states over legitimate violence and claims to seize and redistribute property. The crime is one of deliberately operating outside the law of a state-based system and committing unauthorised acts which impinge upon it, not one of acting for mere personal gain.[48] Put simply, the words 'for private ends' must be understood broadly. All acts of violence that lack state sanction are acts undertaken 'for private ends'.

It is sometimes thought, however, that the 1937 Nyon Arrangement on Submarine Warfare,[49] drafted during the Spanish Civil War, supports the proposition that states can commit piracy.[50] This involves a considerable overstatement. The Nyon Arrangement's preamble refers to indiscriminate acts of unrestricted submarine warfare which 'should be justly treated as acts of piracy' and countered with 'special collective [defensive] measures against [such] piratical acts by submarines'. The nine operative articles are not at all concerned with international criminal law or, in any ordinary sense, piracy. They lay down rules of engagement with submarines, and create what might be thought of as an early type of naval exclusion zone[51] in the Mediterranean (requiring compliance with certain conditions if submarines are to have safe passage). The preambular references to 'piracy' are simply an example of the term's use for condemnatory rhetorical effect, not strict legal

---

[44] *Harvard Research*, 798.   [45] McDougal and Burke, p. 808.
[46] Halberstam, 'Terrorism on the high seas', 276–84.
[47] *United States v. Brig Malek Adhel*, 43 US (2 How.) 210 (1844), 232; cf. *Re Piracy Jure Gentium* [1934] AC 586 at 594 and *Harvard Research*, 817–18.
[48] Rubin, *Law of Piracy*, p. 143.   [49] (1937) 181 LNTS 135.
[50] *Oppenheim*, 8th edn, pp. 612–14; cf O'Connell, p. 973; Halberstam, 'Terrorism on the high seas', 281; [1955] I YBILC 43–4. Contra, *Oppenheim*, 9th edn, pp. 750–1.
[51] See Doswald-Beck, *San Remo Manual*, pp. 181 ff.; Heintschel von Heinegg, 'Law of armed conflict at sea', 464 ff.

meaning.[52] The Arrangement's operative articles concern collective defence of neutral shipping, not crimes. The applicable law is that of the use of force to defend flag vessels, not international criminal law, let alone the law of piracy. There is simply no need to expand the ordinary understanding of piracy to encompass what would now be regarded as war crimes or (in times of peace) acts of state responsibility.[53]

Returning to subjective intent, '[i]t is undesirable to permit the collateral motives or purposes of an offender to control the matter of state jurisdiction'.[54] The view, expressed above, that subjective motives are irrelevant is supported by the *Castle John* case, concerning Belgian Greenpeace protesters who took violent action against a Dutch vessel in international waters to draw attention to its polluting activities.[55] A Belgian court found that the protestors' political motivation provided no defence. By committing acts of violence 'in support of a personal point of view' Greenpeace members had committed an act of piracy and could thus not rely upon the rule of exclusive flag-state jurisdiction to exclude the jurisdiction of the Belgian courts.[56] This is the only approach to take. The rule against piracy exists to protect the freedom of navigation and the safety of persons upon the high seas. This function is not served by reading the definition as inherently excluding acts with a subjective 'political' motive.

Treaty law, as a form of state practice, might be considered ambivalent as to whether political motivations may exclude criminal responsibility for acts of violence at sea. The Convention for the Suppression of Unlawful Acts against the Safety of Maritime Navigation (SUA Convention) expressly criminalises acts including seizing 'control over a ship by force or threat thereof' or performing 'an act of violence against a person on board a ship if that act is likely to endanger the safe navigation of that ship'.[57] Notably, however, it does not, like a number of later terrorism suppression treaties, expressly exclude the 'political offence exemption' from applying to extradition requests regarding such offences.[58] Is such an omission to

---

[52] Rubin, *Law of Piracy*, pp. 295–7; see also Fitzmaurice's arguments in [1955] I YBILC, 43–44, 56; Lauterpacht, 'Insurrection et piraterie', 525.

[53] See the exchanges in the ILC over Nationalist China's seizure of Polish ships: [1955] I YBILC 37 ff.

[54] *Harvard Research*, 823.

[55] *Castle John v. NV Mabeco* (Belgium, Court of Cassation, 1986) 77 ILR 537.

[56] *Ibid.*, 540.   [57] SUA Convention, Article 3.

[58] International Convention for the Suppression of Terrorist Bombings 1997, 2149 UNTS 256; Article 11; International Convention for the Suppression of Terrorist

be interpreted as suggesting that such offences may have a relevant political character? Given that the SUA Convention was a response to politically motivated attacks against shipping in the 1980s, including the *Achille Lauro*, one would be tempted to conclude that the entire structure of the Convention would be rendered abortive if politically motivated violence were excluded from its scope.[59] However, one must recall the long-running debate in the UN General Assembly as to whether acts in furtherance of self-determination could constitute terrorism.[60] It was not until 1985 that a General Assembly resolution condemned, without defining, terrorist tactics 'wherever and by whomever committed'.[61] The same resolution, however, upheld the legitimacy of self-determination struggles,[62] one possible inference being that there might still be *legitimate* acts of politically motivated violence. The now-standard UN phrase, that acts of terrorism 'are in any circumstances unjustifiable, whatever the considerations of a political, philosophical, ideological, racial, ethnic, religious or any other nature that may be invoked to justify them', did not emerge until the 1994 Declaration on Measures to Eliminate International Terrorism.[63] However, the new SUA Protocol on suppression of traffic in WMD does expressly exclude any 'political offence' ground to refuse extradition for Protocol offences.[64] Thus, while there might have been some ambiguity in the treaty practice at the time of the SUA Convention's conclusion, it would be hard to say that subsequent practice has demonstrated a persistent consensus in the international community that political motives can excuse otherwise criminal acts, such as hostage-taking, upon the high seas. Indeed, there appears to

---

Financing 1999, (2000) 39 ILM 268; Article 14; International Convention for the Suppression of Acts of Nuclear Terrorism 2005, Article 15, annexed to 'Report of the Ad Hoc Committee established by General Assembly resolution 51/210 of 17 December 1996' (4 April 2005), UN Doc. A/59/766.

[59] To paraphrase Lord Browne-Wilkinson in *R v. Bow Street Metropolitan Stipendiary Magistrate and others, ex parte Pinochet Ugarte (No. 3)* [2000] 1 AC 119 at 205, and (2000) 119 ILR 135 at 156.

[60] See Cassese, *International Criminal Law*, pp. 120–6.

[61] GA Res. 40/61 (9 December 1985), para. 1.

[62] *Ibid.*, eighth preambular paragraph.

[63] Para. 3, as Annexed to GA Res. 49/60 (17 February 1994). See also International Convention for the Suppression of Terrorist Bombings, Article 5; International Convention for the Suppression of Terrorist Financing, Article 6; International Convention for the Suppression of Acts of Nuclear Terrorism, Article 6.

[64] Protocol of 2005 to the Convention for the Suppression of Unlawful Acts against the Safety of Maritime Navigation (1 November 2005), IMO Doc. LEG/CONF.15/21, Article 11*bis*.

be a clearly emerging consensus in UN practice that the deliberate targeting of civilians in an armed conflict or self-determination struggle anywhere and by any party is always unacceptable.[65] We thus do not need to resolve the debate over the definition of terrorism to conclude that political motivations alone will not prevent an act being characterised as one committed for private (that is, non-public) ends. Civil war insurgents boarding another state's flagged vessel and taking civilian hostages in international waters will thus always be pirates, regardless of their motives. Similar politically motivated criminal attacks will also be piracy, whether we also call them terrorism or not.

In practice, the most likely reason why politically inspired hostage-taking in international waters will not be piracy is that such attacks are seldom staged from one vessel against another, an essential element of piracy.[66] Incidents such as the *Achille Lauro* and *Santa Maria* involved a group of passengers seizing the vessel from within; under such circumstances the flag state will retain exclusive jurisdiction. The usual argument made for extending the customary law of piracy to acts of terrorism is the asserted need for 'universal jurisdiction' over such crimes.[67] In this context it is again important to distinguish prescriptive and enforcement jurisdiction. Regarding enforcement jurisdiction, the law of piracy codified under UNCLOS primarily provides a right of interference on the high seas and allows pirates to be subjected to the national law of the capturing warship.[68] UNCLOS contains only a duty to suppress piracy on the high seas;[69] it does not expressly provide for, in the manner of many terrorism suppression treaties, state prosecution of offenders discovered within their territorial jurisdiction for acts committed elsewhere. However, it has long been assumed that a suspected pirate 'may be tried and punished by any nation into

---

[65] See the preamble to each of the terrorism suppression conventions, cited above at n. 58; High-level Panel on Threats, Challenges and Change, A More Secure World: Our Shared Responsibility (2 December 2004), UN Doc. A/59/565, 48 at para. 160; A.-M. Slaughter and W. Burke-White, 'An international constitutional moment' (2002) 43 HILJ 1; cf. ICTY, *Prosecutor v. Kupreški*, Case No. IT-95–16-T (14 January 2000), 204, at para. 521, www.un.org/icty/kupreskic/trialc2/judgement/kup-tj000114e.pdf.

[66] G. Constantinople, 'Towards a new definition of piracy: the *Achille Lauro* incident' (1986) 26 *Virginia Journal of International Law* 723 at 734, and 742.

[67] Halberstam, 'Terrorism on the high seas', 289; Garmon, 'International law of the sea', 271; cf. J. Noyes, 'An introduction to the international law of piracy' (1990) 21 CWILJ 105 at 109.

[68] UNCLOS, Articles 105 and 107.   [69] Ibid., Article 100.

whose jurisdiction he may come'[70] and such exercises of universal enforcement jurisdiction still occur. The US Navy has arrested Somali pirates in international waters who were subsequently delivered to and prosecuted by Kenyan authorities.[71] While assimilating maritime terrorism to piracy would therefore provide territorial jurisdiction over individual terrorists after they had fled the high seas, this consequence would not be severable from the customary right of high-seas intervention.

Creating such a right would involve a significant loss of control by the flag state over its hijacked vessel. When a ship has been seized internally, it may be a very sensitive matter as to how one secures the release of hostages. Granting every state in the world simultaneous authority to board the ship seems unlikely to promote their safety. One can well imagine most states being reluctant to assent to a rule granting universal boarding rights, not qualified by a consent requirement, over their flag vessels while in the hands of hostage-takers or internal mutineers. If the flag state wishes to waive its exclusive jurisdiction and call upon other states' naval forces to assist, it may, as happened in the *Santa Maria* incident.[72] The contention that any unlawful violence committed upon the high seas, including mutiny by passengers, constitutes piracy at customary international law[73] simply runs counter to the 'great weight' of academic opinion and treaty practice.[74]

Some commentators have assumed that terrorist vessels, flying a flag of convenience, would be immune from interference on the high seas and would face little likelihood of the flag state exercising effective enforcement jurisdiction over their activities.[75] As argued above, however, politically motivated violence involving an attack in international waters by one vessel against another falls within the scope of piracy at general international law or under UNCLOS. The words 'for private

---

[70] *Lotus Case*, 70, per Judge Moore (Dissenting Opinion); cf. *Harvard Research*, 852–6; Brownlie, p. 229; Shaw, pp. 549–50.

[71] US Navy News, 'Suspected pirates captured off Somali coast', 21 January 2006, www.news.navy.mil/search/display.asp?story_id=22026; BBC News, 'Jail sentence for Somali pirates', 1 November 2006, http://news.bbc.co.uk/go/pr/fr/-/1/hi/world/africa/6105262.stm.

[72] Halberstam, 'Terrorism on the high seas', 286.

[73] *Ibid.*, 273; *Oppenheim*, 8th edn, p. 609; contra, *Oppenheim*, 9th edn, pp. 751–2.

[74] *Harvard Research*, 810; cf. the ILC rapporteur's view in [1955] I YBILC, 42–3; and UNCLOS, Article 102; High Seas Convention, Article 16.

[75] Garmon, 'International law of the sea', 268.

ends' are to be interpreted broadly. Further, as seen in international treaty practice, a violent act's political motivation should not be seen as relevant to its characterisation as an ordinary crime. The words 'for private ends' simply emphasise that the violence involved lacks state sanction or authority. This lack of authority is a question that may be tested objectively and without reference to subjective motives. The only possible exception is a limited one for insurgencies attacking the government vessels of their state of nationality. Even so, the test is not the subjective motivation of the insurgents, but turns on the objective questions of its status as an insurgency at international law and its choice of targets under the laws of war. Where a vessel on the high seas was suspected of having been used in a terrorist attack, it could be boarded and searched on suspicion of piracy under Article 110, and such offenders could be subsequently prosecuted if discovered within state territory.

1.5 Special elements and geographical limits of the offence

Piracy consists of ... any *illegal* acts of violence or detention, or any act of depredation, committed for private ends by the crew or the passengers of a private ship or a private aircraft, and directed ... *on the high seas*, against another ship or aircraft, or against persons or property on board such ship or aircraft; ... [or] against a ship, aircraft, persons or property in a *place outside the jurisdiction of any State*.[76]

This definition raises two further issues for consideration: the significance of the phrase 'piracy consists ... of any *illegal* acts' and the territorial scope of the 'the high seas' and places 'outside the jurisdiction of any State'. To be an offence, must piracy consist of acts possessing an inherently or additionally illegal character? And what of acts occurring within areas of special or limited state jurisdiction, such as the EEZ or contiguous zone?[77]

It was the ILC that inserted the 'ambiguous'[78] and 'bootstrapping'[79] words 'any illegal acts' into the Harvard Draft definition. While this has been described as making the definition legally 'incomprehensible', the words remain capable of being given unstrained meanings.[80] The words '[a]ny ... acts' were clearly intended to broaden, not narrow,

---

[76] UNCLOS, Article 101 (emphasis added).
[77] Noyes, 'Introduction to the international law of piracy', 108.
[78] *Ibid.*, 107.   [79] McDougal and Burke, p. 811.
[80] A. Rubin, 'Revising the law of piracy' (1990) 21 CWILJ 129, 136; cf. Rubin, *Law of Piracy*, p. 344.

the range of conduct captured by the definition.[81] An alternative view is that this serves to emphasize that the act must 'be dissociated from a lawful authority',[82] as discussed above regarding 'private ends'. The definition would be rendered unnecessarily complicated if before an act constituted piracy it also had to be demonstrably illegal under some state's internal law. Indeed, an argument along these lines was put by Greece for the deletion of the word 'illegal' altogether.[83] The view that these words are intended only to expand the range of covered conduct is clearly preferable.

The more pressing issue is the geographic extent of state jurisdiction over piracy. Universal jurisdiction to prescribe crimes such as war crimes or breaches of the Geneva Conventions of 1949 inheres in all states, regardless of where the offences were committed.[84] By contrast, while all states have jurisdiction over piracy, that jurisdiction only exists where the prohibited acts are committed on the high seas or 'outside the jurisdiction of any State'.[85] Violence committed against vessels within territorial or internal waters is not piracy at international law. The geographic scope of piracy is thus unusually limited for a crime subject to universal jurisdiction,[86] and discussing it in the same terms as other universal crimes may not be entirely helpful.[87]

This exclusion of areas within territorial jurisdiction from prescriptive and enforcement jurisdiction over piracy raises the question of piracy within the contiguous zone and EEZ. Such areas are not 'outside the jurisdiction of any State' in the sense that no degree of coastal state jurisdiction exists; however, the limited jurisdiction granted over such waters does not extend to repressing piracy. During the third UN Conference on the Law of the Sea Peru twice suggested that the

---

[81] McDougal and Burke, pp. 811–12.

[82] Crockett, 'Toward a revision of the international law of piracy', 82.

[83] UN Conference on the Law of the Sea, Official Records, Vol. IV: Second Committee (High Seas: General Régime), UN Doc. A/CONF.13/40, p. 83.

[84] *Oppenheim*, 9th edn, pp. 469–70; Brownlie, pp. 303–5; Shaw, p. 594.

[85] UNCLOS, Article 101(a).

[86] Note, however, O'Keefe's suggestion that 'universal jurisdiction' simply describes jurisdiction in the absence of other accepted links between prosecuting state and offence: O'Keefe, 'Universal jurisdiction', 745, 755.

[87] E.g. *Attorney-General of Israel v. Eichmann* (District Court, 1968) 36 ILR 5 at 26; *Attorney-General of Israel v. Eichmann* (Supreme Court, 1968) 36 ILR 277 at 298; *Arrest Warrant Case*, President Guillaume (Separate Opinion), 37–8 at para. 5; Judge Koroma (Separate Opinion), 62–3 at para. 9; Judges Higgins, Kooijmans and Buergenthal (Joint Separate Opinion), 79 at paras. 52 and 54; contra, Judge Bula-Bula (Separate Opinion), 121 at para. 64.

definition of piracy should be amended to include acts committed within an EEZ: both suggestions were rejected.[88] The ambiguity is compounded by UNCLOS' final text, as Article 86 states:

The provisions of this Part [VII, including the piracy provisions] apply to all parts of the sea that are not included in the exclusive economic zone, in the territorial sea or in the internal waters of a State, or in the archipelagic waters of an archipelagic State.

While this might be taken to exclude the high-seas regime from applying in the EEZ, it is better thought of as preventing any assumption that it applies automatically and in its entirety. The drafting was intended to reflect 'the unified character of the oceans (in particular the exclusive economic zone and the high seas)' and to embody the proposition that 'the regime of the high seas [applied] in the exclusive economic zone, except with respect to [coastal state sovereignty over] resources'.[89] This view is reinforced by Article 58(2), providing that so far as it is not incompatible with the rights apportioned to the coastal state, the regime of the high seas applies in the EEZ.[90] Thus the residual application of the high-seas regime of criminal law enforcement to the EEZ and contiguous zone should not be controversial.

During the negotiation of the UN Narcotics Convention some states, chiefly Brazil,[91] took the view that foreign states required the coastal state's permission before engaging in law enforcement action within its EEZ.[92] A number of other states maintained that coastal states had no rights that could be infringed by a flag state authorising a third-party interdiction when its vessel was within a coastal state's EEZ.[93] This resulted in the Narcotics Convention's use of a tortuous formula granting jurisdiction to interdict suspect vessels 'exercising freedom of navigation' in accordance with international law.[94] This compromise language has not been repeated in the 2005 SUA Protocol. The Protocol's reference instead to boarding any vessel 'located seaward of any State's

---

[88] *UNCLOS Commentary*, III, pp. 183–4, 199–200.   [89] *Ibid.*, pp. 68–9.

[90] UNCLOS, Article 58(2).

[91] Roach and Smith, *United States Responses*, pp. 415–16.

[92] The debate is recorded in Official Records: Narcotics Convention Conference, 17th meeting, UN Doc. E/CONF.82/C.2/SR.17 (8 December 1988), paras. 1–9, 13–15, 20–23, 26–29, 47–52; 29th meeting, UN Doc. E/CONF.82/C.2/SR.29 (15 December 1988), paras. 1–128 and annex; cf. *UN Practical Guide*, p. 113.

[93] *Ibid.*, especially UN Doc. E/CONF.82/C.2/SR.17 at paras. 12 (Netherlands), 26 (UK), 28 (USSR), 47 (Argentina); cf. Marston (1988), 529.

[94] *Ibid.*, especially E/CONF.82/C.2/SR.29; UN Narcotics Convention, Article 17(3).

territorial sea'[95] may indicate that states now generally accepted that law enforcement action taken by a foreign state's law-enforcement vessels within an EEZ but outside territorial waters is permissible so long as it does not interfere with the subject matters reserved to the coastal State's jurisdiction. The same reasoning should apply to the contiguous zone. This appears consistent with discussion in the MV 'Saiga' case, insofar as the International Tribunal for the Law of the Sea (ITLOS) rejected arguments that coastal states could claim additional heads of subject matter jurisdiction over their EEZ beyond those enumerated in UNCLOS by reference to a pressing 'public interest'.[96] While UNCLOS does not preclude new customary coastal state rights arising in the EEZ, there is little practice supporting any rule of exclusive and general coastal state criminal enforcement jurisdiction in the EEZ.[97]

1.6 Modern forms of piracy

Scholars in the 1920s thought piracy 'chiefly of historical interest',[98] and eminent writers as late as 1962 considered it no longer a significant problem.[99] While high-seas depredations may no longer rival those of commissioned privateers in Renaissance times, in the twenty-first century the crime is far from obsolete. High-seas piracy remains a significant problem for the safety of international shipping[100] and a subject of concern to the International Maritime Organization (IMO)[101] and the International Maritime Bureau (IMB), a division of

[95] See SUA Protocol 2005, Article 8bis(5).

[96] The M/V 'Saiga' (No. 2), (1999) 38 ILM 1323 at 1350–1; cf. Judge Nelson (Separate Opinion), 1389; Judge Vukas (Separate Opinion), 1398–1403; Judge Laing (Separate Opinion), 1415; contra, Judge Zhao (Separate Opinion), 1383–4; note Keyuan's proposed residual interest in safety of navigation in the EEZ or even primary criminal jurisdiction over pirates captured there: Z. Keyuan, 'Issues of public international law relating to the crackdown of piracy in the South China Sea and prospects for regional cooperation' (1999) 3 SJICL 524 at 530, and 'Enforcing the law of piracy in the South China Sea' (2000) 31 JMLC 107 at 111.

[97] M/V 'Saiga' (No. 2), Judge Vukas (Separate Opinion), 1402.

[98] Dickinson, 'Is the crime of piracy obsolete?', 334.

[99] McDougal and Burke, p. 806; cf. UN Conference on the Law of the Sea, Official Records, Vol. IV: Second Committee (High Seas: General Régime) (9 April 1958), UN Doc. A/CONF.13/40, pp. 78–9.

[100] See the 23 March 2003 submission of the International Chamber of Shipping and the International Shipping Federation to the IMO Maritime Safety Committee, IMO Doc. MSC 77/19/3.

[101] Churchill and Lowe, p. 209; see also the IMO Maritime Safety Committee's monthly circulars on Acts of Piracy and Armed Robbery against Ships, www.imo.org/Circulars/mainframe.asp?topic_id=334.

the International Chamber of Commerce.[102] It is a problem which has generally been on the rise since the early 1980s. While there was a progressive downward trend in reported incidents in 2004–6, 2007 saw something of a resurgence.

The IMO Maritime Safety Committee reports on such attacks, usually under the title 'acts of piracy and armed robbery against ships'. This title reflects the legal distinction between acts occurring on the high seas ('piracy') and those committed in territorial waters or ports ('armed robbery'), thus avoiding the traditional confusion of international and domestic offences.[103] In collecting these figures the IMO secretariat must rely in large part on information from non-governmental organisations and shipping companies themselves, as coastal states often fail to report (or are not informed of) these incidents.[104] IMO figures for reported instances of piracy and armed robbery against ships in 2004–7 are reproduced below, followed by total figures including both acts committed and reported attempts. The IMB 'piracy' reports are less useful, due to their failure to distinguish between attacks in territorial and international waters.[105]

While '[m]ost of the attacks worldwide had occurred or been attempted in the coastal State's concerned territorial waters while the ships were at anchor or berthed',[106] over a quarter of all reported incidents in 2004–7 occurred in international waters and would constitute piracy or attempted piracy. Some cite the preponderance of attacks occurring 'within a state's territorial waters' as demonstrating the UNCLOS definition of piracy to be inadequate.[107] This approach conflates attacks in port and in territorial waters. To suggest that events occurring *in port* should attract jurisdiction over piracy would be extraordinary. The lack of international jurisdiction over such attacks in

---

[102] See the IMB's weekly 'Piracy Report', www.icc-ccs.org/prc/piracyreport.php.

[103] R. Balkin, 'The International Maritime Organization and maritime security' (2006) 30 TMLJ 1 at 10. IMO piracy circulars include a standard footnote to this effect.

[104] Submission of the International Chamber of Shipping and the International Shipping Federation (23 March 2003), IMO Doc. MSC 77/19/3. Shipping organisations, however, may have their own reasons for under-reporting. See text accompanying n. 109, below.

[105] Indeed, the reports reject the UNCLOS definition of piracy as too narrow: ICC International Maritime Bureau, *Piracy and Armed Robbery Against Ships: Annual Report, 1 January – 31 December 2004* (Barking, UK: ICC International Maritime Bureau, 2005).

[106] Report of the Maritime Safety Committee on its Seventy-Ninth Session (15 December 2004), IMO Doc. MSC 79/23, 101; see also 2004 Piracy Report, 1.

[107] Barrios, 'Casting a wider net', 155; cf. Stiles, 'Reforming current international law', 309.

Table 1. *IMO figures for acts of piracy and armed robbery against ships in 2004 reported as actually committed*

Region								
	Far East		Africa			South America		
	Malacca Strait	South China Sea	Indian Ocean	East Africa	West Africa	Atlantic	Caribbean	Pacific
International waters (54 total acts)	20	17	7	3	3		3	1
Territorial waters (42)	3	16	8	4	10		1	
Port areas (146)	12	53	16	0	30	8	21	6

Source: Reports on Acts of Piracy and Armed Robbery against Ships: Annual Report – 2004, IMO Doc. MSC.4/Circ.64 (5 May 2005), Annex 2 (2004 Piracy Report).

Table 2. *IMO figures for acts of piracy and armed robbery against ships in 2005 reported as actually committed*

Region								
	Far East		Africa			South America		
	Malacca Strait	South China Sea	Indian Ocean	East Africa	West Africa	Atlantic	Caribbean	Pacific
International waters (23 total acts)	8	5	2	9	1	1	1	1
Territorial waters (45)	2	20	11	8	4		2	
Port areas (124)		56	26	5	16	2	11	8

Source: Reports on Acts of Piracy and Armed Robbery against Ships: Annual Report – 2005, IMO Doc. MSC.4/Circ.81 (22 March 2006), Annex 2 (2005 Piracy Report).

Table 3. *IMO figures for acts of piracy and armed robbery against ships in 2006 reported as actually committed*

Region								
	Far East		Africa			South America		
	Malacca Strait	South China Sea	Indian Ocean	East Africa	West Africa	Atlantic	Caribbean	Pacific
International waters (28 total acts)	12	1	4	5				12
Territorial waters (58)	14	11	7	8	6	4	5	14
Port areas (87)	24	26	3	13	4	3	5	24

Source: Reports on Acts of Piracy and Armed Robbery against Ships: Annual Report – 2006, IMO Doc. MSC.4/Circ.98 (13 April 2007), Annex 2 (2006 Piracy Report). One incident in each of the North Sea and Arabian Sea included in totals, not tables.

Table 4. *IMO figures for acts of piracy and armed robbery against ships in 2007 reported as actually committed*

Region								
	Far East		Africa			South America		
	Malacca Strait	South China Sea	Indian Ocean	East Africa	West Africa	Atlantic	Caribbean	Pacific
International waters (37 total acts)	4	7	6	7	9	2		
Territorial waters (101)	1	33	11	13	26	8	1	2
Port areas (67)	1	15	15	7	17	2	3	5

Source: Reports on Acts of Piracy and Armed Robbery against Ships: Annual Report – 2007, IMO Doc. MSC.4/Circ.115 (10 April 2008), Annex 2 (2007 Piracy Report). Included in total figures but not the table are one incident in international waters in each of the Arabian Sea and North Atlantic Ocean, five incidents in territorial seas in the Persian Gulf and one in the Mediterranean, and two incidents in ports in the Mediterranean.

Table 5. *Combined IMO figures for acts of piracy and armed robbery against ships in 2004 reported as having been either committed or attempted*

Region								
	Far East			Africa		South America		
	Malacca Strait	South China Sea	Indian Ocean	East Africa	West Africa	Atlantic	Caribbean	Pacific
International waters (97 total acts)	42	24	14	9	4		3	1
Territorial waters (60)	4	27	10	4	12		2	1
Port areas (173)	14	62	17		41	9	23	7

Source: 2004 Piracy Report, Annex 2.

Table 6. *Combined IMO figures for acts of piracy and armed robbery against ships in 2005 reported as having been either committed or attempted*

Region								
	Far East			Africa		South America		
	Malacca Strait	South China Sea	Indian Ocean	East Africa	West Africa	Atlantic	Caribbean	Pacific
International waters (65 total acts)	18	9	8	26	1	1	1	1
Territorial waters (64)	1	25	13	17	5		3	
Port areas (137)	2	60	30	6	17	2	12	8

Source: 2005 Piracy Report, Annex 2.

Table 7.   *IMO figures for acts of piracy and armed robbery against ships in 2006 reported as having been either committed or attempted*

Region								
	Far East			Africa		South America		
	Malacca Strait	South China Sea	Indian Ocean	East Africa	West Africa	Atlantic	Caribbean	Pacific
International waters (60 total acts)	9	17	2	18	10			
Territorial waters (78)	4	23	16	10	8	6	6	5
Port areas (100)	9	26	35	3	13	4	4	6

Source: 2006 Piracy Report, Annex 2. Four attempted incidents in the Mediterranean or Arabian Sea added to totals but not table.

Table 8.   *IMO figures for acts of piracy and armed robbery against ships in 2007 reported as having been either committed or attempted*

Region								
	Far East			Africa		South America		
	Malacca Strait	South China Sea	Indian Ocean	East Africa	West Africa	Atlantic	Caribbean	Pacific
International waters (88 total acts)	10	13	11	33	12	2		1
Territorial waters (120)	1	38	13	18	31	8	1	3
Port areas (72)	1	16	16	9	17	2	3	5

Source: 2007 Piracy Report. Included in total figures but not the table are one incident in international waters in the North Atlantic Ocean, five in international waters and two in territorial waters in the Arabian Sea, five incidents in territorial seas in the Persian Gulf and one in Mediterranean territorial seas, and two incidents in ports in the Mediterranean and one in the North Sea.

the territorial sea is clearly a matter of the jealousy with which littoral states view any encroachment upon their exclusive competence within the 12-n.m. limit. Excluding attacks in port, half of all reported incidents at sea actually occur in international waters.

While the IMO figures show that piracy remains a concern, especially off East Africa and in the South China Sea and the Malacca Strait, the level of reported incidents might not be thought especially significant compared with the sheer volume of international maritime traffic. Two things, however, must be borne in mind.

First, there is evidence of coastal state under-reporting. While some states may simply not be aware of all incidents that occur, others may be reluctant to concede that there are any well-grounded concerns about the safety of maritime traffic off their coasts. The extraordinary rise in all incidents reported (including incidents in port and the territorial sea) in the period 1984–2004 from fewer than fifty annually to 300 to 400 annually may be as suggestive of improved reporting as changing historical conditions. Indeed, it was only in 1995 that the IMO secretariat began issuing monthly circulars, a quarterly analysis and an annual report on reported attacks on shipping.[108] The possibility arises that the maritime community only began reporting incidents systematically after the introduction of this procedure, seeing the value in such information being widely available. Nonetheless, ship owners may still be reluctant to report incidents for fear of losing clients or of increased insurance premiums or to avoid the delays (and therefore costs) attendant on any criminal investigation.[109] Also there are consistently higher numbers of 'actual', as opposed to 'attempted', incidents reported, which might suggest that attempts are under-reported. One, admittedly unverifiable, estimate is that 50 per cent of all attacks against shipping (including those in port and territorial waters) go unreported.[110]

Second, the raw figures do not disclose qualitative data. For example, it appears that in 2001 in Indian waters most incidents involved boardings or attempted boardings of merchant vessels by relatively small

---

[108] IMO Secretariat, 'Reports on Acts of Piracy and Armed Robbery against Ships' (18 October 2004), IMO Doc. MSC 79/16.

[109] J. Vagg, 'Rough seas? Contemporary piracy in South East Asia' (1995) 35 *British Journal of Criminology* 63 at 65; J. Burnett, *Dangerous Waters: Modern Piracy and Terror on the High Seas* (New York: Plume, 2003), 10; Keyuan, 'Issues of public international law', p. 537 n. 58.

[110] See Maritime Institute of Malaysia, 'Piracy cases in Malacca Strait down', News Flash service, 1–11 November 2006 (quoting Noel Choong of the IMB), www.mima.gov.my/mima/htmls/mimarc/news/newsflash_files/news-cut/nov06.htm.

groups armed with knives from small boats. Most such boarders fled when confronted, and generally ships' masters preferred not to press complaints.[111] While many such incidents, especially those closer to land, may be capable of being treated as ultimately more of a nuisance than a real threat, that is certainly not the case for all. In one 2005 incident against the carrier TM *Buck*,

[e]ight pirates armed with automatic weapons and grenades in two speedboats fired upon the ship ... Master took evasive manoeuvres ... sent distress alert and all crew closed doors and hid in superstructure. Two grenades hit a lifeboat, which caught fire. Pirates continued shooting and at 1000 UTC [Co-ordinated Universal Time] they boarded using a portable ladder. Pirates could not enter superstructure but continued shooting at the bridge. Pirates left at 1100 UTC ... there were bullet holes in superstructure and master's cabin window. No injuries to crew.[112]

While the IMO secretariat figures generally show a downward trend in reported incidents since 2000, albeit with a spike in 2007, there remain numerous incidents in which 'crews were violently attacked by groups of five to ten people carrying knives or guns'.[113] In 2007 attacks at sea or in port saw twenty mariners killed, over 153 injured and 194 kidnapped or taken hostage; sixteen ships were hijacked, and one vessel and three crew remained unaccounted for in April 2008.[114] Figures were lower in 2006 with 13 deaths, 112 injuries, 180 kidnappings and 10 hijackings.[115] In 2004, thirty crew and passengers were killed and in 2005 an astonishing 652 crew members were kidnapped.[116]

Hijacking has consistently been described as a serious problem. In south-east Asia organised criminals are known to hijack vessels and steal entire vessels and cargoes: crews are killed or set adrift, the vessel renamed and its distinctive marks repainted at sea to create a 'phantom ship', the pirates themselves boarding with ready-prepared forged registration documents and bills of lading so that hijacked cargoes

---

[111] 'Reports on Acts of Piracy and Armed Robbery against Ships: Coastal States' Reports' (25 March 2003), IMO Doc. MSC 77/19/Add. 1.

[112] IMO Doc. MSC.4/Circ.68 (9 May 2005), Annexe 1, p. 1.

[113] 2004 Piracy Report, 1; see also IMO, Report of the Maritime Safety Committee on its Eightieth Session (24 May 2005), IMO Doc. MSC 80/24, 95; IMO Secretariat, Reports on Acts of Piracy and Armed Robbery against Ships (18 October 2004), IMO Doc. MSC 79/16, 1.

[114] 2007 Piracy Report, 2.   [115] 2006 Piracy Report, 2.

[116] 2004 Piracy Report, 2; 2005 Piracy Report, 1.

and even the ship itself can be sold.[117] Such hijackings are enormously profitable, require 'detailed planning and organization' and 'involve significant economic losses to the shipowners, cargo owners and marine insurers' as well risking crews' lives.[118]

While the level of attacks in the Malacca and Singapore straits has been declining in recent years, and may seem modest compared with east Africa, their strategic importance and the development of regional anti-piracy initiatives make them worthy of special examination. The east African experience of piracy off the coast of Somalia, and proposals to draw upon the Malacca Strait experience, will then be examined.

1.7 Case study: the Malacca and Singapore straits

Situated between ... Thailand, Malaysia and Singapore to the East and the Indonesian island of Sumatra to the West, the Strait of Malacca extends some 900 km from its widest point, about 350 km between northern Sumatra and Thailand, to its narrowest, less than 3 km between southern Sumatra and Singapore. At its shallowest, the Strait of Malacca has a reported depth of just 25 meters. ... Because of its small size and high volume of traffic, said to be around 50,000 vessels a year, the Strait of Malacca remains one of the most important shipping lanes in world ...[119]

---

[117] Report of the UN Secretary General: Oceans and the Law of the Sea, UN Doc. A/56/58 (9 March 2001), paras. 179–180; E. Ellen, 'Contemporary piracy' (1990–1) 21 CWILJ 123 at 125–6, 128; Burnett, *Dangerous Waters*, pp. 9–10, 226–7. The famous *Alondra Rainbow* hijacking was a case where the vessel's name and registry markings were changed at sea and some cargo offloaded by the time of its recapture; see the report in IMO Doc. MSC 72/17/6 (15 February 2000). It has been suggested that such at-sea incidents have declined since 2001 and phantom ships are now more likely to be procured in port by fraud: P. Mukundan, 'Piracy and armed attacks against vessels today' (2004) 10 JIML 308 at 311, 313–14.

[118] R. Beckman, 'Issues of public international law relating to piracy and armed robbery against ships in the Malacca and Singapore straits' (1999) 3 SJICL 512 at 514.

[119] E. Watkins, 'Facing the terrorist threat in the Malacca Strait', *Terrorism Monitor*, Vol. II, Issue 9, 6 May 2004, 8, www.jamestown.org/publications_details. php?volume_id=400&issue_id=2945&Article_id=236671. Another view describes it as 600 n.m. long, varying in width from 600 to 8 n.m.: Admiral B. Sondakh (Chief of Staff, Indonesian Navy), 'National sovereignty and security in the Strait of Malacca' (September 2004), www.mima.gov.my/mima/htmls/conferences/som04/papers/sondakh.pdf. Some consider the Malacca Strait proper only to begin in the narrow area governed by traffic separation schemes. This area is, as described below, entirely within the adjacent territorial seas of the littoral states.

An estimated one-third of the world's trade passes through the Malacca and Singapore straits.[120] In its wider reaches, several hundred kilometres across, large areas of the Malacca Strait are clearly beyond the territorial waters of the littoral states; but at its narrow southern end much of it clearly falls within the territorial jurisdiction of Malaysia, Indonesia and Singapore. These narrow and heavily trafficked areas provide tempting targets for armed robbers operating at sea.[121] Crimes against shipping in this area are most likely to be non-violent, petty theft: vessels may be boarded at night with considerable skill and intruders will take 'whatever cash and negotiable valuables … come easily to hand'.[122] However, attacks on a vessel such as a very large crude carrier (VLCC) in the Strait could have catastrophic consequences. If armed attackers, be they robbers or terrorists, were to commandeer such a ship and disable the crew in the busy and narrow reaches of the Strait, the VLCC could easily 'collide with another ship or break up on the rocks, closing this vital commercial conduit and creating an economic and environmental catastrophe of global proportions'.[123]

The special conditions obtaining in the Straits thus make co-operation among the three coastal states over maritime security particularly important. Beckman has identified three challenges to co-operation to repress piracy in the region. First, 'the entire southern half of the Malacca Strait and the entire Singapore Strait – the areas governed by Traffic Separation Schemes – are within the territorial waters of one of the three coastal states', having the obvious consequence that attacks in this area are not piracy at international law, but internal criminal law matters.[124] Second, it may not always be clear to attacked vessels 'in whose waters the attacks took place … [as] official navigational maps for the Straits indicate the Traffic Separation Scheme, but not the territorial boundaries'.[125] In addition, unresolved boundary delimitation

---

[120] 'Indonesia, Malaysia, Singapore vow to secure Malacca Strait', AFX News Limited, 3 August 2005, www.forbes.com/work/feeds/afx/2005/08/03/afx2169219.html; E Koo, 'Terror on the high seas: southeast Asia's modern-day pirates', *Asia Times*, 19 October 2004, www.atimes.com; Burnett, *Dangerous Waters*, p. 11.

[121] Vagg, 'Rough seas?', 67.

[122] Ellen, 'Contemporary piracy', 123; cf. Mukundan, 'Piracy and armed attacks', 308.

[123] Burnett, *Dangerous Waters*, p. 12; cf. Barrios, 'Casting a wider net', 151; Mark Valencia, *The Proliferation Security Initiative: Making Waves in Asia* (Oxford: Routledge, 2005), p. 19.

[124] Beckman, 'Issues of public international law', 519.   [125] *Ibid.*

issues between the coastal states may further confuse determining the applicable national jurisdiction.[126]

While all states have the right (indeed, the duty to co-operate) to repress piracy in those parts of the Malacca Strait lying beyond territorial waters, Indonesia and Malaysia seem unlikely to take a sanguine view of any such third-party action. Both have generally been highly suspicious of any foreign law-enforcement action in the Strait. As recently as 2004 a US-initiated 'Maritime Regional Security Initiative' to promote information sharing was widely reported as a US plan to police the Malacca Strait, prompting Malaysian and Indonesian criticism.[127] The Malaysian foreign minister has described any proposed third-party assistance in maintaining security in the Strait as 'endanger[ing] Malaysia's sovereignty'.[128] This suspicion of external aid may, however, be softening.

The persistent prevalence of attacks on shipping (both in international and territorial waters) in the years 2000–4[129] led to the area being classified by the London insurance market as a 'war risk' zone from August 2005 to August 2006.[130] Regional concerns have also been raised over some ships transiting the straits using private security contractors.[131] There is an obvious potential for political embarrassment, as the use of such services may be seen as indicating that the coastal states cannot guarantee the security of shipping. While once

---

[126] *Ibid.*, 519 at n. 32.

[127] Testimony of Admiral Thomas B. Fargo, United States Navy, Commander US Pacific Command, Before the House Armed Services Committee, United States House Of Representatives, 31 March 2004, www.shaps.hawaii.edu/security/us/2004/20040331_fargo.html; J. Banusiewicz, 'Officials clarify maritime initiative amid controversy', American Forces Press Service, 4 June 2004, www.defenselink.mil/news/Jun2004/n06042004_200406048.html; A. Basral, 'An Excessive Offer', *Tempo*, No. 43 (IV), 28 June–5 July 2004, www.asiaviews.org/?content=153499ym32d ddw4&headline=20040630222200.

[128] Watkins, 'Facing the terrorist threat', 9.

[129] The total number of attacks (including attempts) against shipping in the Malacca Strait reported to the IMO was 112 in 2000, 58 in 2001, 34 in 2002 and 2003, and 55 in 2004. See IMO Docs. MSC 74/17 (30 March 2001), MSC 75/18 (11 April 2002), MSC 77/19 (25 March 2003), MSC 78/20 (21 April 2004), MSC 80/17 (26 April 2005).

[130] '"Bin Laden effect" prompted Malacca war risk rating', *Lloyd's List*, 12 August 2005, p. 1; M. Hand, 'Attacks hit bid to end Malacca war risk rating: shipowners and governments fear the worst for shipping lane as pirates swoop on UN vessels', *Lloyd's List*, 5 July 2006, p. 1; B. Kates, 'Malacca Strait risk put into perspective', *Lloyd's List*, 5 September 2006, 'Markets', p. 4.

[131] M. Valencia, 'Mercenaries in the Strait of Malacca', *Jakarta Post*, 28 July 2005, www.asiamedia.ucla.edu/Article.asp?parentid=27534; cf. articles cited at n. 120, above.

described as 'uneconomical' in terms of the benefit delivered,[132] the use of security contractors and counter-piracy measures, such as electrically charged barriers to boarding,[133] appears to be on the rise.

Singapore, Malaysia and Indonesia have been co-operating to improve safety in the Strait, commencing co-ordinated patrols of the Strait in July 2004 (MALSINDO patrols). In 2005, joint air surveillance patrols also commenced, with foreign states providing technical assistance.[134] These activities are not without precedent. In 1990–2 Indonesia conducted co-ordinated patrols with each of Malaysia and Singapore (separately) successfully to suppress a wave of armed attacks against shipping around the Riau archipelago.[135] Renewed patrolling since 2004, especially by air, appears to have led to a sharp downturn in attacks across 2004–6,[136] although the 2004 Asian tsunami disaster may also have played a role by destroying 'pirates' craft and equipment'.[137] Nonetheless, significant limitations on the effectiveness of the MALSINDO-co-ordinated patrols remain, in the form of a 'preoccupation with sovereignty' and agreed operational procedures which prevent 'one state from operating in the territorial waters of another'.[138] Thus the MALSINDO patrols are not analogous to the kind of joint patrols conducted under the US ship-rider agreements discussed in Chapter 5.[139] While MALSINDO patrols are co-ordinated and each party is informed of the others' activity, there is no unified operational structure: lines of command, and patrol vessels, remain firmly within respective national jurisdictions.[140] By contrast, the

---

[132] Ellen, 'Contemporary piracy', 124.   [133] Burnett, *Dangerous Waters*, p. 88.

[134] D. Boey, 'More countries urged to join "Eyes in sky" patrols', *Straits Times*, 14 September 2005.

[135] Vagg, 'Rough seas?', 77–8; cf. Keyuan, 'Issues of public international law', 541.

[136] 'Black flag flies high', *Lloyd's List*, 10 January 2008, p. 8; 'Piracy attacks are down as new initiative bears fruit', *Lloyd's List*, 4 July 2007, p. 14; see also Maritime Institute of Malaysia, 'Piracy cases in Malacca Strait down', News Flash service, 1–11 November 2006 (quoting Noel Choong of the IMB), www.mima.gov.my/mima/htmls/mimarc/news/newsflash_files/news-cut/nov06.htm.

[137] The United Kingdom Government's Strategy for Tackling Piracy and Armed Robbery at Sea, IMO Doc. MSC 80/17/1 (4 March 2005), para. 3; Balkin, 'The International Maritime Organization and maritime security', 11 n. 65.

[138] Barrios, 'Casting a wider net', 160.

[139] On doubts as to their effectiveness see M. Valencia, 'Piracy and politics in southeast Asia' in D. Johnson and M. Valencia, *Piracy in Southeast Asia: Status, Issues and Responses* (Singapore: Institute of Southeast Asian Studies, 2005), pp. 103, 104–6, 109–13, 117.

[140] See Sondakh, 'National sovereignty and security in the Strait of Malacca', n. 119 above.

aerial patrols are conducted with combined teams and with foreign governments providing technical assistance, observers and aircraft.[141] This level of co-operation, and indeed foreign involvement, is perhaps possible because these aircraft do not directly engage in any law enforcement action and because overflight is seen as less intrusive by the littoral states. Further signs of growing co-operation between Indonesia, Malaysia and Singapore were also evident in the 27 May 2008 announcement of a trilateral 'Co-operative Mechanism' under Article 43 of UNCLOS, focused on environmental protection and removing navigational hazards in the straits.[142]

A related development is the Regional Cooperation Agreement on Combating Piracy and Armed Robbery against Ships in Asia (ReCAAP), which was concluded in Singapore on 28 April 2005 and entered into force on 4 September 2006.[143] This development follows several conferences and statements identifying the need for closer regional co-operation against piracy.[144] ReCAAP does not provide for joint patrols or grant novel powers of at-sea law-enforcement, but it does provide a framework for greater maritime law enforcement co-operation within the straits. The Agreement restates the UNCLOS obligation to suppress piracy and its definition of the offence. It further defines 'armed robbery' of vessels as, with one small variation, those acts prohibited as

---

[141] N. Khalid (Maritime Institute of Malaysia), 'Maintaining security in the Strait of Malacca: a new dawn' (5 November 2007), 5, www.mima.gov.my/mima/htmls/ papers/pdf/nazery/CSCAP%202007%20_6Nov07_.pdf.

[142] Bernama (Malaysian Official News Agency), 'Malaysia, Singapore and Indonesia implement Cooperative Mechanism to safeguard straits', 27 May 2008, www. bernama.com.my/bernama/v3/news.php?id=335711. On its origins see IMO Press Briefing 29/2007, 18 September 2007, www.imo.org/Safety/mainframe. asp?topic_id=1472&doc_id=8471.

[143] See M. Hayashi, 'Introductory note to the regional cooperation agreement on combating piracy and armed robbery against ships in Asia' (2005) 44 ILM 826; IMO, Report of the Maritime Safety Committee on Its Eightieth Session (24 May 2005), IMO Doc. MSC 80/24, 95; ReCAAP Information Sharing Centre, Adding Value, Charting Trends: Research Report 2007 (undated), p. 5, www.recaap.org/incident/ pdf/reports/2007/Recaap_lowres.pdf (ReCAAP ISC Research Report 2007). ReCAAP had fourteen parties at 8 April 2008: Bangladesh, Brunei, Cambodia, China, India, Japan, South Korea, Laos, Myanmar, Philippines, Singapore, Sri Lanka, Thailand and Viet Nam.

[144] See Hayashi, 'Introductory note', 827; Valencia, 'Piracy and politics in southeast Asia', 106; IMO Secretariat, Piracy and Armed Robbery against Ships: Implementation of the Anti-piracy Project (25 March 2003), IMO Doc. MSC/77/19/1, 1–2; ASEAN Regional Forum, Statement on Cooperation Against Piracy and Other Threats to Security, 17 June 2003, www.aseansec.org/14837.htm.

piracy under UNCLOS when they are committed in territorial waters.[145] Thus, there is no strict requirement that an 'armed robber' be armed. The minor variation on the UNLCOS text is that when committed in territorial waters an offence need only be directed 'against a ship' not 'against another ship', broadening the scope of the treaty crime in territorial waters.[146] ReCAAP was initially open for signature only to a limited group of regional states, but once in force became open to accession by others,[147] and the Netherlands has reportedly considered joining.[148] Malaysia and Indonesia remained outside the organisation as at August 2008.

The 2005 Agreement established an 'Information Sharing Centre', based in Singapore.[149] The Centre serves as a hub for information exchange, statistical analysis and, when called upon, a clearing house for requests for assistance between members in dealing with piracy or maritime armed robbery incidents. It is also to prepare 'non-classified' statistics for the IMO, and to issue 'alerts' to member states if it believes an attack is imminent, and has training and capacity-building functions.[150] The Centre now provides monthly, public reports on its website in a similar format to that used by the IMO.[151]

Perhaps most usefully, ReCAAP obliges each party to establish 'a focal point' for communications with the Centre, allows parties to request law enforcement co-operation either directly from other parties (via focal points) or through the Centre, and obliges parties to 'make every effort to take effective and practical measures for implementing such request[s]'.[152] Focal points also send information on piracy and maritime armed robbery to the Centre through a secure web-based network.[153]

However, unlike the Harvard Draft Convention and some of the US bilateral drug interdiction treaties discussed later, there is no provision for pursuit of a suspect vessel from the high seas by one contracting party into the territorial waters of another.[154] Further, there are two significant savings clauses on territorial questions. The first states that

---

[145] ReCAAP, Article 1(2).
[146] Hayashi, 'Introductory note', 827; ReCAAP, Article 1(2)(a).
[147] ReCAAP, Article 18.
[148] 'ReCAAP success in Asia prompts call for expansion', *Lloyd's List*, 29 February 2008, p. 4.
[149] ReCAAP, Article 4.   [150] *Ibid.*, Articles 7 and 14.
[151] See www.recaap.org/incident/reports.html.
[152] ReCAAP, Articles 9, 10, 11(1).   [153] ReCAAP ISC Research Report 2007, 13.
[154] *Harvard Research*, 832–4; see also Chapter 5, section 6.2.

neither the Agreement nor 'any act or activity carried out under' it shall prejudice any party's position regarding 'any dispute concerning territorial sovereignty or any issues related to the law of the sea'.[155] This wording may leave open the disputed question of law enforcement action by foreign vessels in the EEZ and contiguous zone. On one reading it could be *enabling* of such action: a pirate vessel could be pursued by one party into another's EEZ or contiguous zone, and the pursuer could rely on the treaty to say that the action did not prejudice any claims to law enforcement competence in these areas. Such a reading might, however, seem undercut by the second significant saving provision, stating,

[n]othing in this Agreement entitles a Contracting Party to undertake in the territory of another Contracting Party the exercise of jurisdiction and performance of functions which are exclusively reserved for the authorities of that other Contracting Party by its national law.[156]

This drafting is curious. While at first glance it is a strident assertion of sovereignty, its effect may be nugatory. It is not phrased as a prohibition on action by one party contrary to another party's national law, thus 'internationalising' exclusive jurisdictional competences asserted under domestic law. It simply prevents any suggestion that *this Agreement* allows such action, and is silent as to what might be permissible under UNCLOS. Although it could be construed as reserving the right of parties to assert claims to exclusive policing jurisdiction beyond the 12-n.m. limit, nothing at general international law or under ReCAAP requires such claims be respected. Further, ReCAAP expressly does not displace any rights or obligations arising under UNCLOS or international law.[157]

These savings clauses may nonetheless have a chilling effect on willingness to take action in zones of disputed jurisdictional competence. Coupled with the lack of ability to pursue vessels from the high seas into territorial waters or across adjoining maritime boundaries, the Agreement clearly leaves in place major limitations upon efficient law enforcement co-operation in the most congested and vulnerable areas of the Malacca and Singapore straits. Further limitations arise from clauses on extradition (regarding pirates) and mutual legal assistance (regarding 'armed' robbers). Rather than imposing strict

---

[155] ReCAAP, Article 2(4); cf., Caribbean Area Agreement, Article 30.
[156] ReCAAP, Article 2(5).   [157] *Ibid.*, Article 2(2).

obligations either to extradite or to prosecute, these merely require parties to exercise their best endeavours subject to 'national laws and regulations'.[158]

As regards high seas interdictions, ReCAAP does not expressly restate the authority granted under UNCLOS Article 110, but does impose a further best endeavours obligation, subject to 'national laws and regulations and applicable rules of international law', to 'prevent and suppress piracy', arrest pirates and seize vessels 'committing piracy or armed robbery against ships'.[159] The limited obligation to arrest pirates is silent on the issue of subsequent prosecution and implementing effective national laws. Overall, it is a cautious agreement to promote law-enforcement co-operation, making no significant borrowings from treaty law innovations in other fields. It appears principally concerned with maintaining exclusivity of domestic criminal law-enforcement jurisdiction without making any statement as to the perceived limits as among the parties of that exclusive competence and whether it extends beyond territorial waters.

Nonetheless, the promotion of dialogue among ReCAAP parties, meetings between the Centre and focal points, and recurrent contact between the focal points themselves may all promote mutual confidence, and closer and faster co-operation and exchange of best practice. Claims that ReCAAP has played a significant role in reducing piracy and armed robbery against ships in the region are, however, probably exaggerated, especially while Indonesia and Malaysia remain outside the formal structure. While ReCAAP has been able to point to some successes involving real-time information sharing and responses to incidents leading to prosecutions, the trilateral co-ordinated patrols of Indonesia, Malaysia and Singapore must receive the greatest credit for suppressing such attacks.[160] Indeed this is acknowledged to some extent by the ReCAAP Information Sharing Centre itself, which stated:

[t]he coordinated patrols by Indonesia, Malaysia and Singapore may have contributed to the decrease in incidents in the Straits of Malacca and Singapore. However, the number of incidents taking place closer to shore, in ports and at anchorages, has risen in some years during the period 2003–2007.[161]

---

[158] *Ibid.*, Articles 12 and 13.   [159] *Ibid.*, Article 3(1).
[160] 'Eyes in the sky see strait attacks slashed to zero', *Lloyd's List*, 15 April 2008, p. 1.
[161] ReCAAP Information Sharing Centre, 'The piracy and armed robbery situation in Asia', 28 February 2008, www.recaap.org/news/press.html.

This latter observation, in particular, might suggest that more effective patrolling of the straits has displaced some criminal activities closer to shore.

1.8 Case study: piracy off Somalia

Conflict in Somalia has increasingly extended its reach into the waters off its coasts, with armed groups now attacking foreign vessels not only in the territorial sea but even at distances beyond 200 n.m. from shore. As a consequence, the high seas off Somalia have become a dangerous place: cruise liners have been shot at, aid deliveries jeopardised and the crews of fishing, recreational and aid vessels taken hostage for ransom.[162] Concerns raised in the IMO have now led to two legal instruments which may play a significant role in regional counter-piracy. UN Security Council Resolution 1816 first used powers under Chapter VII of the UN charter to authorise foreign military and law-enforcement action in the Somali territorial sea to repress piracy and armed robbery at sea over an initial six-month period. In parallel, an IMO-organised African regional conference has produced a draft Memorandum of Understanding on piracy which, despite its non-binding form, could create practical and effective structures to combat piracy in the region. Before turning to these instruments, some consideration of their context is required.

In 2005 and 2007 attacks or attempted attacks against shipping in international waters off east Africa exceeded reported incidents for the traditional piracy hot spots of the Malacca Strait and the South China Sea combined.[163] This lawlessness at sea clearly follows principally from the chaos on the Somalian shore.[164] Somalia has lacked a government controlling its entire territory since 1991. Indeed, for a period Somalia was so lacking in any internal governmental structures that from 1992 to 2000 it was in the unique position of 'having a nameplate in the [UN

---

[162] 'Cruise lines turn to sonic weapon', BBC News, 8 November 2005, http://news.bbc. co.uk/go/pr/fr/-/1/hi/world/africa/4418748.stm; 'Somalia: pirates attack UN aid ship, prompting call for action', UN News Centre, 20 May 2007, www.un.org/apps/news/ story.asp?NewsID=22609&Cr=Somalia&Cr1=; 'French troops seize Somali pirates after hostages are freed', *International Herald Tribune*, 11 April 2008, www.iht.com/ articles/2008/04/11/africa/yacht.php.

[163] See Annex 2 to the 2005 and 2007 Piracy Reports.

[164] To a lesser extent conflict in Nigeria has also reached the high seas, with attacks on floating oil production facilities in the EEZ: 'Shell shock Nigerian rebels attack Bonga', *Lloyd's List*, 20 June 2008, p. 1.

General Assembly] but nobody… to sit behind it'.[165] The Transitional Federal Government (TFG), internationally recognised since 2000, has only limited control over Somalian territory. Protracted internal conflict and the absence of effective government has led to a situation allowing pirates

to operate without hindrance at many coastal landing points. In all cases, vessels captured on the high seas are quickly taken to the territorial waters of Somalia and anchored off the landing point where the pirates have established a 'command centre'.[166]

The tactics of some Somali pirates are sophisticated and aggressive. While it was once thought that ships travelling more than 200 n.m. from Somalia's coast were safe from attack, Somali pirates are now using offshore 'mother ships' to stage attacks using smaller craft in international waterways.[167] The mother ship will hang back, hiding 'among … fishing vessels' and not visibly armed, while its small boats 'attack as a pack' armed with 'anti-tank missiles, machine guns and rocket propelled grenades'.[168] Following an attack, pirates can retreat into territorial waters, forcing pursuers to abandon the chase unless authorised to continue by the local government. Naval forces active in the region (including Coalition Taskforce 151, NATO forces and from December 2008 an EU naval force) have co-ordinated their efforts, in particular to establish a patrolled secure shipping lane.

Among the more notorious Somali pirate hijackings was the seizure in February 2007 of the World Food Programme's chartered vessel the MV *Rozen*. The vessel was seized in international waters and taken to an anchorage off the coast of Puntland (a Somalian constituent territory claiming a degree of self-government). Neither federal nor local authorities appeared able to act against the hijackers. Vessel and crew were eventually released after an undisclosed ransom was paid.

---

[165] R. Koskenmaki, 'Legal implications resulting from state failure in light of the case of Somalia' (2004) 73 NJIL 1 at 13.

[166] Report of the Monitoring Group on Somalia pursuant to Security Council resolution 1724 (2006), UN Doc. S/2007/436 (18 July 2007) (Somalia Monitoring Group Report), para. 90.

[167] 'Call to arms to tackle Somalia piracy threat; international shipping community must act to end violent attacks', Lloyd's List, 16 January 2008, p. 15.

[168] M. Nizza, 'Intensifying the hunt against Somali pirates', New York Times Online, 29 November 2007, http://thelede.blogs.nytimes.com/2007/11/29/intensifying-the-hunt-against-somali-pirates/, quoting A. Mwangura, East Africa Seafarers' Assistance Program.

Similarly, in May 2007 the World Food Programme vessel *Victoria* was attacked by pirates, causing one fatality aboard, and was successfully hijacked in international waters a year later, in May 2008.[169] International attention was also captured in late 2008 by several extraordinary hijackings of commercial vessels. September 2008 saw the *Faina*, containing a cargo of small arms and thirty-three Ukrainian battle-tanks, seized and its crew taken hostage. This was followed in November 2008 by the hijacking of the *Sirius Star* and the ransoming of its crew and its cargo of 2 million barrels of oil. At the time of writing, both vessels, along with numerous others, remained held for ransom. While these piracy operations are clearly highly organised, the extent to which they are connected with Somali warlords or armed groups is unverified, as it is rare for anyone to claim responsibility for such attacks, hijackings or kidnappings.

In several hostage-takings, those involved have claimed to be acting to deter illegal foreign fishing in the Somalian EEZ.[170] Overfishing is endemic off African coastlines, and up to 700 foreign vessels – some of them armed – have taken advantage of chaos in Somalia to conduct unlicensed fishing (or fishing 'licensed' only by local warlords), adding to local fishing communities' hardships.[171]

In at least one case the TFG has consented to foreign forces conducting a counter-piracy action on Somalian soil. In April 2008, French helicopters and commandos seized the pirates who had ransomed the crew members of the yacht *Le Ponant* as they returned ashore. The pirates were reportedly Somali fishermen, and they were removed to face trial in Paris with the TFG's permission.[172]

In December 2007 the IMO called for the Somalian TFG to

---

[169] 'Somalia: pirates attack UN aid ship, prompting call for action', UN News Centre, 20 May 2007, www.un.org/apps/news/story.asp?NewsID=22609&Cr=Somalia&Cr1=; 'Aid vessel hijacked off Somalia', BBC News, 18 May 2008, http://news.bbc.co.uk/go/pr/fr/-/1/hi/world/africa/7406818.stm.

[170] 'Fishing for the motives that lie behind piracy: attacks on vessels can often be attributed to social deprivation in coastal regions', *Lloyd's List*, 5 March 2008, p. 19. It is sometimes claimed that foreign vessels are illegally dumping toxic waste in Somalian waters. See UN Doc. S/PV.6046, 15.

[171] *Ibid.*

[172] 'French troops seize Somali pirates', n. 169 above; 'France charges Somali pirates', BBC News, 18 April 2008, http://news.bbc.co.uk/1/hi/world/europe/7355598.stm; on France's co-operation with the TFG in the *Ponant* affair, see also International Maritime Organization, 'France and IMO agree on prevention and suppression of piracy and armed robbery', IMO Media Briefing 14, 15 April 2008, www.imo.org.

advise the Security Council that… it consents to [foreign] warships or military aircraft… entering its territorial sea when engaging in operations against pirates or suspected pirates and armed robbers endangering the safety of life at sea… specifying any conditions attached to the consent given.[173]

Somalia consented to such measures being taken on 27 February 2008. It took several months to achieve a Security Council resolution, despite the Security Council having previously expressed concern about Somalian piracy[174] and encouraged 'Member States whose naval vessels… operate in international waters… adjacent to the coast of Somalia' to take measures to protect merchant shipping and humanitarian aid from piracy 'in line with relevant international law'.[175] In particular the Council had praised France and Denmark's actions in protecting the World Food Programme's convoys.[176] Eventually, it was France, Panama and the United States which introduced a draft resolution before the Council in April 2008 authorising member states to enter Somalia's territorial sea to 'repress acts of piracy and armed robbery'.[177]

On 2 June 2008, the Security Council passed such a resolution, UNSCR 1816, with Somalia's consent. The second preambular paragraph stated that the Council was '*Gravely concerned* by the threat that acts of piracy and armed robbery against vessels pose to the prompt, safe and effective delivery of humanitarian aid to Somalia, the safety of commercial maritime routes and to international navigation'.

The Council then proceeded to determine

that the incidents of piracy and armed robbery against vessels in the territorial waters of Somalia and the high seas off the coast of Somalia exacerbate the situation in Somalia, which continues to constitute a threat to international peace and security in the region.

---

[173] IMO Doc. A 25/Res.1002 (6 December 2007), para. 6; replacing IMO Doc. A 24/Res.979 (6 February 2006), which did not call for such action. See also the UN Security Council presidential statement replying to Resolution 979: UN Doc. S/PRST/2006/11 (15 March 2006).

[174] SC Res. 1676 (10 May 2006); SC Res. 1772 (20 August 2007); SC Res. 1801 (20 February 2008).

[175] SC Res. 1772 (2007), para. 18; SC Res. 1801 (2008), para. 12.

[176] SC Res. 1801 (2008), para. 12. The Netherlands, Canada, NATO and an EU Naval Force have all subsequently performed this role.

[177] 'UN urged to tackle Somali pirates', BBC News, 28 April 2008, http://news.bbc.co.uk/go/pr/fr/-/1/hi/world/europe/7372390.stm; the resolution was ultimately sponsored by Australia, Canada, Denmark, Greece, Italy, Japan, Netherlands, Norway, South Korea, Spain, and the United Kingdom also.

Notably it is the situation in Somalia which constitutes the threat to international peace and security, not piracy and armed robbery as such.[178] The resolution encourages a package of measures, including: increased co-ordination among those states with naval assets off Somalia; better information sharing and co-operation over Somalian piracy among and between states, international bodies and regional organisations; and encouraging states and organisations 'to provide technical assistance to Somalia and nearby coastal States'.[179] Critically, however, UNSCR 1816 uses the words 'all necessary means' – commonly associated with a general authorisation to use military force – and is one of the few occasions when the Council has authorised interdiction operations in a state's territorial sea.[180] Operative paragraph 7 provides:

that for a period of six months from… [2 June 2008], States cooperating with the TFG in the fight against piracy and armed robbery at sea off the coast of Somalia, for which advance notification has been provided by the TFG to the Secretary General, may:

(a) Enter the territorial waters of Somalia for the purpose of repressing acts of piracy and armed robbery at sea, in a manner consistent with such action permitted on the high seas with respect to piracy under relevant international law; and

(b) Use, within the territorial waters of Somalia, in a manner consistent with action permitted on the high seas with respect to piracy under relevant international law, all necessary means to repress acts of piracy and armed robbery.

States authorised to act under the resolution may thus pursue pirate vessels from international waters into Somalian territorial waters or may counter violence against or aboard vessels occurring exclusively within Somalia's territorial sea.

The restrictions upon these powers are readily apparent. First, this initial grant of authority would have expired on 2 December 2008, but for its renewal on that date by UN Security Council Resolution 1846, as discussed below. Second, only states named by the TFG to the Secretary-General as 'co-operating' with it may act under paragraph 7.

---

[178] A point stressed by South Africa in the Security Council: 'Security Council condemns acts of piracy, armed robbery off Somalia's coast', United Nations Department of Public Information press release, 2 June 2008, www.un.org/News/Press/docs/2008/sc9344.doc.htm.

[179] SC Res. 1816 (2008), paras. 2, 3 and 5.

[180] See McLaughlin, 'United Nations mandated naval interdiction operations'.

Authority to use 'all necessary means' is further conditioned by the requirement that such action must occur within Somalia's territorial waters and be 'consistent with action permitted on the high seas with respect to piracy'. This presumably limits action to pursuing and boarding a pirate vessel, seizing it and arresting those aboard. So limited, the words 'all necessary means' cannot encompass striking at pirate command centres on land or, as occurred in the *Ponant* affair, arresting pirates after their return to shore.[181] Such action will still require the TFG's specific authorisation.

Finally, the repeated words of limitation, 'in a manner consistent with action permitted on the high seas with respect to piracy', require scrutiny. International law has little to say about the *manner* in which piracy may be suppressed. Rules governing the conduct of high-seas interdictions remain embryonic, found in a limited case law and inferences from treaties. Briefly, it can be suggested that the use of force in maritime police actions must be necessary and proportionate, and should be preceded by warning shots where practicable.[182]

Notably, UNSCR 1816 does not make the international law of piracy directly applicable in Somalian waters. On the high seas the capturing warship determines where pirates will be tried and may try them before its own courts without consulting others. This raises a question as to the disposition of any pirates captured in Somalian territorial waters under the resolution. Legal authority to pursue or arrest pirate vessels as granted by UNSCR 1816 (enforcement jurisdiction) is not the same thing as authority to try offenders aboard (prescriptive and adjudicative jurisdiction). Under the resolution,

flag, port and coastal States, States of the nationality of victims and perpetrators or [sic] piracy and armed robbery, and other States with relevant jurisdiction under international law and national legislation, [are called upon] to cooperate in determining jurisdiction, and in the investigation and prosecution of persons responsible for acts of piracy and armed robbery off the coast of Somalia, consistent with applicable international law including international human rights law, and to render assistance by, among other actions, providing disposition and logistics assistance with respect to persons under their jurisdiction and control, such victims and witnesses and persons detained [as suspects]...[183]

Clearly any attack against or aboard a vessel at sea may leave multiple states capable of asserting jurisdiction to prosecute if they can lay hands

---

[181] See nn. 162 and 172, above.   [182] See Chapter 10, section 3.3.
[183] SC Res. 1816 (2008), para. 11.

on the offender. On its face, UNSCR 1816 simply lists every conceivable head of jurisdiction, leaving it to the states involved to settle 'disposition and logistics'.[184] For victims and witnesses this is obviously a matter of getting them safely home or on their way, while taking measures to make their evidence available in any subsequent trial. In the case of captured pirates, co-operation 'in determining jurisdiction, … disposition and logistics' might be thought a euphemism for working out to whom they should be handed for prosecution. In fact, there is a prior legal choice to make. The eventual disposition of criminals captured in Somalian territorial waters is either a matter for Somalia (on the theory that enforcement jurisdiction has been exercised with Somalia's consent) or for the interdicting state (on the theory that it has direct authority to deal with the pirates under the UNSCR). The matter may simply be treated in a memorandum of understanding between co-operating states and Somalia. If not, several approaches are possible. On the one hand, the customary principle allowing the state where the offender is present to assert jurisdiction over pirates who have fled the high seas may indicate that the coastal state, if any state, should have jurisdiction to prosecute.[185] Similarly, one could argue that the exercise of criminal jurisdiction within Somalia's territorial waters would ordinarily be its sole concern and Somalia should determine if, how and where captured offenders are to be tried. On the other hand, the UNSCR allows the use of 'all means necessary' to suppress piracy, including action compatible with that taken on the high seas. On a broad understanding of 'all means necessary' and a strained reading of the word 'compatible', this might be thought to extend to the capturing state asserting prescriptive and adjudicative jurisdiction. As states

---

[184] The reference to coastal *states* at first appears odd. The only coastal state that could be involved by virtue of jurisdiction over the territorial sea is Somalia, unless a crime was commenced in an adjacent territorial sea and continued or completed in waters 'off the coast of Somalia'. The jurisdictional claims of port states as such are also not immediately apparent, although the US state of Florida asserts jurisdiction over crimes at sea in certain cases based on its being the port of departure: see Florida Statute 910.006, 'State Special Maritime Criminal Jurisdiction'. What was probable intended was to suggest that the next port of call might receive captured pirates and prosecute them under universal jurisdiction or, as Security Council Resolution 1846 suggests, the SUA Convention.

[185] The ostensible prohibition in UNCLOS, Article 27(5), upon exercising law-enforcement jurisdiction over vessels passing through the territorial sea in respect of crimes committed on the high seas would not apply here as the fleeing vessel would presumably be making for port. The effect of Article 27 is discussed at Chapter 2, section 2.2 and Chapter 9, section 3.2.

exercising this power are meant to be co-operating with Somalia, it seems most likely that the UNSCR leaves the question of disposition to Somalia. However, as a practical matter, given the limited capacity of the Somalian state, the interdicting state having custody will likely have the job of finding a forum to try the suspects.

Paragraph 9 of the Resolution provides that the resolution:

> applies only... [to] Somalia and shall not affect the rights or obligations or responsibilities of Member States under international law, including any rights or obligations under [UNCLOS], with respect to any other situation, and underscores in particular that it shall not be considered as establishing customary international law.

This was clearly intended to meet the concerns of states, such as Indonesia, wishing to avoid any implication that the resolution involved the 'modification, rewriting or redefining' of UNCLOS principles.[186] As discussed above, Indonesia has previously rejected any suggestion that other states might conduct counter-piracy operations within areas of the Malacca Strait falling within its territorial waters.

At the time of writing, a number of further Security Council resolutions dealing with piracy off Somalia had been passed in 2008. Resolution 1838, in operative paragraph 3, exhorts 'States whose naval vessels ... operate on the high seas ... off the coast of Somalia to use on the high seas ... the necessary means, in conformity with international law, as reflected in ... [UNCLOS], for the repression of acts of piracy'. While the reference to 'necessary means' may encompass the use of force, the resolution clearly does not authorise force in any circumstances other than those contemplated under UNCLOS. Although passed under Chapter VII, Resolution 1838 therefore adds nothing to the substantive law governing piracy. More significantly, the key elements of Resolution 1816 were re-enacted in Resolution 1846 of 2 December 2008. The wording of operative paragraphs 7, 9, 11 of Resolution 1816, discussed above, is repeated *mutatis mutandis* as paragraphs 10, 11, 14 of Resolution 1846. Two additions to Resolution 1816 are notable. First, paragraph 9 of Resolution 1848 calls upon states and regional organisations with the capacity to do so 'to take part actively in the fight against piracy and armed robbery at sea off the coast of Somalia', in particular by deploying appropriate military assets and 'through seizure and disposition of boats,

---

[186] 'Security Council condemns acts of piracy, armed robbery off Somalia's coast', United Nations Department of Public Information press release, 2 June 2008, www.un.org/News/Press/docs/2008/sc9344.doc.htm.

vessels, arms and other related equipment used in the commission of piracy and armed robbery off the coast of Somalia, or for which there is reasonable ground for suspecting such use' in a manner consistent with the resolution and international law. It is possible, although not entirely clear, that this creates a novel preventive power to seize and dispose of a vessel or weapons simply on *reasonable suspicion* of involvement in piracy irrespective of the general international law duty to compensate vessels mistakenly interdicted on such grounds. Second, the Security Council notes in paragraph 15 of Resolution 1848 that the SUA Convention 'provides for parties to create criminal offences, establish jurisdiction, *and accept delivery* of persons responsible for or suspected of seizing or exercising control over a ship by force or threat thereof or any other form of intimidation' (emphasis added).[187] This would appear expressly to acknowledge the problems encountered in finding states prepared, both in terms of political will and adequate national laws, to prosecute acts of piracy lacking any connection with their vessels or nationals. The hope seems to be that more states may have national criminal laws implementing their obligations under the SUA Convention than their optional jurisdiction under the law of piracy.

More dramatically still, the Security Council passed on 19 December 2008 Resolution 1851, and decided in paragraph 6,

for a period of twelve months from [19 December 2008] ... States and regional organizations cooperating in the fight against piracy and armed robbery at sea off the coast of Somalia for which advance notification has been provided by the TFG to the Secretary-General may undertake all necessary measures that are appropriate in Somalia, for the purpose of suppressing acts of piracy and armed robbery at sea, pursuant to the request of the TFG, provided, however, that any measures undertaken pursuant to the authority of this paragraph shall be undertaken consistent with applicable international humanitarian and human rights law.

There is only space here for a brief discussion of this grant of authority to conduct counter-piracy operations on Somalian soil. First, it is subject to Somalian consent. It is thus hard to see the utility of the resolution since the TFG has given such consent in the past without a resolution, as in the *Le Ponant* affair. The scope of authority to take 'necessary measures' is limited by Somalia's *request* for such action to be taken and thus does not confer any wider mandate upon forces involved. Worryingly, the

---

[187] See SUA Convention, Articles 3(1)(a), 5, 6, 8 and 10. This point was made again in the preamble to UNSCR 1851 (2008).

resolution refers to 'applicable humanitarian law' which suggests the possible application of the law of armed conflict. This should certainly not be seen as an implicit determination by the Security Council that a state of armed conflict exists between pirates and international naval forces in the region. Despite the rhetoric of classical writers on the topic, pirates have not declared war on the world and are merely civilian criminals, not combatants. The resolution may be better construed as acknowledging that some Somali pirates may also be civil war insurgents and in those cases any international counter-piracy forces on land may be best considered forces intervening in an otherwise internal conflict at the invitation of the government. Despite this resolution being a US initiative, a number of US officials have cast doubt on its usefulness, given 'the difficulties of identifying [the pirates] and the potential risks of harming innocent civilians'.[188] Again, these comments should not be taken to suggest that the law of military targeting would necessarily be applicable to strikes against pirates ashore. Pirates are criminals to be captured using reasonable force, not combatants who may lawfully be killed in armed conflict. Resolution 1851 also calls on states involved in counter-piracy efforts to set up a common centre to co-ordinate their efforts and on all UN member states to help strengthen Somalia's 'operational capacity to bring to justice those who are using Somali territory to plan, facilitate or undertake criminal acts of piracy and armed robbery at sea, and stresses that any measures undertaken pursuant to this paragraph shall be consistent with applicable international human rights law'. Following from this, an internationally funded special chamber of Somalia's (or a neighbouring state's) criminal courts dealing exclusively with piracy would be one possible solution to some of the problems encountered in the relevant state practice.

State practice following the resolutions is instructive, especially as regards some of the practical difficulties involved. States co-operating with Somalia under Resolutions 1816 and 1846 now include Canada, Denmark, France, India, the Netherlands, Russia, Spain, the United Kingdom and the United States. The EU has assumed responsibility for escorting World Food Programme vessels into Somalian ports for twelve months from December 2008. NATO and China are also actively

---

[188] 'Navy head cool on Somalia strikes', BBC News, 13 December 2008, http://news.bbc.co.uk/2/hi/africa/7780981.stm, quoting Vice-Admiral Bill Gortney. Similar comments have been made by US Defense Secretary Robert Gates: 'Indian navy "captures 23 pirates"', BBC News, 13 December 2008, http://news.bbc.co.uk/1/hi/world/africa/7781436.stm.

engaged in maritime counter-piracy operations in the region. While this increased presence has reduced the number of pirate attacks and numerous individual attacks have successfully been repelled,[189] such operations have not been free from complications. On 12 November 2008, British seamen aboard boats belonging to HMS *Cumberland* were fired on by an encircled vessel suspected of piracy. Returning fire in self-defence, they killed the two suspects aboard.[190] On 18 November 2008, the Indian naval vessel *Tabar* fired on and sank a hijacked Thai fishing vessel, mistakenly believing it to be a pirate craft: the lives of as many as fourteen innocent crew were lost as a result.[191] Such incidents raise questions about the use of force in law-enforcement interdictions, a matter discussed further in Chapter 10. On 25 December 2008 it was reported that a German frigate had captured and disarmed a group of pirates and then released them immediately on the orders of the German government, as 'Germany would only bring pirates to justice ... if a German ship was attacked or German citizens were killed or injured'.[192] As noted above, many states do not provide for universal jurisdiction over piracy and can only assert criminal jurisdiction on the basis of the nationality of either victims or the attacked vessel. The episode thus highlights the limited efficacy of addressing piracy as a problem capable of a military solution absent the law-enforcement mechanisms contemplated by Resolution 1846. Between 11 December 2008 and March 2009 the United Kingdom, the United States and the European Union all concluded memoranda of understanding with Kenya providing for the transfer of captured pirates to Kenya for trial.[193]

It should not be presumed that the only 'co-operating states' under UNSCR 1816 will be the United States and European naval powers.

[189] 'Somali pirate clampdown "working"', BBC News, 1 January 2009, http://news.bbc.co.uk/2/hi/africa/7807379.stm.

[190] C. Wyatt, 'Navy shoots pirate suspects dead', BBC News, 12 November 2008, http://news.bbc.co.uk/2/hi/uk_news/7725771.stm.

[191] 'India navy defends piracy sinking', BBC News, 26 November 2008, http://news.bbc.co.uk/2/hi/south_asia/7749486.stm.

[192] 'German navy foils Somali pirates', BBC News, 25 December 2008, http://news.bbc.co.uk/2/hi/africa/7799796.stm. It has been suggested that the UK Royal Navy has been advised not to take pirates into custody for fear that they may make asylum claims: M. Woolf, 'Pirates can claim UK asylum', *Sunday Times*, 13 April 2008, www.timesonline.co.uk/tol/news/uk/article3736239.ece.

[193] C. Philp and R. Crilly, 'Allies seek power to pursue Somali pirates on land and sea', *The Times,* 12 December 2008, 51; EU–Kenya Exchange of Letters of 6 March 2009, Official Journal of the EU, L.79/49–L.79/59.

Notable steps towards a regional counter-piracy arrangement were taken shortly before UNSCR 1816.

The IMO held a conference in Tanzania in April 2008[194] to discuss the establishment of a regional counter-piracy arrangement similar to ReCAAP.[195] Rather than a treaty text, the Tanzanian conference produced a draft non-binding regional memorandum of understanding (the draft MOU). The choice of a non-binding instrument followed some participants' concerns that 'it would take significantly longer... to gain parliamentary support for entering a binding agreement'.[196] The draft MOU would not establish a single information-sharing centre. Instead it provides that Kenya, Tanzania and Yemen would offer their services as designated communications and reporting 'centres' and that each participant should appoint a single national focal point for information exchange.[197] In addition, the draft MOU goes further than the ReCAAP model, anticipating regional co-operation through use of 'ship-riders'. Ship-rider agreements are discussed in more detail in Chapter 5. Briefly, these agreements first emerged in US bilateral drug interdiction treaties; they involve placing a designated law enforcement officer from one party ('the ship-rider') aboard the vessel of another party ('the host State').[198] The ship-rider is then able to board the vessels of their flag state and enforce flag-state law once aboard, possibly with the assistance of host-state officers. Ship-riders may also have the power to authorise the pursuit of a vessel into the territorial waters of their designating state. In practice, most formal ship-rider agreements include provisions allowing for the exercise of such boarding and pursuit powers in limited cases even when no ship-rider is embarked.[199] The draft MOU does not go this far, but does provide a mechanism by which a state participant may request ad hoc permission from a

---

[194] At the time of writing, this had been followed by a 29 January 2009 counter-piracy Code of Conduct concluded in Djibouti. It similarly provides for ship-riders and information sharing centres based in Kenya, Tanzania and Yemen. The comments made here about regional co-operation apply equally to this newer instrument.

[195] Discussed above at n. 143.

[196] IMO Secretariat, Report: Sub-regional Meeting on Piracy and Armed Robbery against Ships in the Western Indian Ocean, Gulf of Aden and Red Sea Area, 14 to 18 April 2008, TC 0153–08–2000 (IMO Sub-Regional Meeting Report) (copy on file with author).

[197] Article 8, Memorandum of Understanding Concerning the Repression of Piracy and Armed Robbery Against Ships in the Western Indian Ocean, the Gulf of Aden, and the Red Sea (Draft Regional Counter-Piracy MOU), IMO Sub-Regional Meeting Report, Annex 7.

[198] Byers, 'Policing the high seas', 539.   [199] See Chapter 5, section 6.2.

coastal state to continue pursuit of a suspected pirate vessel into its territorial waters.[200] The ability to make such requests is obviously greatly facilitated by the creation of single points of contact under the draft MOU.[201]

The draft MOU also borrows a saving provision on national jurisdiction from ReCAAP Article 2:

Nothing in this Agreement entitles a Party to undertake in the territory of another Party the exercise of jurisdiction and performance of functions which are exclusively reserved for the authorities of that other Party by its national law.

This must, however, be read as subject to the express authority of participants to grant permission for foreign law enforcement vessels to continue pursuit into their territorial waters and then give 'specific instructions as to the actions that the Pursuing Participant may take.'[202] Despite the saving clause, such instructions could obviously include conferring a degree of authority to board and seize the vessel pending local authorities' arrival.

If adopted and implemented, the MOU could provide some improvements over the ReCAAP model, offering a framework for effective regional counter-piracy operations beyond information sharing. Whether it is adopted, and how it is implemented, remains to be seen.

Despite the promise of UNSCR 1816 and the draft MOU, if the view that politically motivated violence cannot be piracy is correct then Somalians attacking shipping beyond territorial waters have a simple defence. They may claim to be acting as civil-war insurgents and not for private ends, or to be fulfilling a necessary public function in the absence of effective government by preserving fishing grounds from foreign over-exploitation. The flaws in the 'private ends' argument have already been noted. One could also point to the fact that no relevant IMO or UNSCR resolution has countenanced the possibility that some of these acts may not be illegal for reasons of political motivation. The generality of these resolutions may provide evidence of states' understanding of the law, and thus support a common-sense interpretation of the law over any supposed political exception. As

[200] Draft Regional Counter-Piracy MOU, Article 4(5).
[201] On the need for 'competent authorities' capable of granting such requests, see Chapter 5, section 7.
[202] Draft Regional Counter-Piracy MOU, Article 4(5).

discussed, the historical rule preventing insurgents from being considered pirates applied only to insurgents who confined themselves to attacking the vessels of the government they sought to overthrow.[203] That is clearly not the case here. As for fisheries-preserving 'eco-piracy', performing a public function in default of effective government is certainly a principle of state responsibility.[204] Simply because a state may become responsible for such acts, however, does not mean the actors involved become cloaked with state immunity.[205] Even if it could, many cases would simply not fit the 'eco-pirate' claim: the first pirates to claim to be acting to deter foreign fishing held to ransom the crew of a barge, not a fishing vessel.[206]

1.9 Conclusion

While the evidence demonstrates that piracy remains a significant hazard in international waters, especially off the coast of east Africa, there appear to be few reported cases of vessels being boarded in international waters in order to repress the crime.[207] This is not altogether surprising. It has long been noted that pirates are at best difficult to apprehend at sea,[208] and at-sea boarding of unco-operative vessels is a difficult, costly and dangerous exercise. That said, the experience of co-operative drug interdiction in the Caribbean would tend to indicate that significant at-sea law enforcement operations can be conducted, given sufficient resources and training.[209] While there is an undoubted right at international law to conduct shipping interdictions to suppress piracy, it remains at best an emerging field for co-operative law enforcement and one that is significantly less sophisticated than that surrounding either drug interdiction practice or the new SUA Protocol on WMD interdiction discussed in later chapters. It remains to be seen whether emerging state practice on regional co-operation changes that picture.

---

[203] See n. 32, above.
[204] ILC Articles on State Responsibility, Article 9.
[205] See text accompanying n. 39, above, and discussion in Chapter 11, section 5.
[206] See n. 170, above. Politically motivated protest is also no defence to piracy: n. 55, above.
[207] On the 1999 Indian high-seas seizure of the hijacked *Alondra Rainbow* and the ensuing piracy trial, see W. Langewiesche, *The Outlaw Sea: Chaos and Crime on the World's Oceans* (London: Granta, 2004), pp. 70–80.
[208] Dickinson, 'Is the crime of piracy obsolete?', 338.
[209] See Chapter 5.

2 The slave trade

'Various international human rights treaties refer to slavery or related concepts without explicitly providing any definition.'[210] The same may be said of UNCLOS.[211] Under general international law slavery, including the transport of slaves, involves the exercise of rights of ownership over a person;[212] while 'practices similar to slavery', not necessarily covered by slavery itself, include debt bondage and child labour.[213] The focus of this section is on the narrow category of slavery proper.

In the nineteenth century the slave trade was not recognised as a practice prohibited by international law.[214] Unsurprisingly, then, it was never historically established that there was a *customary* right to board ships suspected of being engaged in slaving.[215] While the United Kingdom asserted such a general international law right of visitation (principally against US vessels) in the earlier part of the nineteenth century, it later expressly abandoned any such claim, preferring to conclude bilateral and multilateral conventions.[216] Any right of visit and search, therefore, 'derive[d] from treaty and not from customary international law'.[217] In the period 1831–90 numerous treaties, culminating in the multilateral General Act of Brussels, were concluded, providing for reciprocal rights of visit and inspection over vessels suspected of slaving.[218] However, the Slavery Convention 1926 and the Supplementary Slavery Convention 1956 failed to re-enact any measures for the suppression of the trade by sea, leaving only a 'crumbling structure' of nineteenth-century law in place.[219]

---

[210] ICTY, *Prosecutor v. Kunarac*, Judgement, Case No. IT-96–23-T, 22 February 2001, para. 533.

[211] See UNCLOS, Articles 99 and 110(1)(b).

[212] Slavery Convention 1926, (1927) 60 LNTS 253, Article 1.

[213] Article 1, Supplementary Convention on the Abolition of Slavery, the Slave Trade, and Institutions and Practices Similar to Slavery 1956, 266 UNTS 3 (Supplementary Slavery Convention), entered into force 7 December 1953. The UN treaty database lists ninety-six parties to the Slavery Convention as amended by the Supplementary Slavery Convention.

[214] *Le Louis* (1817) 165 Eng. Rep. 1464 at 1475–8; *The Antelope* (1825) 23 US (10 Wheat.) 66 at 115.

[215] R. Reuland, 'Interference with non-national ships on the high seas: peacetime exceptions to the exclusivity rule of flag state jurisdiction' (1989) 22 VJTL 1161 at 1190; Rosemary Rayfuse, *Non-Flag State Enforcement in High Seas Fisheries* (Leiden: Martinus Nijhoff, 2004), p. 55; McDougal and Burke, p. 881.

[216] McDougal and Burke, pp. 767, 881 ff.; Byers, 'Policing the high seas', 536.

[217] Hunnings, 'Pirate broadcasting', 426.

[218] Reuland, 'Interference with non-national ships', 1192–4.   [219] *Ibid.*, 1194.

The Geneva Convention and UNCLOS both include a right of visit and inspection by warships of foreign vessels suspected of slaving;[220] and in both treaties this right is limited to confirming a vessel's right to fly its flag. Despite the obligation of every flag state to prevent and punish the use of its vessels as slave transports,[221] no right of interference beyond boarding and inspection is conferred. Thus a warship encountering a foreign-flagged vessel actually engaged in the slave trade is limited to informing the flag state,[222] or possibly seizing the vessel if inspection reveals it to be stateless. While some contend that the reiteration of this limited right of visit and search in successive modern treaties evidences that it has now achieved customary status,[223] there remains no support for the exercise of seizure jurisdiction in such cases.[224]

While this limited right could, perhaps, be exercised in the most extreme cases of contemporary human trafficking, there is little recent or relevant state practice. As noted above, debt-bondage and the forced labour of children under 18 are among 'institutions and practices similar to slavery', but such practices are not necessarily forms of slavery per se. It is therefore doubtful whether cases of people being trafficked by sea into forms of exploitation less severe than classical slavery would give rise to the general international law right of visit and inspection.[225]

In 2001, the MV *Etirino* was suspected of carrying from Benin 200 child slaves.[226] Trafficking in children is prevalent in Benin, and many are trafficked to Gabon by land, sea or air.[227] When the *Etirino* eventually docked in Benin it was found to be carrying only some forty-three

---

[220] High Sea Convention, Article 22; UNCLOS, Article 110.
[221] High Sea Convention, Article 13; UNCLOS, Article 99.
[222] Churchill and Lowe, p. 212.
[223] Reuland, 'Interference with non-national ships', 1195–6; F. Lenzerini, 'Suppressing slavery under customary international law' (2000) 10 IYBIL 145 at 155.
[224] *Third Restatement of Foreign Relations Law*, II, pp. 84, 86 n. 3.
[225] See Chapter 8, section 3. Note, however, reports of exploited fishing crews effectively imprisoned on vessels and kept in conditions approaching slavery: US State Department, *Trafficking in Persons Report* (2007), p. 9, www.state.gov/g/tip/.
[226] Lenzerini, 'Suppressing slavery under customary international law', 179; 'Suspicion falls on Benin "slave ship"', BBC News, 21 April 2001, http://news.bbc.co.uk/1/hi/world/africa/1289032.stm.
[227] L. Potts, 'Global trafficking in human beings: assessing success of the United Nations Protocol to Prevent Trafficking in Persons' (2003) 35 GWILR 230 at 246; Mike Thomson, 'In the grip of Benin's child traffickers', BBC News, 31 May 2005, http://news.bbc.co.uk/1/hi/world/africa/4589731.stm.

young persons (reports vary due to difficulties in establishing their ages).[228] Subsequent investigations revealed that 'at least a dozen … appeared to have been potential slaves'.[229] Although the Benin government called for international assistance in locating the ship, it was not boarded at sea but was forced to return after being refused entry to ports in Gabon and Cameroon.[230] There were also reports in September 2001 that the Cameroonian military had rescued Togolese children (aged 18 months to 17), who were being trafficked into Gabon as child labourers, from aboard a sinking vessel.[231] However, it is not clear that in either case these exploited child labourers were slaves in the strict sense of having been bought and sold as property (although some may have been) and neither case involved interdiction. The case of rescuing children from a sinking vessel is more properly characterised as conducted under the obligation to preserve life at sea.[232]

Unlike piracy, it can fairly be said that the maritime interdiction of the slave trade is chiefly a matter of historical concern. Trafficking in human beings, often rhetorically described as the modern face of slavery, is discussed in Chapter 8.

3 Conclusion

Piracy and the slave trade are the only instances of universal rights to board vessels suspected of involvement in an offence defined at international law. That is, any duly authorised public vessel of any state, irrespective of whether it is directly affected by the vessel's conduct, may interdict upon suspicion of piracy or slaving. As has been seen, however, these rights are quite limited. Jurisdiction to suppress piracy by at-sea interdiction is chiefly constrained by the 'two vessels' and special geographical elements of the offence. Interdiction rights

---

[228] 'Les enfants de l'Etireno étaient quarante-trois', Le Monde, 19 April 2001, www.lemonde.fr/web/recherche_breve/1,13–0,37–700761,0.html.

[229] 'Ship children "were slaves"', BBC News, 30 April 2001, http://news.bbc.co.uk/1/hi/world/africa/1305547.stm; 'The slave children', BBC News, 5 October 2001, http://news.bbc.co.uk/1/hi/programmes/correspondent/1519144.stm; Potts, 'Global trafficking in human beings', 246.

[230] 'Benin seeks help over "slave" ship', BBC News, 16 April 2001, http://news.bbc.co.uk/1/hi/world/africa/1276620.stm; '"Slave ship" timeline', BBC News, 17 April 2001, http://news.bbc.co.uk/1/hi/world/africa/1281391.stm.

[231] 'Child slaves returned to Togo', BBC News, 24 September 2001, http://news.bbc.co.uk/1/hi/world/africa/1560392.stm.

[232] See UNCLOS, Article 98, and Chapter 8, below.

in the case of slaving are limited to search, not seizure, and general enforcement jurisdiction remains with the flag state. Despite these significant limitations, the model of allocating universal rights of interdiction capable of unilateral exercise has not generally been followed in other fields of maritime policing activity.

5   Drug trafficking

1 Introduction

Interdicting drug smugglers is a well-recognised head of coastal state jurisdiction over vessels within national waters.[1] It may be impractical, however, to wait for traffickers to enter territorial or contiguous waters before taking action.[2] Drug-running 'mother ships' may sit in international waters, distributing their cargo to faster, smaller boats to convey ashore at night. Major treaties creating high-seas boarding rights to address this problem are the 1988 UN Narcotics Convention,[3] a 1990 Spanish–Italian treaty,[4] the 1995 Council of Europe Agreement,[5] and numerous US bilateral agreements with neighbouring states. Most create procedures allowing one party to request permission to board another's flag vessel, without imposing any obligation to permit arrests or seizure. It is convenient to begin with the historic bilateral practice between the United States and the United Kingdom, culminating in the 1981 US–UK Exchange of Notes, which may have influenced later developments.[6]

---

[1] Convention on the Territorial Sea and the Contiguous Zone 1958, 516 UNTS 205, Article 19(1)(d); UNCLOS, Article 27(1)(d).

[2] *UN Practical Guide*, p. 3. The majority of US drug interdiction practice certainly now occurs upon the high seas: data on file with author, provided by the US Coast Guard.

[3] UN Convention against Illicit Traffic in Narcotic Drugs and Psychotropic Substances 1988, (1989) 28 ILM 497, entered into force 11 November 1990, 183 parties at 14 March 2008.

[4] Treaty between the Kingdom of Spain and the Italian Republic to Combat Illicit Drug Trafficking at Sea 1990, 1776 UNTS 229 (Spanish–Italian Treaty).

[5] Agreement on Illicit Traffic by Sea, Implementing Article 17 of the United Nations Convention against Illicit Traffic in Narcotic Drugs and Psychotropic Substances 1995, Europ TS No.156 (Council of Europe Agreement). Entered into force 1 May 2000, 13 parties at 8 August 2008.

[6] W. Gilmore, 'Drug trafficking by sea: the 1988 United Nations Convention against Illicit Traffic in Narcotic Drugs and Psychotropic Substances' (1991) 15 *Marine Policy* 183, 191.

2 US–UK bilateral practice on smuggling

Modern treaty law on smuggling interdiction has its origin in the 1924 Liquor Treaty between the United States and the United Kingdom, which aimed at combating rum-running during Prohibition. The United States had, in the years preceding the treaty, taken to arresting vessels 'hovering' in international waters if by means of their small boats (or boats coming out from shore) they had participated in running liquor ashore.[7] At the time, the United Kingdom vigorously opposed such action as incompatible with international law and in order to avoid what it saw as an attempt to extend the effective breadth of the territorial sea.[8] The historic difference in viewpoints is explained in *US v. Postal*, itself a 1979 case where a smuggling vessel was interdicted outside territorial waters and in admitted breach of the High Seas Convention. There the Court observed that the United States

has long adhered to the objective principle of territorial jurisdiction, which holds that it has jurisdiction to attach criminal consequences [including interdiction] to extraterritorial acts ... intended to have [or having] effect in the United States ... The United States has exercised this competence in enacting the statutes ... prohibit[ing] conspiracies to ... import controlled substances.[9]

This conflation of jurisdiction to prescribe and enforce meant that the objective territoriality principle was thought to allow extraterritorial enforcement, not merely prescriptive, action.[10] The United Kingdom, and other states, protested against such enforcement action as incompatible with international law. Thus the concern of the United States to conclude the Liquor Treaty was not motivated by any US doubts about

---

[7] See *Grace and Ruby*, [1922] 283 Fed. 475; *Frances Louise,* [1924] 1 Fed. (2nd) 1004; *Marjorie E. Bachman*, [1925] 4 Fed. (2nd) 405; contra, *Henry L. Marshall*, [1923] 292 Fed. 486; William Masterson, *Jurisdiction in Marginal Seas with Special Reference to Smuggling* (New York: Macmillan, 1929), pp. 220 ff.

[8] Masterson, *Jurisdiction in Marginal Seas*, pp. 304–21, 326–52.

[9] *US v. Postal* 589 F.2d 862, 885 (1979).

[10] For other criticisms see C. Connolly, '"Smoke on the water": Coast Guard authority to seize foreign vessels beyond the contiguous zone' (1980–1) 13 *NYU Journal of International Law and Policy* 249 at 283–90; R. Canty, 'Limits of Coast Guard authority to board foreign flag vessels on the high seas', (1998) 23 TMLJ 123. On objective territorial prescriptive jurisdiction see Lowe, 'Jurisdiction', pp. 343–5; *Annotated Commander's Handbook*, pp. 232–44; *Lotus Case*, 37 per Judge Loder (Dissenting Opinion), 76–8 per Judge Moore (Dissenting Opinion).

the validity of seizures beyond the three-mile limit but by a desire to avoid the repeated protests that the British had lodged... It was absolutely clear ... that the British [would protest against] ... any interference not justified by the treaty ... Therefore, it was assumed that Great Britain would assert the rights of its vessels and their crews under international law not to be subjected to adjudication. Without such objection, the doctrine embodied in the *Ker* case would apparently have validated the jurisdiction of the court notwithstanding the violation of international law.[11]

That is, under national law, US courts could proceed against defendants detained in breach of international law unless and until there was a diplomatic protest.

US statute law had also previously allowed US officials limited law enforcement rights against foreign-flagged vessels in designated high-seas 'customs enforcement areas'.[12] The Coast Guard also has statutory powers to seize stateless vessels[13] and the Federal Court has consistently upheld the view that US drug-smuggling law can be applied against stateless vessels on the high seas irrespective of any direct nexus between the conduct and the United States.[14] Such statutes were originally passed in order to protect national 'customs and public health interests' under an expansive interpretation of a state's ability to assert 'protective' or objective territorial jurisdiction at international law.[15] Thus, the Liquor Treaty provided that

His Britannic Majesty agrees that he will raise no objection to the boarding [and inspection] of private vessels under the British flag outside the limits of territorial waters by the authorities of the United States [and their being taken into US ports for adjudication] where such vessels were suspected of liquor-smuggling and those suspicions proved justified upon boarding and inspection.[16]

The wording allowed both sides to maintain positions of principle: the US position that it had a right of non-consensual high-seas enforcement

---

[11] *US v. Postal*, 883.

[12] *Third Restatement of Foreign Relations Law*, II, p. 54; Connolly, '"Smoke on the water"', 270–3 and 308–10.

[13] *United States v. Cortes*, 588 F.2d 106 (1979), 110; Connolly, '"Smoke on the water"', 317–18.

[14] See *US v. Bravo* 489 F.3d 1 (2007) at 7–8; *US v. Tinoco*, 304 F.3d 1088 (2002) at 1108, and the cases discussed therein.

[15] *US v. Romero-Galue*, 757 F.2d 1147 (1985), 1152 and n. 13, 1154 and n. 21; *US v. Postal*, 884; cf. Connolly, '"Smoke on the water"', 259–60.

[16] Convention between the United Kingdom and the USA respecting the Regulation of the Liquor Traffic 1924, (1924) Treaty Series No. 22, Article 2.

to protect its interests, the UK position that such actions breached international law.[17]

A similar bilateral approach was taken in 1981 regarding narcotics smuggling, principally marijuana. Unusually in modern practice, the 1981 Agreement is non-reciprocal, permitting US authorities to board UK vessels, and not vice versa.[18] It grants boarding and seizure rights in advance: no express consent to particular interdictions is required, provided they occur within defined high-seas areas including the Caribbean Sea, the Gulf of Mexico and all waters within 150 miles of the US Atlantic coast.[19] Permission is conditioned upon the United Kingdom being subsequently notified of both interdiction and any intended prosecution. The United Kingdom may object to the 'continued exercise of United States jurisdiction over the vessel' within fourteen days of its arriving in port or within thirty days to US prosecution of any UK national.[20] US criminal law is therefore that applied to any smuggling discovered.[21]

Rather than granting positive permission to interdict, the UK government agrees that it will not object to an interdiction where US authorities 'reasonably believe' that a UK vessel is carrying 'drugs for importation into the United States' in violation of US law.[22] This was apparently done to 'avoid any implication' that the Coast Guard is 'acting on behalf of' or with the positive authorisation of the United Kingdom.[23] Despite the bilateral history supporting the use of such a formula to avoid setting precedents or abandoning principles, it is difficult to see how it vests positive jurisdiction in US authorities at international law rather than merely waiving rights regarding otherwise internationally wrongful conduct.

Regardless, two developments now make the formula obsolete. First, statute law now requires US authorities to obtain flag-state consent

---

[17] O'Connell, p. 643; Connolly, '"Smoke on the water"', 261–8.

[18] Agreement to Facilitate the Interdiction by the United States of Vessels of the United Kingdom Suspected of Trafficking in Drugs 1981, 1285 UNTS 197 (US–UK Exchange of Notes).

[19] Ibid., para. 9.   [20] Ibid., paras. 4 and 5.

[21] M. Havers, 'Good fences make good neighbours: a discussion of problems concerning the exercise of jurisdiction' (1983) 17 International Lawyer 784 at 789.

[22] US–UK Exchange of Notes, Para. 1.

[23] J. Siddle, 'Anglo-American cooperation in the suppression of drug smuggling' (1982) 31 ICLQ 726 at 740; W. Gilmore, 'Narcotics interdiction at sea: US–UK co-operation', (1989) 13 Marine Policy 218 at 219; a similar formula is used in practice by Canada; see Official Records: Narcotics Convention Conference, 29th meeting, UN Doc. E/CONF.82/C.2/SR.29, 14.

before interdicting a vessel in international waters,[24] overturning the judicial concept of objective territorial enforcement jurisdiction. Second, the Notes' requirement that drugs interdicted must be bound for the United States has proved cumbersome. Following the statutory changes, this requirement introduces an additional element in domestic prosecutions – proof of destination – not present under the UN Narcotics Convention.[25] In practice, most US–UK interdictions now rely on that Convention.

3 The 1988 UN Narcotics Convention

Article 108(1) of UNCLOS requires all states to co-operate in suppressing illicit high-seas drug trafficking. Article 108(2), however, provides only that any state with 'reasonable grounds for believing' that *its* flag vessel 'is engaged in illicit traffic … *may* request' other states' co-operation (emphasis added). This omits the more usual situation, where a state seeks to interdict a suspected smuggler flying *another* state's flag.[26]

The UN Narcotics Convention addresses this lacuna. Article 17 provides a framework for seeking flag-state consent to interdict. Article 17(3) provides that a party with 'reasonable grounds' to suspect that a vessel 'flying the flag or displaying marks of registry of another Party' and 'exercising freedom of navigation' is engaged in illicit traffic, may request from the ostensible flag state 'confirmation of registry and, if confirmed, … authorization … to take appropriate measures'. There is no obligation to authorise interdiction.[27] The words 'exercising freedom of navigation' are significant, as this drafting could encompass all vessels outside territorial waters, including those within a party's EEZ.[28]

---

[24] Maritime Drug Law Enforcement Act, 46 App. USCA §1903(c) and n. 4 (repealed 6 October 2006); see now 46 USCA §70502(c).

[25] Personal communications: discussion with Wayne Raabe, US Department of Justice, 30 March 2005; discussion with Annabelle Bolt, Her Majesty's Revenue and Customs, 17 May 2005; contra, Gilmore (1990), 378, and the apparent result in *US v. Beirman* (US District Court) (1988) 84 ILR 206 at 212–14. See Canty, 'Limits of Coast Guard authority', 124, 131, on policy considerations.

[26] Gilmore, 'Drug trafficking by sea: the 1988 United Nations Convention', 185.

[27] Official Records: Narcotics Convention Conference, 28th meeting, UN Doc. E/CONF.82/C.2/SR.28, para. 7.

[28] Marston (1988), 529; cf. V. Gualde, 'Suppression of the illicit traffic in narcotic drugs and psychotropic substances on the high seas: Spanish case law' (1996) 4 SYBIL 91, 95. See also discussion in Chapter 4, section 1.5.

Although some states have maintained that all interdictions within the EEZ require coastal state consent, it is not apparent that drug-smuggling interdictions could interfere with a coastal state's limited EEZ rights.[29]

Article 17(4) provides that – following a request under Article 17(3) – the flag state may authorise the boarding state to, *inter alia*,

    (a) board the vessel;
    (b) search the vessel; and
    (c) if evidence of involvement in illicit traffic is found, take appropriate action with respect to the vessel, persons and cargo on board.

This disjunctive list emphasises that permission to board does not necessarily include permission to seize, and that flag states may reserve their position on seizure until evidence of illicit traffic is discovered.[30]

The Convention also contains certain obligations and a permissive grant of national prescriptive jurisdiction. Articles 17(7) and (9) require that parties respond 'expeditiously' to requests and consider entering 'bilateral or regional [interdiction] agreements … to enhance the [Convention's] effectiveness'. Article 4(1)(b)(ii) provides that parties *may* establish national prescriptive jurisdiction over offences committed aboard foreign-flagged vessels upon which they have been

authorized to take appropriate action pursuant to Article 17, *provided* that such jurisdiction shall be exercised only on the basis of agreements … referred to in paragraphs 4 and 9 of that Article. (emphasis added)

Article 4(1)(b)(ii) thus allows prosecutions before the courts of the boarding state where interdictions have occurred consensually under the Narcotics Convention procedures *or* a further Article 17(9) bilateral or regional agreement. The Spanish Audiencia Nacional has held that the Convention, coupled with Panama's providing ad hoc written consent 'through diplomatic channels' to the interdiction of the Panamanian flagged vessel *Archangelos* and subsequent Spanish

---

[29] See Chapter 4, section 1.5; *UN Practical Guide*, p. 113; Roach and Smith, *United States Responses to Excessive Maritime Claims*, pp. 415–17.

[30] *UN Practical Guide*, p. 115; Gilmore, 'Drug trafficking by sea', 190; Official Records: Narcotics Convention Conference, 29th meeting, UN Doc. E/CONF.82/C.2/SR.29, para. 8 and note paras. 108, 123–4, on the use of '*inter alia*' to give flag states 'the maximum flexibility' to authorise a variety of actions including those listed.

proceedings, was sufficient at international law to give Spanish courts jurisdiction over smuggling offences committed aboard while in international waters.[31] A similar result followed in a UK case where the US private vessel *Battlestar* was interdicted by permission given under the Convention.[32]

4 The 1990 Spanish–Italian Treaty

The 1990 Spanish–Italian Treaty (the 1990 Treaty) grants comprehensive permission in advance to interdict, considerably streamlining the UN Narcotics Convention approach. Where there is reasonable suspicion that 'ships displaying the flag' of one party are engaged in smuggling offences outside territorial waters, 'each party recognizes the other's *right to intervene* [aboard] as its agent'.[33] The reference to 'ships displaying the flag' of the other party may indicate that this right of intervention is granted on the basis of presumptive flag-state authority (discussed below).[34] Article 5(2) permits parties to 'pursue, arrest and board' the other party's flag vessels and 'check documents, question persons on board and, if reasonable suspicion remains, search the ship, seize drugs and arrest the persons involved and ... escort the ship to ... port'. If a party 'intervenes without adequate grounds for suspicion, it may be held liable for any loss or damage incurred' unless acting on the flag state's request.[35]

The flag state is said to have a 'preferential jurisdiction', by which it retains exclusive jurisdiction to prosecute unless it expressly cedes it to the boarding state.[36] This makes express what the disjunctive list of powers which may be granted a boarding state under the UN Narcotics Convention implies. The treaty also provides that '[o]n ships sailing under national flags, police powers granted by the respective legal systems remain valid.'[37] This appears to envisage the non-displacement of the flag state's law during an interdiction, rather than requiring interdicting state officials to apply the flag state's policing law. The result must follow that once preferential jurisdiction is renounced, the applicable substantive criminal law is that of the boarding state.

---

[31] Gualde, 'Suppression of the illicit traffic', 102–3. Upheld in *Rigopoulos v. Spain,* European Court of Human Rights, Request Number 37388/97, Judgment of 12 January 1999.

[32] *R v. Dean and Bolden* [1998] 2 Cr. App. R. 171, 173–5.

[33] Spanish–Italian Treaty, Articles 4(2) and 5(1) (emphasis added).

[34] Chapter 5, section 7.   [35] Spanish–Italian Treaty, Article 5(4).

[36] *Ibid.*, Articles 4(2) and 6.   [37] *Ibid.*, Article 5(1).

In any event, as both Spain and Italy are parties to the UN Narcotics Convention, that Convention would allow the boarding state to exercise prescriptive jurisdiction and conduct subsequent prosecutions under Articles 17(9) and 4(1)(b)(ii).[38]

Despite these concepts of 'preferential jurisdiction' and 'agency', the treaty is completely silent on the transfer of suspects in the boarding state's custody to the flag state if preferential jurisdiction is not relinquished. This is especially surprising given that a vessel could be *escorted to port* before a decision on the exercise of preferential jurisdiction has been made.[39] The apparent assumption that suspects can simply be surrendered to the flag state is not without difficulties, as discussed in the next section. In 1994 Spain concluded a broadly similar treaty with Portugal, although it provides for reciprocal as-of-right interdictions only where 'circumstances prevent ... prior [flag state] authorization being obtained in a timely manner'.[40]

5 The 1995 Council of Europe Agreement

The 1995 Council of Europe Agreement likewise builds upon the UN Narcotics Convention model of case-by-case flag-state authorisation, and also uses concepts of 'preferential jurisdiction' and perhaps boarding state 'agency'. The Agreement entered into force in 2000 with three ratifications, and now has thirteen parties.[41] The slow pace of ratification perhaps reflects subsequent advances in European law enforcement co-operation, reducing the need for subject-specific treaties. It may also reflect potential national difficulties in implementing two aspects of the Agreement. First, the Agreement assumes that suspects arrested by the boarding state may be 'surrendered' without extradition to the flag state should it assert its preferential jurisdiction and undertake the prosecution of offences discovered by the boarding state.[42] The choice of language on deeming and surrender reflects some states' view that the boarding state's enforcement jurisdiction is essentially one loaned by the flag state.[43] This view is further reflected in the provision that where prosecution is not left to the boarding

---

[38] Vienna Convention on the Law of Treaties 1969, 1155 UNTS 331, Article 30(4)(a).
[39] Spanish–Italian Treaty, Article 5(2).
[40] *UN Practical Guide*, p. 157.
[41] As of 8 August 2008; see www.coe.int.   [42] Article 3.
[43] W. Gilmore, 'Narcotics interdiction at sea: the 1995 Council of Europe Agreement' (1996) 20 *Marine Policy* 3 at 11.

state, '[m]easures taken by the intervening State against the vessel and persons on board may be deemed to have been taken as part of the procedure of the flag State'.[44]

The Council of Europe explanatory report suggests that under this 'legal fiction' 'measures taken against the vessels and persons on board [by the boarding state] may be deemed to have been taken as part of the proceedings of the flag State'.[45]

Quite apart from the delays and complexities attendant on extradition, the 'surrender' provision also appears designed to attempt to avoid the constitutional difficulties some states would face in extraditing to the boarding state nationals discovered aboard their flag vessel; or similar difficulties in cases where a boarding state has discovered one of its own nationals aboard, removed them into its custody and is then required to return him or her to the flag state for trial. While there is no reported case law on that point under the Agreement, the very same 'semantic distinction' between extradition and surrender did not prove successful in obviating problems of rendering nationals to foreign authorities in the context of European Arrest Warrant procedures, and a number of states had to amend their constitutions to comply.[46] Even so, 'surrender' under the European Arrest Warrant is less automatic than the choice of verb might imply: at most, it is a simplified form of extradition involving a judicial process and a degree of human rights scrutiny, which may take up to ninety days.[47] A rather more unconditional concept of 'surrender' applies when state parties are requested to deliver a suspect to the International Criminal Court (ICC); indeed, such 'requests' are binding and within some state parties are subject only to the most limited review by national courts.[48] The

---

[44] Article 14(5).

[45] Council of Europe, Explanatory Report: Agreement on Illicit Traffic by Sea implementing Article 17 of the United Nations Convention against Illicit Traffic in Narcotic Drugs and Psychotropic Substances (1994), http://conventions.coe.int/Treaty/en/Reports/Html/156.htm, para. 14.

[46] Z. Deen-Racsmány, 'Lessons of the European arrest warrant for domestic implementation of the obligation to surrender nationals to the International Criminal Court' (2007) 20 LJIL 167 at 169.

[47] N. Vennemann, 'The European arrest warrant and its human rights implications', (2003) 63 ZaöRV 103 at 109, 112–19.

[48] Rome Statute of the International Criminal Court 1998, 2187 UNTS 3 (entered into force 1 July 2002, 106 parties at 1 June 2008), Article 89(1); International Criminal Court Act 2001 c.17 (UK) s. 5; International Criminal Court Act 2002 (No.41 of 2002) (Australia), s. 23.

surrender process, however, remains subject to judicial control and review at the ICC level before a Pre-Trial Chamber.[49] Any suggestion in the word 'surrender' that suspects aboard an interdicted vessel may simply be handed over to the flag state by the boarding party may thus create difficulties regarding both national law and international human rights guarantees.

The second potential problem is the law applicable during boardings. In contrast to the Spanish–Italian treaty, the Agreement expressly provides that enforcement action taken aboard a vessel 'shall be governed by the law of the intervening State'.[50] The consequences if preferential jurisdiction is then asserted are unclear. Before the flag state asserts jurisdiction its flag vessel could have been searched, evidence seized and witnesses interviewed under one of twelve different sets of police powers, possibly compromising subsequent prosecutions before its courts.[51]

Article 26 addresses questions of responsibility, including joint or shared state responsibility, for the conduct of interdictions. The Article provides for recourse against the boarding state alone for loss, damage or injury suffered:

(1) 'as a result of negligence or some other fault attributable to the [boarding] State';
(2) following 'action … taken in a manner which is not justified' under the Agreement; or
(3) where 'the suspicions prove to be unfounded and provided that the vessel boarded, the operator or the crew have not committed any act justifying them'.

Liability in the first instance rests with the flag state where it has requested the boarding state's intervention aboard the vessel.[52] Liability provisions are more fully discussed in Chapter 12.

---

[49] R. Cryer, 'Implementation of the International Criminal Court Statute in England and Wales' (2002) 51 ICLQ 733 at 737.
[50] Article 11(1).
[51] See Chapter 11. By contrast Articles 41(2) and (5)(a), Convention Applying the Schengen Agreement 1990, (1991) 30 ILM 84, requires police officers engaged in cross-border hot pursuit to comply with the law of the territorial state and denies them powers of formal arrest outside their own jurisdiction.
[52] Articles 4 and 26(3).

6 US bilateral agreements

6.1 *High-seas interdictions*

The United States has extensive experience in conducting drug interdictions under a network of bilateral treaties with twenty-four states.[53] These treaties address consensual boarding in international waters and enforcement (seizure) jurisdiction over vessels, their cargo or crew. They also often provide for 'ship-rider' law enforcement personnel and interdictions in either party's territorial waters.

The US–Guatemala agreement[54] is typical in providing for either actual or presumed consent to boarding flag vessels. While consent must be requested,

[i]f there is no response ... within two (2) hours ... the requesting Party will be deemed to have been authorized to board the suspect vessel for the purpose of inspecting ... documents, questioning the persons on board, and searching the vessel to determine if it is engaged in illicit traffic.[55]

The same mechanism is contained in US agreements with Honduras,[56] Nicaragua,[57] Panama[58] and Venezuela.[59] Under the agreements with

[53] Antigua and Barbuda, Bahamas, Barbados, Belize, Colombia, Costa Rica, Dominica, Dominican Republic, Grenada, Guatemala, Guyana, Haiti, Honduras, Jamaica, Malta, Nicaragua, Panama, St Kitts and Nevis, St Lucia, St Vincent and the Grenadines, Suriname, Trinidad and Tobago, the United Kingdom, and Venezuela.

[54] Agreement between the United States and Guatemala Concerning Cooperation to Suppress Illicit Traffic in Narcotic Drugs and Psychotropic Substances by Sea and Air 2003, available at http://guatemala.usembassy.gov/uploads/images/COB7Udl1HS7y04mWhEcLNg/usguatmaritimeagreemente.pdf (Guatemala Agreement).

[55] Article 7(3)(d); cf. Art. 7(3)(c).

[56] Implementing agreement between the US and Honduras Concerning Cooperation for the Suppression of Illicit Maritime Traffic in Narcotic Drugs and Psychotropic Substances 2000, KAV 5963 (Honduras Agreement), Article 6(1).

[57] Agreement between the USA and Nicaragua Concerning Cooperation to Suppress Illicit Traffic by Sea and Air, 2001, KAV 5964 (Nicaragua Agreement), Article 9(1).

[58] Supplementary Arrangement between the US and Panama to the Arrangement for Support and Assistance from the US Coast Guard for the National Maritime Service 2002, KAV 6074 (Panama Supplementary Agreement), Article 10(6).

[59] Agreement between the US and Venezuela to Suppress Illicit Traffic in Narcotic Drugs and Psychotropic Substances by Sea 1991, TIAS 11827 (Venezuela Agreement), Article 4.

Colombia,[60] Barbados[61] and Jamaica[62] consent may be presumed after three hours. Deemed consent only arises, however, if there is *no* response: responses stating that more time is required to consider the request will 'stop the clock'.[63] The Haitian and Costa Rican agreements provide automatic consent to boarding where boarding officials act upon reasonable suspicion.[64]

The treaties contain various provisions on seizure where a crime is detected following boarding. The US–Haiti agreement is typical: it provides that where illicit traffic is uncovered, US officials may detain persons and cargo 'pending expeditious disposition instructions' from Haiti.[65] As under the Council of Europe Agreement, Haiti retains 'the primary right to exercise jurisdiction' over detained vessels, cargoes and persons but may waive it to 'authorize the enforcement of United States law against the vessel'.[66] Similar language is found in three other treaties.[67] Under the Nicaraguan and Colombian agreements only the United States may waive its jurisdiction and authorise the enforcement of foreign law against its flag vessel, presumably reflecting the other parties' constitutional constraints.[68] However, under Colombian national law, where the United States first initiates criminal proceedings in respect of offences detected aboard a Colombian vessel in international waters, US criminal law will apply to the Colombian flag vessel to the exclusion of Colombian criminal law.[69] The Venezuelan

---

[60] Agreement between the United States and Colombia to Suppress Illicit Traffic by Sea 1997, KAV 4867 (Colombia Agreement), Article 8.

[61] Agreement between Barbados and the United States Concerning Cooperation in Suppressing Illicit Maritime Drug Trafficking 1998, KAV 5337 (Barbados Agreement), Article 14, (using a 'will not object' formula).

[62] Agreement between the US and Jamaica Concerning Cooperation in Suppressing Illicit Maritime Drug Traffic 1998, KAV 5155 as amended by the 2004 Protocol to the Agreement, KAV 6387 (Jamaica Agreement (as amended)), Article 8.

[63] Commentary appended to J. Ashley Roach, 'Proliferation Security Initiative (PSI): countering proliferation by sea' in M. Nordquist *et al.* (eds.), *Recent Developments in the Law of the Sea and China* (Dordrecht: Martinus Nijhoff, 2006), p. 351 at p. 360.

[64] Agreement between the United States and Costa Rica Concerning Cooperation to Suppress Illicit Traffic 1999, KAV 5643 (Costa Rica Agreement), Article 5, Agreement between the United States and Haiti Concerning Cooperation to Suppress Illicit Maritime Traffic 1997, KAV 6079 (Haiti Agreement), Article 5.

[65] *Ibid.*, Article 14.   [66] *Ibid.*, Article 16.

[67] Costa Rica Agreement, Article 6, Honduras Agreement, Art. 7(1); Barbados Agreement, Article 15.

[68] Nicaragua Agreement, Article 10; Colombia Agreement, Article 16.

[69] See Colombia Agreement, Article 16.

treaty simply requires an expeditious 'decision by the flag State as to which Party is to exercise enforcement jurisdiction'.[70]

Seven US bilateral narcotics interdiction treaties[71] and one multilateral convention[72] provide for 'ship-riders', a designated official of one state who can travel aboard the other party's law enforcement vessels and provide on-the-spot consent to interdiction of their state's flag vessels and enforce the flag state's criminal law once aboard. Typically, this results in an official of a central American state being placed on a US Coast Guard vessel, allowing that state to retain formal control over interdictions.[73] In practice the use of ship-riders is the exception rather than the rule, although Jamaican and Bahamian ship-riders on US Coast Guard patrols are not uncommon. Two factors may account for this. The first is smaller states' capacity to spare personnel to act as ship-riders. The second is the practical issues for the Coast Guard in 'receiving' a ship-rider. These include storage of the ship-rider's weapons and ammunition (if any), cabin-space, laundry costs, who will have tactical control during interdictions and the extent of the ship-rider's authority to authorise warning shots or disabling fire.[74] Such issues are commonly treated in memoranda of understanding.

6.2 Territorial-sea interdictions

If a suspect vessel on the high seas or in territorial waters can outrun a pursuing government vessel and enter another state's territorial waters, pursuit must ordinarily cease. The issue arises sharply in relation to Caribbean drug-traffickers' use of 'go-fast' modified speedboats, or the ease with which pirates operating in the Malacca Strait

---

[70] Article 8.
[71] Barbados Agreement, Articles 3 and 4; Costa Rica Agreement, Article 4; Haiti Agreement, Articles 4–10; Honduras Agreement, Article 4; Jamaica Agreement (as amended), Articles 7–9; Nicaragua Agreement, Articles 4 and 5; Agreement Concerning a Cooperative Ship-rider and Over-flight Drug Interdiction Program (US–Bahamas exchange of notes) 1996, KAV 4743 (Bahamas Agreement), paras. 1–2.
[72] Agreement Concerning Co-operation in Suppressing Illicit Maritime and Air Trafficking in Narcotic Drugs and Psychotropic Substances in the Caribbean Area 2003 (Caribbean Area Agreement), Articles 8–10. Text available in William C. Gilmore (ed.), *Agreement Concerning Co-operation in Suppressing Illicit Maritime and Air Trafficking in Narcotic Drugs and Psychotropic Substances in the Caribbean Area* (London: The Stationery Office, 2005). Not in force as of March 2008, presently ratified only by France, the United States, Jamaica and Belize, www.state.gov/p/inl/rls/nrcrpt/2008/vol1/html/100778.htm.
[73] Byers, 'Policing the high seas', 539.
[74] Personal communication, Lt. Commander Brad Kieserman (US Coast Guard), 1 April 2005.

may evade capture by moving from the territorial waters of one littoral state to another.[75]

The Harvard Draft Convention on Piracy suggested permitting what might be dubbed 'reverse hot pursuit' or 'pursuit and entry'. Its draft Article 7 provided that pursuit of a suspected pirate vessel commenced in international waters could be continued into another state's territorial waters unless prohibited by that coastal state.[76] If seizure occurred in foreign waters, the interdicting state was to tender the vessel and crew for adjudication to the coastal state; if the tender was refused, the interdicting state could take enforcement jurisdiction.[77] The proposal has not been widely adopted. Article 23(2) of the 1958 High Seas Convention, as re-enacted in Article 111(3) of UNCLOS, terminates any right of hot pursuit once 'the ship pursued enters the territorial sea of its own country or of a third State'.[78] While only directly applicable to hot pursuit commenced from territorial waters and adjacent regulatory zones, the same rule must apply to pursuit commenced on the high seas.

'Pursuit and entry' provisions have, however, been included in US bilateral drug interdiction treaties and the Caribbean Area Agreement on drug interdiction.[79] Articles 11 and 12 of the Caribbean Area Agreement are representative of the general practice. Article 11 provides that law enforcement operations in territorial waters are subject to the coastal state's authority, are to be carried out 'by, or under the direction of', its law enforcement authorities and may only be carried out by other states with its consent. Similar provisions exist in a number of US bilateral treaties.[80] Article 12 provides possible exceptions,

---

[75] See Gilmore, *Agreement Concerning Co-operation*, p. 4; Stiles, 'Reforming current international law', 309. The use of go-fasts is now the common practice: *US v. Sinisterra*, 237 Fed.Appx. 467 (2007), 468–9.

[76] *Harvard Research*, 744 and 833; cf. Gidel, I, p. 337.   [77] *Ibid.*

[78] UNCLOS, however, refers to 'state' not 'country' throughout.

[79] See n. 72, above.

[80] Barbados Agreement, Article 5; Colombia Agreement, Article 4 (exclusively reserving such operations to the coastal state); Costa Rica Agreement, Article 3; Agreement between the US and Dominica concerning Maritime Counter-Drug Operations 1995, TIAS 12630 (Dominica Agreement), Article 2; Agreement between the US and the Dominican Republic concerning Maritime Counter-Drug Operations 1995, TIAS 12620 as amended by the 2003 Protocol to the Agreement, KAV 6186 (Dominican Republic Agreement (as amended)), Article 2; Agreement between the US and Grenada concerning Maritime Counter-Drug Operations 1995, TIAS 12648 (Grenada Agreement), Article 2; Guatemala Agreement, Article 3; Haiti Agreement, Article 3; Honduras Agreement, Article 3; Nicaragua Agreement, Article 3;

allowing one party to pursue a suspect vessel from international waters into the territorial waters of another party and take measures (including boarding and 'secur[ing] the vessel and persons on board') to prevent its escape, pending 'expeditious disposition instructions' from the coastal state as to which state will take law enforcement jurisdiction. Such pursuit and entry is permitted in one of two cases.[81] The default rule is that it is only permissible where express consent is sought and received.[82] Parties may alternatively notify the depository that they will allow pursuit and entry where notice is given *and* there is no ship-rider aboard the pursuing vessel *and* no coastal state vessel 'is immediately available'.[83] This notice must be provided prior to entry 'if operationally feasible', but otherwise 'as soon as possible'.[84]

Bilateral treaty provisions on pursuit and entry are somewhat varied. Several options may be used singly or in combination in any given agreement:

(1) case-by-case permission in advance is required in all circumstances;[85]

(2) pursuit into territorial waters is allowed, provided pursuing authorities give notice as early as practicable, including notice subsequent;[86]

(3) permission in advance is given to pursue vessels into territorial waters in order to 'maintain contact' with the suspect vessel pending instructions from the coastal state (including authorisation to interdict), often subject to a condition that the pursuing state has ascertained that no coastal state enforcement vessel 'is immediately available'. Some allow boarding to secure a suspected crime scene without prior consent (usually where option 4 is also used). This option is normally *excluded* where a ship-rider is present on the

---

Agreement between the US and Saint Kitts and Nevis concerning Maritime Counter-Drug Operations 1995, KAV 4231 (Saint Kitts and Nevis Agreement), Article 2; Agreement between the US and Santa Lucia concerning Maritime Counter-Drug Operations 1995, KAV 4240 (Saint Lucia Agreement), Article 2; Agreement between the US and Saint Vincent and the Grenadines concerning Maritime Counter-Drug Operations 1995, TIAS 12676 (Saint Vincent and the Grenadines Agreement), Article 2; Agreement between the US and Suriname concerning Maritime Law Enforcement 1999, KAV 5631 (Suriname Agreement), Article 3; and cf. Jamaica Agreement (as amended), Article 10(4).

[81] Caribbean Area Agreement, Article 12(1).

[82] *Ibid.*   [83] *Ibid.*   [84] *Ibid.*

[85] Jamaica Agreement (as amended), Article 10.

[86] Costa Rica Agreement, Article 4(6); Honduras Agreement, Article 5(1); Suriname Agreement, Article 6.

pursuing vessel and capable of giving permission to enter territorial waters;[87] and

(4) the foreign state is given consent in advance and without any prior requirement of pursuit to enter the coastal state's territorial waters where it has detected a suspect vessel in those territorial waters and board it, pending final disposition instructions from the coastal state. Such provisions usually do not extend to flag vessels of the coastal state.[88]

Pursuit and entry does not concern flag-state jurisdiction, but rather the vesting of a parallel jurisdiction in a foreign state by the *territorial* sovereign (which retains primary jurisdiction). Reliance on coastal state jurisdiction clearly dispenses with any need for flag-state authorisation. Rights of innocent passage do not apply, given the express permission in UNCLOS Article 27(1)(d) to take drug-enforcement action against foreign vessels, quite apart from the plenary competence of states in their territorial sea (as discussed in Chapter 2, section 2.2).

Given the diversity of options and the language of individual treaties, it would clearly be a mistake to suggest that any regional custom has emerged.[89] The treaties usually contain a provision formally requiring express consent but stating that such consent is provided by the treaty. This negates any claim that a general right exists, independent of treaty and absent express consent, to conduct such pursuits. That said, many agreements embody options 2 and 3, accepting the idea – within a treaty arrangement – of pursuit into territorial waters without prior notice.

---

[87] Agreement between the US and Antigua and Barbuda concerning Maritime Counter-Drug Operations 1995, KAV 4238 (Antigua and Barbuda Agreement), Article 8; Barbados Agreement, Article 6; Agreement between Belize and the US Concerning Maritime Counter-Drug Operations 1992, TIAS 11914 (Belize Agreement), Article 8; Costa Rica Agreement, Article 4(6); Dominica Agreement, Article 8; Dominican Republic Agreement, Article 8; Grenada Agreement, Article 8; Guatemala Agreement, Article 6; Haiti Agreement, Article 9; Honduras Agreement, Article 5(1); Nicaragua Agreement, Article 6(2)(b) and (3); Panama Agreement, Article 6(4); Saint Kitts and Nevis Agreement, Article 8; Saint Lucia Agreement, Article 8; Saint Vincent and the Grenadines Agreement, Article 8; Suriname Agreement, Article 6.

[88] Antigua and Barbuda Agreement, Article 8; Dominica Agreement, Article 8; Dominican Republic Agreement, Article 8; Grenada Agreement, Article 8; Guatemala Agreement, Article 6; Haiti Agreement, Article 9; Nicaragua Agreement, Article 6(2)(c) and (3); Panama Agreement, Article 6(5); Saint Kitts and Nevis Agreement, Article 8; Saint Lucia Agreement, Article 8; Saint Vincent and the Grenadines Agreement, Article 8; Suriname Agreement, Article 6.

[89] See *Right of Passage Case (Merits)*, [1960] ICJ Rep. 6 at 39–43; *Asylum Case*, [1950] ICJ Rep. 266 at 276–278.

7 Conclusion: practical issues in drug interdiction under treaty arrangements

At-sea interdictions are logistically complex, potentially dangerous and often very expensive. Only a limited number of states have the resources and trained personnel to conduct them.[90] These well-resourced boarding states, when seeking to interdict flag vessels from less-resourced states, face a common problem. Even when the flag state is party to a relevant treaty, it may be difficult to find an official with authority under national law to grant an interdiction request (a 'competent authority'). Some states may have multiple competent authorities and requests could involve contacting them all. In practice, boarding states will seek to establish a single point of contact in advance, and keep a list of 'current contacts' updated by diplomatic notes.

Article 17 paragraphs (3) and (4) of the UN Narcotics Convention create a further procedural obstacle, requiring that the requested flag state confirm registry before authorising interdiction. This can cause significant delays if the competent authority lacks 'round-the-clock access to their national register of shipping', which may be maintained by a different agency.[91] Even where the competent authority has such access, completing a search may take days. Malefactors may seek registration in states known to have inefficient registries in order to frustrate interdiction. Further, requiring confirmation of *registry* is inconsistent with UNCLOS Article 91, which acknowledges that vessels may hold nationality through a right to fly a flag independent of registration.[92] National legal systems commonly only require vessels of a certain size to register, and smaller vessels may be entitled to fly the flag of their owner's state of nationality without registration.[93] In *Battlestar*, mentioned above, an English court found that the requirements of Article 17 paragraphs (3) and (4) could not be met where a

---

[90] The author is indebted to Captain J. Ashley Roach (Ret.)(US Department of State), Lt. Commander Brad Kieserman (US Coast Guard), Wayne Raabe (US Department of Justice) and Annabelle Bolt (HM Revenue and Customs) for their assistance in explaining issues discussed here. Any views expressed, or interpretative errors made, remain the author's.

[91] Roach, 'Proliferation Security Initiative', 389.

[92] The point was noted at the time of drafting by the German Democratic Republic: Official Records: Narcotics Convention Conference, E/CONF.82/C.2/ SR.29, para. 71.

[93] O'Connell, p. 753; Lowe and Churchill, 'The International Tribunal for the Law of the Sea', 474–5; Meyers, pp. 149–50; cf. [1956] I YBILC, 67 ff.

ship had a right to fly a state's flag but was not formally registered in that state.[94]

Even in wealthy states, confirming registry may prove troublesome. The United States circumvents time-consuming searches of both federal and state registries by a doctrine of 'presumptive flag-state authority'.[95] It takes the view that a ship ostensibly claiming its nationality (by flag, markings of registry or the master's verbal assertion when hailed) is assumed to be subject to its jurisdiction and it may thus authorise boarding. This reflects a pragmatic view that the vessel will ultimately prove to be (i) a US vessel, in which case the permission is valid; (ii) without nationality, making US permission irrelevant; or (iii) also, on inspection, carrying other flags or evidence of registry – in which case it can again be assimilated to a stateless vessel.[96] Alternatively, it could be justified by the recognised jurisdiction to prevent abuse of claims to nationality.[97]

The doctrine of presumptive authority could cover the lacuna regarding small, unregistered vessels otherwise entitled to fly a state flag. Nevertheless, the approach is not widely followed. The reticence of some states may reflect either a doctrinal view that one cannot grant an authority one may have no power to give or concern that a state granting permission to board a vessel ultimately discovered not to be subject to its jurisdiction may become jointly liable for any wrongfully conducted interdiction. However, in practice, presumptive flag-state authority is an operative concept in any agreement containing deemed authority to board a vessel flying one party's flag either generally (as in the US–UK Exchange of Notes, the Spanish–Italian Treaty, and US agreements with Haiti and Costa Rica) or after the elapse of a number of hours from an unanswered request (as in some US bilateral treaties). Such practices could only be justified by an assumption of presumptive flag-state authority. On any view *requiring* registry checks to confirm flag-state power these agreements would be purporting to grant a permission that the flag state potentially lacked competence to give. Further, some recent WMD interdiction treaties require verification of 'nationality', not 'registry'.[98] This may suggest a lower standard than confirming registration and contemplate presumptive flag-state authority.

---

[94] *R v. Dean and Bolden*, 182; cf. 179–80, wrongly finding the *Battlestar* stateless, but upholding interdiction on other grounds.

[95] *Ibid.*, 173–5.

[96] UNCLOS, Article 92(2); Roach, 'Proliferation Security Initiative', 390.

[97] *Oppenheim*, 9th edn, p. 737.   [98] See Chapter 9, section 5, and Chapter 9, section 6.

6 Fisheries management

1 Introduction

The freedom to fish, a fundamental historical freedom of the high seas, was first justified on the basis that fish were an inexhaustible resource.[1] Before the introduction of industrial fishing technology this may have been a reasonable assumption.[2] But open access to high-seas fisheries as a global commons has led to over-exploitation. Attempts to manage diminishing fish stocks in international law have taken two forms. First, coastal state authority to regulate fisheries has been extended seaward. While this increases regulatory control over some stocks, it has two limitations: high-seas fisheries remain unregulated and it creates 'straddling' or 'highly migratory' stocks. Second, states have established a variety of regional fisheries management organisations (RFMOs) to co-operate in managing the high-seas fishery for certain stocks in a defined area (management area) by prescribing management and conservation measures (measures). RFMOs form the principal

---

[1] Christian Wolff, *Jus gentium methodo scientifica pertractatum*, (trans. J. Drake) reproduction and translation of 1764 edn, vol. II (Oxford: Clarendon Press, 1934), p. 69; Emer de Vattel, *The Law of Nations*, reproduction and translation of 1758 edn, (trans. C. Fenwick) vol. III (Washington, DC: Carnegie Institution, 1916), p. 106; although Grotius appears to have noted 'in a way it can be maintained that fish are exhaustible' (qua dici quodammodo potest pisces exhauriri), Hugo Grotius, *The Freedom of the Seas or the Right which Belongs to the Dutch to Take Part in the East Indian Trade* (trans. R. Magoffin) (translation of *Mare Liberum sive de iure quod batauis competit ad indicana commerici: Dissertatio*), reproduction of 1688 edn (New York: Oxford University Press, 1916), p. 43.

[2] C. Roberts and J. Hawkins, 'Extinction risk in the sea', (1999) 14 *Trends in Ecology & Evolution* 241 at 241; J. Caddy and L. Garibaldi, 'Apparent changes in the trophic composition of world marine harvests: the perspective from the FAO capture database' (2000) 43 *Ocean & Coastal Management* 615 at 649–50.

subject of this chapter. High-seas fisheries management arrangements not involving at-sea boarding and inspection are not discussed.[3]

An RFMO's effectiveness may be undermined by fishing not in accordance with its adopted measures, so-called 'illegal, unreported or unregulated' fishing (IUU fishing).[4] Illegal fishing is fishing conducted by vessels of any nationality within waters under national jurisdiction in contravention of national laws and regulations; or fishing by vessels which contravenes RFMO measures binding upon the vessel's flag state.[5] Unreported fishing describes catch subject to reporting requirements which goes un- or under-reported to a coastal state authority or RFMO.[6] Unregulated fishing is fishing by stateless or non-party vessels in an RFMO management area in a manner contrary to RFMO measures.[7]

RFMOs have developed various strategies to regulate parties' total catch, induce non-party compliance and deter IUU fishing. Frequently, these have been borrowed and adapted to local conditions by other RFMOs. One can thus discuss various commonly used RFMO measures. This chapter discusses, first, the international law of fisheries jurisdiction and RFMOs' role in fisheries regulation. An overview of the most common RFMO regulatory measures is then presented, placing interdiction in its proper context as a *subsidiary* enforcement measure.

Despite the abundance of at-sea fisheries inspection practice under RFMOs, no RFMO provides for non-flag-state *prosecution* of RFMO violations. Enforcement jurisdiction is at best limited to conducting preliminary investigations and escorting vessels to port in serious cases. The issues of concurrent jurisdiction of principal interest to this book

---

[3] See R. Churchill, 'The Barents Sea loophole agreement: a "coastal state" solution to a straddling stock problem' (1999) 14 IJMCL 467; E. Molenaar, 'Participation, allocation and unregulated fishing: the practice of regional fisheries management organisations' (2003) 18 IJMCL 457; R. Rayfuse, 'The United Nations Agreement on Straddling and Highly Migratory Fish Stocks as an objective regime: a case of wishful thinking?' (1999) 20 AYBIL 253 at 276–7; Arrangement between the Government of New Zealand and the Government of Australia for the Conservation and Management of Orange Roughy on the South Tasman Rise 1998, www.dfat.gov.au/geo/new_zealand/roughy.pdf.

[4] The term originated in CCAMLR: W. Edeson, 'The international plan of action on illegal unreported and unregulated fishing: the legal context of a non-legally binding instrument' (2001) 16 IJMCL 603 at 605.

[5] UN Food and Agriculture Organization, International Plan of Action to Prevent, Deter and Eliminate Illegal, Unreported and Unregulated Fishing, 2001 (FAO Action Plan), www.fao.org/documents/show_cdr.asp?url_file=/DOCREP/003/y1224e/y1224e00.HTM, Article 3.1.

[6] Ibid., Article 3.2.   [7] Ibid., Article 3.3.

thus arise in a circumscribed context. Nonetheless, although most fisheries regimes involve only search and not seizure measures, fisheries practice still illustrates key difficulties in any multilateral interdiction regime. These include operational issues regarding the conduct of boardings, the political difficulties of reaching agreement on the use of force in policing a legal (as opposed to criminal) activity and the potential for conflict between states over the status of a foreign boarding party under flag-state law. The potential for conflict between national jurisdictions arises as, despite the fact that fisheries inspectors enforce RFMO rules, they do so under a 'network of reciprocal measures ... rather than a truly international control system in the sense of a system applied independently and uniformly by an intergovernmental organization'.[8] It has long been observed that fisheries inspections continue to be conducted by nationally appointed inspectors and their activities remain primarily an extension of member states' 'national [fisheries] control systems'.[9]

2 Jurisdiction over fisheries

2.1 The assertion of fisheries zones prior to UNCLOS

The freedom to fish has long existed in tension with coastal states' interests in fisheries adjacent their coast. The permissible extent of any exclusive fisheries zone (whether extending beyond the territorial sea or not) caused difficulties at all three UN Conferences on the Law of the Sea from 1958 onwards. Indeed, the 1960 Conference solely concerned this question; the proposal which 'narrowly' failed would have entitled coastal states to a 6-n.m. territorial sea and a 'contiguous fishing zone to a maximum limit of twelve nautical miles'.[10] The difficulty was compounded by claims over maritime natural resources precipitated by the United States' proclamations on the continental shelf and 'contiguous' high seas fisheries.[11] The US fisheries proclamation did not assert exclusive jurisdiction over fisheries superjacent to its continental shelf but rather a power to declare discrete fishing

---

[8] J. Carroz and A. Roche, 'The international policing of high seas fisheries', (1968) 6 CYBIL 61 at 88.

[9] *Ibid.*   [10] *UNCLOS Commentary*, II, p. 495.

[11] Proclamation by the President with Respect to the Natural Resources of the Subsoil and Sea Bed of the Continental Shelf [Proclamation No. 2667], (1946) 40 AJIL Sup. 45; Proclamation by the President with Respect to Coastal Fisheries in Respect of Certain Areas of the High Seas [Proclamation No. 2668], (1946) 40 AJIL Sup. 47.

'conservation zones' and to seek agreement with other states having a history of 'legitimately' fishing those waters.[12] This potentially collaborative management approach was not widely followed.

From 1947 a number of Latin American states asserted jurisdiction over natural resources, including fisheries, in the seas adjacent to their coastlines to a distance of 200 n.m.[13] The United States eventually declared a 200-n.m. fisheries zone in 1977, following at least twenty-seven states in the Americas, Africa, Europe and the sub-continent.[14] This practice resulted in the creation of the exclusive economic zone under UNCLOS; indeed, the EEZ had, given the multitude of prior unprotested claims, certainly become 'part of international law long before the [Convention's] entry into force'.[15]

UNCLOS provides that a coastal state may, 'in the exercise of its sovereign rights' in the EEZ, 'take such measures, *including boarding, inspection, arrest and judicial proceedings*, as may be necessary to ensure compliance' with its laws.[16] This grant of enforcement jurisdiction is tempered by requirements that arrested vessels and crews 'shall be promptly released' on reasonable bond; penalties for EEZ fisheries violations may not generally include imprisonment; and coastal states, when detaining foreign vessels, shall notify the flag state of action taken.[17] However, expanding state jurisdiction seawards simply displaces management issues. UNCLOS, therefore, elaborates a high-seas fishing regime.

2.2 UNCLOS fisheries management obligations

UNCLOS's fisheries provisions defer much to subsequent agreement, consisting largely of duties to negotiate, co-operate and take 'necessary measures'. As necessity seldom dictates precise legal arrangements, implementing 'necessary measures' also requires negotiation and cooperation.

Subject to other UNCLOS rules and treaty obligations, state parties remain free to fish on the high seas.[18] Article 117, however, requires parties to

---

[12] *Ibid.*; *UNCLOS Commentary*, II, p. 494.
[13] A. Hollick, 'The origins of 200-mile offshore zones' (1977) 71 AJIL 494.
[14] *UNCLOS Commentary*, II, p. 494 and n. 2.
[15] Churchill and Lowe, p. 161; *Libya/Malta Continental Shelf Case*, [1985] ICJ Rep. p. 13 at p. 33.
[16] UNCLOS, Article 73 (emphasis added).   [17] *Ibid.*, Article 73(2)–(4).
[18] *Ibid.*, Articles 87(1)(e) and 116.

take, or to cooperate with other States in taking, such measures for their respective nationals as may be necessary for the conservation of the living resources of the high seas.

This is not merely a duty to regulate all flag vessels,[19] as it also refers to *nationals*. Arguably it requires parties to enforce UNCLOS conservation obligations against their nationals regardless of the nationality of the vessel they fish upon, at least where the flag state fails in its own conservation duties. This approach is endorsed by the UN Food and Agriculture Organization (FAO) and required by the South East Atlantic Fisheries Organization Convention (SEAFO Convention). The FAO's International Plan of Action on IUU Fishing states that, following UNCLOS

and without prejudice to the *primary responsibility* of the flag state on the high seas, each State should, to the greatest extent possible, take measures or cooperate to ensure that nationals *subject to their jurisdiction* do not support or engage in IUU fishing.[20]

While the Plan is non-binding it represents a view, reached by consensus in a major international organisation, as to what UNCLOS permits. This clearly suggests that a state of nationality may exercise enforcement jurisdiction in respect of IUU fishing where a flag state does not, once its national re-enters its territory.[21]

The SEAFO Convention draws on the FAO Plan's wording.[22] While such provisions do not mandate high-seas interdiction to exercise control over nationals, they do allow for 'preventative measures before, or corrective measures after, nationals' violate RFMO measures.[23] There have been no reports to SEAFO indicating such practice yet; however, SEAFO first adopted management measures only in 2005. In terms of non-UNCLOS party practice, the US Lacey Act makes it a crime for US nationals to violate any applicable fisheries regulations anywhere.[24]

---

[19] See *UNCLOS Commentary*, III, p. 294.
[20] FAO Action Plan, para. 18 (emphasis added).
[21] Cf. *Lotus Case*, Judge Moore (Dissenting Opinion), 71–2.
[22] SEAFO Convention, Article 13(6)(a).
[23] A. Jackson, 'The Convention on the Conservation and Management of Fishery Resources in the South East Atlantic Ocean, 2001: an introduction' (2002) 17 IJMCL 33, 45.
[24] 16 USC §§3371–3378; see criminal prosecutions in *US v. Cameron*, 888 F.2d 1279 (1989) (violating International Pacific Halibut Commission regulations); *Wood v. Verity*, 729 F.Supp. 1324 (1989) (violating Bahamian EEZ regulations); and forfeiture proceedings in *US v. 594,464 Pounds of Salmon, More or Less*, 687 F.Supp. 525 (1987)

UNCLOS requires states to co-operate 'in the conservation and management of [high seas] living resources'. In any high-seas area where multiple states fish, those states 'shall enter into negotiations with a view to taking' necessary measures to conserve the fishery and shall, 'as appropriate, co-operate to establish ... regional fisheries organizations'.[25] This duty to co-operate, where 'appropriate', to establish RFMOs is also expressed in articles dealing with highly migratory fish species.[26]

These general duties are given more concrete expression in relation to several categories of fishery: (i) anadromous and catadromous species; (ii) 'straddling stocks', fisheries straddling either two or more adjacent EEZs or an EEZ and a contiguous high-seas area; (iii) highly migratory species; and (iv) high-seas fisheries beyond national jurisdiction. Anadromous species are migratory fish that return to a state's internal waters to spawn. Conversely, catadromous species are ordinarily river-dwelling species, which spawn in the sea. The latter have attracted little or no state practice. Anadromous species, particularly salmon, are more significant. Article 66 acknowledges the 'primary interest in and responsibility for' anadromous species of the 'state of origin' in whose rivers they originate. Article 66 generally restricts fishing for them to EEZ areas, except where this would cause other states 'economic dislocation'. All states fishing for the stock (whether legally or not) 'shall make arrangements' to implement Article 66 'where appropriate, through regional organizations'.[27] Any action to prevent prohibited high-seas fishing thus requires agreement among fishing states.

Article 63 on straddling stocks and Article 64 on highly migratory species are important to subsequent developments. Article 63 provides that the states interested in a stock not entirely contained within one EEZ

shall seek, either directly or through appropriate ... regional organizations, to agree upon the measures necessary to coordinate and ensure [its] conservation and development ...

This may occur where the one fish stock overlaps adjacent EEZs, or where the one stock occurs both within an EEZ and 'in an area beyond

---

(Taiwanese Salmon regulations); *US v. Proceeds from Sale of Approximately 15,538 Panulirus Argus Lobster Tails*, 834 F.Supp. 385 (1993) (Turks and Caicos Islands fishing restrictions); *US v. 144,774 pounds of Blue King Crab*, 410 F.3d 1131 (2005) (Russian Federation fishing and resource protection laws).
[25] UNCLOS, Article 118.   [26] *Ibid.*, Article 64.   [27] *Ibid.*, Article 66(5).

and adjacent to [that] zone'.[28] In the latter case the duty to seek to agree upon conservation measures only applies to that high-seas fishery. Under Article 63, co-operation through appropriate regional organisations is merely an alternative to direct negotiations. The same is not true of Article 64 on highly migratory species, which provides that

[t]he coastal state and other states whose nationals fish in the region for the highly migratory species listed in Annex I shall cooperate directly or through appropriate international organizations with a view to ensuring conservation and ... optimum utilization of such species ... both within and beyond the exclusive economic zone. In regions for which no appropriate international organization exists ... [the fishing] states ... shall cooperate to establish such an organization and participate in its work.

Annex I lists 17 species, including some tuna, mackerel, swordfish and marlin. The article imposes a duty upon all states fishing for a listed species in a 'region' to establish an RFMO, if none exists, and then to 'participate' in it. Articles 63 and 64 thus provide RFMOs with a role in fisheries management without specifying what further rights or powers, including enforcement, such organisations might exercise. This point was taken up by the 1995 Straddling Fish Stocks Agreement.

3 The 1995 Straddling Fish Stocks Agreement

3.1 RFMOs and third parties

The 1995 Straddling Fish Stocks Agreement (FSA)[29] represents a remarkable effort to create a regulatory framework for sustainable management of international fisheries and add detail to some of the 'too general' UNCLOS provisions on fisheries regulation.[30] The FSA assigns a central role to RFMOs in the co-operative management of straddling and highly migratory stocks.[31] The FSA's regional emphasis

---

[28] *Ibid.*, Article 63(2).

[29] The United Nations Agreement for the Implementation of the Provisions of the United Nations Convention on the Law of the Sea of 10 December 1982 relating to the Conservation and Management of Straddling Fish Stocks and Highly Migratory Fish Stocks 1995, 2167 UNTS 88 (FSA). Entered into force 11 November 2001, 71 parties at 16 July 2008.

[30] Jean-Pierre Lévy and Gunnar G. Schram, *United Nations Conference on Straddling Fish Stocks and Highly Migratory Fish Stocks: Selected Documents* (The Hague: Martinus Nijhoff, 1996), p. 3.

[31] FSA, Articles 8–13.

'draws heavily' on models provided by the North Atlantic Fisheries Organization (NAFO) and Central Bering Sea Convention.[32]

However, any approach based on voluntary regulation may create 'free-rider' problems. To counter this, the FSA aims at creating a regime where 'only those who play by the rules may fish'.[33] The question is how far it has gone, or may go, to achieve this. First, FSA members are *obliged* to 'give effect to their duty to cooperate' in fisheries management by joining any RFMO competent to establish measures over a stock fished by their flag vessels.[34] Further, where states fish on the high seas for a straddling or highly migratory fish stock and there is no RFMO management structure in place, those fishing states 'shall co-operate to establish such an organization or ... other appropriate arrangement[] ... and shall participate in [its] work'.[35]

Article 8(4) attempts to give teeth to these provisions, providing that '[o]nly those states which are members of such an organization ... or which agree to apply ... [its] measures ... shall have access to the fishery resources to which those measures apply'.

Further, Article 17 of the FSA provides that an RFMO non-member state 'is not discharged from the [UNCLOS and FSA] obligation to cooperate' in conserving and managing fish stocks and it must not authorise its flag vessels to fish for straddling or highly migratory fish stocks covered by RFMO measures.

The consistent use of 'state' rather than 'state party' in these and other FSA provisions could suggest that the FSA purports to require even non-parties to refrain from fishing within an RFMO-managed area unless they join it or follow its measures voluntarily.[36] Indeed, in face of the strenuous objections to this ambiguous wording made by some states during the FSA drafting conference, the chairman reiterated the parties' understanding that the provisions would apply to FSA parties only.[37]

Ultimately, one need conclude neither that the FSA binds non-parties nor that its effects are limited only to FSA members. The FSA provides

---

[32] R. Barston, 'The law of the sea and regional fisheries organisations' (1999) 14 IJMCL 333 at 349.

[33] D. Balton, 'Strengthening the law of the sea: the new agreement on straddling fish stocks and highly migratory fish stocks' (1996) 27 ODIL 125 at 138.

[34] FSA, Article 8(3).   [35] *Ibid.*, Article 8(5).

[36] See generally Rayfuse, 'United Nations Agreement on Straddling and Highly Migratory Fish Stocks'.

[37] *Ibid.*, 268.

an agreed framework for co-operative fisheries management and a series of minimum enforcement provisions. The FSA acknowledges that parties will need to enter still further, negotiated agreements. There are thus multiple tiers of obligation where a state is

(1) party only to UNCLOS;
(2) party to UNCLOS, and the FSA, but not relevant RFMOs;
(3) party to relevant RFMOs, the FSA and UNCLOS; or
(4) party to a relevant RFMO and UNCLOS, but not the FSA.

Article 17 deals with case 2: in effect, FSA parties have covenanted not to let their nationals fish where they are not parties to the relevant RFMO. Cases 3 and 4 are simple, in that the state has consented to RFMO measures, although only in case 3 will they have consented to the FSA 'default boarding regime' (see section 3.3, below).

It must not be assumed that where an RFMO regime exists in a particular place, its existence has no consequence for states that are, as in case 1, party to UNCLOS and not the FSA. Such states are still bound by UNCLOS Article 117 to co-operate in taking necessary conservation measures. While this does not mean that catch limits or quota allocations set under a regional FSA arrangement would be binding upon a new entrant to the fishery which was not an FSA party, that new entrant – if an UNCLOS party – must still co-operate with the RFMO. Whether this duty to co-operate implies any stricter obligations can only be assessed in the light of state practice.

3.2 Provision for boarding and inspecting vessels

Articles 18, 19, 21 and 22 provide the FSA enforcement scheme. As flag states, each FSA member must

- ensure that their vessels comply with RFMO measures and do not engage in activities undermining their effectiveness (including through imposing conditions upon fishing licences);
- not authorise its vessels to fish unless it can regulate their conduct effectively;
- enforce RFMO measures 'irrespective of where violations occur'; and
- impose sanctions 'adequate in severity' to ensure compliance and deter violations.[38]

---

[38] FSA, Articles 18(1), 18(2), 18(3) and 19; the duty of effective regulation has created controversy; see *The Grand Prince (Belize v. France)*, ITLOS Case No.8, 20 April 2001, www.itlos.org, Judges Caminos, Marotta Rangel, Yankov, Yamamoto, Akl, Vukas, Marsit, Eiriksson and Jesus (Joint Dissenting Opinion), para. 16.

These flag state duties apply *independently* of RFMO membership; all FSA parties must thus ensure their vessels' compliance with all RFMO measures everywhere. Non-flag interdiction is allowed, even required, under the FSA but is divided into

- boarding and inspection;
- investigation; and
- enforcement action.

While FSA powers of boarding and inspection may be exercised unilaterally by the interdicting state, powers of investigation and enforcement rest primarily with the flag state, although it may authorise the interdicting state to exercise them to some extent. This raises the same issues of 'preferential' jurisdiction discussed in Chapter 5. Article 21 contains various boarding and inspection rights which FSA parties must implement, or formulate adequate alternatives to, regarding RFMOs in which they are members.[39] Article 22 contains a default set of procedures applying where such RFMO procedures are not adopted within two years.[40] Articles 21 and 22 together thus provide a minimum default code for RFMO boarding and inspection.

3.2.1 Inspection

Unlike most drug interdiction treaties, the FSA provides express consent to boarding and inspection in all cases in advance, irrespective of any reasonable suspicion that the boarded vessel is engaged in illicit conduct. Under Article 21(1) the 'duly authorized inspectors' of an FSA state party which is also a member of the relevant RFMO may 'board and inspect' the flag vessel of any other FSA state party present within the RFMO management area to ensure compliance with RFMO measures. While the line between 'boarding and inspection' and 'investigation' is somewhat nebulous, where inspection reveals 'clear grounds for believing' that a vessel has acted contrary to applicable RFMO measures, the inspector may secure evidence and must contact the flag state.[41] Parties are required under Article 21(2) to establish procedures, through RFMOs, to implement Article 21. This process encountered problems in the Western and Central Pacific Fisheries Commission, and the experience suggests that the boarding rights contained in the FSA may be qualified by the practical necessity of agreeing implementation

---

[39] FSA, Article 21(2) and (15).   [40] *Ibid.*, Article 21(3).   [41] *Ibid.*, Article 21(5).

procedures, despite the default implementation provisions in Article 22.[42] Inspecting states must also

require [their] inspectors to observe generally accepted international regulations, procedures and practices relating to the safety of the vessel and the crew, minimize interference with fishing operations and ... avoid action ... adversely affect[ing] the quality of the catch on board. The inspecting State shall ensure that boarding and inspection is not conducted in a manner that would constitute harassment.[43]

The generality of this provision raises numerous areas for potential disagreement between boarding and inspecting states, greatly undermining its utility.

3.2.2 Investigation

If inspection reveals clear grounds for believing that the vessel has breached relevant RFMO measures, the flag state must either investigate or authorise the boarding state to do so.[44] Where the flag state investigates it must 'promptly inform the inspecting state of the results ... and any enforcement action taken'.[45] Where evidence gathered during an authorised boarding state-conducted investigation warrants enforcement action, the flag state must again either take enforcement action or authorise the boarding state to do so.[46] Curiously, if the flag state assumes enforcement jurisdiction in this case, no obligation to report to the boarding state arises. Despite the mandatory language, there is no means of scrutinising the effectiveness of any flag-state enforcement action, other than the limited reporting requirements.

3.2.3 Enforcement

Under FSA Article 21, the boarding state may secure evidence and direct a vessel into port where, following boarding and inspection,

(1) there 'are clear grounds for believing a vessel has committed a serious [FSA] violation' (including fishing without a licence, fishing with prohibited gear, and failing to maintain accurate catch records);

(2) the flag state fails to respond to a request to investigate within three days; or

---

[42] See Chapter 2, section 3.2.   [43] FSA, Article 21(10).   [44] *Ibid.*, Article 21(6).
[45] *Ibid.*, Article 21(6)(a).   [46] *Ibid.*, Article 21(7).

(3) the flag state fails to respond (in an unspecified timeframe) to evidence warranting enforcement action.[47]

This limited power to direct a vessel into port remains subject to the flag state's right 'at any time' to require an inspecting state to release the vessel to it, 'along with full information on the progress and outcome of [the] investigation [conducted]'.[48]

Article 21(14) creates a degree of port-state inspection and control by applying all of Article 21, *mutatis mutandis*, to situations where a state party has 'clear grounds for believing' that another FSA party's fishing vessel has contravened RFMO measures and that vessel has subsequently entered its 'national jurisdiction'. However, the application of the entirety of Article 21 undoubtedly includes a flag state's right to require that the vessel be released into its custody.

3.2.4 State responsibility

FSA Article 21(18) provides that 'States shall be liable for damage or loss attributable to them arising from action' taken under Article 21 where it 'is unlawful or exceeds that reasonably required in the light of available information' to implement its provisions. Allegations of unlawfully conducted at-sea fisheries inspections are discussed in relation to NAFO but otherwise there seems to be little state practice. Issues of state responsibility for wrongful interdiction are discussed further in Chapter 12.

3.2.5 Stateless vessels

Like Article 110 of UNCLOS and Article 17(2) of the UN Narcotics Convention, FSA Article 21(17) provides that a state may board and inspect a fishing vessel on the high seas on reasonable suspicion of statelessness. It too is somewhat ambiguous regarding further enforcement measures, simply providing that '[w]here evidence so warrants, the state may take such action as may be appropriate in accordance with international law.' This wording is capable of accommodating divergent views as to prescriptive and enforcement jurisdiction over stateless vessels at general international law.[49]

3.3 *The FSA 'default' boarding scheme for subsequent RFMOs*

For RFMOs established after the FSA entered into force, the FSA contains procedures for implementing Article 21 boarding and inspection

---

[47] *Ibid.*, Article 21(8) and (11).   [48] *Ibid.*, Article 21(12).   [49] See Chapter 2, section 3.2.

rights. Article 21(3) provides that the Articles 21 and 22 rules and procedures ('the default FSA rules') will apply to an RFMO after two years unless, or until, the RFMO creates its own inspection procedures. Some non-FSA parties have argued that to base RFMO inspection measures on the default FSA rules is effectively to bind third parties to rules lacking their consent and which they have opposed in other forums.[50] The point may have some validity insofar as individual RFMOs allow measures to be adopted by majority, not consensus or unanimity. However, it is absurd to suggest that RFMOs, when looking for guidance in drafting their own rules, may not have regard to other treaties unless all RFMO members have subscribed to them. Indeed, the entire Articles 21 and 22 default boarding and inspection scheme can be displaced where RFMO members agree on an 'alternative mechanism which effectively discharges the[ir] obligation … to ensure compliance with the [RFMO's] conservation and management measures'.[51] Nonetheless, any arguments that the FSA default rules have customary status must account for this repeated opposition by some fishing states (notably Japan and China) to their replication in later RFMO agreements.[52]

The FSA default rules require examination in some detail. The Article 22 default boarding procedures operate to implement the Article 21 provisions described in section 3.2 above, and appear beguilingly straightforward. Article 22(1) provides that an inspecting state shall ensure that its authorised inspectors

    (a) present credentials to the master of the vessel and produce a copy … of the relevant conservation and management measures … ;

    (b) initiate notice to the flag State at the time of the boarding and inspection;

    (c) do not interfere with the master's ability to communicate with the authorities of the flag State …;

    (d) provide a copy of a report on the boarding and inspection to the master and to the authorities of the flag State, noting thereon any objection or statement which the master wishes to have included … ;

---

[50] See Rayfuse, *Non-Flag State Enforcement*, pp. 136, 189, 304–5, 307–8, 339, 341 (on Japan); cf. 189 (on China) and 304 (on Korea). Note also Argentina's position that UN General Assembly resolutions referring to the FSA must not be interpreted as suggesting that it is binding on non-members: Report of the Twenty-Sixth Meeting of the Commission for the Conservation of Antarctic Marine Living Resources (2007), 188.

[51] FSA, Article 21(15).

[52] Rayfuse, *Non-Flag State Enforcement*, references above, n. 50.

(e) promptly leave the vessel following completion of the inspection if they find no evidence of a serious violation; and

(f) avoid the use of force except when and to the degree necessary to ensure the safety of the inspectors and where the inspectors are obstructed in the execution of their duties....[53]

An inspector has authority under Article 22(2) to 'inspect the vessel, its licence, gear, equipment, records, fish products and any relevant documents necessary to verify compliance' with relevant RFMO measures. The flag state must ensure that the master co-operates, facilitates prompt and safe boarding and disembarkation, does not 'obstruct, intimidate or interfere with' inspectors and allows the inspector to communicate with the flag and inspecting states while aboard (Article 22(3)). If the master refuses boarding, the flag state must suspend the vessel's authorisation to fish and order it to return to port immediately (Article 22(4)). These obligations are additional to those in section 3.2 above, such as Article 21(4) requirements that inspectors have regard to the 'safety of the vessel and the crew' and 'minimize interference with fishing'.

Are these provisions adequate? The attitude of the first RFMO faced with the duty of implementing Article 22 in default of agreed procedures, the Western and Central Pacific Fisheries Commission, is telling. The Commission reached a 'gentleman's agreement' not to implement the FSA default rules before concluding its own Article 21 measures.[54] Commission members considered that a subsidiary agreement would, in any event, need to be reached on how to implement operationally the default FSA rules.[55] As further negotiations would thus be needed to implement *any* inspection scheme, it was deemed expedient to continue negotiating a complete package of tailored boarding and inspection arrangements. This strongly indicates that the default rules may be of limited utility.

Examining other RFMO boarding manuals, such as that agreed by the parties to the Bering Sea Convention, indicates the further matters requiring agreement in order to implement a boarding and inspection scheme.[56] The Bering Sea 'doughnut hole' fishery, conducted in

---

[53] On implementation, note for example the incorporation of these provisions into s. 87F, Fisheries Management Act (Cth) (No. 162 of 1991) (Australia).

[54] Personal communication: Dr John Kalish, Department of Agriculture, Fisheries and Forestry (Australia), 11 January 2006.

[55] See Chapter 6, section 5.7.

[56] The Convention on the Conservation and Management of Pollock Resources in the Central Bering Sea 1994, (1994) 34 ILM 67.

an enclosed high seas area between EEZs proclaimed off the Russian Federation's east coast and the Alaskan west coast, is not discussed at length here.[57] The high-seas fishery has effectively collapsed,[58] but a set of boarding and inspection arrangements has been concluded among the Convention parties should fishing ever resume. In the interim, a very few such boardings have been conducted in respect of scientific and trial fishing in the area.[59] The Bering Sea Convention boarding and inspection manual makes provision for matters such as

- acceptable methods of hailing a vessel, the international signals to be used and their meaning in an inspection context (including, for example, 'SQ3', meaning 'You should stop or heave to; I am going to board you');
- the channel fishing vessels must monitor for instructions (a practical choice is 16 VHF-FM, the universal safety channel which all vessels should monitor continuously); and
- parties' obligation to equip vessels with a safe, SOLAS-compliant pilot ladder along with a safety line and ladder illumination to allow boarding.[60]

Further, parties must agree upon, and publicise, the credentials inspectors will present. This can be vital if masters are to distinguish

[57] See Rayfuse, *Non-Flag State Enforcement*, ch. 6, section 5; Stuart Kaye, *International Fisheries Management* (London: Kluwer Law International, 2001), pp. 308 ff. D. Balton, 'The Bering Sea doughnut hole convention: regional solution, global implications' in Olav Schramm Stokke (ed.), *Governing High Seas Fisheries: The Interplay of Global and Regional Regimes* (Oxford University Press, 2001), p. 143; for Annual Reports of the Conference of Parties to the Bering Sea Convention, see www.afsc.noaa.gov/refm/cbs/.

[58] Trial fishing cruises have routinely caught as little as one pollock: Report of the Eleventh Annual Conference of the Parties to the Convention on the Conservation and Management of Pollock Resources in the Central Bering Sea (5–8 September 2006), Appendix 4 and Attachment 3, www.afsc.noaa.gov/refm/cbs/11th_annual_conference.htm.

[59] The conference reports do not always describe these inspections. Two Chinese vessels were inspected in 2007 (personal communication, Lt. Commander Lisa Ragone, US Coast Guard, 22 April 2008). The last such at-sea inspection detailed in reports, however, was in 2001: Report of the Seventh Annual Conference of the Parties to the Convention on the Conservation and Management of Pollock Resources in the Central Bering Sea (16–19 September 2002), Attachment 9, www.afsc.noaa.gov/refm/cbs/7th_annual_conference.htm.

[60] Annual Conference of the Convention on the Conservation and Management of Pollock Resources in the Central Bering Sea, *Boarding and Inspection Manual*, p. 2 (copy on file with the author); on commonly used signals see *Annotated Commander's Handbook*, pp. 388–9.

between lawful boarding and a ruse by pirates.[61] Given the FSA's deference to the enforcement procedures actually established under RFMOs, and its reliance upon their existence, it remains necessary to enquire into practice at the RFMO level.

4 Common measures in international fisheries management: the International Commission for the Conservation of Atlantic Tunas precedent

At-sea inspection is only one part of most RFMOs' package of regulatory measures, if they resort to interdiction at all. An RFMO's primary function is to agree upon conservation and management measures. In this respect RFMOs have a 'wide margin' to adopt measures as they see fit.[62] The International Court of Justice (ICJ) has held that there are few constraints on this discretion.

[I]n order for a measure to be characterized as a 'conservation and management measure', it is sufficient that its purpose is to conserve and manage living resources and that ... it satisfies various technical requirements. ... Typically, ... states describe such measures by reference to such criteria as: the limitation of catches through quotas; the regulation of catches by prescribing periods and zones in which fishing is permitted; and the setting of limits on the size of fish which may be caught or the types of fishing gear which may be used.[63]

The only limiting criteria appear to be 'purpose' and satisfaction of 'various technical requirements'. The ICJ provides little guidance on the latter, beyond reference to various conventions.

The most fundamental measure an RFMO can take is setting an annual total allowable catch (TAC) for a fish stock within its management area and apportioning catch quotas among participating states. Allied measures might include restrictions on the season in which that stock may be caught and on the equipment that can be used (such as net mesh size). RFMOs will also have reporting requirements in order to establish whether a party's fishing fleet has reached its quota.

---

[61] Personal communication: Deirdre Warner-Kramer (Senior Atlantic Fisheries Officer) and Holly Koehler (Foreign Affairs Officer), US Department of State, 3 April 2006.

[62] M. Orellana, 'The law on highly migratory fish stocks: ITLOS jurisprudence in context' (2004) 34 GGULR 459 at 475.

[63] *Fisheries Jurisdiction Case (Spain v. Canada)*, ICJ Reports 1988, pp. 432, 461.

The question is how to enforce conservation measures and deter non-compliant IUU fishing. The most common conservation and management measures adopted by RFMOs to monitor or induce compliance (hereafter 'measures'), other than at-sea boarding and inspection, include

- catch documentation schemes,
- deterring re-flagging,
- satellite vessel monitoring systems (VMS),
- so-called 'positive' and 'negative' lists, and
- diplomatic demarches or trade restrictive measures ('sanctions').

Where such enforcement measures aim at influencing non-parties' behaviour, they may be referred to as non-contracting party (NCP) schemes.[64] Before examining interdiction's role within this framework it is useful to sketch how these other enforcement measures operate.

The International Commission for the Conservation of Atlantic Tunas (ICCAT) was 'the first RFMO to tackle the problems of non-member fishing in a comprehensive way'.[65] It was thus ICCAT that first introduced many of the measures now commonly implemented by other RFMOs. ICCAT's establishing treaty expressly provided for high-seas inspection measures and an international joint inspection scheme was even adopted in 1975, although it was only brought into force in June 2007.[66] ICCAT practice thus illustrates that RFMOs may prefer a range of measures as an alternative to reciprocal at-sea boarding and inspection, and some may well be more effective than interdiction in the fisheries context.

In 1992 ICCAT began implementing a catch documentation scheme, under which Atlantic bluefin tuna could not enter contracting party markets without ICCAT catch documents 'validated by a government

---

[64] See FSA, Article 33(2); Molenaar, 'Participation, allocation and unregulated fishing', 473–80; D. Warner-Kramer, 'Control begins at home: tackling flags of convenience and IUU fishing' (2004) 34 GGULR 497 at 511 ff.

[65] Warner-Kramer, 'Control begins at home', 511.

[66] International Convention for the Conservation of Atlantic Tunas 1966, 673 UNTS 63, Article 9(3). The text of the 1975 ICCAT Scheme of Joint International Inspection is found in ICCAT, Report for Biennial Period, 1974–75, Part II (1975), Annexe 7, Appendix II (ICCAT Scheme 1975). It was brought into force from 13 June 2007 by ICCAT Recommendation 2006–05; see ICCAT Report for biennial period 2006–07, Part I (2006), Vol. 1, 145. ICCAT reports can be found at www.iccat.int/pubs_ biennial.htm.

official of the [fishing vessel's] flag state'.[67] As the 'vast majority of Atlantic bluefin tuna … is destined for ICCAT member-country markets', the scheme had the effect of requiring non-party compliance if they were to sell their catch.[68] The scheme was later extended to swordfish and bigeye tuna.[69]

In 1994 ICCAT was also the first RFMO to threaten trade sanctions against non-parties whose actions undermined its measures. This was done to deter non-parties from granting their nationality to vessels formerly flagged by an ICCAT party, thus allowing them to conduct unregulated fishing in the management area. In 1995 ICCAT imposed trade sanctions on Panama, Belize and Honduras, typically prohibiting the import of the relevant fish species (tuna or swordfish) from the sanctioned states. As a result, Panama adopted stricter regulations, prompting the flight of long-line fishing vessels to other registries or fisheries.[70]

Registry-hopping, increasing numbers of IUU vessels of uncertain registry, and evidence that 'some vessel owners were "laundering" catch made by one vessel flagged to a state under sanction to another of the company's vessels under a "clean" flag' prompted the adoption of list systems in 2002.[71] The creation of a 'positive list' required ICCAT parties to register all flag vessels over 24 metres long licensed to fish in the management area. RFMO measures obliged parties to prohibit fishing for, transhipment of, or landing of regulated stocks by their flag vessels not on the positive list.[72] It also required that catch documents only be validated for listed vessels. Parties were further required to prohibit landings, transhipment and imports from vessels on a 'negative list' of IUU vessels. Such port-state enforcement may be among the most effective means of deterring IUU fishing. While IUU vessels can simply sail on to other ports, the ports an RFMO 'can effectively close' are usually those 'nearest the relevant fishing ground'.[73] Port-state measures can thus 'widen the circumference of controls, effectively forcing IUU vessels to sail further to unload', thus decreasing their 'efficiency and profits'.[74]

---

[67] Warner-Kramer, 'Control begins at home', 512.

[68] *Ibid.*, 512–13.   [69] *Ibid.*, 516.   [70] *Ibid.*, 514–15.   [71] *Ibid.*, 516.

[72] Recommendation by ICCAT Concerning the Establishment of an ICCAT Record of Vessels Authorized to Operate in the Convention Area, ICCAT Doc. GEN 2002–22, www.iccat.es/Documents/Recs/compendiopdf-e/2002–22-e.pdf, para 7(a).

[73] R. Baird, 'CCAMLR initiatives to counter flag state non-enforcement in Southern Ocean fisheries' (2006) *Victoria University of Wellington Law Review* 733 at 740.

[74] *Ibid.*

In addition, all RFMOs 'have introduced or are about to introduce mandatory VMS for vessels operating within their areas of competence.'[75] A VMS can allow a vessel's position to be continually and automatically monitored by satellite, making the misreporting of where catches were taken and the forgery of catch documentation more difficult.[76] Such VMS data are usually reported to national authorities but may also be reported centrally to the RFMO secretariat in real time.[77] The use of such measures within individual RFMOs is discussed further below.

The long-delayed implementation in 2007 of ICCAT's boarding and inspection scheme ('the Scheme') will only briefly be discussed here for a number of reasons. First, there is as yet no reported practice under the Scheme. Second, it has been implemented as adopted in 1975 and thus is much less detailed than many other schemes which have been amended and developed in the light of experience across the intervening years.

Inspectors and inspection vessels under the Scheme are appointed by and remain responsible to their nominating state. They must carry an ICCAT identification document and the inspection vessel must fly an ICCAT pennant. Masters of vessels flagged to ICCAT members must permit inspectors to board their vessels. Inspectors must carry out their inspection 'so that the vessel suffers the minimum interference and inconvenience', and must restrict themselves to 'ascertainment of the facts' relevant to the adopted ICCAT measures in force.[78] Inspectors may affix an identification mark to any fishing gear which appears to be in contravention of ICCAT measures, and may photograph the gear and inspect catches.[79] The inspection report must be signed in the presence of the master, who may attach observations.[80] The flag state must 'consider and act on reports of foreign inspectors ... on a similar

---

[75] Report submitted in accordance with paragraph 17 of General Assembly Resolution 59/25, to assist the Review Conference to implement its mandate under paragraph 2, Article 36 of the United Nations Fish Stocks Agreement, 4 January 2006, UN Doc A/CONF.210/2006/1, 47 at para. 223; note the European Commission's prosecution of Greece for failure to implement Commission VMS requirements aboard its fishing vessels: *Commission of the European Communities v. Greece*, European Court of Justice, 14 April 2005 [Case C-22/04], http://curia.eu.int/jurisp/cgi-bin/gettext.pl?lang=fr&num=79949585C19040022&doc=T&ouvert=T&seance=ARRET.

[76] Baird, 'CCAMLR initiatives to counter flag state non-enforcement', 747–8.

[77] The first such centralised vessel monitoring system was in the Commission for the Conservation of Antarctic Marine Living Resources; see CCAMLR Conservation Measure 10–04, www.ccamlr.org/pu/e/e_pubs/cm/drt.htm.

[78] ICCAT Scheme 1975 (see n. 66, above), Article 5.   [79] *Ibid.*, Articles 10–13.

[80] *Ibid.*, Article 5.

basis ... to the reports of national inspectors'.[81] There are no defined 'serious violations' that might warrant a vessel being directed into port, or reporting requirements on action taken in respect of cited violations, both common features of later schemes. It remains to be seen how the ICCAT boarding and inspection scheme will operate in practice.

5 The practice of regional fisheries management organisations

5.1 Introduction

The present discussion will be limited to the current practice of RFMOs which have adopted and implemented non-flag-state at-sea boarding and inspection regimes (commonly called 'enforcement schemes' or 'schemes').[82] This limits relevant RFMOs to

- The International Commission for the Conservation of Atlantic Tunas (as discussed above);
- the North Pacific Anadromous Fish Commission;
- the North-East Atlantic Fisheries Commission;
- the Northwest Atlantic Fisheries Organization;
- the Commission for the Conservation of Antarctic Marine Living Resources;
- the Annual Conference of the Convention on the Conservation and Management of Pollock Resources in the Central Bering Sea (discussed above as the Bering Sea Convention);
- the South East Atlantic Fisheries Organization; and
- the Western and Central Pacific Fisheries Commission.

Other than ICCAT none of these RFMOs includes fisheries for highly migratory species (the 'tuna RFMOs'). Indeed, none of the tuna RFMOs undertake at-sea boarding and inspection measures; while some have discussed, or even adopted, at-sea non-flag enforcement schemes, none except ICCAT have brought them into force.[83] The tuna RFMOs will thus not be discussed in any detail here. Tuna RFMO practice, however,

[81] *Ibid.*, Article 8.
[82] On the historical origins and practices of RFMOs see generally Rayfuse, *Non-Flag State Enforcement*.
[83] See *ibid.*, pp. 145, 151–6 (on the Inter-American Tropical Tuna Commission), 163–80 (on the history of the International Commission for the Conservation of Atlantic Tunas' 1975 scheme), 189–90 (on the Indian Ocean Tuna Commission), 196 (on the General Fisheries Commission for the Mediterranean), and 202–3 (on the Commission for the Conservation of Southern Bluefin Tuna).

'reveals a veritable "bee-hive" of activity aimed at establishing effective alternative [enforcement or verification] mechanisms'.[84] The tuna RFMOs' reluctance to embrace interdiction is thus not a question of enthusiasm for enforcement, but a choice of means. While at-sea boarding and inspection may be important in catching individual violators at the 'micro' level, the 'macro' violations likely to endanger a fishery are more probably the result of overfishing by entire national fleets,[85] in which case trade documentation and port-state controls are likely to be more effective.

There is not space here to discuss all eight RFMOs identified above in detail.[86] In particular, there is nothing to add to previous discussion of the boarding and inspection schemes adopted by ICCAT and parties to the Bering Sea Convention, as there is little or no relevant state practice. In respect of the remaining six RFMOs, the aim will be to highlight the limited role interdiction plays in high-seas fisheries practice and examine what the fisheries experience may suggest about interdiction in other contexts.

5.2 The North Pacific Anadromous Fish Commission

5.2.1 Background

The North Pacific Anadromous Fish Commission (NPAFC) was created under the Convention for the Conservation of Anadromous Stocks in the North Pacific Ocean (NPAF Convention).[87] Its history is closely tied to the UN General Assembly's driftnet fishing moratorium. '[W]ithin the Commission it is said that enforcement is conducted pursuant to the [NPAF] Convention and in support of the Moratorium'[88] called for in repeated UN General Assembly Resolutions since 1991.[89]

---

[84] *Ibid.*, 343.
[85] Personal communication: Leo Strowbridge, Department of Fisheries and Oceans (Canada), 27 January 2006.
[86] See Rayfuse, *Non-Flag State Enforcement.*   [87] TIAS 11465.
[88] Rayfuse, *Non-Flag State Enforcement*, p. 135.
[89] See GA Res. 44/255 (1989); also cited in National Oceanic and Atmospheric Administration, 2007 Report of the Secretary of Commerce to the Congress of the United States Concerning U.S. Actions Taken on Foreign Large-Scale High Seas Driftnet Fishing, 24 (copy on file with author) (NOAA Report 2007) are GA Res. 45/197 (1990), 46/215 (1991), 50/25 (1995), 51/36 (1996), 52/29 (1997), 53/33 (1998), 54/32 (1999), 55/8 (2000), 57/142 (2002), 58/14 (2003), 59/25 (2004), 60/31 (2005) and 61/105 (2006), and UNGA Driftnet Decisions 47/443 (1992), 48/445 (1993), and 49/436 (1994). See: www.nmfs.noaa.gov/ia/intlbycatch/docs/CONGO07RPT.pdf. (Earlier reports under the same title are cited as 'NOAA Report 2006', 'NOAA Report 2005' and 'NOAA Report 2004'. Copies on file with author.)

Although it is generally accepted that the General Assembly cannot legislate new international principles and that the driftnet moratoria have no binding effect, the major driftnet fishing states have declared their intent to observe the recommended moratoria.[90] Concerns over driftnet fishing's impact in the South Pacific in particular led to South Korea, Taiwan and Japan voluntarily ceasing their driftnet operations.[91]

The NPAF Convention came into force in 1993 between Japan, the United States, Canada and Russia as original parties; South Korea acceded in 2003. While China has declined invitations to join, its co-operation with the NPAFC is routinely praised as excellent.[92] The Convention aims to prevent directed fishing for certain salmon species within the management area, minimise incidental catch of salmon in other fishing operations and prohibit the retention of such incidental catch.[93] This is consistent with the UNCLOS Article 66 duty not to take anadromous fish outside EEZ areas (see section 2.2 above). The parties are also to co-operate to prevent trafficking in fish taken in violation of the Convention.[94] The management area constitutes the oceans north of 33°N and beyond the EEZs of coastal states, covering an enormous area of the North Pacific ocean and smaller non-contiguous areas within the Bering Sea and the Sea of Okhotsk.

5.2.2 Boarding and inspection under the Convention

The Convention lays out a reciprocal boarding and inspection scheme in relatively few provisions. Duly authorised officials of any state party may board any other party's fishing vessel upon reasonable suspicion that it is contravening the Convention and inspect the vessel (including gear and logbooks) and question persons aboard.[95] Inspections must occasion 'the minimum interference and inconvenience' to vessels.[96] The inspecting state may arrest a person or vessel it reasonably believes to have contravened the Convention and conduct further investigations 'if necessary'.[97] The flag state is to be notified promptly, but if it cannot immediately be contacted or take delivery of arrested persons or vessels, they may be taken to a designated port or kept under arrest within

---

[90] William T. Burke, *The New International Law of Fisheries: UNCLOS 1982 and Beyond* (Oxford: Clarendon, 1994), p. 107.
[91] *Ibid.*, p. 102, n. 59.   [92] E.g., NOAA Report 2005, 22.
[93] NPAFC Convention, www.npafc.org, Articles 3 and 4 and Annexe I.
[94] *Ibid.*, Article 3(3).   [95] *Ibid.*, Article 5(2)(a).   [96] *Ibid.*   [97] *Ibid.*, Article 5(2)(b).

the management area.[98] The flag state must investigate and prosecute appropriate cases and immediately take action to prevent persons or vessels 'conducting further operations' violating the Convention.[99] Only the flag state may try violations and impose penalties.[100]

5.2.3 Third-party co-operation: the US–China ship-rider agreement

Support for the driftnet moratorium helps to explain co-operative action within the NPAFC area by non-parties, especially China. In 1993 China concluded a ship-rider and boarding agreement with the United States,[101] allowing either party (but in practice the United States) to visit and inspect the other's flag vessels fishing in the management area. Earlier in 1993 China had given ad hoc permission for NPAFC parties to board and inspect a number of Chinese vessels in the management area.[102] The Agreement is said to be about 'effective cooperation and implementation' of the driftnet moratorium, sidestepping China's relationship with the NPAFC.[103]

The Agreement is simply drafted. One party may request permission to board the other party's vessel. The presumption is in favour of joint boarding and inspection, with the requesting party being joined by flag-state enforcement officials in a 'reasonable time' or accompanied by a flag-state 'ship-rider'.[104] Where the flag state either does not immediately reply that it is sending its own officers, or replies that it cannot do so, 'the requesting party shall initiate the visit and verification [of nationality]'.[105] Boarding-state officials may 'verify … flag and registry, and examine the vessel …, together with its equipment and records, fishing gear, catch and logs' to determine the vessel's involvement in activities 'inconsistent' with the moratorium.[106] If such evidence is found, it is transmitted to the flag state for action.[107] Where inspection reveals the vessel to have neither party's nationality, it is for the boarding state to take further action (presumably

---

[98] Ibid.   [99] Ibid., Article 5(2)(c).   [100] Ibid., Article 5(2)(d).

[101] Memorandum of Understanding between the Government of the United States of America and the Government of the People's Republic of China on Effective Cooperation and Implementation of United Nations General Assembly Resolution 46/215 of December 20, 1991, entered into force 3 December 1993, KAV 3727. (US–China Ship-rider MOU).

[102] Rayfuse, Non-Flag State Enforcement, pp. 130–1.

[103] US–China Ship-rider MOU, above note 101, Preamble.

[104] Ibid., paras. 2 and 4.   [105] Ibid., para 3.

[106] Ibid., para. 5.   [107] Ibid., para. 8.

by contacting the 'true' flag state or by assimilating it to a stateless vessel).[108] In practice the US Coast Guard has one or more Chinese ship-riders available out of Kodiak, Alaska, each fishing season, who can 'deploy aboard a USCG aircraft or cutter' to conduct an inspection when a suspect vessel is detected.[109] The Agreement, originally of one year's duration, has frequently been extended, most recently until 31 December 2009.[110]

Japan has also reported controlling salmon imports from non-parties Taiwan, China and North Korea by 'implementing [an] import approval system as a supplementary method of enforcement to the NPAFC Convention'.[111] This is effectively a unilateral catch documentation scheme.

5.2.4 NPAFC high-seas enforcement practice

IUU driftnet fishing activities by non-members has been a persistent NPAFC concern. In 1993–9 a significant number of at-sea boardings, and even enforcement actions, were conducted against non-member vessels. A lull in detection and enforcement action against IUU vessels in 2000–2 gave the impression that NPAFC enforcement activity had had a deterrent effect. A sharp rise in suspect vessels sightings in 2003 suggested either a resurgence of IUU activity, or its sporadic conduct. Sightings declined again in 2004, while the 2005 and 2006 data, including an enormous leap in vessel sightings, suggest that IUU fishing may have moved from targeting salmon to squid.

In 2004 Rayfuse attributed NPAFC's general success to high levels of co-operation and resource co-ordination.[112] Further,

there is nothing for the parties *not* to cooperate over. Since high seas fishing for salmon is prohibited [irrespective of the driftnet moratorium], no issues of allocation of high seas catch arise.[113]

As noted, the NPAFC saw a considerable amount of enforcement activity in its early years. In 1993–2000 some thirteen vessels were apprehended, and significantly more were sighted or boarded. Of

---

[108] *Ibid.*, para. 9.
[109] K. Riddle, 'Illegal, unreported, and unregulated fishing: is international cooperation contagious?' (2006) 37 ODIL 265 at 287.
[110] NOAA Report 2006, 23.
[111] NPAFC Secretariat, 11th Annual Report (2003) at Annexe 3, at 6(1); and see NPAFC Secretariat, 12th Annual Report (2004) at 5(1).
[112] Rayfuse, *Non-Flag State Enforcement*, p. 135.   [113] *Ibid.*

these, enforcement action was taken under US national law regarding four vessels apprehended by the US Coast Guard. These were found to be stateless (in the case of one vessel with a Taiwanese master), or were rendered constructively stateless when the flag state refuted their claimed registry (as China did in the cases of the *Cao Yu 6025* and *Ying Fa*), or were submitted to US jurisdiction by ad hoc flag-state consent (in the case of Honduran vessel *Arctic Wind*).[114] Otherwise, vessels were boarded either under the Convention, the US–China ship-rider agreement or following flag-state consent. These vessels were then referred to their flag state, often China, for enforcement action. A number of vessels were also seized by the Russian Border Guard within the Russian EEZ for activities apparently conducted on the high seas: in the case of the *Zhong Xin 37*, a five-day hot pursuit in 1998 ended with Russian authorities using 'disabling fire', 'which killed two people and wounded three'.[115] The legal basis for such action is unclear. Less forcefully, in 1997 Japan boarded, within its territorial sea, the Chinese vessel *Nanao 5508*, which had been sighted driftnet fishing within the NPAFC area and was found with salmon aboard.[116] Information was forwarded to China for follow-up, and Japan took no enforcement action.[117] The *Nanao 5508* may well have been boarded on the basis of the master's consent.[118]

The 'high water mark' of NPAFC enforcement action came in 1999, when eleven IUU fishing vessels were sighted and three apprehended.[119] Of these, two were Russian and one was Chinese. Fourteen tonnes of salmon were seized.[120]

Little enforcement action was taken in 2000–1,[121] and no at-sea enforcement activity was reported in 2002. However, 2003 saw a spike in sightings and enforcement action. The US Coast Guard reported that it had sighted

---

[114] *Ibid.*, pp. 131–3; on the *Cao Yu 6025* see also NPAFC Annual Report 1997, 26 and the NPAFC Newsletter, vol. 1 (2), 1997, 1, www.npafc.org/new/publications.html.

[115] Rayfuse, *Non-Flag State Enforcement*, p. 132; however, the NPAFC Newsletter vol 2(2), 1998, 1 refers to the 'Zhong Zin 37' being arrested for 'illegally fishing in the Russian EEZ'. No reference is made to lethal force being used. It appears that this was one of five Chinese vessels first detected by US Coast Guard vessels.

[116] Rayfuse, *Non-Flag State Enforcement*, pp. 131–2.

[117] See NPAFC Annual Report 2007, 26.

[118] On master's consent boardings, see n. 171 below.

[119] Rayfuse, *Non-Flag State Enforcement*, pp. 132–3.   [120] *Ibid.*, p. 132.

[121] *Ibid.*, p. 133; NPAFC Secretariat, 2001 Annual Report (2001) (NPAFC Report 2001), 38–9; NPAFC Secretariat, 10th Annual Report (2002) at Appendix 1.

[t]wenty-seven suspected HSDN [high-seas driftnet] vessels … four were boarded and turned over to PRC for prosecution, two Korean vessels were boarded and evidence of large-scale HSDN fishing was turned over to Korea for further action. One Russian vessel ARONT was sighted with HSDN fishing gear on board and reported to the Russian authorities for further action.[122]

South Korea later reported that it prosecuted both of its vessels, and imposed substantial fines.[123]

In 2004, twenty-two 'driftnet capable' vessels were sighted in the management area.[124] Eleven of these were Chinese. The only reported boarding in 2004 was by Japan, which found the driftnet vessel *Chun Jin No 1* with 'more than 10 tons of pink salmon' aboard.[125] The vessel carried only expired Georgian certificates of registration, but its captain, crew and owning company were all Taiwanese.[126] Following the investigation, Japanese officers handed the captain 'a warning paper' which demanded that he 'stop fishing and leave the NPAFC Convention Area'.[127] Despite Japan's lack of authority to make this demand of a non-party vessel, unless it was considered stateless, the vessel complied. Taiwanese authorities subsequently prosecuted the captain under national law, revoking his licence and imprisoning him for five months.[128] No boardings of driftnet vessels were reported in 2005 or 2006.[129]

In 2005 there were twenty-four potential IUU vessel sightings in the NPAFC area. The United States, however, noted that

in recent years, HSDN activity seems to have shifted from targeting salmon to squid, with tuna as bycatch … [and] the NPAFC enforcement scheme cannot be … [effective] against non-salmon non-Party HSDN fishing threats. The nature of the threat (target species and vessel flags) requires that the Parties work multilaterally through both enforcement and diplomatic channels to bring pressure on these fishing vessels and their flag states to end such operations.[130]

---

[122] NPAFC Secretariat, 11th Annual Report (2003) at 6(1); note also Chinese reports at Annexe 3.

[123] NOAA Report 2004, 8.

[124] Though this may include some double-reporting: NOAA Report 2004, 7.

[125] NPAFC Annual Report 2004, at 5(1).

[126] *Ibid.* Note that a lapse in registration may not deprive a vessel of its right to fly a flag: *The MV Saiga Case (No 2)*, (1999) 38 ILM 1323, 1339 ff., at paras. 59–74.

[127] NPAFC Annual Report 2004, Appendix 4.   [128] NOAA Report 2005, 9.

[129] See: NOAA Report 2005, 5–9; NOAA Report 2006, 10, 15.

[130] NPAFC Annual Report 2005, at 5(1), www.npafc.org/new/publications/Annual%20 Report/2005/13th%20Annual%20Meeting/ENFO.htm; cf. Riddle, 'Illegal, unreported, and unregulated fishing', 279.

Figures for 2006 indicate a dramatic jump from twenty-four to ninety-eight sightings of suspected IUU vessels, largely reported by the Japanese Coast Guard and Canadian aerial surveillance. As these figures are for sightings, not vessels, there is a risk of double-counting. Further, due to changes in the time of year of NPAFC patrolling there is 'uncertainty as to whether the increased … sightings represent[s] a real increase in … large-scale high seas driftnet fishing … or whether enforcement efforts have uncovered an existing IUU fishery'.[131]

Although these new challenges may require a change in the NPAFC's focus, its essential methods of surveillance and seeking non-party flag state co-operation are unlikely to change.

Indeed, 2007 showed that the traditional approach to enforcement in the NPAFC area is far from obsolete. Forty-seven IUU driftnet vessels were sighted and seven apprehensions were made.[132] Six of these involved vessels boarded under the US–China ship-rider MOU, several of which were found to be fishing for shark, swordfish and tuna while others appeared equipped and ready for such fishing. The similarly named vessels *Lu Rong Yu 1961*, *Lu Rong Yu 2659*, *Lu Rong Yu 2660*, *Lu Rong Yu 6105* and *Lu Rong Yu 6007* – as well as the *Zhe Dai Yuan Yu 829* – were all arrested by a Chinese ship-rider embarked on a US Coast Guard cutter for violations of Chinese law. One further suspect Chinese fishing vessel fled and evaded capture, and a Malaysian vessel was also questioned by a US Coast Guard cutter over its driftnet fishing.[133]

A Russian patrol vessel intercepted the *Rong Shen 828* at a position approximately 215 n.m. east of Onekotan in the Russian Kuril Islands.[134] The vessel was pursued for two and a half hours, before a Russian inspection team boarded and found 90 tonnes of salmon aboard, 70 per cent of it later determined to be of Russian origin. The vessel was found to have an Indonesian home port and crew. The vessel was escorted approximately 300 n.m. to a Russian port and Indonesia was notified.

---

[131] NOAA Report 2006, 5; see also NPAFC Annual Report 2007, at Part I, section 3 (Enforcement Activities), www.npafc.org/new/publications/Annual%20Report/2007/EECM/Activities.htm.

[132] NOAA Report 2007, 7.

[133] NOAA Report 2007, 8. In the latter case a chase occurred with the vessel 'conduct[ing] evasive manoeuvres and attempt[ing] to conceal nets and gear on deck'. NOAA laconically describes the US cutter 'performing right of approach questioning alongside the vessel to gather register information'. The master eventually 'lowered registry documents to the cutter small boat for examination'.

[134] *Ibid.*, 13; giving the vessel's position as 47°21′N, 159°25′E. Distances given in this paragraph are the author's approximations.

It is not clear if Russia regarded the vessel as having been intercepted, or pursuit of it having commenced, within its EEZ. The fact that Russia has asked Indonesia's permission to prosecute the skipper suggests not, making the legal basis of the interception questionable. While the vessel had taken salmon of Russian origin, if it did so upon the high seas this act – though prohibited – would not have granted any jurisdiction to Russia beyond its EEZ.[135]

5.2.5 Conclusion

The effectiveness of NPAFC boarding and inspection, and even seizure and prosecution, has rested upon the voluntary co-operation of non-parties: South Korea (before its accession), China and Taiwan. China's posture has been critical, authorising interdiction of suspected IUU fishing vessels either under the US ship-rider agreement or through rendering vessels constructively stateless by refuting claims of registry. Without Chinese co-operation under the ship-rider agreement it is difficult to envisage an effective high-seas inspection regime in the area, despite isolated cases such as the Japanese boarding of *Chun Jin No 1* and the apparent high-seas seizure by Russia of the *Rong Shen 828*.

5.3 The North-East Atlantic Fisheries Commission

The North-East Atlantic Fisheries Commission (NEAFC) was established under the Convention on Future Multilateral Cooperation in North-East Atlantic Fisheries 1980 (NEAF Convention).[136] The NEAFC management area consists of three entirely separate high-seas areas: the Reykjanes Ridge–Azores area, and parts of the Norwegian and Barents seas.[137] The NEAFC enforcement scheme allows reciprocal non-flag boarding and inspection as among the RFMO parties, while enforcement jurisdiction rests with the flag state. Non-flag inspectors have some limited powers in the case of serious violations. The parties to the NEAF Convention are the EU, Denmark (in respect of the Faroe Islands and Greenland), Iceland, Norway and the Russian Federation.

The NEAF Convention applies to all fisheries resources in this management area other than marine mammals, sedentary species and certain highly migratory species and anadromous stocks governed

---

[135] See the discussion of UNCLOS, Article 66, at n. 27 above.
[136] 1285 UNTS 129 (NEAF Convention). Entered into force 17 March 1982.
[137] See the map at www.neafc.org/about/ra.htm.

by other conventions.[138] 'Despite these seemingly extensive exclusions, the Convention and Regulatory areas encompass a large range of species not all of which are yet subject to regulatory measures'.[139] The Commission can 'make recommendations concerning measures of control' to be applied in the management area, providing the basis for the NEAFC's extensive and frequently updated Scheme of Control and Enforcement (The Scheme).[140] The first NEAFC Scheme was adopted in November 1998, along with a 'Scheme to Promote Compliance by Non-Contracting Party Vessels', and entered into force in July 1999. This development resulted from a review of NEAFC arrangements in the light of the FSA.[141]

5.3.1 The NEAFC inspection scheme

Articles 15–19 and 28–33 of the Scheme govern at-sea inspections and detail boarding procedure, inspectors' powers, masters' duties and applicable 'safeguards'. Many provisions are similar to those in the NAFO Scheme, discussed below, although some are more extensive. Under the Scheme parties must

- permit inspections by other states of their fishing vessels,
- oblige their masters to co-operate, and
- ensure that inspections are 'carried out in a non-discriminatory manner' which aims at 'an equitable distribution of inspections … based upon fleet size, taking into account the time spent in the Regulatory Area'.[142]

Where inspections result in a flag state being notified of an infringement committed by one of its fishing vessels it must promptly 'consider the evidence', 'conduct any further investigation necessary … and, whenever possible, inspect the fishing vessel concerned'.[143] State parties must 'consider and act on' reports from other parties' inspectors 'on the same basis as reports from its own inspectors'.[144] The parties must designate competent authorities for receiving NEAFC inspection reports.[145]

---

[138] NEAF Convention, Article 1(2).
[139] Rayfuse, *Non-Flag State Enforcement*, p. 209.
[140] NEAF Convention, Article 8(1); see www.neafc.org/measures/index.html.
[141] E. Molenaar, 'The concept of real interest and other aspects of co-operation through regional fisheries management mechanisms' (2000) 15 IJMCL 475 at 521.
[142] NEAFC Scheme of Control and Enforcement 2008 ('NEAF Scheme 2008'), Article 15(3), available at www.neafc.org/measures/docs/scheme_2008.pdf.
[143] NEAFC Scheme 2008, Article 28(4).   [144] *Ibid.*, Article 28(5).   [145] *Ibid.*, Article 3(2).

Boardings may only be carried out from nationally designated inspection vessels bearing NEAFC markings,[146] and '[n]o boarding shall be conducted without prior notice by radio [or other signal] being sent to the fishing vessel ... whether or not such notice is acknowledged as received.'[147] No more than two inspectors from one state party may participate in inspecting another state party's flag vessel.[148] Given that inspectors are nationally designated and deployed on nationally designated vessels, this seems likely to limit most boarding parties to two inspectors.[149] An inspection may not exceed four hours, and there are limits on inspectors' ability to interrupt fishing operations.[150]

The Scheme in previous editions expressly stated that designated inspectors, while bound by NEAFC rules, remain accountable to, and under the operational control of, the state appointing them.[151] This provision was adopted from the ICCAT Scheme and remains present in the NAFO Scheme.[152] It is curiously absent from the NEAFC Scheme's current edition, although it remains clear that inspectors act as organs of their appointing state and not in any sense as officers of NEAFC.[153] An inspector has express authority to

examine all relevant areas, decks and rooms of the fishing vessels, catch (whether processed or not), nets or other gear, equipment, and any relevant documents which the inspector deems necessary to verify the compliance with the measure established by NEAFC and to question the master or a person designated by the master.[154]

An inspector may also request the master's assistance, and the master has certain duties to render assistance.[155] Where an infringement is found it must be noted in a report, and inspectors must 'immediately attempt to communicate with an inspector or designated authority' of the flag state.[156] In cases of suspected infringements inspectors shall also 'take all necessary measures to ensure security and continuity of the evidence for subsequent dockside inspection' including affixing

---

[146] *Ibid.*, Article 16.   [147] *Ibid.*, Article 18(1).   [148] *Ibid.*, Article 18(6).

[149] Though see *ibid.*, Article 16(5), on jointly operated inspection vessel.

[150] *Ibid.*, Article 18(3) and (5).

[151] NEAFC Scheme 2006, Article 15(2); see www.neafc.org/measures/docs/scheme-2006.pdf.

[152] See ICCAT Scheme 1975 (entered into force 2007) (see n. 66, above), Article 7; NAFO Scheme 2008 (n. 232, below), Article 30(2).

[153] NEAFC Scheme 2008, Articles 15(1) and (3).   [154] *Ibid.*, Article 18(2).

[155] *Ibid.*, Articles 18(8) and 19.   [156] *Ibid.*, Article 28(1).

identification marks to any fishing gear appearing to contravene NEAFC measures.[157]

Masters' duties under Article 19 of the Scheme include facilitating safe boarding; cooperating with the inspection (including an express prohibition on obstructing or intimidating inspectors); allowing inspectors to communicate with the flag state and their designating boarding state; providing access to relevant areas and rooms, catch, nets and other equipment, and relevant documents; and, if Article 29 serious violations are discovered, providing 'reasonable facilities, including, where appropriate, food and accommodation, for the inspectors' for as long as they remain aboard. This last provision lacks any direct equivalent in the NAFO Scheme of at-sea boarding and inspection, where master's duties are more limited.[158]

Serious infringements warranting stronger action are defined and dealt with consistently with FSA Article 21. Serious infringements under Article 29 of the Scheme include

- fishing without valid flag-state authorisation;
- 'fishing without or after attainment of a quota';
- using prohibited gear;
- 'serious mis-recording of catches';
- 'repeated failure to comply' with VMS and continuous catch reporting requirements;
- obstructing inspectors;
- 'directed fishing' for prohibited stocks;
- 'falsifying or concealing' a vessel's markings or registration;
- 'disposing of evidence';
- multiple violations which cumulatively 'constitute a serious disregard of conservation and management measures'; and
- transhipping catch to, or conducting certain joint operations with, non-parties[159] or providing services to listed IUU vessels.

Under Article 30, where an inspector has 'clear grounds for believing' a vessel has committed a serious infringement, he must notify the flag state promptly. The flag state must then organise an inspection by one of its inspectors within seventy-two hours. 'In order to preserve the evidence, the inspector shall take all necessary measures

---

[157] *Ibid.*

[158] See NAFO Scheme 2008 (n. 232 below), Article 33. However, under Article 27, each NAFO party's fishing vessels must carry at all times a state-appointed observer, whom the captain must feed and house.

[159] Other than co-operating non-parties, as described below.

[including remaining aboard] to ensure security and continuity of the evidence whilst minimising interference with and inconvenience to the operation of the vessel' either until a flag-state inspector arrives or until required to leave by the flag state.[160] The flag state 'shall, if evidence so warrants, require the fishing vessel to proceed immediately to a port' for inspection and may authorise the inspecting state to exercise this power.[161] If ordered to port, and if the flag state consents, an inspector from another state party may board the vessel, accompany it to port and be present at the inspection.[162] Where a vessel suspected of a serious infringement is not called to port, the flag state must provide 'due justification' to the NEAFC Secretary and the inspecting state.[163] While the serious infringements system is highly detailed, prosecution remains entirely a flag-state matter. The Scheme provides no penalties if a flag state fails to implement its obligations; '[i]nstead, the medium of public scrutiny is invoked' to encourage compliance.[164]

As regards safeguards provisions, inspectors must 'avoid the use of force except when and to the degree necessary to ensure the[ir] safety' and may not carry firearms during inspections.[165] Inspectors may not interfere with a master's ability to communicate with the flag state.[166] The rights in tension under any compulsory system of inspections are neatly captured in Article 15(5), providing that,

[w]ithout limiting the capability of inspectors to carry out their mandates, inspections shall be made so that the fishing vessel, its activities and the catch retained on board do not suffer undue interference and inconvenience.

5.3.2 The NEAFC Non-Contracting Party Scheme

The NEAFC Non-Contracting Party Scheme (NCP Scheme) is contained in Chapter VII of the NEAFC Scheme. It requires all sightings of non-party and stateless vessels to be reported to the Secretariat, as they are presumed both to be 'undermining the effectiveness of' NEAFC measures[167] and to constitute IUU fishing for reporting purposes and the exchange of information with other RFMOs.[168] The NCP Scheme does not distinguish the treatment of non-party (but flagged) and stateless vessels, seemingly requiring the master's consent for boarding and

---

[160] NEAFC Scheme 2008, Article 30(3) and (4).   [161] *Ibid.*, Article 30(5) and (6).
[162] *Ibid.*, Article 30(8).   [163] *Ibid.*, Article 30(7).
[164] Rayfuse, *Non-Flag State Enforcement*, 206.   [165] NEAFC Scheme 2008, Article 15(4).
[166] *Ibid.*, Article 18(9).   [167] *Ibid.*, Article 44(1).   [168] *Ibid.*, Articles 42 and 43.

inspection in either case.[169] Indeed, the NCP Scheme obliges NEAFC inspectors encountering non-party vessels to seek such consent.[170] The NCP Scheme thus contemplates seeking to inspect non-party flag-state vessels on the basis of the master's consent alone, a notoriously controversial proposition.[171] Where any non-contracting party vessel has been boarded, Article 38(1) provides:

[w]here evidence so warrants, a Contracting Party may take such action as may be appropriate in accordance with international law. Contracting Parties are encouraged to examine the appropriateness of domestic measures to exercise jurisdiction over such vessels.

This is, in part, another coy provision on enforcement jurisdiction over stateless vessels: without asserting that it is permissible, it appears to directly encourage the adoption of national laws permitting extraterritorial enforcement action against stateless vessels.[172]

There have been few recent instances of NEAFC consensual non-party boardings and inspections. In 2004, for example, 101 non-party vessels were observed fishing in the regulatory area (almost all Dominican); of these only one was reported to have allowed at-sea boarding, while twelve were listed as having refused boarding.[173] More recently, it appears that Norway inspected the Georgian-flagged *Marlin* in 2007 some 250 n.m. or more from the Norwegian coast.[174] The *Marlin* was, however, receiving a transhipment of fish from the vessel of a state party – itself clearly subject to inspection – making this perhaps an exceptional case. In earlier years, some Enforcement Committee reports had noted the refusal of most non-party vessels to

---

[169] *Ibid.*, Articles 1(g) and 38.   [170] *Ibid.*, Article 38(1).

[171] The *Annotated Commander's Handbook*, p. 240, asserts that obtaining the master's consent to 'consensual boarding' for inspection purposes alone involves no exercise of law-enforcement jurisdiction and thus does not require flag-state consent. Such consent would still be needed prior to any enforcement action. See the facts in *US v. Biermann* (1988) 678 F. Supp. 1473, discussed at (1989) 83 AJIL 99–100; cf. G. Palmer, 'Guarding the coast: alien migrant interdiction operations at sea' (1997) 29 *Connecticut Law Review* 1565 at 1568 n. 15. Germany has, apparently, taken a similar view and Denmark considers its masters competent to authorise boarding by a foreign state: Philipp Wendel, *State Responsibility for Interferences with the Freedom of Navigation in Public International Law* (Berlin: Springer, 2007), pp. 167–8.

[172] See Chapter 2, section 3.2.

[173] NEAF Commission, Report of the Seventh Meeting of the Permanent Committee on Control and Enforcement, 6–7 October 2004, 13–19, www.neafc.org/reports/peccoe/docs/peccoe_oct-2004_final.pdf.

[174] It is listed as having been inspected at '6801N-00054E' in NEAFC Doc PE 2007/02/10; see www.neafc.org/reports/peccoe/oct07/index-docs.htm.

permit boarding and inspection.[175] The number of non-party boardings actually conducted, as reported in Commission documents, would thus appear to number only two or three, and those all occurred only with the master's consent.

In practice the NCP Scheme is enforced by two means: maintaining lists of IUU vessels to be sanctioned through national action, and diplomatic action or trade sanctions against flag states. Regarding the first, the NEAFC compiles a list of vessels presumed to be engaged in IUU fishing on the basis of submitted observation reports ('the A list').[176] The NEAFC Permanent Committee on Control and Enforcement (PECCOE) then recommends to the NEAF Commission which vessels should be transferred to a list of 'confirmed' IUU vessels ('the B list').[177] Contracting parties may not allow A-list vessels to land their catches in their ports, irrespective of whether those fish were taken in the regulatory area, or allow their nationals or flag vessel to support or re-supply A-list vessels.[178] B-list vessels are subject to various further disabilities, chiefly being prohibited from *entering* any party's ports.[179] The NEAFC now shares B-list data with NAFO, CCAMLR and SEAFO, and inclusion on lists compiled by these other organisations entails inclusion on the NEAFC's lists also.[180]

Non-contracting party vessels must also be inspected in members' ports to gather information about their activities in the management area.[181] NEAFC members send diplomatic demarches to the flag state of listed vessels, seeking their co-operation in upholding the effectiveness of NEAFC measures.[182] Trade restrictive measures, consistent with World Trade Organization obligations, may be taken against the

---

[175] NEAF Commission, Report of the Second Meeting of the Permanent Committee on Control and Enforcement, 17–18 October 2001, 5, www.neafc.org/reports/peccoe/docs/peccoe_oct-01_final.pdf; Report of the Third Meeting of the Permanent Committee on Control and Enforcement, 28–29 May 2002, 2, www.neafc.org/reports/peccoe/docs/peccoe_may_2002_final.pdf.

[176] NEAFC Scheme 2007, Article 44.   [177] *Ibid.*   [178] *Ibid.*, Article 45(1).

[179] *Ibid.*, Article 45(2).

[180] *Ibid.*, Article 44(6). The NEAFC website now includes useful links to both NAFO and CCAMLR lists of IUU vessels; see www.neafc.org/measures/index.html. In some RFMOs any mutual recognition of IUU vessel lists has proved contentious; see Report of the Twenty-Sixth Meeting of the Commission for the Conservation of Antarctic Marine Living Resources (2007) (CCAMLR-XXVI), 54 and cf. Argentina's comments at 37.

[181] NEAFC Scheme 2007, Article 40.

[182] *Ibid.*, Article 46; on diplomatic action see the PECCOE reports cited at n. 173 and n. 175 above and n. 187 below.

flag state if it does not address its vessels' IUU fishing activities.[183] In addition, the NEAFC launched on 1 May 2007 a significant set of port-state controls for all NEAFC members in respect of landings of frozen fish by all foreign vessels.[184] (In practice, effectively all deep-sea fishing factory ships will land frozen fish.) These controls require, *inter alia*, that the ship's master make prior notification to port state authorities of the catch on board and that the ship's flag state verify that documentation before that catch is landed.[185] Such verification must include confirmation that the vessel was engaged in authorised fishing, has fished within quota and that its fishing was VMS monitored.[186] Without flag-state verification, no landings will be authorised.[187]

A non-party may apply for the status of a co-operating non-contracting party. A co-operating non-contracting party must undertake to respect NEAF Commission measures, provide relevant fishery data to the Commission and report on compliance measures taken.[188] The major benefit of successful application for such status is that a co-operating non-contracting party's vessels are exempt from automatic inclusion on the A list (and thus cannot move to the B list) unless they fail to comply with certain conditions or are observed fishing in breach of the co-operation agreement.[189] Present co-operating non-contracting parties are Belize, Cook Islands, Canada, Japan and New Zealand.

NEAFC reports of non-contracting party vessels observed in the management area in the 2002–6 reporting periods consistently show eleven to thirteen presumed IUU vessels.[190] In the period since 2000–1

---

[183] *Ibid.*; Warner-Kramer, 'Control begins at home', 520; Molenaar, 'Participation, allocation and unregulated fishing', 475. Brazil has within CCAMLR, with some support from Argentina, disputed whether RFMOs have a 'legal basis' for such trade measures against non-parties. The WTO compatibility of such measures was supported by Italy, Georgia and Belgium and the EU. See CCAMLR-XXVI, 42–4 and 58–60.

[184] See NEAFC Scheme 2008, Articles 20–27.   [185] *Ibid.*, Articles 22 and 23.

[186] *Ibid.*, Article 23.

[187] On the experience of these measures in their first five months see NEAF Commission, Report of the Permanent Committee on Control and Enforcement, 9–10 October 2007, 8–11, www.neafc.org/reports/peccoe/docs/peccoe_oct_2007.pdf.

[188] NEAFC Scheme 2008, Article 34.   [189] *Ibid.*, Article 44(1) and (2).

[190] NEAF Commission, Report of the Permanent Committee on Control and Enforcement, 11–12 October 2005, 36–7, www.neafc.org/reports/peccoe/docs/peccoe_oct-2005.pdf (PECCOE Report 2005), and NEAFC Annual Enforcement Review 2005–2006, NEAFC Doc. AM 2006/53, www.neafc.org/reports/annual-meeting/am_2006/index-docs.htm.

the nationality of IUU vessels in the area has changed. Sightings of vessels flagged by Belize have dropped, while new flags in the region such as Georgia and Liberia have emerged. Dominica now accounts for more than half of all non-party sightings annually.

5.3.3 Conclusions on NEAFC practice

PECCOE produces detailed annual reports on the reciprocal inspection programme, and the violations detected. In the 2004–5 year some 275 at-sea inspections were conducted in the regulatory area, with 22 infringements detected.[191] In 2005–6, 191 inspections were conducted and 23 infringements detected.[192] The figures for 2006–7 show 166 inspections and 26 infringements.[193] In practice the majority of inspections are conducted by vessels from the EU, with about a third of inspections performed by vessels from the Faroe Islands, Iceland and Norway.[194] Russia's persistent failure to contribute an inspection vessel has long been noted. The majority of vessels inspected in 2004–5 where infringements were detected were Russian, their most common infringement being fishing for herring without flag-state authorisation.[195] It would seem that the NEAFC scheme of reciprocal inspection among the contracting parties functions without significant controversy.

The NEAFC's port-state measures supplement diplomatic processes which together are generally regarded as successful alternatives to high-seas boarding and inspection of non-party flag vessels.[196] The NCP scheme has generally been described as a 'success story' within the NEAF Commission.[197] In 2005 this confidence appeared to rest on the 'delisting [namely deregistration] of a number of vessels from Dominica, which

---

[191] *Ibid.*, 35.

[192] See NEAFC Annual Enforcement Review 2005–2006, n. 190, above.

[193] At the time of writing, the author relied upon contracting parties' 'Article 32 reports' submitted to PECCOE to produce figures for 2006–7. See the documents at www.neafc.org/reports/peccoe/oct07/index-docs.htm.

[194] PECCOE Report 2005, 35.

[195] *Ibid.*, 25–32. A rough guide to abbreviations used in NEAFC reports can be found in the Annexes to the NEAFC Scheme. Comparable data is not available in PECCOE reports for other years.

[196] Port State control measures are found in Chapter 5 of the NEAFC Scheme 2007. Their impact is discussed in NEAF Commission, Report of the Permanent Committee on Control and Enforcement, 3–4 October 2006, 11 ff, www.neafc.org/reports/peccoe/docs/peccoe_oct-2006.pdf (PECCOE Report 2006 B).

[197] *Ibid.*, 11.

had left these vessels nowhere to go' and Belize's co-operation with the Commission over its B-listed vessel *Sunny Jane*.[198] Belize also chose to apply for co-operating non-party status after this incident. The *Sunny Jane* was not directly involved in IUU fishing, but rather in the transhipment at sea of a suspected IUU catch taken in the NEAFC regulatory area.[199] 'Belize authorities had also [subsequently] carried out inspections [on the *Sunny Jane* while in port in the Netherlands] and given a prohibition to sail order.'[200] The vessel was eventually released and its contentious cargo was presumed to have been discharged in Agadir. Belize later 'fined and de-flagged' the vessel.[201] Belize is now widely regarded as having taken significant steps to fulfil its flag-state obligations, including entering contractual arrangements with port states for the inspection of its flag vessels which might never otherwise enter port in Belize.[202] Panama and the Bahamas have also now applied for co-operating non-party status after the B-listing of one vessel of each flag.[203]

5.4 The Northwest Atlantic Fisheries Organization

On 1 January 1979, the Convention on Future Multilateral Cooperation in the Northwest Atlantic Fisheries came into force among seven signatories: Canada, Cuba, the European Economic Community, East Germany, Iceland, Norway, and the Soviet Union.[204] The Convention established The Northwest Atlantic Fisheries Organization (NAFO), 'to contribute through consultation and cooperation to the optimum utilization, rational management and conservation of the fishery resources of the Convention Area'.[205] To this end it has adopted

---

[198] *Ibid.*, 11; NEAF Commission, 24th Annual Meeting of the North-East Atlantic Fisheries Commission, 14–18 November 2005, 28, www.neafc.org/reports/.

[199] See also NEAF Commission, Report of the Permanent Committee on Control and Enforcement, 4–5 April 2006, 10, www.neafc.org/reports/peccoe/docs/peccoe_april-2006.pdf (PECCOE Report 2006 A).

[200] NEAF Commission, 24th Annual Meeting, 28. A more detailed account of the incident is found in Report of the North East Atlantic Fisheries Commission Performance Review Panel (2007), 71–2, www.neafc.org/news/docs/performance-review-final-edited.pdf.

[201] PECCOE Report 2006 B, 8.

[202] Personal communication: Deirdre Warner-Kramer and Holly Koehler, US Department of State, 3 April 2006.   [203] PECCOE Report 2008, 13–14, 16–17.

[204] Northwest Atlantic Fisheries Organization, *Convention on Future Multilateral Cooperation in the Northwest Atlantic Fisheries* (Dartmouth: The Commission, 2004), v. Significant treaty amendments were approved on 28 September 2007, not yet in force. They are not relevant to the present discussion.

[205] *Ibid.*

a scheme of control and inspection (the Scheme). The Scheme's present operation is best understood in the context of the 1995 dispute between Canada and Spain over turbot fisheries within the NAFO area and adjacent to the Canadian EEZ, particularly the *Estai* incident.

5.4.1 The *Estai* incident

Responding to evidence of declining fish stocks, the NAFO Fisheries Commission in 1994 issued a 'proposal', setting a total allowable catch (TAC) for Greenland halibut at 27,000 tons.[206] Such 'proposals' are binding among the parties unless a party objects within sixty days.[207] The European Community (EC) did not object to the TAC, but did object to its subsequent distribution among members which was, on a split vote, overwhelmingly allocated to Russia and Canada.[208] The EC, following its objection, set its own unilateral quota of 18,630 tons, as it was entitled to.[209] What might constitute the historically 'correct' EC share of the halibut fishery is controversial. The argument can be made that the EC (principally through Spanish and Portuguese vessels) was a late and rapacious entrant to Grand Banks halibut fishing, at the expense of other NAFO parties – especially Canada. The Spanish and Portuguese halibut NAFO fishery commenced only in 1986, but soon accounted for 75 per cent of the catch.[210]

Outside NAFO, Canada had taken steps towards unilateral enforcement of its own fisheries management laws in high-seas areas adjacent to its EEZ. Its Coastal Fisheries Amendment Act 1994 purportedly prohibited foreign vessels, of nationalities prescribed by regulations, from 'fish[ing] or preparing to fish for a straddling stock in contravention' of NAFO measures within the NAFO area.[211] The extraterritorial enforcement powers granted under Canadian law were extensive:

[e]very power of arrest, entry, search or seizure or other power that could be exercised in Canada … may be exercised … on board the [suspect] foreign fishing vessel.[212]

---

[206] P. Davies, 'The EC/Canadian fisheries dispute in the northwest Atlantic' (1995) 44 ICLQ 927 at 930–1.

[207] *Ibid.*   [208] *Ibid.*

[209] L. De La Fayette, 'The Fisheries Jurisdiction Case (*Spain v. Canada*), Judgment on Jurisdiction of 4 December 1998' (1999) 48 ICLQ 664 at 665.

[210] Davies, 'The EC/Canadian fisheries dispute', 930.

[211] See An Act to amend the Coastal Fisheries Act, Statutes of Canada, 1994, c.14, s.2.

[212] *Ibid.*, s.7.

It is generally accepted that this legislation formed part of Canada's attempt to pressure the FSA drafting conference into producing an effective enforcement regime.[213]

The same day that the EC adopted its unilateral quotas for Greenland halibut, the relevant Canadian regulations were amended to cover Spanish and Portuguese vessels and a NAFO prohibition 'on fishing for Greenland halibut from 3 March to 31 December'.[214] The subsequent high-seas seizure of the *Estai* on 9 March 1995 for halibut fishing resulted in strong condemnation from both Spain and the EC.[215] Canada responded that 'the arrest of the *Estai* was necessary in order to put a stop to the overfishing of Greenland halibut by Spanish fishermen'.[216] Despite the undeniable orthodoxy of the EC's legal position, the incident nonetheless won concessions for Canada regarding high-seas enforcement of NAFO measures. The dispute was resolved by an agreement between the EC and Canada to seek to strengthen the NAFO enforcement regime and to implement between themselves an interim inspection regime (the Canada–EC Agreement).[217] The terms of the Canada–EC Agreement were ultimately adopted as NAFO measures and incorporated into the boarding and inspection scheme discussed below.[218]

The Canada–EC Agreement provided for the deployment of observers with certain limited enforcement powers aboard all NAFO member vessels fishing in the NAFO area.[219] The Agreement also required Canada to repeal its fisheries regulations as they applied to Spain and Portugal.[220] The vigour with which the international community in general opposed Canada's action certainly precluded the development of any customary rule along the lines of Canada's initial extraterritorial legislation.[221]

---

[213] Davies, 'The EC/Canadian fisheries dispute', 935; cf. C. Joyner, 'On the borderline? Canadian activism in the Grand Banks', in Olav Schramm Stokke (ed.), *Governing High Seas Fisheries: The Interplay of Global and Regional Regimes* (Oxford University Press, 2001), p. 207 at p. 222.

[214] De La Fayette, 'The Fisheries Jurisdiction Case', 666.

[215] *Fisheries Jurisdiction Case (Spain v. Canada)*, [1998] ICJ Rep., p. 432 at p. 443.

[216] *Ibid.*

[217] Canada–European Community: Agreed Minute on the Conservation and Management of Fish Stocks 1995, (1995) 34 ILM 1260 (Canada–EC Agreement).

[218] Joyner, 'On the borderline?', 218.

[219] Canada–EC Agreement, Paragraph A.2 and Annex I, Point II.11.A, Point II.3.

[220] Canada–EC Agreement, Paragraph C.1.

[221] Byers, 'Policing the high seas', 538; Joyner, 'On the borderline?', 219; José A. de Yturriaga, *The International Regime of Fisheries: From UNCLOS 1982 to the Presential Sea*

Some have argued that the *Estai*'s seizure could have been justified by a state of necessity.[222] (While Canada frequently stressed that its actions were 'necessary' to stop overfishing, it is not clear that Canada expressly relied on the doctrine of necessity.) A state invoking necessity inherently acknowledges that its conduct is not in conformity with an international obligation, but raises a plea that circumstances existed precluding its actions being wrongful.[223] The elements required to raise a 'defence' of necessity at general international law are:

(1) 'an "essential interest" of the State ... must have been threatened';
(2) the threat must constitute a 'grave and imminent peril';
(3) 'the act [in question] ... must have been the only means of safeguarding that interest';
(4) the act 'must not have "seriously impair[ed] an essential interest" of the state towards which the obligation existed'; and
(5) 'the state which is the author of the act must not have "contributed to the occurrence of the state of necessity"'.[224]

These conditions are to be regarded as cumulative and strict, as the defence is 'exceptional'.[225] On the first criterion, there is a credible argument that the fishery represented an essential Canadian interest. It was a straddling stock, and fishing outside the Canadian EEZ was bound to have effects on exclusive Canadian interests within the EEZ. There is certainly support for the idea that essential interests could extend to environmental issues,[226] and that necessity might justify extraterritorial action to avert 'a threat to a vital ecological interest' in certain cases.[227] However, it is difficult to see how the actions of a few vessels constituted a 'grave and imminent peril' to the continued existence of the fish stock. Even if this was conceded, unilateral enforcement was hardly 'the only means of safeguarding ... [Canada's] interest' while negotiations continued within the framework of a

---

(The Hague: Martinus Nijhoff, 1997), p. 246; cf. *Military and Paramilitary Activities in and Against Nicaragua (Nicaragua v. US)*, Merits, [1986] ICJ Rep. 14, 98 at para. 186.

[222] O. Akiba, 'International law of the sea: the legality of Canadian seizure of the Spanish trawler (*Estai*)' (1997) 37 *Natural Resources Journal* 809 at 809.

[223] *Gab íkovo-Nagymaros Project (Hungary/Slovakia)*, [1997] ICJ Rep. 7 at 40–1.

[224] *Ibid.*, 40–1, referring to Article 33 of the ILC Draft Articles on State Responsibility, [1980] II YBILC, 34; cf. Shaw, pp. 712–13.

[225] *Ibid.*, 40–1; cf. Brownlie, p. 448; [2001] II(2) YBILC, 80–3 at (1), (2), (11) and (14).

[226] *Ibid.*, 41.

[227] [1980] II YBILC, 40 at para. 16; but cf. [2001] II(2) YBILC, 80 at (6).

standing fisheries organisation.[228] Finally, there is the requirement that the state asserting necessity had not itself 'contributed to the particular state of necessity'. There is little doubt that Canada had made a substantial contribution to the overfishing of halibut and depletion of its stocks.[229] While the EC's contribution to the state of necessity may have been significantly the greater, there is a strong rationale for maintaining a high threshold on the availability of the doctrine of necessity to prevent its abuse.[230] Further, ITLOS appeared hostile in the *Saiga* case to the unilateral assertion of novel enforcement jurisdiction by a coastal state to protect alleged vital national interests within the EEZ, let alone beyond it.[231] It is thus difficult to argue either that the Canadian action can be accepted as contributing to the formation of a new rule of international law allowing unilateral high-seas interdictions for environmental purposes, or as a viable example of a situation where necessity might excuse such an action.

5.4.2 The present NAFO boarding and inspection scheme

The NAFO at-sea inspection regime is contained in Articles 28–43 of the NAFO Conservation and Enforcement Measures (the Scheme).[232] The Scheme is not sufficiently different from the NEAFC Scheme to warrant separate discussion. On many points the drafting of the two is virtually identical, though the NEAFC drafting has tended to be more detailed, especially in areas noted above such as masters' duties during inspection.

5.4.3 The NAFO non-contracting party scheme

The NAFO Scheme in Articles 46–54 sets out a regime to encourage compliance by non-contracting parties (NCP Scheme), which is similar in many respects to the NEAFC NCP Scheme. Inspectors encountering NCP vessels fishing in the NAFO area *must* request courtesy boardings 'if appropriate' (Article 48). Once, however, it was widely realised that the information gathered through such consensual boardings was being used to bring diplomatic pressure upon flag states, 'consent ...

---

[228] Yturriaga, *International Regime of Fisheries*, p. 254.

[229] Davies, 'EC/Canadian fisheries dispute', 937; Akiba, 'International law of the sea', 825.

[230] [2001] II(2) YBILC, 80 at (2); on instances of abuse see Harris, *Cases and Materials on International Law*, p. 529 n. 78.

[231] MV '*Saiga*' (No. 2), (1999) 38 ILM 1323 at 1351 para. 131.

[232] NAFO FC Doc. 08/1, www.nafo.int/fisheries/frames/regulations.html (NAFO Scheme 2008).

essentially dried up'.[233] There is thus no recent reported boarding and inspection practice under the NCP Scheme.

The NAFO NCP Scheme also contains a two-list system for suspected and confirmed IUU vessels and a series of port-state sanctions similar to those found in the NEAFC Scheme.[234] The effectiveness of port-state and diplomatic measures is perhaps demonstrated by the very few non-party vessels sighted in the NAFO area: only seven or eight vessels annually in the 2003–5 period (usually flagged to Dominica or the Dominican Republic);[235] declining to only five Georgian-flagged vessels in 2005–6, all of which were subsequently reported as having been scrapped.[236] As of mid-2008, no new IUU vessels had been sighted in the NAFO area since 31 July 2006.

5.4.4 NAFO practice under the scheme

As noted above, consent to NAFO inspections from non-party flag states has 'dried up'.[237] One is thus only able to assess current practice regarding the reciprocal inspection scheme that applies among the parties. Unfortunately, NAFO parties regard such information as confidential.[238] NAFO has publicised the fact that

[a]t-sea inspections in the NAFO Regulatory Area are frequent and random … Of the 401 at-sea inspections carried out in 2004, 18 (i.e. 4.5%), indicated that the vessel inspected might have violated NAFO regulations. These numbers are similar to those found in 2003 when 20 out of 352 inspections resulted in citations.[239]

The public Annual Compliance Review provides no detail as to the distribution of violations by flag state, or the number of inspections conducted by flag state. It does show that in 2005 some 326 at-sea inspections were conducted, resulting in thirty-one 'citations' for Scheme

---

[233] Rayfuse, *Non-Flag State Enforcement*, p. 251.   [234] NAFO Scheme, Articles 51–54.

[235] NAFO, Meeting Proceedings of the General Council and Fisheries Commission September 2005–August 2006: Report of the Standing Committee on the Fishing Activities of Non-Contracting Parties in the Regulatory Area (STACFAC), 2005 at Annexe 3, www.nafo.int/publications/meetproc/2006/mp-05–06.html.

[236] NAFO, Meeting Proceedings of the General Council and Fisheries Commission September 2006–August 2007: STACFAC Report 2006 at item 6, www.nafo.int/publications/frames/gen-mp-06–07.html; see the IUU vessel table at www.nafo.int, last visited 8 August 2008.

[237] Rayfuse, *Non-Flag State Enforcement*, pp. 250–1.

[238] Personal communication: Ricardo Federizon, NAFO Fisheries Commission Coordinator, 2 May 2006.

[239] See the NAFO website: www.nafo.int/fisheries/frames/fishery.html.

infringements, and that in 2006 there were 361 such inspections and 22 'citations' issued.[240] The Scheme clearly involves a very large number of at-sea inspections annually.

The Scheme's operation has not been without controversy. Rayfuse characterises the 'reality of NAFO' as 'basically a fight to the death between two … deeply distrustful, highly antagonistic and mutually incompatible view points',[241] these two views being that of Canada, as the most directly affected coastal state, and those European states (whose own fisheries may be over-capitalised or failing) claiming a tradition of fishing these waters.[242] The level of detail in the NAFO Scheme thus sets the stage for subsequent disputes between parties regarding its good faith implementation and effective flag-state follow-up.[243]

There have been two instances in which criminal complaints have been made in Portugal against individual Canadian-appointed NAFO inspectors.[244] Both have now been dismissed or discontinued prior to trial. The first, dating to 1999, involved the vessel *Calvao*. The complaint related to an alleged slander resulting from a conversation on land between an inspector and the vessel's master after an at-sea inspection and the vessel's subsequent return to a Portuguese port in the Azores.[245] The facts, however, do not directly concern the conduct of the inspection itself. In 2000, in the course of inspecting the Portuguese-flagged *Santa Mafalda*, a Canadian inspector temporarily removed a logbook to the inspection vessel for photocopying.[246] Subsequently, an allegation was made that the logbook was not voluntarily supplied to the inspector but was removed (contrary to Portuguese law) from a private area not subject to lawful search.[247] It should be noted that while '[i]nspectors have the authority to examine all relevant areas, decks and rooms' aboard, there is only express reference in the Scheme to their summarising the fishing logbook on a provided form.[248] The case was eventually discontinued in 2006.[249] Regardless of the precise (and no doubt disputed) facts of the *Santa Mafalda* case, it raises both practical and legal issues.

---

[240] See NAFO Annual Compliance Review 2007, NAFO/FC Doc. 07/23, http://archive.nafo.int/open/fc/2007/fcdoc07-23.pdf.

[241] Rayfuse, *Non-Flag State Enforcement*, p. 256.   [242] *Ibid.*   [243] *Ibid.*, pp. 238, 257.

[244] Not in Spain as reported in Rayfuse, *Non-Flag State Enforcement*, pp. 257–8.

[245] Personal communication: Amos Donoghue (Senior Counsel, International Law Section), Department of Justice, Canada, 1 February 2006.

[246] *Ibid.*   [247] *Ibid.*   [248] NAFO Scheme 2008, Article 32(5) and (6).

[249] Personal communication: Amos Donoghue, n. 245 above.

Practically speaking, such threatened prosecutions create a chilling effect on inspectors' willingness to conduct boardings and inspections (as opposed to non-boarding surveillance). The NAFO Scheme itself provides inspectors with no express immunity from prosecution for their official acts. Further, vessels fishing in violation of their licensed catch quota or their flag state's national quota commonly maintain two sets of fishing logs: an accurate set for the vessel's owners, and a separate set for inspectors. If certain areas are effectively 'off-limits' to inspectors by operation of national law, concealing such logs becomes easy. It is thus hardly surprising that the idea of 'immunity for NAFO inspectors' has been 'mooted in Canadian circles'.[250]

Such scenarios also implicate state immunity. NAFO inspectors remain 'under the operational control of' and 'responsible to' the state appointing them.[251] One would expect them to be treated in the same manner as other state officials, who are generally held immune in foreign courts for their official, non-commercial actions. These issues are explored further in Chapter 11.

5.5 The Commission for the Conservation of Antarctic Marine Living Resources

5.5.1 Introduction

The management area of the Commission for the Conservation of Antarctic Marine Living Resources (CCAMLR) is vast, remote and inhospitable; encompassing all waters south of 60°S and the adjacent 'Antarctic Convergence' marine ecosystem. CCAMLR's establishing convention expressly requires at-sea observation, boarding and inspection.[252] Conditions, however, often make at-sea boarding dangerous or impossible, and parties may perceive interdictions as simply too costly and often resulting in poor flag-state follow-up.[253] CCAMLR parties have focused on other measures to deter IUU fishing, such as VMS

---

[250] Rayfuse, Non-Flag State Enforcement, p. 258.

[251] NAFO Scheme 2008, Article 30(2); this formula was also formerly used in NEAFC – see text accompanying nn. 151–153, above – and was first used in ICCAT Scheme 1975 (n. 66 above), Article 7.

[252] Ibid., and Convention for the Conservation of Antarctic Marine Living Resources 1980, (1980) 19 ILM 841 (CAMLR Convention), Article XXIV(1) and (2)(a). There are twenty-five states members of the Commission, and a further nine states parties to the Convention.

[253] Rayfuse, Non-Flag State Enforcement, p. 282; cf. the Commission's website, www.ccamlr.org/pu/e/gen-intro.htm.

requirements and catch documentation schemes.[254] The principal concern has been the lucrative trade in IUU fishing for toothfish (*Dissostichus* spp.):

Fishing vessels flying various flags and most often involving Spanish interests ... engage in long-term fishing cruises in ... the Southern Ocean. The wealth of the fish – especially Patagonian toothfish – in the vast expanses of the Southern Ocean, and the relatively remote chance of being caught while fishing in the economic zones of France (Kerguelen and Crozet Islands) and Australia (Heard and McDonald Islands), are the main [incentives]... The financial stakes are considerable, given that a full cargo of Patagonian toothfish can equal or exceed the value of the fishing vessel involved.[255]

Australia has described the practice as 'a highly organised form of transnational crime'.[256] Maritime enforcement action in the CCAMLR area has principally resulted from Australian and French enforcement action in EEZs surrounding their Antarctic island possessions. France and Australia have both characterised such actions as national-law enforcement of the CAMLR Convention, and this approach has gone unprotested in the Commission.[257] Australia has in the past not sought to enforce the Convention within the EEZ proclaimed over its continental Antarctic claim, due to, among other concerns, its limited recognition by other states.[258]

---

[254] Rayfuse, *Non-Flag State Enforcement*, pp. 278–82; a general CCAMLR catch documentation scheme was introduced in 2006–7: Report of the Twenty-Sixth Meeting of the Commission (2007) (CCAMLR-XXVI), 180–2. All Commission reports are available at www.ccamlr.org.

[255] T. Treves, 'Flags of convenience before the law of the sea Tribunal' (2004–5) 6 SDILJ 181 at 181–2; cf. R. Baird, 'Coastal state fisheries management: a review of Australian enforcement action in the Heard and McDonald Islands Australian fishing zone' (2004) 9 DLR 91 at 97.

[256] Report of the Twenty-First Meeting of the Commission (2002) (CCAMLR-XXI), 162 at para. 5.3.

[257] See Report of Members' activities in the Convention Area: Australia 2004–05, www.ccamlr.org/pu/e/e_pubs/ma/04–05/australia05.pdf; as to whether the EEZs are legally declared, see *Monte Confurco Case (Seychelles v. France)*, ITLOS Case No. 6, 18 December 2000, www.itlos.org, Judge Vukas (Declaration); *Volga Case (Russia v. Australia)* (2003) 42 ILM 159 at 179–181, Judge Vukas (Declaration); cf. UNCLOS, Article 121(3), and the UK position on Rockall Island: Barston, 'Law of the sea and regional fisheries organisations', 349.

[258] See *Humane Society International Inc v. Kyodo Senpaku Kaisha Ltd* [2005] FCA 664 (27 May 2005) at paras. 2, 13, 14, www.austlii.edu.au/au/cases/cth/federal_ct/2005/664. html. On the application of Australian environmental law to this area, see the decision on appeal: [2006] FCAFC 116 (14 July 2006), paras. 7–9, http://austlii.law. uts.edu.au/au/cases/cth/FCAFC/2006/116.html. The Australian government has now suggested that it may challenge the legality of Japanese whaling in this area: Prime

There have been some signs that IUU fishing is diminishing. It has been estimated that the IUU catch in the CCAMLR area, as a percentage of total catch, has declined from 72.4 per cent in 1996–7 to 16.5 per cent in 2003–4.[259] In 2005–6, it was estimated the IUU toothfish catch was only 30 per cent of 2001–2 levels.[260] That said, in 2006–7 it was estimated that in some divisions of the CCAMLR management area the IUU catch was ten times the maximum TAC set by the Commission,[261] and in recent years the total tonnage of the IUU catch appears to have been increasing.[262] There is no doubt that IUU fishing remains an extremely serious issue for the Commission.[263]

Both France and Australia have reported a decline to zero in sightings of IUU fishing vessels in their Antarctic EEZs in recent years.[264] They have attributed this to surveillance activity within their Antarctic EEZ areas, although this appears simply to have displaced IUU fishing to adjacent CCAMLR waters.[265] 'Australia [has] reported that the current flags of such [displaced IUU] vessels include Democratic People's Republic of Korea, Equatorial Guinea, Sierra Leone and Togo.'[266] In 2007 France reported to CCAMLR that it had 'undertaken diplomatic demarches … to Togo and Equatorial Guinea, with the aim of obtaining permission to board, inspect and detain any of their flag vessels in the Convention Area, including on the high seas'.[267] France 'received no response from Togo', but it did receive a diplomatic note from Equatorial Guinea in September 2007 'which authorises France to take action, if required, in order to combat IUU fishing in the Convention Area'.[268] Indeed, it appears that by a separate letter dated 3 August

Minister Kevin Rudd, press conference, 17 January 2008: www.pm.gov.au/media/Interview/2008/interview_0030.cfm.

[259] Report of the Twenty-Third Meeting of the Commission (2004) (CCAMLR-XXIII), 140.
[260] Report of the Twenty-Fifth Meeting of the Commission (2006) (CCAMLR-XXV), 153–4.
[261] CCAMLR-XXVI, 38–9.   [262] CCAMLR-XXV, 31; CCAMLR-XXVI, 177.
[263] See the extended debate in CCAMLR-XXVI, 38–44.
[264] See Rapport des activités des membres: France, 2002–3, www.ccamlr.org/pu/e/e_pubs/ma/02-03/france.pdf; 2003–4, www.ccamlr.org/pu/e/e_pubs/ma/03-04/france04.pdf; 2004–5, www.ccamlr.org/pu/e/e_pubs/ma/04-05/france05.pdf; Report of Members' Activities in the CCAMLR Area: Australia, 2006–7, www.ccamlr.org/pu/e/e_pubs/ma/06-07/aus07.pdf; CCAMLR-XXVI, 177.
[265] CCAMLR-XXV, 153–4; CCAMLR-XXVI, 176–7.   [266] CCAMLR-XXVI, 176.
[267] Ibid., 177. The UK also had high-level talks with Togo and Equatorial Guinea, although it does not appear that it sought an agreement on boarding and inspection: Report of Members' activities in the Convention Area: United Kingdom 2006-2007, 2, www.ccamlr.org/pu/e/e_pubs/ma/06-07/uk07.pdf.
[268] Ibid.

2007, 'Togolese authorities authorised the boarding and inspection of Togolese-flagged vessels listed in the NCP-IUU List by patrol vessels of CCAMLR Members'.[269] No practice under these arrangements has yet been reported.

5.5.2 The CCAMLR System of Inspection

The System of Inspection[270] is functionally very similar to that applied in NEAFC and NAFO, allowing high-seas boarding by nationally designated inspectors and requiring follow-up or enforcement action to be undertaken by the flag state. It is, however, considerably less detailed and contains no 'serious violations' provision allowing a vessel to be directed into port. Given the remoteness of the CCAMLR area, this would be impractical. Again, there is no system of sanction if a flag state fails to take effective action, although their reports on action taken are circulated to other CCAMLR member states by the Commission, providing a degree of scrutiny.[271]

5.5.3 Enforcement under the System of Inspection

In the reporting year 2003–4, members appointed forty-four inspectors, twenty of whom 'were actually deployed at sea' and '11 vessels were inspected' (all by UK-appointed inspectors).[272] In 2004–5 South African inspectors conducted '[t]en inspections of foreign-flagged vessels (six Spanish and four Japanese)'; and the United Kingdom reported conducting ten at-sea inspections.[273] In 2005–6 four inspectors deployed at sea (out of forty-six appointments) conducted fouteen at-sea inspections: thirteen conducted by the United Kingdom and one by Australia.[274] In 2006–7 there were seventy-three designated inspectors and twenty-seven at-sea inspections conducted; similarly, twenty-three

---

[269] *Ibid.*

[270] See CCAMLR, *Basic Documents* (2005), 'Part 9: Text of the CCAMLR System of Inspection', 104–12, www.ccamlr.org/pu/e/e_pubs/bd/toc.htm (CCAMLR Scheme).

[271] CCAMLR Scheme, para IX.

[272] CCAMLR-XXIII, Annexe 5: Report of the Standing Committee on Implementation and Compliance, 147, www.ccamlr.org/pu/e/e_pubs/cr/04/a5.pdf.

[273] Report of Members' activities in the Convention Area: South Africa 2004–05, www.ccamlr.org/pu/e/e_pubs/ma/04–05/southafrica05.pdf; Report of Members' activities in the Convention Area: United Kingdom 2004–05, www.ccamlr.org/pu/e/e_pubs/ma/04–05/uk05.pdf; and Report of the Twenty-Fourth Meeting of the Commission (2005) (CCAMLR-XXIV), Annex 5: Report of the Standing Committee on Implementation and Compliance, 146, www.ccamlr.org/pu/e/e_pubs/cr/05/a5.pdf.

[274] CCAMLR-XXV, 162.

were conducted by the United Kingdom and one by Australia.[275] In 2006–7 only one infringement was found. In the same year some controversy resulted from the refusal of one Polish and four Chinese vessels to allow inspectors to board.[276]

The practice, while not insignificant, is hardly extensive. Further, it is obvious that a reciprocal system of inspection among contracting parties and Commission members has at best a limited impact on IUU fishing of the type of most concern to CCAMLR: fishing conducted under the flags of non-co-operating parties. Of more interest, then, is the collateral means of enforcement provided by the exercise of Australian and French EEZ jurisdiction over toothfish fisheries.

5.5.4 Co-operation between Australia and France

Within the CCAMLR area, in addition to the unenforced claim discussed above, Australia claims EEZs in respect of Heard Island and the adjacent MacDonald Islands. France claims EEZs surrounding the highly dispersed Kerguelen Islands, Crozet Islands, Saint-Paul Island and Amsterdam Island. Despite being only partially contiguous, these various EEZs are described as an 'Area of Cooperation' under an Australian–French treaty (the Co-operation Treaty).[277]

The Co-operation Treaty is a self-described 'first step', principally authorising one party to seek permission to conduct fisheries surveillance in the other party's waters and to exchange resulting information.[278] It contemplates subsidiary agreements providing for 'law enforcement operations possibly accompanied by forcible measures'.[279] The Treaty does provide that hot pursuit commenced by one party may continue through the other party's territorial sea, provided it is informed and no 'physical law enforcement or other coercive action against the vessel pursued' is taken while within that territorial sea.[280]

---

[275] CCAMLR-XXVI, 165–7.

[276] *Ibid.* There was a technical dispute about whether in the case of the Polish vessel the inspector appeared on the CCAMLR list; China disputed that it was bound by the Scheme of Inspection in the period when it was a 'contracting party' but not a Commission 'member'.

[277] Treaty between the Government of Australia and the Government of the French Republic on Cooperation in the Maritime Areas Adjacent to the French Southern and Antarctic Territories (TAAF), Heard Island and the McDonald Islands 2003, [2005] ATS 6 (Cooperation Treaty 2003); commentary in Australian National Interest Analysis [2004] ATNIA 9, www.austlii.edu.au/au/other/dfat/nia/2004/9.html.

[278] Cooperation Treaty 2003, Articles 3, 5 and Annexe III, Article 1(d).

[279] *Ibid.*, Annexe III, Articles 1(e) and 2; cf. Article 4.

[280] *Ibid.*, Article 3(3) and (4).

This is practical in a remote environment where suspect vessels in one party's EEZ may attempt to break pursuit by entering the other's territorial sea.

Within this Co-operation Treaty framework, Australia and France concluded a ship-rider agreement on 8 January 2007, which is not yet in force.[281] It provides for the embarkation of 'controllers' from one party aboard the enforcement vessels of the other party, who may conduct 'co-operative enforcement' measures. Co-operative enforcement means, in effect, the fisheries laws of one party being carried out from the platform of the other party's vessel. As the choice of terminology suggests, it is the ship-riding controller who has authority to conduct enforcement action in respect of violations of the fisheries laws of their designating state. Such enforcement activity may not be carried out without a controller present. Thus, for example, a French controller aboard an Australian vessel could authorise the pursuit of a vessel engaged (directly or by its small boats) in IUU fishing within the French Antarctic EEZs and the enforcement of French law against that vessel. This obviously allows a law-enforcement platform with an embarked controller to operate throughout the Co-operation Area.

The agreement provides unusual detail as to the applicable national law during an interdiction and the consequences of any wrongful conduct occurring. The agreement expressly states that 'cooperative enforcement activities ... shall be conducted in conformity with the law applicable in the maritime zone in which the activities are undertaken or, in the case of hot pursuit, the maritime zone from which a hot pursuit is commenced'.[282] This provision is clearly applicable both to the boarding of a vessel and to conduct once aboard. It contrasts with drug interdiction treaty provisions which expressly provide that the officers of an interdicting state should comply with the boarding state's applicable national laws.[283] The treaty reinforces this point, through a relatively standard 'safeguards clause' providing that '[e]ach Party shall ensure that its Controllers ... act in accordance with its

---

[281] Agreement on Cooperative Enforcement of Fisheries Laws between the Government of Australia and the Government of the French Republic in the Maritime Areas Adjacent to the French Southern and Antarctic Territories, Heard Island and the McDonald Islands, [2007] ATNIF 1 (Australian–French Cooperative Enforcement Agreement).

[282] Ibid., Article 3(4).

[283] See Council of Europe Agreement, Article 11(1); Caribbean Regional Arrangement, Article 22; and other treaty practice discussed at Chapter 10, section 3.3.3 ('Rule 6').

applicable national laws and policies and with international law and accepted international practices' during an interdiction.[284] Each party is to inform the other of 'applicable laws and policies' and 'cooperative enforcement activity involving the use of force against a fishing vessel shall require the joint authorisation of both Parties'.[285] The treaty appears to contemplate that in all cases, seized vessels and arrested crew should be 'handed over as soon as possible to the authorities' of the controller's designating state.[286] The difficulties of surrender without extradition have been noted elsewhere, but are less likely to arise in a ship-rider-controlled interdiction.[287] Uniquely among ship-rider treaties, the Australian–French agreement deals with state immunity, Article 5(2) providing that

Officers of one Party shall enjoy immunity from the criminal, civil and administrative jurisdiction of the other Party for acts performed in the course of carrying out cooperative enforcement activities pursuant to and consistent with this Agreement.

Issues of state immunity are discussed further in Chapter 11.

As noted, the ship-rider agreement is not yet in force and the Co-operation Treaty has so far only been relied upon to conduct several joint patrols.[288] Nonetheless the Co-operation Area has seen a great deal of national EEZ enforcement practice.

5.5.5 Australian enforcement practice in its Antarctic EEZs

The first IUU fishing in the Australian Antarctic EEZ was detected in 1996.[289] In the period 1997–2005, nine vessels were arrested by Australian authorities. Only one of these, the *Taruman*, was arrested in international waters, with the consent of the flag state, Cambodia.[290] It was suspected of IUU fishing for toothfish in the Australian EEZ off Macquarie Island, outside the CCAMLR area. All other arrests were

---

[284] Australian–French Cooperative Enforcement Agreement, Article 3(5). On 'safeguard clauses' see Chapter 10, section 2.

[285] Australian–French Cooperative Enforcement Agreement, Articles 3(6) and (8).

[286] *Ibid.*, Article 6.   [287] See Chapter 5, section 5 and Chapter 9, section 7.

[288] Australia, Report of Members' activities in the Convention Area, 2004–5, 3, www.ccamlr.org/pu/e/e_pubs/ma/04–05/australia05.pdf (Australian CCAMLR Report 2004–2005).

[289] CCAMLR-XXI, 162.

[290] Australian CCAMLR Report 2004–5, 6; CCAMLR-XXV, Annexe 5: Report of the Standing Committee on Implementation and Compliance, 155, www.ccamlr.org/pu/e/e_pubs/cr/06/a5.pdf.

Table 1. *Australian interdictions in the Australian EEZs, 1997–2005*

Fishing vessel name	Flag state	Date of arrest
Salvora	Belize	16 October 1997
Aliza Glacial	Panama	17 October 1997
Big Star	Seychelles	21 February 1998
South Tomi	Togo	12 April 2001
Lena	Russia	6 February 2002
Volga	Russia	7 February 2002
Viarsa	Uruguay	28 August 2003
Maya V	Uruguay	22 January 2004
Taruman	Cambodia	6 September 2005

made within the Australian Antarctic EEZs. These nine arrests may be summarised as shown in Table 1.[291]

Some of the cases often involved lengthy hot pursuits in difficult conditions: the *South Tomi* was pursued for fifteen days across 3,300 n.m.;[292] when first pursued in 2001, the *Lena* 'evaded a civilian patrol vessel for 14 days before finally escaping';[293] and the *Viarsa* pursuit lasted twenty-one days and covered 3,900 n.m.[294]

Australia's prosecutions of early CCAMLR cases in 1997–8 in respect of the *Salvora*, the *Aliza Glacial* and the *Big Star* had mixed results. Despite the imposition of fines and the forfeiture of large securities in both the *Salvora* and *Big Star* cases, the *Salvora* was spotted illegally fishing in the French EEZ within a year of its arrest.[295] The sale of the seized *Aliza Glacial* to new owners before forfeiture proceedings could commence prompted a change in Australian law.[296] Section 106A of the Fisheries Management Act now provides for automatic forfeiture of any vessel present within an Australian EEZ area and engaged in

[291] Australian CCAMLR Report 2004–5; Baird, 'Coastal state fisheries management', 103.

[292] Baird, 'Coastal state fisheries management', 100.

[293] R. Baird, 'Illegal, unreported and unregulated fishing: an analysis of the legal, economic and historical factors relevant to its development and persistence' (2004) 5 MJIL 299 at 326.

[294] Baird, 'Coastal state fisheries management', 100 and 102.

[295] Australian Fisheries Management Authority, Annual Report 1998–9, 180, www.afma.gov.au/information/publications/corporate/annual/ar88_89/ar88_89.pdf; S. O'Kelly, 'Spanish fishermen illegally prowling the Antarctic', *Mail on Sunday*, 30 January 2000, p. 54.

[296] *Bergensbanken ASA v. The Ship 'Aliza Glacial' & Ors* [1998] 1642 FCA (17 December 1998), www.austlii.edu.au/au/cases/cth/federal_ct/1998/1642.html.

unauthorised fishing.[297] A vessel may be seized upon reasonable suspicion of being engaged in unauthorised fishing, and will be forfeited unless the owner can prove it was not involved in a fisheries offence.[298] It is apparently the Australian government's view that

if a foreign fishing [vessel] is sighted illegally fishing in Australian waters then that vessel … is automatically forfeited to the Commonwealth and becomes the property of the Commonwealth and might be liable to seizure anywhere in the world as Australian property.[299]

This possibility has caused some disquiet, but Australia has not attempted such action yet.[300]

Of the later Australian cases, several were disposed of without raising any noteworthy points of law. Crews and masters were fined, and catch confiscated, in both the *Lena* and *South Tomi* cases.[301] The *Maya V* also ended in convictions and forfeiture of the vessel.[302] The crew of the *Viarsa* went free in November 2005 after being acquitted by a jury in Perth; it was the crew's second trial, the first being abandoned when the jury failed to return a verdict.[303] The master and fishing master of the *Taruman* were found guilty and fined in Sydney in September 2006 and the vessel and catch were forfeited.[304]

Vessels that have been forfeited to Australia as a result of illegal fishing within its EEZ are sold by a tender process. The conditions of the tenders allow for the successful tenderer either to scrap the vessel, to re-register it as a fishing vessel if the operator meets stringent

---

[297] Fisheries Management Act 1991 (No. 162 of 1991) (Cth), see ss. 95(1)(a) and (b), 95(2) and 106A; and Fisheries Legislation Amendment Act (No 1) 1999 (No. 143 of 1999) (Cth).

[298] M. White and S. Knight, 'Illegal fishing in Australian waters: the use of UNCLOS by Australian courts', (2005) II JIML 110 at 119; Fisheries Management Act 1991 (Cth), ss. 106E–106H.

[299] Senator Ian Macdonald, Minister for Fisheries, Forestry and Conservation, 'New chapter in maritime law – attempt to claim back the *VOLGA* rejected', 13 March 2004 (press release), www.mffc.gov.au/releases/2004/04042m.html.

[300] White and Knight, 'Illegal fishing in Australian waters', 120.

[301] Macdonald (press release), n. 299 above; AFMA, Annual Report 2001–2, 74, www.afma.gov.au/information/publications/corporate/annual/ar01_02/ar01_02_00.pdf.

[302] AFMA, Annual Report 2004–5, 98; Australia, Report of Members' activities in the [CAMLR] Convention Area, 2004–5, 2, www.ccamlr.org/pu/e/e_pubs/ma/04–05/australia05.pdf.

[303] R. Pash, 'No convictions from epic sea chase', *The Australian*, 5 November 2005.

[304] M. White, 'Australian maritime law update: 2006 – Part I' (2007) 38 JMLC 293 at 297; Senator E. Abetz, Minister for Fisheries, Forestry and Conservation, 'Taruman finding welcomed', 26 September 2006 (press release), www.mffc.gov.au/releases/2006/06116aj.html.

conditions and probity checks to ensure no involvement in IUU fishing, or for it to be sunk to provide an artificial reef or dive wreck.[305]

The *Lena* and *South Tomi* were sunk as diving wrecks, the *Viarsa 1* was demolished in Indian ship-breaking yards, and as at August 2008 the tender process seemingly continues regarding the *Taruman* and *Maya V.*[306]

The most litigated Australian seizure was that of the *Volga* (which with the *Lena* appeared to be part of a co-ordinated IUU fleet),[307] proceedings being brought both in Australian courts and before ITLOS. In both the international and national proceedings the issue of whether Australia had complied with the UNCLOS requirements for valid exercise of the right of hot pursuit was agitated.[308] UNCLOS Article 111(6)(b) expressly provides that a ship sighted within a zone of coastal-state jurisdiction may not be arrested outside it unless it was ordered to stop and subsequent pursuit was 'without interruption'. It seems likely that hot pursuit was improperly commenced, as the *Volga*, through an error of calculation, was not signalled to stop until it was 'a few hundred metres outside' the Australian EEZ.[309] However, the legality of the hot pursuit was not ruled on in any proceedings. The ITLOS case was a prompt-release proceeding under Article 292 of UNCLOS, concerning solely the reasonableness of the bond imposed by Australia upon the *Volga*.[310]

Similarly, Australian forfeiture proceedings were resolved on the basis that under section 106A of the Fisheries Management Act the *Volga* was already Commonwealth property and Australian law entitled the Commonwealth to recover its property, even on the high seas.[311] The vessel was condemned and in separate proceedings the fishing master and two crew members were fined.[312] As regards hot pursuit, the federal court found that the relevant Australian legislation[313] 'did not fully reflect the requirements of the Convention' and omitted, *inter alia*, 'the requirement for an order to stop'.[314]

---

[305] 'Report of Members' Activities in the CCAMLR Area: Australia', 2006–7, 2.

[306] *Ibid.*; Macdonald (press release), n. 299 above; AFMA, Annual Report 2001–2, 74.

[307] *Volga Case*, Statement in Response of Australia (7 December 2002), 5, www.itlos.org; see also *Volga Case (Russia v. Australia)* (2003) 42 ILM 159, Judge Anderson (Dissenting Opinion), 191, and Judge ad hoc Shearer (Dissenting Opinion), 193.

[308] UNCLOS, Article 111; cf. cases and authorities listed in Chapter 2, n. 65.

[309] *Volga Case*, 165.   [310] *Ibid.*, 175.

[311] *Olbers Co Ltd v. Commonwealth of Australia* [2004] FCAFC 262 (16 September 2004), at para. 22, www.austlii.edu.au/au/cases/cth/FCAFC/2004/262.html.

[312] AFMA, Annual Report 2003–4, 113.

[313] Fisheries Management Act 1991 (Cth), s. 87.

[314] *Olbers v. Commonwealth*, para. 19; see UNCLOS, Article 111(4).

Ultimately, Russia does not appear to have protested against the validity of the hot pursuit or the effect of the Australian forfeiture laws within CCAMLR. Instead Russia declared that the *Volga* would be 'deregistered by Russia immediately upon completion of the court hearings in Australia'.[315]

There have been no recent cases of IUU fishing detected in the Australian Antarctic EEZs, and not for want of policing efforts. Despite significant numbers of Indonesian IUU fishing vessels in Australia's northern continental waters placing extraordinary demands on Australian maritime law-enforcement capabilities,[316] Australia remains committed to continuing patrols in the Southern Oceans.[317]

5.5.6 Enforcement practice in the French Antarctic EEZs

The relevant French practice is extensive. Between 1997 and 2001 alone it apprehended eighteen vessels 'in the Kerguelen and Crozet EEZs'.[318] These interdictions may be summarised as shown in Table 2.[319]

Table 2.   *French interdictions in the French EEZs, 1997–2001*

Fishing vessel name	Flag state	Date of arrest
Belgie III	Belize	1997
Arbumasa XXV	Belize	1997
Kinsho Maru	Argentina	1997
Magallanes	Argentina	1997
Vierasa Doce	Argentina	1997 and again in 1998
Mar Del Sur Dos	Belize	1998
Suma Tuna	Belize	1998
Praia do Restello	Portugal	1998
Explorer	Panama	1998
Golden Eagle	Vanuatu	1998
Ercilla	Chile	1998
Antonio Lorenzo	Chile	1998
Mar del Sur Uno	Chile	1998
Camouco	Panama	1999
Grand Prince	Belize	2000
Monte Confurco	Seychelles	2000
Vedra	São Tomé and Príncipe	2000
Castor	St Vincent and Grenadines	2001

---

[315] Report of the Twenty-Second Meeting of the Commission (2002) (CCAMLR-XXII), 42.
[316] M. White and C. Forrest, 'Australian maritime law update: 2005' (2006) 37 JMLC 299 at 300–1.
[317] CCAMLR-XXV, 43; White, 'Australian maritime law update: 2006 – Part I', 297.
[318] Report of the Twentieth Meeting of the Commission (2001) (CCAMLR-XX), 123.
[319] *Ibid.*

Unfortunately, France has made no detailed reports to the Commission on these arrests or the outcomes of any prosecutions. Such paucity of reporting is widespread among CCAMLR parties.[320] Fortunately, the submissions in the ITLOS prompt-release cases concerning the *Camouco*, the *Monte Confurco* and the *Grand Prince* are instructive as to the French enforcement experience generally.[321] Of eighteen masters arrested, only one has been tried and punished, the rest having demonstrated a tendency to vanish.[322] Further, in the period to 2000, the *Camouco* was the only case in which penalties were paid after first-instance proceedings, all other prosecutions being successfully appealed.[323] Nonetheless, after its release in 1999 the *Camouco* was sighted within a French EEZ again in 2000–1.[324] It has been said of IUU fishing vessels that

These vessels often change their names. They very often change their flags and are very often the property of so-called 'one ship companies'. This is a very useful formula by which to hide the identity of the true interests of the people for whom they are working … It is also a useful means by which to avoid [fines] … These vessels are organised in a network. They communicate with each other [in code] … [and are] ready to help each other and are extremely efficient at doing so.

Having increasing difficulty finding ports for unloading illegal catches, these vessels show a lot of imagination. They are able to unload their catches, on the high seas, on to smaller vessels that can take the catches straight to port.[325]

The one-ship company structure of ownership would also explain the fact that proceedings were generally not pursued against vessels' legal owners,[326] although France has argued that such a choice of defendant is not available to it in criminal cases.[327]

Only a few points from the ITLOS cases require discussion here: the advertence to duties to co-operate in the *Camouco* case, and the effect of national confiscation proceedings on ITLOS prompt-release proceedings. The *Camouco*, a Panamanian vessel with a Spanish master,

---

[320] See CCAMLR-XXII, 171.

[321] *Camouco Case (Panama v. France)*, (2000) 39 ILM 666; *Monte Confurco Case (Seychelles v. France)*, ITLOS Case No. 6, 18 December 2000; *Grand Prince Case (Belize v. France)*, ITLOS Case No.8, 20 April 2001, www.itlos.org.

[322] ITLOS/PV.00/6/Rev.1 (7 December 2000), 6.

[323] ITLOS/PV.00/6/Rev.1 (7 December 2000), 26.

[324] Rapport des Activités des Membres: France, 2000–2001, 3, www.ccamlr.org/pu/e/e_pubs/ma/00–01/France.pdf.

[325] ITLOS/PV.00/6/Rev.1 (7 December 2000), 6.

[326] ITLOS/PV.00/2/Rev.1 (27 January 2000), 19.

[327] ITLOS/PV.00/8/Rev.1 (8 December 2000), 12.

was boarded on 28 September 1999 by the French surveillance frigate *Floréal* 160 n.m. *within* the Crozet Islands' EEZ.[328] France alleged that the *Camouco* concealed its name and registration marks, and jettisoned documents and fresh-caught toothfish before being boarded;[329] the vessel had 6 tonnes of frozen toothfish in the hold.[330] The inference would seem strong that the *Camouco* had been fishing for toothfish within the French EEZ and that its crew knew that it was doing so illegally. The applicant contended, however, that the toothfish aboard were caught just outside the French EEZ. Judge Anderson noted that, if accepted, this contention would only raise new questions, as the fish would clearly then have been taken within the CCAMLR area.[331] While Panama is not a CCAMLR party, it joined UNCLOS in 1996, and duties of co-operation with CCAMLR and negotiation with France would arise under UNCLOS Articles 63(2) and 64. The point is discussed further below.

In the *Grand Prince* case Belize attempted to bring prompt release proceedings regarding a vessel already forfeited to France in a successful national prosecution for fishing in the Kerguelen Islands' EEZ only 95 miles from shore.[332] The French account of its capture strongly indicated IUU fishing activity: a longline had been cut during a helicopter overflight; the factory 'had very recently been used'; there were lines prepared with bait; there were 18 tonnes of toothfish aboard; and twenty-nine freshly caught toothfish were also found aboard.[333] While some of the catch might have been taken outside the EEZ, there could be little question that the vessel was captured in the act of illegal fishing.

On 23 January 2001 a French criminal court 'ordered the confiscation of the vessel', declaring its order 'immediately enforceable notwithstanding … [any] appeal'.[334] France argued before ITLOS that the prompt-release proceedings were thus without object, the vessel in question being already the property of the French state. If such arguments were accepted by ITLOS, coastal states could obviously seek timely forfeiture proceedings to prevent the release of IUU vessels through ITLOS procedures. This issue was not ultimately addressed by the Tribunal. Judge Anderson noted, however, that in prompt-release cases the Tribunal is obliged not to 'prejudice to the merits of any case before the

---

[328] *Camouco*, 672, paras. 25–28.
[329] ITLOS/PV.00/2/Rev.1 (27 January 2000), 4; *Camouco*, 672, para. 29.
[330] *Ibid.*   [331] *Camouco*, Judge Anderson (Dissenting Opinion), 692.
[332] *Grand Prince*, para. 39. The original refers to 'miles', not 'nautical miles'. This may be an error.
[333] *Ibid.*   [334] *Ibid.*, para. 50.

appropriate domestic forum, and the release of a vessel declared forfeit could severely prejudice 'enforcement of the court's order' as the vessel would likely 'flee the ... jurisdiction ... and never return'.[335] Judge Laing expressed an equally forceful contrary view that

confiscation of a [foreign] vessel ..., even if valid according to national law, cannot, *per se*, be accepted by an international adjudicatory body if ... it would exclude the jurisdiction of that body.[336]

Ultimately, Belize's case failed for want of jurisdiction on other grounds.[337] There is a clear policy tension, however, between effective prosecution of IUU fishing and the possibility of using prompt-release proceedings to enable a vessel to escape prosecution.[338] The same issue has been agitated in later cases. In the *Juno Trader* the Tribunal rejected the respondent's contention that the applicant lacked standing as it found, on the facts, that 'whatever may be the effect of a definitive change in the ownership of a vessel upon its nationality, ... there is no legal basis in ... this case for holding that there has been a definitive change in the nationality' seemingly because the Belizean confiscation order was subject to appeal and could not be treated as final.[339] This result would appear to preclude any future argument that Australian legislation resulting in the mere *deemed* forfeiture (subject to an action for recovery) of IUU vessels would bar the Tribunal's jurisdiction.[340] Also, this result would appear to be confirmed by the reasoning of the Tribunal in *Tomimaru*, which emphasised that 'a decision to confiscate a vessel does not prevent the Tribunal from considering an application for prompt release of such vessel *while proceedings are still before the domestic courts* of the detaining state'.[341] Indeed, the Tribunal went so far as to say,

---

[335] *Grand Prince*, Judge Anderson (Separate Opinion); cf. V. Bantz, 'Views from Hamburg: the *Juno Trader* case or how to make sense of the coastal state's rights in the light of its duty of prompt release' (2005) 24 UQLJ 415, 424. Similar views are expressed in the Separate Opinion of Judge Jesus in the *Tomimaru* case, see n. 341 below.

[336] *Grand Prince*, Judge Laing (Separate Opinion), para. 10.

[337] See Lowe and Churchill, 'International Tribunal for the Law of the Sea', 473–6; Treves, 'Flags of convenience'.

[338] Bantz, 'Views from Hamburg', 428. See the French concerns in *Monte Counfurco* of 'systematic' use of Article 292 by private interests implicated in IUU fishing: ITLOS/PV.00/6/Rev.1 (7 December 2000), 5–6, 12; ITLOS/PV.00/8/Rev.1 (8 December 2000), 4.

[339] ITLOS Case No.13, 18 December 2004, para. 63. See Bantz, 'Views from Hamburg', 425.

[340] Australia did not make this argument in the *Volga* case. See ITLOS/PV.02/04 (13 December 2002), 16.

[341] *Tomimaru Case (Japan v. Russian Federation)*, ITLOS Case No. 15, 6 August 2007, para. 78, www.itlos.org (emphasis added).

A decision to confiscate eliminates the provisional character of the detention of the vessel rendering the procedure for its prompt release without object. Such a decision should not be taken in such a way as to prevent the shipowner from having recourse to available domestic judicial remedies, or as to prevent the flag state from resorting to the prompt release procedure set forth in the Convention; nor should it be taken through proceedings inconsistent with international standards of due process of law. In particular, a confiscation decided in unjustified haste would jeopardize the operation of article 292 of the Convention.[342]

This might be taken as suggesting that the Tribunal has a further power to consider whether domestic forfeiture proceedings constitute an abuse of right or are inconsistent with international standards.[343] It may also be taken, on a slightly more strained reading, as 'imply[ing] that coastal states should not confiscate a fishing vessel immediately after its arrest or detention, so as to give time for the flag state to apply for its release upon the posting of a bond'.[344] Not all judges of the Tribunal, however, would appear to support such approaches.[345]

In the result, it appears that only finalised forfeiture proceedings may bar ITLOS's jurisdiction in prompt-release proceedings. Even then the Tribunal might in limited circumstances be prepared to review proceedings for consistency with (as yet undefined) international standards of due process.[346]

5.5.7 Conclusion

In cases where a vessel's flag state is bound by the FSA and the vessel engages in IUU high seas fishing in the CCAMLR area and later passes into a coastal state's EEZ, the coastal state may assert jurisdiction over both EEZ and high-seas offences under FSA Article 21(14). It seems curious, therefore, that no express reliance has been placed on this provision in French and Australian interdictions of vessels flagged by an FSA party, especially the Russian Federation, where it may have been ambiguous whether IUU activity occurred within the EEZ or the CCAMLR area or most likely both. The reason may be that the entirety of Article 21 applies in such situations. As noted above, this would

---

[342] *Ibid.*, para. 76.   [343] *Ibid.*, per Judge Nelson (Declaration), 2.

[344] *Ibid.*, Judge Jesus (Separate Opinion), para. 8.

[345] *Ibid.*; see the opinions of Judges Nelson and Jesus, referred to above.

[346] If a confiscating state wishes to avoid such review, it can simply 'litigate … the amount of the bond' and not claim forfeiture bars proceedings: B. Oxman, 'The "*Tomimaru*" (Japan v. Russian Federation)' (2008) 102 AJIL 316, 322.

necessarily include the flag state's right to insist on the vessel being released into its custody under Article 21(12), thus perhaps undermining the usefulness of Article 21(14) in extending national jurisdiction. This provision may, nonetheless, partially explain the absence of protest within the CCAMLR Commission regarding French and Australian enforcement practice from those affected states which are parties to both the CCAMLR and the FSA, being Argentina, Russia and Uruguay.

Of the other principal flags involved in IUU fishing for Patagonian toothfish between 1997 and 2005, Chile is a party to the CCAMLR but not the FSA, Panama is a party to neither the CCAMLR nor the FSA, and Belize became a party to the FSA as of 14 July 2005 but is not a CCAMLR party. Belize, under the FSA, is now bound not to license its vessels to fish in the CCAMLR management area and must, as discussed above, permit boarding and inspection.[347] In the broader CCAMLR area the principal flags associated with IUU fishing as at 2008 were China (a CCAMLR member), Togo, Equatorial Guinea, North Korea, Cambodia, Sierra Leone and the Marshall Islands.[348] The position of Togo and Equatorial Guinea has been noted above. Of the rest only the Marshall Islands is a party to the FSA. A number of the listed vessels had been reflagged from the registries of Belize, Uruguay and Georgia.

This, however, leaves open the questions raised by Judge Anderson in the *Camouco* case regarding the UNCLOS obligations of a non-RFMO member and non-FSA party towards RFMO management measures. Under UNCLOS Article 63, states fishing for a stock straddling the boundary of an EEZ 'shall seek, either directly' or through 'appropriate' RFMOs to agree upon 'necessary' conservation and management measures.[349] Failure to open negotiations either with the coastal state or the relevant RFMO would clearly breach this duty, but what course of action would be open to RFMO members in respect of such a refusal to negotiate? Recourse to compulsory dispute resolution, including seeking interim measures from ITLOS, might be available. While compulsory dispute resolution is generally beyond the scope of this book, the *Southern Bluefin Tuna* cases (SBT cases) should briefly be mentioned insofar as parties might seek ITLOS interim measures to prevent IUU fishing pending a negotiated or arbitrated outcome.[350]

---

[347] FSA, Article 17(1) and (2).

[348] CCAMLR IUU vessel list as of 14 August 2008, www.ccamlr.org.

[349] Of the flag states appearing on the consolidated 2003–7 CCAMLR IUU vessel list, only North Korea is not an UNCLOS party.

[350] (*New Zealand and Australia v. Japan*) (1999) 38 ILM 1624.

The SBT cases arose in the context of alleged breaches of UNCLOS Articles 64 and 116–119 and might thus be expected to provide some guidance in cases turning on Articles 63, 117 and 118. In the SBT cases ITLOS was prepared to order provisional measures pending a negotiated settlement which included setting total allowable catches (TACs) for Australia, New Zealand and Japan and requiring Japan to cease unilateral experimental fishing. However, in the SBT cases the parties had reached agreement on TACs some years before within the Commission on southern bluefin tuna. The Tribunal's interim measures consisted of maintaining the status quo pending further negotiations. It would be a different matter to impose TACs on a non-party to a RFMO pending dispute resolution over IUU fishing on the high seas.

5.6 The South East Atlantic Fisheries Organization

The South East Atlantic Fisheries Organization (SEAFO) was established under the Convention on the Conservation and Management of Fishery Resources in the South East Atlantic Ocean 2001 (SEAFO Convention),[351] the first RFMO treaty concluded after the FSA opened for signature. The FSA forms a vital backdrop to the SEAFO Convention, but equally the SEAFO Convention is an illustration of how the FSA text has been adapted to meet regional conditions.[352] Principal coastal states involved in negotiating the Convention were Angola, Namibia, South Africa and the United Kingdom (in respect of St Helena and its dependencies of Tristan da Cunha and Ascension Island).[353] Distant-water-fishing states were also represented, including the European Community, Japan, Norway, the Russian Federation and the United States from the outset, and Ukraine, Iceland, Poland and South Korea later.[354] Despite this, SEAFO membership remains small. The Convention entered into force in 2003 following ratification by Namibia, Norway and the European Community. Angola has since joined.[355] South Africa has expressed interest in membership, but was not a party as at August 2008.[356] Japan has indicated its willingness to

---

[351] (2002) 41 ILM 257 (SEAFO Convention).
[352] Jackson, 'Convention on the Conservation and Management of Fishery Resources', 48.
[353] *Ibid.*, 41.   [354] *Ibid.*, 33–4.
[355] See the Commission website: www.seafo.org/About%20Seafo/membership.htm.
[356] SEAFO, Report of the 2nd Annual Meeting of the Commission, 2005 (SEAFO Report 2005), 22, and SEAFO, Report of the 4th Annual Meeting of the Commission, 2007 (SEAFO Report 2007), 3, www.seafo.org.

co-operate with SEAFO by implementing the Commission's adopted measures, but its continued fishing presence in the SEAFO area as a non-party is of concern to the Commission.[357]

The management area is, broadly speaking, a vast rectangle of ocean west of the African continent commencing 'at the outer limit of waters under national jurisdiction'.[358] The SEAFO Convention alone applies both to straddling fish stocks and discrete stocks occurring only within the high-seas area covered. While the former are covered by the FSA, the latter are covered only by the general duty of co-operation under UNCLOS Article 117.[359] Highly migratory fish stocks were excluded from SEAFO's purview to avoid any conflict with ICCAT, given the overlap in their management areas.[360] Key stocks covered by the SEAFO Convention include 'orange roughy, alfonsino, sharks, swordfish, armourhead, deep sea red crab, [and] Patagonian toothfish'.[361]

The Convention's provisions on flag-state responsibility draw heavily on FSA Articles 18 and 19.[362] Requirements include flag-state authorisation to conduct fishing in the management area, 'reporting of vessel position and catch [including by VMS]', transhipment controls, and a scheme for on-board observers.[363]

Of more interest for present purposes is the difficulty encountered in negotiating a SEAFO boarding and inspection regime for inclusion in the Convention, resulting in the issue being left for determination by a Compliance Committee within the Commission.[364] A key issue in negotiations was whether to allow non-flag-state boarding and inspection as envisaged by FSA Article 21, or whether SEAFO should adopt an 'alternative mechanism' under Article 21(15).[365] SEAFO has yet to establish a compliance committee but has adopted a series of interim compliance measures including

---

[357] SEAFO Report 2005, 4; SEAFO Report 2007, 3–4 and 5–6.

[358] Jackson, 'Convention on the Conservation and Management of Fishery Resources', 36 and n. 7; SEAFO Convention, Article 4; the map on SEAFO's website wrongly includes EEZs around several islands, such as Ascension Island: www.seafo.org/About%20Seafo/map.jpg.

[359] Jackson, 'Convention on the Conservation and Management of Fishery Resources', 38 and 47.

[360] *Ibid.*, 38.   [361] SEAFO Report 2005, 4.   [362] See Chapter 6, section 3.2.

[363] Jackson, 'Convention on the Conservation and Management of Fishery Resources', 43; SEAFO Convention, Article 14.

[364] SEAFO Convention, Article 16.

[365] Jackson, 'Convention on the Conservation and Management of Fishery Resources', 43–4.

- compulsory VMS and scientific observer requirements,[366]
- establishing a positive list of authorised vessels (and requirements that members take certain regulatory steps regarding such vessels),[367]
- rules on transhipment of catch,[368] and
- establishing a system of IUU vessel lists and member-state measures similar to the NEAFC and NAFO NCP schemes.[369]

Given that three of the four existing SEAFO members (Namibia, Norway and the European Community) have ratified the FSA, the default FSA rules on boarding and inspection must be taken to apply as between them as more than two years have passed without SEAFO adopting its own measures. There should thus be no legal obstacle to reciprocal boarding to ensure compliance with the Commission's VMS and scientific observer requirements, transhipment prohibitions and other measures. The point appears to have gone unconsidered at the SEAFO annual meetings, and no such practice has been reported. At the 2007 meeting the SEAFO Commission concluded that 'the time is not yet ripe to implement' a 'full-fledged' monitoring and compliance system including at-sea boarding and inspection.[370] It preferred, perhaps understandably given limited participation and resources, to focus on port-state measures.[371]

5.7 The Western and Central Pacific Fisheries Commission

The Western and Central Pacific Fisheries Commission (WCPFC) is the first RFMO established after the entry into force of the FSA, and could thus be expected to provide a case study of the practical effect of the FSA default boarding and inspection rules. Its constitutive instrument, the Convention on the Conservation of Highly Migratory Fish Stocks in the Western and Central Pacific Ocean 2000 (WCPF Convention),[372] expressly provides for the coming into force (for *all* parties) of the measures in FSA Articles 21 and 22 within two years if the WCPFC has

---

[366] Conservation Measure 07/06 Relating to Interim Measures to Amend the Interim Arrangement of the SEAFO Convention, paras. 15, 22–24, www.seafo.org.

[367] *Ibid.*, para. 3.

[368] Conservation Measure 03/06 On an Interim Prohibition of Transshipments-At-Sea in the SEAFO Convention Area and to Regulate Transshipments in Port.

[369] Conservation Measure 08/06 Establishing a List of Vessels Presumed to have Carried Out Illegal, Unreported and Unregulated (IUU) Fishing Activities. Indeed, SEAFO now includes all vessels listed as IUU vessels by CCAMLR, NAFO and NEAFC on its own IUU lists: see SEAFO Report 2007, 5.

[370] SEAFO Report 2007, 6.   [371] *Ibid.*, 6 and Annex 9.   [372] [2004] ATS 15.

not adopted boarding and inspection measures of its own.[373] As noted above, the FSA itself makes no provision for such essential operational matters as how inspectors would hail the vessel, what credentials they would present, what information they would record, and who would be the competent flag-state authority to notify of the boarding and of any infringements discovered. The WCPF Convention provides no such further detail, merely requiring in Article 6(2) that the master and crew of a party's vessel

shall immediately comply with every instruction and direction given by an authorized and identified [inspection] officer of a member of the Commission, including to stop, to move to a safe location, and to facilitate safe boarding and inspection …

Unsurprisingly, there was disagreement among the parties at the WCPFC Technical and Compliance Committee's first meeting as to whether these provisions could be implemented without further operational agreements. The issue of formulating more precise boarding procedures was referred to a working group in 2005[374] on the understanding among parties that FSA Articles 21 and 22 would not be applied in the interim.[375]

While it might be tempting to attribute this delay to members with a history of opposing non-flag boarding measures (such as Japan),[376] the reasons were essentially practical. The Commission secretariat identified as outstanding issues among WCPFC members before boardings and inspections could commence matters including

- whether only state members of the Commission – or also 'regional integration organizations' and 'fishing entities' with Commission membership – would be entitled to conduct boardings (a gloss on the prospect of a Taiwanese vessel boarding and inspecting a Chinese vessel);
- whether inspectors would be entitled to board only upon reasonable suspicion of contraventions (as in the NPAFC), or whenever they encounter a Commission member's vessel in the commission area;

---

[373] *Ibid.*, Article 26(2).
[374] WCPFC, Report of the First Meeting of the Technical and Compliance Committee, 5–9 December 2005 (TCC Report 2005), www.wcpfc.int/tcc1/index.htm#Report, 9, at paras. 38–39.
[375] Personal communication: Dr John Kalish, Department of Agriculture, Fisheries and Forestry (Australia), 11 January 2006.
[376] Rayfuse, *Non-Flag State Enforcement*, pp. 136, 189, 304–5, 307–8, 339, 341.

- how to assign responsibility for boardings and inspections which are either improperly conducted or which result 'in unreasonable delays'; and
- the 'degree of force that may be used'.[377]

The working group came back with an inspection scheme in 2006, which was adopted without amendment by the Commission. The scheme which was finally adopted replicated, almost verbatim, the NEAFC Scheme on boarding and inspection[378] and the language of FSA Articles 21(18) and 22(1)(f) on state responsibility and the use of force.[379] While the WCPFC Scheme only appears to contemplate contracting Parties conducting inspections, the Scheme 'shall also apply in [its] entirety as between a Contracting Party and a Fishing Entity, subject to a notification to that effect to the Commission from the Contracting Party concerned'.[380] Thus fishing entities will only be allowed to inspect the vessels of consenting states.

If such wrangling is to be the common experience among newly established RFMOs, it would seem that Articles 21 and 22 promise much and deliver little, other than prompting parties to consider adopting tailored enforcement schemes. Issues relating to the use of force by fisheries inspectors are taken up again in Chapter 10, where the WCPFC Scheme is considered in more detail.

6 Countermeasures and custom: a general international law of fisheries interdiction?

Rayfuse has made several provocative arguments suggesting that a general international law of fisheries enforcement may be possible. First, she has proposed that there may be a general international law

---

[377] Boarding and Inspection Procedures (Secretariat Paper), 10 November 2005, WCPFC/TCC1/15 (Rev.1), www.wcpfc.int/tcc1/pdf/WCPFC-TCC1-15.pdf.

[378] See Draft Boarding and Inspection Procedures, Articles 17–26, WCPFC Doc. TCC2-2006/Attachment K; WCPFC, Summary Report of the Second Meeting of the Technical and Compliance Committee, 28 September–3 October 2006, 14, www.wcpfc.int/tcc2/index.htm; WCPFC, Summary Report: Third Regular Session of the Commission for the Conservation and Management of Highly Migratory Fish Stocks in the Western and Central Pacific Ocean, 11–15 December 2006, para. 156 and Annex O (WCPFC Report 2006), www.wcpfc.int/wcpfc3/index.htm.

[379] WCPFC Boarding and Inspection Procedures, Conservation and Management Measure 2006–08, Articles 28 and 45, (See WCPFC Report 2006, Annexe O). See also discussion in Chapter 6, section 3.2 and at Chapter 10, section 3.

[380] *Ibid.*, Article 6

obligation to *grant consent* to boarding and inspection by a non-flag-state vessel in an RFMO context. This formulation appears to reflect the difficulty of demonstrating a customary right of boarding and inspection per se. Second, she makes the subsidiary argument that refusing such consent may constitute a breach of an international obligation allowing countermeasures to be taken. This second argument is further extended by the claim that boarding and inspection could then be undertaken *as a countermeasure*. Third, Rayfuse suggests, in the alternative, that RFMO members could use the law of countermeasures to justify boarding the fishing vessels of RFMO parties – and even perhaps non-parties – where they are acting contrary to RFMO measures. These arguments shall be addressed in order.

6.1 A general international law right of boarding or duty to permit it

Rayfuse's argument under this head runs as follows. First, as many RFMOs have adopted consensual boarding regimes they acknowledge a duty to adopt such schemes.[381] Second, implicit in this duty to adopt is a duty to consent to such boardings.[382] Third, states are, however, *free not to implement* boarding schemes according to 'the nature of the fishery involved, the practical suitability of at sea boarding and inspection as an effective compliance and enforcement mechanism … and the existence of suitable and equally effective alternatives'.[383]

On the first limb of the argument, setting aside controversies about *opinio juris*, it is possible in certain cases to deduce the existence of general rules of international law from a plurality of treaties, subordinate instruments and declarations of principles cast in similar terms. The prohibition on racial discrimination is an obvious example.[384] However, Rayfuse is unable to contend that there is a general international law of boarding and inspection due to the myriad RFMO boarding and inspection schemes actually adopted. The argument can only be that there is an obligation to adopt such schemes irrespective of their precise content. The second step in the argument is less controversial. There is no doubt a duty to implement international obligations in good faith.[385] Being party to a boarding scheme prima facie requires a state to allow boardings in accordance with its terms. The purported

---

[381] Rayfuse, *Non-Flag State Enforcement*, p. 344.   [382] *Ibid.*   [383] *Ibid.*

[384] See, e.g., *European Roma Rights Centre v. Immigration Officer at Prague Airport* [2005] 1 All ER 527 at 559–60, per Lord Steyn.

[385] *Nuclear Tests Cases*, [1974] ICJ Rep. 457 at 473; *Border and Transborder Armed Actions Case*, [1988] ICJ Rep. 69 at 105.

rule has to be qualified, in the third step, by a sweeping exception that where 'appropriate' states might choose not to implement the schemes they are obliged to adopt. This concession is necessary to accommodate the tuna RFMOs which almost universally lack boarding regimes.[386] The practical non-existence of boarding regimes in tuna fisheries, however, has little to do with effective alternatives. Put simply, most tuna RFMO measures do not require boarding to verify compliance. Where RFMO measures consist of closed fishing areas or national TACs, boarding individual vessels is irrelevant in assessing compliance.[387] Port-state measures or at-sea observations will be sufficient. Perhaps such fisheries are not 'specially affected' by the purported rule and their practice is not an exception, but simply irrelevant. Nonetheless, the proposed rule remains tenuous: an abstract duty to adopt a set of rules on a particular subject which have no identifiable minimum content.

Further, in her own survey of state practice, Rayfuse finds that 'many members of RFMOs, in particular the distant water fishing nations, are not parties to the FSA and have objected to its non-flag boarding and inspection provisions' being integrated into RFMO measures.[388] There is thus little indication that RFMO members generally accept the existence of any universal obligation to adopt at-sea boarding measures.[389] It is a conclusion that goes against the weight of the evidence, and that is reached on the basis of inferring *opinio juris* from acts alone.[390]

6.2 A general international law obligation to co-operate with RFMOs

As regards non-members, Rayfuse finds that 'state practice indicates both the assertion and the acceptance of a customary duty to co-operate through the medium of RFMOs', thus effectively elevating FSA Article 8 to general international law.[391]

---

[386] Rayfuse, *Non-Flag State Enforcement*, p. 343. As noted above, the ICCAT Scheme 1975 came into force in 2007.

[387] Personal communication: discussion with Deirdre Warner-Kramer, Senior Atlantic Fisheries Officer, and Holly Koehler, Foreign Affairs Officer, US Department of State, Washington DC, 3 April 2006.

[388] Rayfuse, *Non-Flag State Enforcement*, p. 341.

[389] Rayfuse raises the argument that some dissenters may be 'persistent objectors', *ibid.*, p. 136.

[390] *North Sea Continental Shelf Cases*, [1969] ICJ Rep. 3 at 44, but see 246–7, per Judge Sørensen quoting H. Lauterpacht, *The Development of International Law by the International Court* (London: Stevens, 1958), p. 380; cf. Brownlie, pp. 8–9.

[391] R. Rayfuse, 'Countermeasures and high seas fisheries enforcement' (2004) 51 NILR 41, 55 and 59.

RFOs have authorized ... 'courtesy boardings' and boardings and arrests of stateless vessels and, in some cases, have even exercised powers of arrest and detention against non-member vessels. Importantly, non-members have acquiesced in these assertions of jurisdiction by, *inter alia*, applying to become members or cooperating non-parties, by not objecting to transhipment bans, by agreeing to implement catch documentation schemes, by providing lists of vessel names and information on fishing activities and by agreeing to non-flag boarding and inspection and, in some cases, prosecution.[392]

The use of the term 'acquiescence' in this context may be misleading. There are certainly cases where states which are non-parties to RFMOs have *consented* to RFMO boardings, but there are no identifiable cases where states have acquiesced in the unilateral assertion of inspection rights by RFMO members *after the event*, unless one (controversially) counts isolated instances of master's consent such as the *Chun Jin No 1*.[393] Stronger evidence of such acquiescence might be thought to be found in the incidents in which Japan and Russia appear to have boarded vessels within their territorial sea or EEZ suspected of engaging in activities undermining the NEAF Convention on the high seas. However, in the cases of *Zhong Xin 37* and *Rong Shen 828* it is not entirely clear as to whether the vessels involved were in fact arrested for illegal fishing within the Russian EEZ.[394] Reports are either ambiguous or contradictory. It is also not clear on what legal basis Japan boarded the *Nanao 5508*, but it notably left enforcement action to the flag state, China.[395] This suggests it may have been a courtesy or master's consent boarding. These instances are thus of little assistance.

While broader state practice by non-RFMO members may show a willingness to co-operate with RFMOs, there is little evidence that this co-operation results from a sense of legal obligation. Indeed, much of the co-operation in economic or regulatory matters (catch documentation, transhipment prohibitions, etc.) simply demonstrates the effectiveness of trade measures taken against non-parties under RFMO management schemes. For example, the impact on Belize of having its vessels on NEAFC negative lists led to its subsequent application to become a co-operating non-party (a principal advantage of which is that its vessels are no longer automatically considered as potential IUU vessels).[396]

---

[392] *Ibid.*, 58–9 (footnotes omitted).
[393] Lacking any current registration, it may have been a stateless vessel in any event; though see n. 126 above.
[394] See the discussion above at n. 115 and n. 134.
[395] See above at n. 117.   [396] See Chapter 6, section 5.3.2.

On non-RFMO members consenting to RFMO boarding and inspection, Rayfuse cites the numerous instances of China's co-operation with the NPAFC prior to the conclusion of its ship-rider MOU with the United States.[397] However, this is more readily attributed to Chinese support for the General Assembly's pelagic driftnet-fishing ban than any wider customary rule. Rayfuse herself noted that consent to (once frequent) NAFO courtesy boardings 'essentially dried up' once it was realised that the information gained was being used diplomatically to pressure flag states to discipline IUU vessels.[398] One should also consider the state practice in NEAFC, where a majority of non-party vessels *refused* requests for courtesy boardings.[399] Evidence that non-RFMO parties feel obliged to give effect to their duty to co-operate with RFMOs by permitting boarding and inspection is thus scant and the argument that they must do so is unconvincing.

6.3 Countermeasures

Rayfuse also argues that states are obliged – in general and as a result of UNCLOS Article 117 – to co-operate with RFMOs. If their lack of co-operation undermines the effectiveness of RFMO measures, she concludes that the law of countermeasures may then justify non-consensual boarding and inspection. Assessing this argument requires a brief review of the law of countermeasures.

Under limited circumstances states may unilaterally take action to secure their rights under international law. The principal form of such self-help is taking countermeasures:[400] the suspension of the performance of an international obligation by an injured state in order to induce a wrongdoing state to resume compliance with their obligations.[401] That is, state A is considered 'injured' and is entitled to take peaceful countermeasures against state B if state B breaches an obligation owed to it.[402] A is also 'injured' if it is 'specifically affected' by B's breach of an obligation owed to a group of which A is a part,

---

[397] Rayfuse, 'Countermeasures and high seas fisheries enforcement', 58 n. 112 and 59 n. 118.

[398] Rayfuse, *Non-Flag State Enforcement*, p. 251.   [399] See Chapter 6, section 5.3.

[400] D. Bederman, 'Counterintuiting countermeasures' (2002) 96 AJIL 817 at 818; E. Cannizzaro, 'The role of proportionality in the law of international countermeasures' (2001) 12 EJIL 889 at 890; [2001] II(2) YBILC, 128–9.

[401] ILC Articles on State Responsibility, Article 49; see commentary in [2001] II(2) YBILC, 128–31.

[402] ILC Articles on State Responsibility, Article 42; commentary in [2001] II(2) YBILC, 117 at (2).

or if B's breach radically affects the position of all members of the group with respect to the obligation's continued performance.[403] This concept of a 'specifically affected' state thus contemplates that a state may, in some circumstances, take unilateral action in the collective interest.

Might there, however, be a wider rule of general international law allowing a state to take countermeasures to protect a collective interest irrespective of whether it has suffered a specific injury? The ILC Articles on State Responsibility only expressly contemplate a non-injured state demanding cessation of the breach of obligation and reparation to those injured.[404] The Articles are, however, without prejudice to the question of what measures a state, other than an injured state, might take in respect of an obligation 'owed to a group of states including that state, ... established for the protection of a collective interest of the group'.[405] Thus the Articles do not (and do not purport to) address the issue of 'collective interest' countermeasures.[406] The ILC commentary, after reviewing the 'embryonic' and 'controversial' relevant state practice,[407] concludes that

the current state of international law on countermeasures taken in the general or collective interest is uncertain. State practice is sparse and involves a limited number of States. At present there appears to be no clearly recognized entitlement of states ... [other than an injured state] to take countermeasures in the collective interest.[408]

It is certainly possible to view the ILC's assessment of state practice as 'over-cautious' and to conclude that 'at least in the case of *systematic or large-scale* breaches of international law, ... a settled practice [exists] of countermeasures by states not individually injured'.[409] However, the relevant practice is almost exclusively limited to trade or economic measures taken in response to widespread human rights abuses or territorial invasions.[410] Rayfuse's argument for interdiction

---

[403] ILC Articles on State Responsibility, Article 42; cf. E. Weiss, 'Invoking state responsibility in the twenty-first century' (2002) 96 AJIL 798 at 802 ff.

[404] ILC Articles on State Responsibility, Article 48.

[405] *Ibid.*, Articles 54 and 48.

[406] [2001] II(2) YBILC, 129 at (8); Rayfuse, 'Countermeasures and high seas fisheries enforcement', 49.

[407] [2001] II(2) YBILC, 129 at (8).   [408] *Ibid.*, 139 at (6).

[409] Christian J. Tams, *Enforcing Obligations* Erga Omnes *in International Law* (Cambridge University Press, 2005), p. 231 (emphasis added).

[410] [2001] II(2) YBILC, 138–9; Tams, *Enforcing Obligations*, 209–28.

as a countermeasure regarding collective interest obligations thus faces two problems. First, if there is currently a rule or practice permitting collective interest countermeasures it appears limited to 'systematic or large-scale' cases of fundamental legal obligations concerning human rights abuses or acts of aggression.[411] It is not clear that overfishing ranks with such breaches. Second, the counter-measures taken in such collective-interest cases have never extended beyond economic measures to more muscular enforcement action.[412] On present state practice, the argument appears constrained to being one about what the law might become, not what it presently is. Those proposing that countermeasures may currently be taken in the col-lective *environmental* interest are thus still required to demonstrate that any state taking such action would be entitled to do so as an injured state.

Turning to high-seas fisheries, the general obligation upon states to co-operate or take measures 'for the conservation of the living resources of the high seas' under Article 117 of UNCLOS is an obliga-tion so diffuse that it is difficult to see how one individual state is directly injured by another state's individual (or even repeated) breach of it. Indeed, there is significant scope for disagreement as to what might constitute a 'breach' of an obligation to co-operate in the first place. It is also hard to conceive how one state could radically change the position of all others regarding continued high-seas conservation efforts, absent a single state by its efforts alone fishing a particular stock almost to extinction.

In the context of *inter partes* enforcement of RFMO measures, breaches might be easier to judge, but again specific injury to an individual state in respect of a communal resource may be difficult to demonstrate. Rayfuse argues

> each member state [of an RFMO] incurs expenses related to the running of the organization and accepts the restriction of its own nationals' high seas fisher-ies activities ... Where restrictions are not complied with by a state which is under a duty to cooperate ... then each member which has complied will be specifically affected ... [and] one, or all, ... [RFMO members] would be entitled to resort to countermeasures.[413]

---

[411] *Ibid.* The ILC commentary cites eight such episodes, Tams cites thirteen.
[412] On non-consensual interdiction as a prohibited use of force, see Chapter 10.
[413] Rayfuse, 'Countermeasures and high seas fisheries enforcement', 64.

This argument could even be said to apply to RFMO non-members on the basis that the Article 117 duty of co-operation in conservation efforts has been 'further delineated' by Article 8 of the FSA to expressly require that state parties co-operate with, through, or by becoming members of, RFMOs.[414] Even if one accepts the difficult argument that FSA Article 8 represents customary law, there is a clear problem with conflating the non-members' general duty to co-operate with RFMOs with the specific obligations upon RFMO members to implement agreed conservation measures. A duty to co-operate with an organisation is not the same as a duty to comply with its rules (see section 3.1, above).

The more significant problem with this approach is that it confuses loss of an opportunity and actionable injury. The fact that RFMO members have made sacrifices for the general interest and have an interest in the effective operation of an RFMO does not mean that they are injured as RFMO members or FSA parties by a non-member's conduct which undermines that RFMO's effectiveness. RFMO member states do not have proprietary rights to the fish in the high-seas management area and cannot acquire ownership through their altruistic self-restraint. The only right RFMO members have upon the high seas is the same right all other states enjoy: the right to fish. Non-party fishing in an RFMO area, even fishing in contravention of RFMO measures, is not stealing from those RFMO members who abide by the rules. Such unregulated fishing does not affect their right to fish, only the potential profitability of those fishing efforts. This compels the conclusion that RFMO members are not 'injured' or 'specifically affected' in the sense required to invoke countermeasures by non-compliant or non-party fishing in RFMO management areas. This argument might be subject to one exception. Where a 'straddling stock', or single biomass, of fish is fished partially on the high seas and partially within a coastal state's EEZ it may be that a coastal state could be considered specifically injured if, by analogy with high-seas pollution, unregulated or delinquent fishing of the high-seas portion of the stock was such that conservation of the stock required the coastal state to close its EEZ fishery entirely.[415] This appears to be the only case where international law might acknowledge that a lost opportunity to fish amounts to a state

---

being specifically affected, and then seemingly because of the close connection with a state's *exclusive* rights.

6.4 Conclusions on unilateral enforcement

As a matter of policy, a truly effective fisheries law should be enforceable. A general right permitting unilateral interdiction of suspected IUU vessels may well be a laudable aim for the law's future development. However, present state practice supports no such rule. Attempting to achieve the same ends by invoking countermeasures is difficult, given present practice regarding general interest countermeasures.

Further, RFMO memberships have proved themselves far from toothless in their ability to induce compliance by other, principally economic and regulatory, means.[416] Unilateral enforcement puts this effectiveness at risk. Where there exists a standing management body it seems incongruous to allow individual members to take unilateral measures against other members (at least without express agreement in advance) or against 'outsiders' (at least without the RFMO's consent).[417] Unilateral action in the common interest is more readily justified where there is *no* pre-existing forum for collective action. Further, unilateral action by one member against another may undermine the RFMO's credibility and increase the incentives for the targeted member to leave an RFMO and enjoy the benefits of being subject only to very general duties to co-operate.

7 General conclusions

On the present state of RFMO law and practice there is no general international law of boarding and inspection applicable to all high-seas fisheries. The minimum rules in FSA Articles 21 and 22 have not proved operationally capable of implementation without further agreement on significant practical details. Arguments that any perceived deficiency in the enforcement machinery available to RFMOs could be supplied by the law of countermeasures also face fatal obstacles.

The lack of uniform rules or even widespread support for interdiction as the cornerstone of fisheries enforcement has several explanations. Some fisheries, notably the great majority of 'tuna RFMOs', are governed by measures where interdiction is not an effective or necessary tool to

---

[416] See Chapter 6, section 4.
[417] Cf. Cannizzaro, 'The role of proportionality', 913–14.

assess compliance. Port states have implemented controls precluding the unloading and transhipment of fishing catches by vessels or flag states known to be fishing in a manner undermining RFMO measures, and such actions have often proved effective.[418] Further, interdiction may not be an effective compliance mechanism in every high-seas fishery. Some RFMOs have noted the difficulty of patrolling vast high-seas management areas.[419] Even where suspect vessels are discovered through aerial surveillance their remote location may make surface investigation (let alone interdiction) impossible.[420]

The fisheries experience is not, however, irrelevant to the present project. It demonstrates that in a multilateral setting there may be significant obstacles to reaching agreement on the minimum procedures necessary to implement an interdiction regime. Experience has shown that there may be difficulty reaching agreement on issues including the call signs and hails to be used to initiate boarding, communication with flag states and the designation of points of contact, the form of credentials to be presented by inspectors, whether boardings may be conducted as of right or only upon reasonable suspicion of violations and the powers and immunities of inspectors, especially as regards the use of force. State responsibility for wrongful boarding, or boarding occasioning undue interference with fishing operations, has also been a recurrent concern. Such issues are further examined in Chapters 10–12.

---

[418] See Chapter 6, section 4.
[419] See the CCAMLR website, www.ccamlr.org/pu/e/gen-intro.htm.
[420] NOAA Report 2005, 4 (copy on file with author).

7   Unauthorised broadcasting on the high seas

1 Introduction

Jurisdiction over unauthorised broadcasting from the high seas ('unauthorised broadcasting'), sometimes inaccurately called 'pirate broadcasting', is the most unusual form of criminal jurisdiction created under UNCLOS. The evolution of this limited treaty jurisdiction can only be understood in historical context.

2 A short history of unauthorised broadcasting

Unauthorised broadcasting from the high seas was principally a western European problem, peaking in the mid 1960s and largely vanishing thereafter,[1] although sporadic broadcasting continued into the 1980s.[2] Broadcasting regulation explains why the problem was so localised in time and place. In 1965 radio broadcasting in thirteen European states was a state monopoly without advertising.[3] Prior to state regulators permitting domestic commercial radio stations this created an economic niche for commercial broadcasting (especially for popular music) operating outside national jurisdiction.[4] Even at its height such broadcasting was never extensive. From 1958 to 1965 possibly as few

[1] Reuland, 'Interference with non-national ships', 1224 n. 216 and n. 217.

[2] Answers to questions in Parliament reproduced in (1984) 55 BYIL 554, and (1985) 56 BYIL 490–1; *Public Prosecutor v. KVD and LMT* (Netherlands, Local Court of Amsterdam) (1976) 74 ILR 200; cf. Reuland, 'Interference with non-national ships', 1224 n. 217.

[3] United Kingdom, France, West Germany, Netherlands, Belgium, Switzerland, Austria, Italy, Spain, Portugal, Ireland, Sweden, Denmark, Norway and Finland: Hunnings, 'Pirate broadcasting', 416.

[4] H. Van Panhuys and M. Van Emde Boas, 'Legal aspects of pirate broadcasting: a Dutch approach' (1966) 60 AJIL 303 at 309; H. Robertson Jr, 'The suppression of pirate radio broadcasting: a test case of the international system for control of activities outside

as eleven unauthorised high-seas stations operated on anything more than a temporary basis.[5]

Far from being victimless, unauthorised broadcasts may jeopardise public safety, interfering with emergency frequencies and sea and air traffic control channels.[6] However, the interest most affected was undoubtedly the coastal state's economic interest in regulating valuable space on the radio communications spectrum.[7] Denmark, Finland, Norway and Sweden took the first effective measures against unauthorised broadcasting, implementing relatively uniform legislation on 1 August 1962.[8] The 'common basic scheme' of these laws was to criminalise acts by nationals; broadcasts intended to be received, or causing interference, in the legislating state ('effects' or 'objective territorial' jurisdiction);[9] and ancillary activities such as participating in or financing broadcasting or re-supplying ships involved.[10] This resulted in police actions, prosecutions and stations closing.[11] This quasi-uniform legislation[12] was based on International Telecommunication Union (ITU) Regulations,[13] which these countries had themselves proposed. However, the ITU regulations did not contain or authorise any assertion of extra-territorial maritime enforcement jurisdiction.[14] Belgium also passed a law against unauthorised broadcasting, extending only to prosecuting Belgian nationals or foreigners involved in offences committed on Belgian ships, once present in Belgium.[15]

The initial UK reaction was, like that of Belgium, restrained. Despite there being at least five stations broadcasting from vessels or fixed platforms outside its territorial sea, no specific legislation was passed. The

---

national territory' (1982) 45 *Law & Contemporary Problems* 71 at 72, 76; Churchill and Lowe, p. 212.

[5] Hunnings, 'Pirate broadcasting', 410; Robertson, 'Suppression of pirate radio broadcasting', 71.

[6] D. Smith, 'Pirate broadcasting' (1967–8) 41 SCLR 769 at 772; J. Evensen, 'Aspects of international law relating to modern radio communications' (1965) 115(II) *Recueil des Cours* 477 at 565–6.

[7] M. Hanna, 'Controlling pirate broadcasting' (1977–8) 15 SDLR 547 at 547–8; cf. Hunnings, 'Pirate broadcasting', 413; Smith, 'Pirate broadcasting', 773.

[8] Hunnings, 'Pirate broadcasting', 419.   [9] *Ibid*.; Smith, 'Pirate broadcasting', 782.

[10] Hunnings, 'Private broadcasting', 418–19.

[11] *Ibid*., 419–20; Hanna, 'Controlling pirate broadcasting', 553.

[12] M. Bos, 'La liberté de la haute mer: quelques problèmes d'actualité' (1965) 12 NILR 337 at 352.

[13] (1963) 2 ILM 345.   [14] Robertson, 'Suppression of pirate radio broadcasting', 73–4.

[15] Van Panhuys and Van Emde Boas, 'Legal aspects of pirate broadcasting', 324; Bos, 'La liberté de la haute mer', 353.

UK referred only Radio Caroline to the ITU International Frequency Registration Board for action. This caused Panama to cancel the vessel's registration, but did not result in transmissions ceasing.[16] While the now stateless vessel could have been subjected to British jurisdiction under UK law,[17] no further steps were taken, as UK radiotelegraphy legislation did not extend 'to the [high seas] area of its operation'.[18] Further, it was thought such action would have compromised 'traditional British concept[ions] of the freedom of the seas'.[19]

Difficult jurisdictional issues arose regarding unauthorised broadcasts from fixed platforms outside territorial waters. Platforms required no registration and were not subject to any flag-state jurisdiction. Three such stations were established in the Thames estuary on disused War Department forts.[20] These were eventually brought within territorial waters through redrawing baselines to enclose the estuary.[21] The fourth such case was Radio Nordzee. Radio Nordzee broadcast from a fixed platform on the Dutch continental shelf for several months in 1964 until the Dutch parliament extended national criminal jurisdiction to such platforms and a police action closed the station.[22] This was controversial at the time among academics and Dutch legislators, but went unprotested by other states.[23] The provisions of the 1958 Continental Shelf Convention do not appear to have been invoked, perhaps because its references to coastal-state jurisdiction over fixed continental shelf platforms seemed only to cover structures constructed by the coastal state itself.[24] A coastal state would now be justified in asserting both prescriptive and enforcement jurisdiction over fixed platforms upon its continental shelf under UNCLOS.[25] Indeed, the idea that Holland's

---

[16] Hunnings, 'Pirate broadcasting', 422.

[17] *Molvan v. Attorney General for Palestine* (Privy Council) (1948) 15 ILR 115; cf. J. Woodliffe, 'Some legal aspects of pirate broadcasting in the North Sea' (1965) 12 NILR 365 at 371–3.

[18] O'Connell, p. 815.

[19] See Woodliffe, 'Some legal aspects of pirate broadcasting', 366.

[20] Hunnings, 'Pirate broadcasting', 422–3.

[21] Van Panhuys and Van Emde Boas, 'Legal aspects of pirate broadcasting', 310 n. 35.

[22] *Ibid.*, 326 ff. (legislation appended at 340–1); Hunnings, 'Pirate broadcasting', 423.

[23] Hunnings, 'Pirate broadcasting', 428 ff.; Hanna, 'Controlling pirate broadcasting', 554 ff.; Van Panhuys and Van Emde Boas, 'Legal aspects of pirate broadcasting', 314 n. 53 and 315 ff. The report of the Dutch government's commission of experts on international law appears in (1965) 12 NILR 202 (Dutch Report).

[24] Convention on the Continental Shelf 1958, 499 UNTS 311, Article 5(2) and (4); cf. Evensen, 'Aspects of international law', 574, 578.

[25] Articles 60(1)(b) and (2), and 80.

actions in 1964 supported such a rule was discussed at the time.[26] The officially articulated rationale, however, was the less satisfactory idea of a 'legal vacuum': that international law would not tolerate persons placing themselves beyond all national jurisdictions and thus the state most contiguous to their activities, where those activities affected its legal interests, could assert jurisdiction.[27] This doctrine never gained wide currency. Rather than establish any new principle, the Radio Nordzee incident is best thought of as an 'exceptional illegality' demonstrating the need for a new jurisdictional rule.

Unauthorised broadcasting was first defined as a treaty crime under a 1965 European Agreement,[28] closely modelled on the common Nordic legislation.[29] The European Agreement makes it an offence to transmit broadcasts capable of being received in the territory of *any* party but only requires parties to establish jurisdiction based on the nationality of the offender or vessel, or the territory from which ancillary offences of supporting unauthorised broadcasting were committed.[30] While parties remained free to establish jurisdiction on other bases,[31] the form of jurisdiction contemplated was neither universal nor analogised to piracy. Jurisdiction to prosecute was founded upon jurisdiction over nationals, jurisdiction over acts aboard flag vessels and on the basis of territorial jurisdiction over accessorial crimes of supporting unauthorised broadcasting. The conduct proscribed may in some cases have been extraterritorial, but jurisdiction to enforce was clearly preconditioned upon the existence of recognised heads of jurisdiction and the presence of the offender within territorial jurisdiction. No reciprocal rights of high-seas boarding were created. These were perhaps unnecessary, as the European Agreement's ancillary crimes proved highly effective. '[B]y prohibiting the purchase of advertising time by nationals, the agreement … [disrupted] the [broadcasters'] major source of revenue'.[32] For example, in 1964 Radio Caroline cost approximately £275,000 to run and took £750,000 in advertising, principally from cigarette companies.[33]

---

[26] Van Panhuys and Van Emde Boas, 'Legal aspects of pirate broadcasting', 331 and 337.

[27] *Ibid.*, 332–4; Robertson, 'Suppression of pirate radio broadcasting', 93–4; Dutch Report, 203.

[28] European Agreement for the Prevention of Broadcasting transmitted from Stations outside National Territory 1965, (1965) 4 ILM 115, 634 UNTS 239 (European Agreement), entered into force 19 October 1967, nineteen parties at 29 April 2008, http://conventions.coe.int/.

[29] Hunnings, 'Pirate broadcasting', 433.   [30] European Agreement, Articles 1 and 3.

[31] Evensen, 'Aspects of international law', 576.

[32] Hanna, 'Controlling pirate broadcasting', 563.

[33] Commonwealth of Australia, *Hansard*, House of Representatives, (1967) Vol. 56, 122.

Criminalising the provision of supplies and equipment to unauthorised broadcasters was also highly effective.

This territorial and nationality based approach was that ultimately followed in a 1967 UK statute (1967 Act).[34] The approach was similar to the common Nordic legislation, although it made no provision for objective territorial jurisdiction. It criminalised unauthorised broadcasting in territorial waters, or by British subjects on the high seas, as well as acts of support committed or commenced within UK territory and advertising on such stations.[35] Like the European Agreement and Nordic legislation it contained no high-seas enforcement provisions.[36] Radio Caroline was thus able to continue broadcasting from two ships outside UK territorial waters, so long as it only took advertising from outside the United Kingdom and 'service[d] the ships outside Britain'.[37]

Outside Europe, Australia passed legislation on the subject, although in a less detailed form than the United Kingdom's 1967 Act, and principally as a deterrent measure.[38] While the bill was before the federal parliament, there had only been three attempts at unauthorised broadcasting. The first – rather comical – Australian effort at 'pirate' broadcasting was Radio Gloria. A Sydney university student wrote to the Postmaster General's department requesting technical information for an essay on UK pirate broadcasting and used the information supplied to construct a transmitter, Radio Gloria, which made a 90-second broadcast from 3 n.m. outside the Sydney Heads.[39] It was not heard from again. Abortive efforts were also made to establish a student offshore station in Adelaide and a commercial station off Queensland's Gold Coast.[40] Despite proposals to have the Australian act more closely mirror the UK legislation, the law as enacted did not prohibit advertising on such stations,[41] only supplying and equipping them.[42] The Australian legislation applied, rather ambiguously, to any 'person … on a ship outside Australia but in waters adjacent to Australia'.[43] The scope of 'waters adjacent to Australia' was not defined. This appeared to assert a broad jurisdiction, unqualified by considerations of nationality (of either offender or vessel) or any requirement that the broadcast be capable

---

[34] The Marine &c, Broadcasting (Offences) Act 1967 (c. 41) (Broadcasting Act 1967).
[35] Smith, 'Pirate broadcasting', 806–10.   [36] See O'Connell, p. 818.
[37] Ibid., p. 814.   [38] Wireless Telegraphy Act 1967 (No. 59 of 1967) (Cth).
[39] Commonwealth of Australia, Hansard, House of Representatives, (1967) Vol. 56, p. 121.
[40] Ibid., p. 129.   [41] Ibid., pp. 126–31.
[42] Wireless Telegraphy Act 1967, s. 4.   [43] Ibid.

of being received within Australian territory. There were, however, no reported prosecutions under the Act.

With the exception of Radio Nordzee, only two other instances of high-seas enforcement are reported. In 1962 the Danish government, without flag-state consent, arrested the *Lucky Star* and five persons aboard and seized its broadcasting equipment.[44] The action went unprotested, perhaps because all persons aboard were Danish citizens. That the vessel was foreign-flagged does not appear to have concerned the court authorising the warrant for its search and seizure.[45]

The *Lucky Star* incident was cited in 1981 (along with the 1974 draft UNCLOS provision on unauthorised broadcasting) as evidence of a customary rule permitting Dutch authorities to board a Panamanian flagged vessel in international waters to arrest a Dutch national suspected of unauthorised broadcasting and to seize the ship and equipment aboard.[46] While this argument succeeded at first instance, it was rejected by the Supreme Court and was not raised again before the Court of Appeal of The Hague.[47] The Supreme Court's decision turned upon Article 6(1) of the High Seas Convention, providing that derogation from the flag state's exclusive jurisdiction could only occur under treaty. The customary law argument was, in any event, manifestly weak. It would be unusual for a single act of state practice and a draft treaty provision adopted by consensus to create customary law in a field as long-established and involving as many actors as the law of the sea.[48]

Apart from these incidents, no state took high-seas police action regarding unauthorised broadcasting prior to UNCLOS except against its own flag-vessels. As noted above, the European Agreement contains no reciprocal boarding and enforcement provisions. The practice by the most affected states, therefore, does not support a customary right of at-sea non-flag state enforcement.

---

[44] There is confusion as to the vessel's nationality. Some authors thought it Lebanese (Bos, 'La liberté de la haute mer', 351; O'Connell, p. 815), some Guatemalan (Van Panhuys and Van Emde Boas, 'Legal aspects of pirate broadcasting', 319; and C. Rousseau, 'Chronique des faits internationaux' (1963) 67 RGDIP 161 at 161–2). It may have lacked any valid claim to nationality and been stateless: Meyers, p. 317.

[45] 'Denmark: Litigation Concerning the *Lucky Star* (Offshore Broadcasting)' (1963) 2 ILM 343 at 343–5.

[46] *Compania Naviera Panlieve SA v. Public Prosecutor* (Netherlands, Court of Appeal), (1986) 101 ILR 409.

[47] *Ibid.*, 415.

[48] Cf. B. Cheng, 'United Nations resolutions on outer space: "instant" Customary International Law' (1965) 5 *Indian Journal of International Law* 23.

3 Jurisdiction under UNCLOS

One of the principal differences between UNCLOS Article 110 and Article 22 of the High Seas Convention is the inclusion of unauthorised broadcasting as a ground for interdicting a foreign vessel. Further, unauthorised broadcasting is, along with piracy, one of the only two cases where UNCLOS provides express high-seas enforcement jurisdiction going beyond a right of visit and inspection of the vessel's papers. The critical jurisdictional provision is Article 109. Article 109 imposes a general duty upon state parties to 'cooperate in the suppression of unauthorized broadcasting from the high seas.' 'Unauthorized broadcasting' is defined to cover the transmission of television or sound radio broadcasts 'from a ship or installation' (i.e. fixed platform) on the high seas intended for reception by the general public.[49] Enforcement jurisdiction is conferred by Article 109(3) and (4):

3. Any person engaged in unauthorized broadcasting may be prosecuted before the court of:

(a)   the flag State of the ship;

(b)   the State of registry of the installation;

(c)   the State of which the person is a national;

(d)   any State where the transmissions can be received; or

(e)   any State where authorized radio communication is suffering interference.

4. On the high seas, a State having jurisdiction in accordance with paragraph 3 may, in conformity with Article 110, arrest any person or ship engaged in unauthorized broadcasting and seize the broadcasting apparatus.

This list of jurisdictional bases may reflect the view that creating unilateral rights of intervention on the high seas, absent some jurisdictional nexus with the intervening state, is generally undesirable.[50] Jurisdiction under sub-paragraphs 3(d) and (e) may be characterised as an application of the doctrine of constructive presence or objective territoriality. In an innovation not found elsewhere, the fact that the courts of state A have jurisdiction to prosecute a national of state A, engaged in unauthorised broadcasting from a flag vessel of state B, would appear to give state A the right to board B's vessel, arrest the state A national and *any other persons aboard* and seize the vessel and

---

[49] UNCLOS, Article 109(2).
[50] Churchill and Lowe, p. 214; Hunnings, 'Pirate broadcasting', 427.

equipment aboard. Article 109 thus apparently, and unprecedentedly, creates rights of boarding and plenary enforcement jurisdiction on the sole ground of the nationality of *one* offender involved. As a practical matter, a boarding state would more usually be confronted with a situation where it could assert jurisdiction on the basis of objective territoriality or flag jurisdiction, or where all persons aboard are actually its nationals (as in the *Lucky Star*).

In some ways UNCLOS makes more limited use of the effects doctrine than the European Agreement. The European Agreement required each party to take strictly territorial enforcement action in respect of persons who had engaged in unauthorised broadcasts that could be received in *any* state party's territory. That is, enforcement action did not have to be taken by the state in which territorial effects were felt. By contrast, the authority under UNCLOS to board vessels at sea on the basis of objective territoriality may only be exercised by a state where the broadcast can actually be received.

As Article 109 cannot be regarded as codifying pre-existing customary law, it applies only as among the parties to UNCLOS.[51] Its inclusion in UNCLOS, 'fifteen years after the peak of the problem', is sometimes regarded as mysterious,[52] or even as 'an exercise in overkill', compromising freedom of navigation.[53] The simplest reason for its inclusion, however, would no doubt be that nothing prevented the problem from recurring elsewhere in the world. The desirability of direct at-sea enforcement action had been demonstrated by the United Kingdom's difficulties in shutting down unauthorised broadcasters prepared to take foreign advertising and to rely on foreign supply lines.

The present Article 109 was first suggested for inclusion in the draft UNCLOS negotiating text in 1974,[54] when the practical experience of the sponsoring European states would have seemed relatively fresh. It was included with little explanation or debate,[55] other than a comment by France that it was aimed 'particularly [at] commercial and propaganda broadcasts'.[56] There is no evidence, however, that propaganda broadcasts from the sea (as opposed to broadcasts from neighbouring states) had ever been a practical problem.

---

[51] Reuland, 'Interference with non-national ships', 1227–8.
[52] Hanna, 'Controlling pirate broadcasting', 568; cf. Churchill and Lowe, p. 211.
[53] Robertson, 'Suppression of pirate radio broadcasting', 101; similar objections were raised by Israel in 1978 and 1982, see *UNCLOS Commentary*, III, pp. 234–5 and 235 n. 5.
[54] Robertson, 'Suppression of pirate radio broadcasting', 99.
[55] *Ibid.*, 99–100.   [56] *UNCLOS Commentary*, III, p. 233.

4 UK practice after 1982

As late as 1985 the British government took the view that it lacked authority to act directly against foreign-flagged vessels on the high seas making radio broadcasts received in UK territory, even if they later entered a UK port.[57] Eventually national law changed, through a 1990 statutory instrument and amendments to the 1967 Act (collectively, 'the 1990 UK Act').[58] The final effect of the 1990 UK Act was to allow prosecution under UK law of unauthorised broadcasters operating in a defined high-seas area and to allow at-sea enforcement action to be taken against such vessels. Under the enforcement provisions UK officials may 'board and search the [suspect] ship, structure or other object', seize and detain both it and equipment aboard, and arrest persons aboard.[59]

However, despite post-dating the conclusion of UNCLOS, the 1990 UK Act was *not* justified on the basis of Article 109, as the United Kingdom was not yet a party or even a signatory to the Convention. While it was conceded in Parliament that these provisions were modelled on UNCLOS, their inclusion in the 1990 UK Act was said to be justified by a state's jurisdiction over its continental shelf (in the case of broadcasting from fixed structures) and by the ITU Regulations in the case of ships.[60] The first proposition, regarding fixed platforms on the continental shelf, may be sustainable on one of two bases. First, one can take the view that the 1958 Continental Shelf Convention (to which the United Kingdom was a party) gave jurisdiction to the coastal state over all fixed platforms on its continental shelf.[61] Second, one could suggest that between the 1964 Radio Nordzee incident and 1990 the customary law of the continental shelf had evolved to the point where UNCLOS Article 80 simply codified the general law. The proposition that the ITU Regulations mandate high-seas interdiction is, however, dubious. As noted above, the ITU Regulations do not expressly mandate interdiction and the first attempt to implement them by treaty, the European Agreement,

---

[57] (1985) 56 BYIL 490–1.

[58] See Schedule 16 of the Broadcasting Act 1990 (c. 42); and The Marine & c. Broadcasting (Offences) (Prescribed Areas of the High Seas) Order 1990 (Statutory Instruments 1990, No. 2503).

[59] The Marine &c. Broadcasting (Offences) Act 1967, s. 7A, as inserted by Schedule 16 of the Broadcasting Act 1990 (c. 42).

[60] G. Marston (ed.), 'United Kingdom materials on international law' (1990) 61 BYIL 463 at 582–3.

[61] As above at n. 24, one could, however, suggest Article 5 applies only to platforms installed by the coastal state.

did not take that course. Following UK accession to UNCLOS in 1997,[62] there could not now be any question of the 1990 Act's conformity with the United Kingdom's international obligations. However, given that Article 109 does not reflect pre-existing custom, enforcing the 1990 UK Act against the flag vessels of UNCLOS non-parties could perhaps give rise to questions of consistency with general international law. There have been no reported UK cases on the application of this legislation, and it may have had a deterrent effect on operators and owners without the need for interdictions.

5 Conclusion

It is difficult to extrapolate from unauthorised broadcasting law and practice to other contexts. The practice prior to UNCLOS, or subsequent practice not expressly relying upon it (such as the 1990 UK Act), is sporadic and far from uniform. The only significant case involving at-sea enforcement against a foreign-flag vessel was the *Lucky Star*, which has not subsequently been seen as a lawmaking precedent. At best the UNCLOS provision on unauthorised broadcasting provides one specific example where the 'objective territorial' or 'effects' theory of jurisdiction has not proved controversial.[63]

As noted in Chapter 3, UNCLOS defines three high-seas offences which all state parties must co-operate to suppress. However, there is no common rule in regard to high-seas enforcement jurisdiction in each case. The two cases where enforcement jurisdiction is expressly provided for – piracy and unauthorised broadcasting – have markedly different preconditions to the exercise of that jurisdiction. The rules relating to both piracy and pirate broadcasting are better explained by their history than by any common underlying policy rationale or theory.

---

[62] The United Kingdom acceded to UNCLOS on 25 July 1997, not being an original signatory. See www.un.org/Depts/los/convention_agreements/convention_agreements.htm.

[63] UNCLOS, Article 109(3)(d) and (e), Lowe, 'Jurisdiction', pp. 343–5.

8   Transnational crime: migrant smuggling and human trafficking

1 Introduction

The illegal movement of persons by sea may occur in three cases: the slave trade, as discussed in Chapter 4, human trafficking and migrant smuggling. Migrant smuggling involves procuring a person's entry into a state 'of which the person is not a national or a permanent resident' by crossing borders without complying with national migration law *and* doing so for financial benefit.[1] Human trafficking involves the recruitment and transportation of persons, including within one state, by coercive means for purposes of exploitation including sexual exploitation, forced labour and 'slavery or practices similar to slavery'.[2] While legally distinct,[3] these activities overlap significantly in definition and human experience. A person may be trafficked into slavery. A willingly smuggled migrant may be delivered into debt bondage, rendering them trafficked.[4] It is thus 'frequently difficult to legally establish whether there were elements of deception and/or

---

[1] Article 3(a) and (b) and Article 6, The Protocol against the Smuggling of Migrants by Land, Sea and Air, Supplementing the United Nations Convention against Transnational Organized Crime 2000, 40 ILM 384 (2001) (Migrant Smuggling Protocol), entered into force 28 January 2004, 112 parties at 16 April 2008, www.unodc.org/unodc/en/treaties/CTOC/index.html.

[2] Article 3(a), Protocol to Prevent, Suppress and Punish Trafficking in Persons, Especially Women and Children, supplementing the United Nations Convention against Transnational Organized Crime 2000, (2001) 40 ILM 353 (Human Trafficking Protocol), entered into force 25 December 2003, 119 parties at 1 April 2008, www.unodc.org/unodc/en/treaties/CTOC/index.html.

[3] T. Obokata, 'Trafficking of human beings as a crime against humanity: some implications for the international legal system' (2005) 54 ICLQ 445 at 446.

[4] Australian Institute of Criminology and United Nations Interregional Crime and Justice Research Institute, Global Programme Against Trafficking in Human Beings – Rapid Assessment: Human Smuggling and Trafficking from the Philippines, Tenth United

coercion, and whether these were sufficient to elevate the situation from one of voluntary migration (including smuggling), to one of trafficking'.[5]

While there must be deception or coercion to establish trafficking, there is no converse requirement that a smuggled migrant be smuggled *voluntarily*. Thus, where human traffickers or slave traders move persons illegally across a border, they also commit migrant smuggling. The approach taken under various international instruments to maritime jurisdiction over such crimes is inconsistent. Participation in the slave trade, the gravest of these offences, attracts only a right of visit and search, not enforcement jurisdiction.[6] Human trafficking, often described as the modern face of slavery, attracts no search or seizure jurisdiction whatsoever. Interdiction of migrant smuggling vessels occurs either unilaterally or under treaties following the drug interdiction model. State practice in the latter field is complicated by refugee law and obligations regarding safety of life at sea.

The most important instruments for jurisdictional purposes are the separate Protocols to the UN Organized Crime Convention (UN Protocols) dealing with migrant smuggling and human trafficking. Under the UN Protocols only migrant smuggling attracts maritime interdiction. The Human Trafficking Protocol has no such provisions. Interdiction of human trafficking could only occur where it is classified as also being migrant smuggling or slave trading. In the former case a co-operative interdiction regime may apply under the Protocol; in the latter a unilateral right of visit and search, but not seizure, will apply under UNCLOS. The explanation for this difference in legal regimes may be simple pragmatism. 'States the world over consistently have exhibited great reluctance to give up their sovereign right to decide which persons will, and which will not, be admitted to their territory, and given a right to settle there.'[7]

More people are smuggled than trafficked, therefore migrant smuggling is perceived as posing a higher threat to a state's sovereign right

Nations Congress on the Prevention of Crime and the Treatment of Offenders, Vienna, 10–17 April 2000, A/CONF.187/CRP.1, 14–15 (AIC Report).

[5] *Ibid.*, 9.

[6] See Chapter 3; *Third Restatement of Foreign Relations Law, II*, pp. 84 and 86 n. 3.

[7] P. Hyndman, 'Refugees under international law with a reference to the concept of asylum' (1986) 60 ALJ 148 at 153, quoted in *Minister for Immigration v. Khawar* (2002) 210 CLR 1 at 16, per McHugh and Gummow JJ, and in *European Roma Rights Centre v. Immigration Officer at Prague Airport*, [2005] 1 All ER 527 at 544, per Lord Bingham.

to determine who will enter its territory and on what conditions.[8] Further, there is little evidence that trafficked persons are moved by sea in significant numbers, as they tend to enter destination states on valid visas by ordinary scheduled transport.[9]

This chapter first examines current law and practice on migrant smuggling interdiction, being the largest field of relevant state activity. Human trafficking, and the extent to which it may be covered by the law on the slave trade, is then considered. For simplicity, and to avoid conclusory terminology, the term 'irregular migrant' will generally be used rather than 'trafficked person', 'asylum seeker', 'refugee', or 'economic migrant'.

2 Migrant smuggling by sea

2.1 The criminal enterprise of migrant smuggling

Where profit can be made someone will willingly take the associated risks.[10] Undoubtedly, restricted opportunities for legal migration from impoverished to highly developed countries create demand for, and an economic incentive to supply, irregular migration services.[11] Smuggling by sea 'involves a much lower risk of detection' than land and air routes.[12] For example, on the maritime smuggling route from Turkey into Greece it is estimated that 40 to 75 per cent of vessels make landfall undetected (the lower figure being a Coast Guard estimate).[13] Maritime smuggling is also more profitable: smugglers may move more people at lower cost, without requiring (forged) travel documents or bribes for border officials.[14] Obviously, sea transport poses 'serious danger[s] for the migrants'.[15] Indeed, the sea route from

---

[8] E.g. Prime Minister John Howard, Commonwealth of Australia, *Hansard* (House of Representatives), 27 August 2001, No. 13 of 2001, p. 30235; cf. US Presidential Proclamation 4865 of 29 September 1981, 46 FR 48107.

[9] See Chapter 8, section 3.1.

[10] A. Schloenhardt, 'Organised crime and the business of migrant trafficking: an economic analysis' (1999) 32 *Crime, Law and Social Change* 203 at 204 and 206.

[11] *Ibid.*, 228; A. Betts, 'Towards a Mediterranean solution? Implications for the region of origin' (2006) 18 IJRL 652 at 655, 664–5; D. Jones, 'Turkey's booming people trade', BBC News, 5 June 2002, news.bbc.co.uk/1/hi/world/europe/2024943.stm.

[12] Schloenhardt, 'Organised crime and the business of migrant trafficking', 224.

[13] Jones, 'Turkey's booming people trade'; R. Galpin, 'Migrants run Greek gauntlet', BBC News, 5 September 2005, http://news.bbc.co.uk/1/hi/world/europe/4184246.stm.

[14] Schloenhardt, 'Organised crime and the business of migrant trafficking', 224.

[15] *Ibid.*

China to the United States is 'now reserved mostly for the peasantry and villagers', with many educated, urban 'smugglees' preferring the safety of air travel.[16] Reliable figures on maritime migrant smuggling and interdiction at sea are hard to come by, as an IMO reporting procedure established in 2000 goes largely unused.[17]

It is also often assumed that large criminal organisations 'have taken over human smuggling from smaller organizations', attracted by 'low risk and high profits',[18] and that such organised criminal activity resembles a monopolistic corporation: a centralised, hierarchical organisation, driven to expand and destroy competition.[19] The only criminological study conducted of actual migrant smugglers in the United States suggests, however, that it is often a flexible, entrepreneurial activity. Smugglers may form temporary alliances to conduct a single operation; aiming as a group simply to deliver one shipment of clients 'and get paid'.[20] While sharing family connections, home towns or dialect might be advantageous, only a shared commitment to profit is necessary.[21] Rather than being dominated by monopolistic criminal networks, human smuggling is 'a frontier enterprise' open to 'anyone with the right connections'.[22] Similar entrepreneurial flexibility and lack of connection to wider criminal networks has been observed in smuggling practices from Albania into Italy, Turkey into Italy and Greece, and Senegal to the Spanish Canary Islands.[23] State efforts to counter such criminal enterprises are discussed after an analysis of the applicable legal framework.

---

[16] S. Zhang and K.-L. Chin, 'Enter the dragon: inside Chinese human smuggling organizations' (2002) 40 *Criminology* 737, 738–9, although this is now harder after 11 September 2001, see usinfo.state.gov/eap/Archive_Index/Direct_Flights_to_United_States_Desirable_But_Rare.html.

[17] At present, only Italy and Turkey are making reports: 'Unsafe Practices Associated with the Trafficking or Transport of Migrants by Sea: First Biannual Report' (11 January 2008), IMO Doc. MSC.3/Circ.14.

[18] AIC Report, 13.

[19] Schloenhardt, 'Organised crime and the business of migrant trafficking', 211, 214; United Nations Office on Drugs and Crime, *Trafficking in Persons: Global Patterns* (Vienna: UNODC, 2006), p. 35 (UNODC (2006)), www.unodc.org/documents/human-trafficking/HT-globalpatterns-en.pdf.

[20] Zhang and Chin, 'Enter the dragon', 750, 758.

[21] *Ibid.*, 750; cf. UNODC (2006), 35.   [22] Zhang and Chin, 747.

[23] F. Heckmann *et al.*, 'Transatlantic workshop on human smuggling – conference report' (2001) 15 GILJ 167 at 172; Jones, 'Turkey's booming people trade', n. 11 above; M. Bortin, 'Making money in Senegal off human cargo', *International Herald Tribune*, 31 May 2006, www.iht.com/articles/2006/05/30/news/senegal.php.

2.2 The UN Convention against Transnational Organized Crime

The UN Convention against Transnational Organized Crime (UNTOC)[24] aims at the 'the prevention, investigation and prosecution' of offences such as participation in serious organised crime, money laundering, corruption and obstructing justice.[25] Parties must take steps to ensure that such crimes can be prosecuted and the proceeds confiscated.[26] UNTOC is otherwise concerned with international co-operation in exchanging information, extradition, joint operations, requests for mutual legal assistance and the like. It creates a framework for co-ordinated action against transnational crimes between domestic legal systems, focusing on 'eliminat[ing] differences between national systems' and setting effective 'standards for domestic laws'.[27] Perhaps for this reason UNTOC only provides for extraterritorial prescriptive jurisdiction over money laundering.[28] Otherwise, it relies upon states' jurisdiction over flag vessels and nationals (including passive personality).[29] Unauthorised extraterritorial enforcement activities upon the territory of another state are expressly forbidden.[30]

2.3 The Protocol against the Smuggling of Migrants

The UNTOC Migrant Smuggling Protocol[31] provides for the criminalisation of movement of persons across international borders into a state of which they are not a national contrary to local migration law for profit ('migrant smuggling'), and establishes as aggravating circumstances either endangering the lives or safety of migrants or their 'inhuman or degrading treatment, including ... exploitation'.[32] Reference to 'exploitation' acknowledges the possible overlap with human trafficking.

The Protocol's interdiction provisions borrow from the UN Narcotics Convention, obliging states parties to co-operate 'to prevent and suppress' maritime migrant smuggling 'in accordance with the international law of the sea' (Article 7). Article 8 provides that a party may request other parties' assistance where it reasonably suspects that one

---

[24] (2001) 40 ILM 353. Entered into force 29 September 2003, 144 parties as of 27 June 2008, www.unodc.org/unodc/en/treaties/CTOC/signatures.html.

[25] UNTOC, Articles 3, 5, 6, 8 and 23.   [26] Ibid., Articles 12–14.

[27] A. Schloenhardt, 'Trafficking in migrants in the Asia Pacific: national, regional and international responses' (2001) 5 SJICL 697 at 731.

[28] See Article 6(2)(c), where 'outside its jurisdiction' clearly means 'outside its territory'.

[29] UNTOC, Article 15.   [30] Ibid., Article 4.   [31] See n. 1, above.

[32] Migrant Smuggling Protocol, Articles 3 and 6.

of its flag vessels is engaged in migrant smuggling. Requested parties must assist 'to the extent possible within their means'.[33]

Where a party reasonably suspects that another party's flag vessel is smuggling migrants, it may request confirmation of registry and subsequent permission to take action against the vessel, including boarding, search and, upon finding evidence of migrant smuggling, 'appropriate measures … as authorized by the flag State'.[34] This closely follows Article 17 of the UN Narcotics Convention and presumably reflects a similar intent that these measures are 'disjunctive' and sequential.[35] The drafting also replicates the problems attendant upon requiring 'confirmation of registry' prior to any action.[36] Boarding states are prohibited from taking any measures additional to those authorised, except steps permitted under relevant treaties or necessary to 'relieve imminent danger' to human life.[37] Consent to interdict may also be granted on conditions, 'including conditions relating to responsibility and the extent of effective measures to be taken'.[38]

Article 8 also provides that a state party may board a suspect vessel on reasonable suspicion of statelessness, and if 'evidence confirming the suspicion is found, that State Party shall take appropriate measures in accordance with relevant domestic and international law'.[39] This contains the now-familiar ambiguity regarding permissible enforcement jurisdiction over stateless vessels.[40]

Safeguard provisions in Article 9 require the boarding state to ensure 'the safety and humane treatment' of persons aboard and that 'within available means' measures taken are 'environmentally sound'. It must also take account of the need not to 'endanger the security of the vessel or its cargo' nor 'prejudice the commercial or legal interests' of other interested states (including coastal states).[41] Where suspicions giving rise to interdiction prove unfounded, the boarding state must

---

[33] *Ibid.*, Article 8(1).   [34] *Ibid.*, Article 8(2).   [35] See Chapter 5, section 3.

[36] See Chapter 5, section 7.   [37] Migrant Smuggling Protocol, Article 8(5).

[38] *Ibid.*; and cf. UN Narcotics Convention, Article 17(6). On state responsibility see Chapter 12.

[39] Migrant Smuggling Protocol, Article 8(7).

[40] Cf. UNCLOS, Article 110; UN Narcotics Convention, Article 17(2), FSA; Article 21(17); NAFO Scheme 2008, Articles 2(6) and 48(2); and NEAFC Scheme 2008, Articles 1(g) and 38(1); encouraging parties 'to examine the appropriateness of domestic measures to exercise jurisdiction over such vessels'. Regardless, the question whether there must be a further nexus between the wrongful act and the state asserting jurisdiction remains. See Chapter 2, section 3.2 and Chapter 11, section 2.

[41] Cf. UN Narcotics Convention, Article 17(11); UNCLOS, Article 94(1) and (2)(b).

compensate the vessel 'for any loss or damage that may have been sustained, provided that the vessel has not committed any act justifying the measures taken'.[42] Similar safeguard provisions were also adopted in some WMD interdiction treaties and their consequences are discussed in Chapter 10.

Reading the Protocol alongside UNTOC, parties are not expressly required to exercise *prescriptive* jurisdiction over offences committed aboard interdicted foreign vessels. Nor is there any express concept of preferential jurisdiction. Article 8(2)(c) does provide that where migrant smuggling is discovered during an authorised interdiction, the interdicting state may take 'take appropriate measures ... as *authorized* by the flag state' (emphasis added). Ultimately, these words reflect the fact that the exclusive jurisdiction of the flag state will prevail unless it permits the interdicting state to prosecute. By default, then, the rule is one of preferential flag-state jurisdiction.

Article 15(2)(c) may indirectly require states to provide for domestic jurisdiction over offences committed on other parties' flag vessels. It requires each state party to establish jurisdiction over conspiracies or activities undertaken outside its territory 'with a view to the commission of a serious crime [punishable by four years' imprisonment] within its territory'. This will often cover acts undertaken aboard foreign-flag vessels with a view to illegally disembarking migrants in the territory of the interdicting state. Further, where the boarding state is permitted to remove offenders from a flag vessel, it could later gain jurisdiction over them once it has conveyed them into its territory.[43] This follows from the fact that states *may*, under UNTOC (the provisions of which apply *mutatis mutandis* to the Protocol),[44] 'establish its jurisdiction over the offences covered by this Convention when the alleged offender is present in its territory and it does not extradite him or her'.[45]

However, given that the Protocol's jurisdictional provisions are even less specific than those found lacking in the UN Narcotics Convention, it might be expected that states would enter more detailed bilateral agreements to resolve lingering uncertainties. Surprisingly, there is little such practice, migrant smuggling having been generally addressed as a matter of domestic criminalisation, intergovernmental and law

---

[42] Migrant Smuggling Protocol, Article 9(2); see discussion in Chapter 12, section 1.
[43] See discussion in Chapter 9, section 6.
[44] Migrant Smuggling Protocol, Article 1(2).   [45] UNTOC, Article 15(4).

enforcement co-operation[46] and *unilateral* maritime interdiction of smuggling vessels. Selected state practice is discussed below. Italy and Spain are the gateway to Europe for maritime irregular migration across the Mediterranean, and 'Australia and the United States … [are] the two other main destinations for boat people'.[47] In practice, a recurring tension between states' rights and obligations can be perceived, as humanitarian obligations regarding safety of life at sea or under the Refugee Convention[48] frequently affect the permissible exercise of coastal states' rights to prevent irregular migration.

2.4 US practice

The United States ratified the Migrant Smuggling Protocol on 3 November 2005. However, US high-seas interdictions of irregular migrants usually occur under bilateral arrangements, especially those with Haiti and the Dominican Republic, or as a consequence of rescuing irregular migrants in distress. The United States also has agreements regarding the return of interdicted or rescued irregular migrants from Cuba, although these agreements do not mandate interdicting Cuban vessels.

The Coast Guard is the US agency responsible for interdicting irregular migrants.[49] It conducted significant migrant interdiction operations in the course of three mass migrations: the Mariel Boatlift of 1 April 1980–25 September 1980, in which some 125,000 Cuban migrants entered the United States by sea; Operation 'Able Manner' of 15 January 1993–26 November 1994, involving interdicting some 25,000 Haitian migrants; and Operation 'Able Vigil' of 19 August 1994–23 September 1994, involving interdicting some 31,000 Cuban migrants.[50] No other state has such recent and extensive experience of maritime irregular migration. The largest groups of would-be migrants presently interdicted

---

[46] Schloenhardt, 'Trafficking in migrants in the Asia Pacific', 709, 713, 736, 742; US State Department, Trafficking in Persons Report (2007), 57, 80, 102, 109, 129, 132, 133, 137, 140, 149, 152, 170, 180, www.state.gov/g/tip/.

[47] O. Bowcott, '4,000 refugees believed drowned at sea every year', *Guardian*, 9 October 2004, p. 18, quoting Professor Michael Pugh.

[48] Convention relating to the Status of Refugees 1951, 189 UNTS 150, entered into force 22 April 1954 (Refugee Convention); amended by the Protocol Relating to the Status of Refugees 1967, 606 UNTS 267, entered into force 4 October 1967 (Refugee Protocol).

[49] Palmer, 'Guarding the coast', 1569–70; under 14 USC §§2 and 89 the Coast Guard is the agency that enforces immigration laws in 8 USC §§1185(a)(1) and 1324.

[50] Figures from the US Coast Guard website, www.uscg.mil/hq/g-o/g-opl/AMIO/AMIO.htm.

by the Coast Guard are nationals of the Dominican Republic, Cuba, Haiti and Ecuador. In the reporting period ending 30 September 2007, these nationalities accounted for 5,947 of 6,338 interdicted migrants.[51] The numbers from each destination fluctuate significantly each year.

The Coast Guard lacks authority at US law to exercise jurisdiction over foreign flag-vessels in international waters without flag-state consent.[52] It may, however, consistent with US understandings of international law, conduct a visit with the master's consent and seek flag-state permission to exercise jurisdiction thereafter – the master not being considered competent to waive flag-state jurisdiction.[53] For example, in 1996 the Coast Guard requested and obtained the master's consent to visit and inspect a vessel of uncertain nationality, the *Xing Da*.[54] It then obtained presumptive flag-state consent from China to exercise jurisdiction over the vessel and persons aboard, but subsequently considered the vessel presumptively stateless when China did not ultimately confirm its registry.[55]

2.4.1 Haiti

Ever since François 'Papa Doc' Duvalier's military regime of 1957–71 first took power, significant numbers of Haitian irregular migrants have left for the US by boat.[56] Continued political instability has fuelled continued irregular migration. Clearly, the 'best reason to interdict migrants at sea … is that it saves lives'.[57] Migrants leaving Haiti usually travel in overcrowded wooden sailing vessels with no sanitation and unreliable (if any) engines and navigational equipment, which may pose a serious risk to the safety of their passengers and crew.[58] In the event of incidents endangering the safety of life at sea, the Coast Guard is obliged by customary international law, treaty and US national law to assist those in peril.[59]

---

[51] US Coast Guard, www.uscg.mil/hq/g-o/g-opl/AMIO/FlowStats/FY.htm.

[52] Palmer, 'Guarding the coast', 1569; *Third Restatement of Foreign Relations Law*, p. 334, and II, pp. 85 and 88 n. 8; cf. limits placed on Coast Guard action by Executive Order 12807 of 23 May 1992, 57 Fed. Reg. 23, 133 (1992); however, the only such statutory enactment is limited to drug interdiction: 46 App. USCA §1903.

[53] Palmer, 'Guarding the coast', 1568 n. 15; cf. Chapter 6, section 5.3, discussion in n. 171.

[54] Palmer, 'Guarding the coast', 1581–2.   [55] *Ibid.*

[56] K. Bockley, 'A historical overview of refugee legislation: the deception of foreign policy in the land of promise' (1995) 21 *North Carolina Journal of International Law and Commercial Regulation* 253 at 272.

[57] Palmer, 'Guarding the coast', 1572–3.   [58] *Ibid.*

[59] 46 USC §2304; [1956] II YBILC, 281; High Seas Convention, Article 12.

Between 1981 and 1994, under an exchange of notes, the United States had the power to stop either Haitian- or US-flagged vessels suspected of attempting to smuggle migrants into the United States and, upon 'prior notice to Haiti, escort such vessels back to a Haitian port'.[60] Interdictions in this period have erroneously been described as unilateral and 'exceptional measures of enforcement jurisdiction'.[61] In fact, this agreement was used extensively. It gave the United States comprehensive permission in advance to board suspect Haitian flag vessels and 'address inquiries, examine documents and … establish the registry, condition and destination of the vessel and the status of those on board'.[62]

Haiti also agreed to US authorities detaining such vessels, subject to their promptly notifying Haitian authorities of 'action taken'.[63] These broad powers were not subject to there being a Haitian ship-rider aboard, although the United States agreed that there could be a Haitian 'liaison' aboard the US vessels implementing this 'cooperation program'.[64] The agreement expressly provided that Haiti would not prosecute those returned and that the United States did not intend to return those it found to be refugees.[65] The agreement thus appeared to contemplate making individual refugee status determinations before conducting repatriations, presumably to comply with Refugee Convention *non-refoulement* obligations.[66] The Executive Order implementing the US–Haiti Agreement further provided that 'no person who is a refugee will be returned without his consent',[67] although it also 'suspended the entry of undocumented aliens from the high seas and ordered the Coast Guard to intercept vessels carrying such aliens and to return them to their point of origin'.[68]

In practice, the United States conducted preliminary screenings of interdicted persons at sea, 'screening out' those considered economic migrants, and transferring to US territory for further processing those 'screened in' as having a 'credible' refugee claim.[69] Migrant screening

---

[60] Agreement to Stop Clandestine Migration of Residents of Haiti to the United States, (1981) 20 ILM 1198 (Haitian Migrant Agreement).
[61] Churchill and Lowe, p. 217.   [62] Haitian Migrant Agreement, 1199.
[63] *Ibid.*   [64] Haitian Migrant Agreement, 1200.   [65] *Ibid.*
[66] L. Rosenberg, 'The courts and interception: the United States' interdiction experience and its impact on refugees and asylum seekers' (2003) 17 GILJ 199.
[67] Executive Order 12,324, 46 Fed. Reg. 48,109 (1981).
[68] *Sale v. Haitian Centres Council*, 509 US Reports 155 at 160 (1992) (*Sale*).
[69] *Ibid.*, 161–2; Palmer, 'Guarding the coast', 1573–4; the screening process is discussed in *Haitian Centers Council v. McNary*, 969 F.2d 1326, 1329–1333 (1992).

at sea required that numbers interdicted remained at manageable levels. Given safety concerns over the situation in Haiti following the coup that deposed President Aristide in September 1991, the Coast Guard suspended repatriations for some weeks.[70] When repatriation resumed, the situation had changed dramatically.

During the six months after October 1991, the Coast Guard interdicted over 34,000 Haitians. Because so many ... could not be safely processed on Coast Guard cutters, the Department of Defense established temporary facilities at the United States Naval Base in Guantánamo, Cuba, to accommodate them ... Those temporary facilities, however, had a capacity of only about 12,500 persons.[71]

The number of Haitians interdicted aboard unsafe vessels continued to rise, and by the end of May 1992 'no additional migrants could be safely accommodated at Guantánamo' or aboard cutters.[72] The United States faced a choice between allowing Haitians into the country for screening or directly repatriating interdicted migrants without any refugee claims assessment process.[73] President George Bush Sr chose the latter option in issuing the 'Kennebunkport order'.[74] The Kennebunkport order also asserted that the United States understood that Refugee Convention *non-refoulement* obligations did not apply outside US territory.[75] The US Supreme Court upheld this interpretation of the Convention and the legality of turning back migrant vessels in international waters without assessing the refugee status of those aboard.[76]

In the face of sustained humanitarian criticism, President Clinton terminated the formal policy of direct return of interdicted Haitian migrants in May 1994.[77] This involved, first, a return to at-sea screenings and very quickly thereafter, when at-sea facilities were overwhelmed, resuming detention and screening at Guantánamo Bay.[78] 'Approximately 20,000 Haitians were [then] provided safe haven ... on Guantánamo', the majority returning to Haiti voluntarily upon the restoration of President Aristide, who resumed office in October 1994.[79] During this period, the United States also concluded memoranda of

---

[70] *Sale*, 162.   [71] *Ibid.*   [72] *Ibid.*   [73] *Ibid.*
[74] See Executive Order 12807, n. 52 above.   [75] *Ibid.*, §2.
[76] *Sale*, 178–183; and see Chapter 8, section 2.7.
[77] T. A. Alexinikoff, 'Safe haven: pragmatics and prospects' (1994) 35 *Virginia Journal of International Law* 71 at 73; Bockley, 'A historical overview of refugee legislation', 290.
[78] Alexinikoff, 'Safe haven'.   [79] *Ibid.*, 74 and 77–8.

understanding with both Jamaica and the Turks and Caicos Islands in June 1994, allowing US-interdicted Haitians to be processed aboard vessels in Jamaican territorial waters and in an on-shore facility on Grand Turk Island.[80] Agreements to provide further 'safe haven' camps were concluded in July–September 1994 with Dominica, St Lucia, Suriname and Panama.[81]

In 1994, President Aristide terminated the 1981 US–Haitian interdiction agreement.[82] In international waters the US Coast Guard is only authorised to interdict US flag vessels, stateless vessels and foreign vessels pursuant to 'arrangements' with flag states.[83] However, the United States may also effect interdictions outside its contiguous zone as the result of at-sea rescue operations. That is, when a state boards a migrant smuggling vessel in distress and rescues those aboard, it has a choice as to where to disembark rescued persons. For a time, this may have achieved the same effect as interdiction and repatriation, as 'Haiti continue[d] to be responsive to case-by-case requests to permit repatriation of Haitian migrants interdicted at sea' for some years.[84]

From February 2005 it appears to have been US policy to interdict irregular Haitian migrants at sea, take them aboard Coast Guard cutters and involuntarily return them to Haiti.[85] Few, if any, have been 'screened in' for refugee processing, raising doubts about the policy as it is presently being applied.[86] It is not clear on what basis migrants are presently returned to Haiti. However, given that the majority of Haitian migrants are discovered in dangerous and unseaworthy vessels, and absent any specific refugee claims being raised, it seems likely that such craft and the persons aboard are taken to the nearest port as a matter of the law governing rescue at sea.[87] Following a change in smuggling routes which now transit the Turks and Caicos Islands, it also appears that the Coast Guard may interdict such migrants much closer to the Florida coast than previously.[88] There are fears of a new

---

[80] (1994) 5(2) US Department of State Dispatch, 468 and 632.
[81] M. Nash, 'Contemporary practice of the United States relating to international law', (1995) 89 AJIL 96 at 102 n. 6.
[82] Palmer, 'Guarding the coast', 1577.   [83] Executive Order 12807, n. 52 above, §2(b).
[84] Palmer, 'Guarding the coast', 1577.
[85] S. Legomsky, 'The USA and the Caribbean interdiction program' (2006) 18 IJRL 677 at 682.
[86] Ibid.
[87] See the discussion in Chapter 8, section 2.5 below, especially at nn. 170 ff.
[88] M. Lacey, 'Haitians go from dream to nightmare on a hellish voyage', International Herald Tribune, 19 May 2007, www.iht.com/articles/2007/05/20/america/haiti.1-57042.

maritime exodus, prompted by rising food prices and related riots, although as at the time of writing there does not appear to have been any spike in US Coast Guard interdictions.[89]

2.4.2 Cuba

While only 90 n.m. of ocean separate Cuba from Florida, crossing the intervening Gulf Stream can be 'treacherous' for ill-prepared or over-loaded craft.[90] Interdiction of irregular migrants seeking to enter the United States by sea from Cuba often results from masters' requests for urgent assistance or at-sea rescues, the vessels involved often being overcrowded or unsafe. US policy as to what to do with Cubans rescued at sea has varied, usually in reaction to various waves of Cuban migration. This section focuses on the 1980 and 1994 mass migrations from Cuba to the United States, and subsequent bilateral agreements.

In 1980, President Castro declared the Cuban port of Mariel open to any Cuban living in the United States who wished to collect relatives by sea. This was in part prompted by President Carter's statement that refugees from Cuba would be met with 'open arms' and resulted in the 'Mariel Boatlift'.[91] The boatlift was largely conducted by US-flagged vessels owned or chartered by US citizens.

Between April and September 1980 some 125,000 Cuban migrants arrived in the US by boat. These vessels were allowed entry and were only interdicted where lives were at risk. Boatlift vessels were sometimes poorly equipped for the crossing and returned grossly overloaded, and Coast Guard involvement commonly resulted from requests for assistance. Eventually, non-US-flag vessels became involved. In one such early case, Panama granted authority to the US authorities to board the *Rio Indio* and inspect it for violations of Panamanian law, including a Panamanian prohibition on its vessels transporting Cuban migrants.[92] At the time, US practice was relatively generous towards Cuban migrants as the 'Cuban Refugee Adjustment Act permitted the Attorney General to grant permanent resident status' to Cubans

---

php; see current interdiction figures at www.uscg.mil/hq/g-o/g-opl/AMIO/FlowStats/currentstats.html.

[89] J. Delva, 'Haitian food crisis sending refugees to the sea', Reuters, 23 April 2008, www.alertnet.org/thenews/newsdesk/N4M218228.htm.

[90] *Ibid.*

[91] J. Hughes, 'Flight from Cuba' (1999) 36 *California Western Law Review* 39 at 56–8.

[92] B. Stabile and R. Scheina, 'US Coast Guard operations during the 1980 Cuban exodus', www.uscg.mil/hq/g-o/g-opl/.

present within the United States 'for at least one year'.[93] The Act applied to Cuban citizens regardless of refugee status.[94]

In 1994 President Castro prompted another exodus by declaring, following anti-government riots, that Cuba would not prevent departures by sea, nor penalise such attempts under 'illegal exit' laws.[95] Subsequently, great numbers of Cuban 'Balseros', or 'rafters', tried to cross to the United States on 'homemade rafts and boats' with significant loss of life.[96] This prompted Operation 'Able Vigil', a massive Coast Guard search and rescue effort that intercepted between 31,000 and 38,560 migrants, sometimes at the rate of nearly 750 a day.[97]

During Operation Able Vigil President Clinton ordered Cuban migrants to be interdicted and diverted for processing at Guantánamo Bay.[98] Some were also diverted to a temporary 'safe haven' in Panama.[99] This represented a radical shift in policy towards irregular Cuban migrants, as it denied them the benefit of the Cuban Adjustment Act.[100] However, the way had been paved by President Bush's 1992 Executive Order on interdicting migrant smuggling vessels, which had not been expressly limited to the Haitian crisis.[101] The formally agreed US–Cuban position at September 1994 was that 'migrants rescued at sea attempting to enter the United States will not be permitted to enter the United States, but instead will be taken to safe haven facilities outside the United States' whence the two governments would seek to organise their voluntary return.[102] Agreement was also reached to promote legal migration, with the US undertaking to admit a *minimum* of 20,000 Cubans annually.[103]

---

[93] Palmer, 'Guarding the coast', 1577.   [94] Hughes, 'Flight from Cuba', 54.

[95] J. Talamo, 'The Cuban Adjustment Act: a law under siege?' (2002) 8 *ILSA Journal of International and Comparative Law* 707 at 713.

[96] Palmer, 'Guarding the coast', 1577–8.

[97] Compare figures in *ibid.* and at www.uscg.mil/hq/g-o/g-opl/. Differences may reflect reporting periods.

[98] Palmer, 'Guarding the coast', 1578; Bockley, 'A historical overview of refugee legislation', 290.

[99] M. Sartori, 'The Cuban migration dilemma: an examination of the United States' policy of temporary protection in offshore safe havens' (2001) 15 GILJ 319, 329.

[100] Talamo, 'Cuban Adjustment Act', 715.

[101] Executive Order 12807, n. 53 above.

[102] See Cuba–United States: Joint Communiqué [9 September 1994] and Joint Statement on Normalization of Migration, Building on the Agreement of September 9, 1994 [2 May 1995], (1996) 35 ILM 327 at 329 ('1994 Joint Communiqué' and '1995 Joint Statement' respectively).

[103] *Ibid.*, 330.

Facilities at Guantánamo were initially overwhelmed, and even once conditions improved its limited holding capacity pressured the United States to negotiate a bilateral solution.[104] The rafters crisis was resolved by a May 1995 amendment to the agreed position of September 1994.[105] Thereafter, the policy was that

Cuban migrants rescued at sea while attempting to reach the United States will be taken back to Cuba, where U.S. consular officials will meet them at the dock and advise them how to apply to ... [migrate] through existing legal mechanisms.[106]

The policy was now one of involuntary and automatic repatriation. Despite these measures, irregular migration continued.

Since 1994, leaving Cuba by raft has become 'nearly futile', due to efficient Coast Guard interdictions under the 1995 agreement.[107] This has encouraged increased recourse to migrant smugglers since 1998,[108] and smugglers have proven capable of 'maintain[ing] an advantage over law enforcement agencies'.[109] Their vessels are usually speedboats, 'thirty feet in length with two or more outboard engines'; detecting such craft at night is 'nearly impossible' without detailed intelligence to confine the search area.[110] Even when detected, smuggling vessels can often outrun pursuit, given the safety risks in trying to stop over-loaded, speeding vessels at night.[111]

While US policy is that irregular migrants are to be stopped as far from shore as practicable, Coast Guard policy is only to stop vessels over which it has jurisdiction at international law as well as authority under US national law.[112] The 1994 and 1995 US–Cuba Agreements do not provide express permission to interdict vessels. The 1994 Agreement referred only to 'migrants rescued at sea', while the 1995 Agreement states that 'Cuban migrants intercepted at sea by the United States ... will be taken to Cuba'.[113] The agreements might be

---

[104] Sartori, 'Cuban migration dilemma', 344–9.
[105] 1995 Joint Statement.
[106] M. Nash, 'Contemporary practice of the United States relating to international law' (1995) 89 AJIL 761 at 765; cf. the 1995 Joint Statement.
[107] D. Brown, 'Crooked straits: maritime smuggling of humans from Cuba to the United States' (2002) 33 UMIALR 273, 278.
[108] *Ibid.*, 274.   [109] *Ibid.*, 282.   [110] *Ibid.*, 283.   [111] *Ibid.*
[112] US Coast Guard, *Maritime Law Enforcement Manual*, ch. 6, 'Immigration Law Enforcement', at C.1.c.1 and B.2.a.1-B.2.a.2, B.3, www.uscg.mil/hq/g-o/g-opl/AMIO/ FOIA_Docs.pdf; United States, Presidential Decision Directive 9: Repatriation Process, 18 June 1993, www.fas.org/irp/offdocs/pdd9.txt.
[113] See 1994 Joint Communiqué and 1995 Joint Statement.

taken to provide tacit authorisation to interdict Cuban nationals. The practice has certainly gone unprotested. Alternatively, if rafts are not 'ships' or 'vessels' under UNCLOS,[114] then the jurisdiction exercised over foreign nationals on the high seas might be analogised to that exercised over persons aboard stateless vessels. That is, absent the immunity from interference conferred by being aboard a flag vessel, persons in international waters may be interdicted by foreign law enforcement vessels.[115] Finally, one might argue that, under any conditions, rafting in the Gulf Stream constitutes a hazard to life occasioning a compulsory duty of rescue, irrespective of the rafter's wishes.

Migrant-smuggling speedboats are legally more complex. The United States clearly has the power in its contiguous zone to prevent (although not punish) violations of its migration law, which could involve escorting the vessel, or transporting those aboard, back to Cuba under the 1995 Agreement. However, the mere fact that such a vessel might not be registered in Cuba, or might display no national markings, does not mean that it is stateless. Whether a speedboat enjoys nationality is contingent upon either registration or a right to fly a flag (which may follow from the owner's nationality).[116] Interdicting such vessels beyond the contiguous zone may thus present problems. In practice, however, such vessels often cannot be interdicted other than close to shore, due to resource and operational constraints.[117]

2.4.3 The Dominican Republic

The Dominican Republic lies 60 n.m. from Puerto Rico, a territory of the United States, making it an attractive departure point for migrant smuggling.[118] From 1994 the Coast Guard redirected resources to patrolling the Mona Passage between the Dominican Republic and Puerto Rico, following the decline in Haitian and Cuban irregular migration.[119] Migrant interdictions in the Mona Passage rapidly increased thereafter, from 371 migrants in 1994 to 3,375 in 1995 and 6,273 in 1996.[120] The fiscal year 1996 represented a peak. In subsequent years

---

[114] UNCLOS does not define these terms: O'Connell, pp. 747–50; [1950] I YBILC, 189; [1955] I YBILC, 10.
[115] Cf. Guy Goodwin-Gill, *The Refugee in International Law*, 2nd edn (Oxford: Clarendon Press, 1996), p. 161.
[116] See Chapter 5, section 7.
[117] US Coast Guard, *Maritime Law Enforcement Manual*, ch. 6 at C.1.c.1.
[118] Palmer, 'Guarding the coast', 1579.   [119] *Ibid.*   [120] *Ibid.*

(1997–2007) anywhere between 499 and 5,014 Dominican nationals have been interdicted.[121]

The 2003 US migrant interdiction agreement with the Dominican Republic (US–Dominican Republic Agreement) contains a ship-rider clause, allowing a Dominican Republic official aboard a US government vessel *inter alia* to authorise pursuit of a fleeing vessel into Dominican Republic waters and to enforce the Dominican Republic's laws therein.[122] US ship-riders on Dominican Republic vessels have similar powers. Any boarding, search or seizure may only be conducted by the national ship-rider; the other party's officials may assist if requested, strictly within the terms of the request.[123] US law enforcement vessels may, as of right, enter Dominican Republic waters to render 'emergency assistance' to suspected migrant smuggling vessels in 'danger or distress', provided they notify local authorities.[124]

In international waters, Article 8 grants the United States rights to board, inspect and search a Dominican-flagged vessel reasonably suspected of smuggling migrants, or of their 'unsafe transport', by sea. This permission is comprehensive and no case-by-case authorisation is needed. The United States may also detain suspect vessels if evidence of migrant smuggling offences is found, pending 'expeditious disposition instructions' from the Dominican Republic. The Dominican Republic agrees to facilitate interdicted migrants' return; and both parties pledge to prosecute migrant smugglers.[125] Article 8 is without prejudice to other international law justifications for boarding a vessel, including master's consent.

Jurisdiction under the ship-rider clause seems straightforward: the ship-riding officer conducts enforcement action and enforces coastal-state law. Regarding US interdiction of Dominican Republic vessels in international waters, Article 9(1) provides that the Dominican Republic has 'the primary right to exercise jurisdiction' but may waive it and 'authorize the enforcement of United States law against the vessel, cargo and/or persons on board'. This form of primary jurisdiction is familiar from the drug interdiction treaties. Article 9(2) provides that

---

[121] www.uscg.mil/hq/g-o/g-opl/.

[122] Agreement Between the Government of the United States of America and the Government of the Dominican Republic Concerning Cooperation in Maritime Migration Law Enforcement 2003, KAV 6187 (US–Dominican Republic Migrant Agreement). The agreement is still in force.

[123] *Ibid.*, Article 4(5).   [124] *Ibid.*, Article 5(6).   [125] *Ibid.*, Article 10.

[i]n cases arising in the contiguous zone of a Party, not involving suspect vessels fleeing from the waters of that Party or suspect vessels claiming nationality in the Party, in which both Parties have the authority to exercise jurisdiction to prosecute, the Party which conducts the boarding and search shall have right to exercise jurisdiction.

The words 'in which both Parties have the authority to exercise jurisdiction to prosecute' assume that there could be simultaneously valid enforcement – or at least adjudicative – jurisdiction on the basis of flag-state jurisdiction and coastal-state authority in the contiguous zone. As discussed further regarding WMD interdiction treaties,[126] this would only be the case where a vessel of state A, by its actions in the contiguous zone of state B, infringes customs laws in the territorial sea of B, and where these acts also constitute a crime in A. This usually arises where a mother ship offloads prohibited goods to smaller vessels to smuggle them ashore. The same practice could, and does, occur in migrant smuggling. Transferring passengers to smaller boats at sea, however, can be highly dangerous and may even involve passengers jumping aboard the smaller vessel when lifted by waves to the mother ship's deck height.[127]

2.5 Australian practice

2.5.1 Political co-operation

Australia is one of forty-two participant governments in the 'Bali Process' co-operative forum on migrant smuggling.[128] Since 2000 Australia has co-operated with Indonesia to prevent potential illegal migrants leaving Indonesia for Australia, diverting such persons into International Organization for Migration and UN High Commissioner for Refugees (UNHCR) channels.[129] Australia has also entered into confidential bilateral arrangements concerning migrant smuggling with Thailand (6 July 2001), Cambodia (March 2002), South Africa (2 August

---

[126] See Chapter 9, section 5.

[127] P. Keefe, 'The snakehead: the criminal odyssey of Chinatown's Sister Peng', *New Yorker*, 24 April 2006, p. 78.

[128] www.baliprocess.net/. On regional co-operation and model legislation to counter human smuggling and trafficking, see Schloenhardt, 'Trafficking in migrants in the Asia Pacific', 713–14, 722–9; J. Cavenagh, 'Australian practice in international law 2004' (2006) 25 AYBIL 463 at 693.

[129] J. French (ed.), 'Australian practice in international law 2003' (2004) 24 AYBIL 337 at 438.

2002) and Nauru (9 December 2002).[130] None of these created boarding rights over flag vessels and all preceded the Migrant Smuggling Protocol coming into force.[131]

2.5.2 Maritime interdiction of irregular migrants and the *Tampa* incident

Australian migrant interdiction practice changed sharply in 2001. Previously, the navy had intercepted irregular migrant vessels and brought them into port 'for reception and processing by relevant agencies'.[132] Since 2001 Australian policy has been 'to detect, intercept and deter vessels transporting unauthorized arrivals from entering Australia through the North-West maritime approaches'.[133] This involves interdictions by the Australian navy, assisted by Australian Customs aerial surveillance (Coastwatch). Where possible, vessels interdicted since 2001 have been returned to the high seas, a change prompted by a sudden surge in irregular maritime migration in 1998–2001.

In 1997–98 only 13 vessels carrying 157 people attempted to enter Australia. In 1998–99, 42 vessels carrying 926 people arrived. In 1999–2000, 75 boats arrived, bringing 4,175 people. In 2000–01, … [54 boats brought] 4,137 arrivals… There were no unauthorized boat arrivals in 2002–03 and 2004–05.[134]

In the period to 30 January 2007 it appears that only forty-three unauthorised people seeking asylum arrived, in a single boat.[135]

---

[130] P. Scott (ed.), 'Australian practice in international law 2001' (2002) 22 AYBIL 371, 371; J. Garratt and J. Chew (eds.), 'Australian practice in international law 2002' (2003) 23 AYBIL 391, 391–5.

[131] Personal communication: Peter McColl, Director, Asia Bilateral Section, International Cooperation Branch, Department of Immigration and Multicultural and Indigenous Affairs (Australia), 15 December 2004.

[132] Senate of Australia, *Senate Select Committee for an Inquiry into a Certain Maritime Incident: Report* (Canberra: Commonwealth of Australia, 2002) (*Australian Senate Report*), xx, www.aph.gov.au/senate/committee/maritime_incident_ctte/report/report.pdf.

[133] See Department of Defence (Australia), 'Operation Relex II', www.defence.gov.au/oprelex2/index.cfm.

[134] Department of Immigration and Multicultural and Indigenous Affairs (Australia), *Managing the Border: Immigration Compliance, 2004–05 edition* (Canberra, 2005), p. 29, (DIMIA (2005)), www.immi.gov.au/media/publications/compliance/managing-the-border/index.htm.

[135] Department of Immigration and Multicultural and Indigenous Affairs (Australia), Fact Sheet 73: People Smuggling, 30 January 2007, www.immi.gov.au/media/fact-sheets/73smuggling.htm.

In 1999–2001, the highest numbers of intercepted migrants were from either Iraq or Afghanistan, the majority transiting Indonesia en route to Australia.[136] Many perished attempting the crossing in over-loaded vessels. In one incident, 353 persons drowned.[137]

The so-called 2001 'Tampa crisis' marked the turning point in Australian policy. On 26 August 2001, Australia co-ordinated search and rescue operations for a sinking Indonesian-flagged vessel, *Palapa 1*, carrying 433 irregular migrants and five crew men.[138] They had been embarked on the unseaworthy vessel by migrant smugglers; four crew men were later prosecuted for migrant smuggling.[139] At the Australian authorities' request, and following its clear international law duty to assist those in distress at sea, the Norwegian container vessel MV *Tampa* successfully rescued those on board.[140] The *Tampa* was then 246 n.m. from the Indonesian port of Merak, and 75 n.m. from the Australian territory of Christmas Island. Although first steaming for Merak, the *Tampa*'s master changed course for Christmas Island when several passengers threatened suicide otherwise.[141] Australian authorities informed him that if he entered Australia's territorial sea intending to disembark rescued persons he would be prosecuted under the Australia Migration Act for 'people-smuggling'.[142] It was, however, the master's view that

Had he sailed to Indonesia he would have exposed the vessel and persons on board to … [numerous dangers] across an open ocean which may have resulted in massive loss of life.[143]

On 27 August 2001, the Australian Prime Minister stated that the government had told the master that the *Tampa* lacked 'permission

---

[136] DIMIA (2005), pp. 30–1.

[137] *Australian Senate Report*, pp. xiii, 466.

[138] D. Rothwell, 'The law of the sea and the MV *Tampa* incident: reconciling maritime principles with coastal state sovereignty' (2002) 13 *Public Law Review* 118 at 118; M. White, '*Tampa* incident: shipping, international and maritime legal issues' (2004) 78 ALJ 101 at 101.

[139] See *R v. Disun* [2003] WASCA 47 (7 February 2003), www.austlii.edu.au/cgi-bin/disp.pl/au/cases/wa/WASCA/2003/47.html.

[140] UNCLOS, Article 98(1)(b); *Victorian Council for Civil Liberties v. Minister for Immigration & Multicultural Affairs* [2001] FCA 1297 (11 September 2001), at para. 35, www.austlii.edu.au/au/cases/cth/federal_ct/2001/1297.html (*VCCL v. Minister*).

[141] *VCCL v. Minister*, para. 18.

[142] Rothwell, 'Law of the sea and the MV *Tampa* incident', 118.

[143] *VCCL v. Minister*, para. 18.

to enter Australian territorial waters'.[144] The *Tampa* crossed into Australian territorial waters on 29 August. The master was advised that this was 'a "flagrant breach of Australian law", and that the Australian Government was initiating "necessary actions to board the vessel under appropriate legal powers"'.[145]

The vessel was subsequently boarded by forty-five Australian SAS troops.[146] These forces initially requested the master to head back out to sea.[147] The master declined, considering it illegal to sail while the *Tampa* lacked the food, 'safety equipment and toilet facilities [needed] to make it seaworthy' for so many passengers.[148] The SAS then provided medical assistance to those aboard. These events raise questions as to the propriety of Australia closing its territorial waters to the *Tampa*, whether Australia had a right to preclude its passage through the territorial sea as 'non-innocent' or whether the *Tampa* had a right to enter Australian ports as a vessel in distress, and whether Australia's actions breached obligations regarding the safety of life at sea or refugee protection.

First, under UNCLOS Article 25(3) a coastal state may suspend 'without discrimination … among foreign ships' rights of innocent passage 'in specified areas of its territorial sea' if that action is 'essential for the protection of its security'. The declaration applying to the *Tampa* alone was clearly discriminatory and the security threat in disembarking 438 rescued persons is difficult to perceive.[149] Closing the territorial sea was thus prima facie 'clearly unlawful'.[150] Notably, the two other possible destinations for the *Tampa*, Indonesia and Singapore, also declared that it would not be admitted to their waters.[151] Mauritania took a similar view when Spain tried to return a migrant vessel to its waters in 2007.[152] There is thus some evidence of states asserting a unilateral right to close their territorial waters to irregular migrant vessels, despite there being no such express power in UNCLOS.

---

[144] Rothwell, 'Law of the sea and the MV *Tampa* incident', 121; cf. *VCCL v. Minister*, para. 35.
[145] *Australian Senate Report*, p. 2. Footnotes omitted.
[146] *VCCL v. Minister*, paras. 26 and 28.   [147] White, '*Tampa* Incident', 103.
[148] *Ibid.*; and *VCCL v. Minister*, paras. 18 and 22.
[149] Rothwell, 'Law of the sea and the MV *Tampa* incident', 122; contra, R. Barnes, 'Refugee law at sea' (2004) 53 ICLQ 47 at 56–7.
[150] Barnes, 'Refugee law at sea', 55.
[151] M. Zanker, 'MV *Tampa*: some law of the sea aspects', paper presented to the Maritime Law Association of Australia and New Zealand, Melbourne, 4 October 2002, 6, www.mlaanz.org/docs/Mark%20Zanker.doc.
[152] See Chapter 8, section 2.6.

The next question is whether the *Tampa* was engaged in innocent passage. This depends on whether one concludes that disembarking the migrants would have been a national migration law offence Australia was entitled to prevent or that Australia was obliged to admit the *Tampa* as a vessel in distress (although not necessarily to allow anyone to disembark). Coastal states may 'take the necessary steps ... to prevent passage which is not innocent' against vessels within their territorial sea.[153] Such non-innocent passage includes unloading any person contrary to the coastal state's immigration laws.[154] One could reasonably have presumed that the *Tampa*'s master intended to disembark at least some rescuees to seek medical attention and

Accordingly, at the time the *Tampa* was boarded ... it would have been reasonable to presume that an illegal unloading of persons ... was about to take place and ... therefore ... the ship was no longer exercising a right of innocent passage.[155]

In this context, the military deployment appears to have been a justifiable preventative action. As no military force was actually used,[156] no consideration of use-of-force issues is required.[157]

Australia, however, asserted that once within its territorial sea it could have exercised full criminal law enforcement jurisdiction over the *Tampa*, including arresting the master. The present author has certainly taken the position that Article 27 is hortatory only and state jurisdiction in the territorial sea is plenary.[158] The master, however, obviously lacked the requisite criminal intent at international law to smuggle migrants for financial benefit.[159]

In any event, turning first to Article 27, it does 'not deal with the fact that the *Tampa* was [rendered] unseaworthy [by the numbers aboard] and in distress'.[160] While UNCLOS does not expressly codify the right of a ship in distress to proceed to port and to be held immune from local law,[161] the existence of both such a right and immunity is not doubted.[162] The right is qualified: entry might be refused if it would risk public health or serious pollution[163] and the coastal state is not

---

[153] UNCLOS, Article 25(1).   [154] Ibid., Article 19(2)(g).
[155] Rothwell, 'Law of the sea and the MV *Tampa* incident', 125.
[156] White, '*Tampa* incident', 103 and 113.   [157] See Chapter 10.
[158] See Chapter 2, section 2.2.   [159] Migrant Smuggling Protocol, Article 6(1).
[160] White, '*Tampa* incident', 106 n. 27.   [161] See UNCLOS, Article 17.
[162] Churchill and Lowe, p. 63; McDougal and Burke, p. 110; O'Connell, pp. 853–5.
[163] Churchill and Lowe, p. 63.

required to allow persons aboard to disembark. Some contend that the doctrine of distress 'reflects not so much a right of entry, as a limited immunity for having so entered'.[164] This is too restrictive. It suggests that a state could prevent such entry, which seems incompatible with the humanitarian purpose of the rule. The general view that it is a right conferring a necessary correlative immunity is clearly preferable. The test of distress is

> that the necessity [of entering port] must be urgent and proceed from such a state of things as may be supposed to produce, on the mind of a skillful mariner, a well-grounded apprehension of the loss of the vessel and cargo or of the lives of the crew.[165]

This rule must also encompass a well-grounded apprehension of the loss of life among persons rescued at sea. 'There is little doubt that the *Tampa*', certified to carry only forty persons, was unseaworthy once 'it had some 438 extra persons onboard'.[166] The *Tampa* was incontestably a vessel in distress and was entitled to enter Australian waters. Australian efforts to close the territorial sea to it not only breached UNCLOS Article 25, but also an elementary rule of international law based on precepts of humanity.[167]

Australia's conduct may also have breached the 1974 International Convention for the Safety of Life at Sea 1974 (SOLAS) to which both Australia and Norway are parties.[168] Chapter I, Regulation 19 of the Annex to SOLAS provides that where a port state's inspecting safety officer finds 'clear grounds' for believing that a ship or its equipment does not conform with its flag-state safety certificate, then the inspecting state shall prevent the ship sailing until it can do so without danger to passengers or crew. It would be pedantic to suggest that as the *Tampa* was not in port for inspection the provision did not apply. The vessel was under the effective control of the Australian military, and the officers aboard had the clearest grounds for knowing that the vessel was unfit to travel and were under a duty not to allow it to sail. This could only be achieved once the rescued persons were unloaded. Eventually Australia discharged this obligation by transferring them

---

[164] Goodwin-Gill, *Refugee in International Law*, p. 164.
[165] *The New York* [1818] 3 Wheat. 59 at 68; cf. *The Rebecca* (1929) 4 RIAA 444 at 447–8.
[166] White, '*Tampa* incident', 109.
[167] Brownlie, pp. 26–7; cf. *Corfu Channel Case*, [1949] ICJ Rep. 4 at 22.
[168] 1184 UNTS 278, as amended.

to HMAS *Manoura* and transporting them to Nauru. However, Australia clearly breached these obligations when it 'invited' the vessel to return to the high seas in an unsafe condition.[169]

The final and larger criticism is that Australia's actions undermined the co-operation necessary to ensure working maritime search and rescue arrangements. While there is both a conventional and customary duty 'to rescue persons in distress' at sea, this basic rule is 'incomplete', containing 'no provision for the disembarkation of rescued persons'.[170] Australia has now published a Protocol on its role in regional search and rescue operations, essentially undertaking to co-ordinate discussions between the master, flag state and state of preferred port of disembarkation with a view to persuading the latter to accept the rescued persons.[171] When Australia is the suggested point of disembarkation, the government will assess 'the appropriateness of accepting the rescued persons, taking into account ... factors including customs, migration and security arrangements'.[172] This Protocol 'fail[s] to address the only major question that needed clarification', whether in similar circumstances the Australian government would relieve a rescuing vessel of an unsafe number of passengers.[173] Nonetheless, it does contrast favourably with Australia's initial position on the *Tampa* crisis, which was that once the rescue was effected it was for Norway (the flag state) and Indonesia (the state of embarkation) to find a solution without further Australian assistance.[174] The position taken under the Australian Protocol is now more or less the position under 2004 amendments to the SOLAS Convention.[175] The amendments emphasise that states are to co-operate to ensure

---

[169] White, '*Tampa* incident', 103.

[170] Barnes, 'Refugee law at sea', 49 and 67; cf. Rothwell, 'Law of the sea and the MV *Tampa* incident', 120–1, 126–7; Zanker, 'MV *Tampa*', 7.

[171] Department of Transport and Regional Services, Protocol for Commercial Shipping Rescuing Persons at Sea In or Adjacent to the Australian Search and Rescue Region, June 2002 (as reissued June 2005), www.amsa.gov.au/Shipping_Safety/ Marine_Notices/2005/documents/Marine%20Notice%208–2005%20-%20Att%20-%20 Guidelines.pdf.

[172] *Ibid.*   [173] White, '*Tampa* incident', 112.

[174] Commonwealth of Australia, Official Hansard, House of Representatives, No. 13, 2001, 30235 (27 August 2001); *VCCL v. Minister*, para. 74; on previous Australian assertions that international law requires the flag state to undertake resettlement of rescued persons, see R.P. Schaffer, 'The singular plight of sea-borne refugees' (1983) 8 AYBIL 213 at 213–14.

[175] See Resolution MSC.153(78) and MSC.155(78) (adopted 20 May 2004, entered into force 1 July 2006), in IMO Doc. MSC 78/26/Add.1.

that 'masters of ships providing assistance by embarking persons in distress at sea are released from their obligations with minimum further deviation from the ship's intended voyage'.[176]

To this end,

> The Contracting Government responsible for the search and rescue region in which such assistance is rendered shall exercise primary responsibility for ensuring such co-ordination and co-operation occurs, so that survivors assisted are disembarked from the assisting ship and delivered to a place of safety[.][177]

This, of course, still does not imply any ultimate responsibility to receive rescued persons. Refugee Convention issues are discussed below.[178]

2.5.3 Australian 'border protection' legislation and practice, 2001–2007

The *Tampa* incident crystallised concern in Australia regarding irregular migrants arriving by sea. Subsequent international law enforcement co-operation, maritime interdiction measures and changes to migration law have been widely credited with the decline, almost to zero, in irregular maritime arrivals since 2001.[179] Australian law now prevents persons arriving on outlying islands 'excised' from the Migration Act's territorial application from making 'on-shore' Australian visa applications or refugee status claims and provides for their removal to a declared country.[180] Those arriving in 'excised' territories or taken aboard Australian naval vessels at sea were until 2008 removed to offshore processing centres, principally in Nauru and Papua New Guinea

---

[176] SOLAS Convention, Chapter V, Regulation 33(1) and 33(1.1), https://mcanet.mcga. gov.uk/public/c4/solas/solas_v/Regulations/regulation33.htm; cf. IMO and UNHCR, *Rescue at Sea: A Guide to Principles and Practice as Applied to Migrants and Refugees* (2006), www.imo.org/includes/blastDataOnly.asp/data_id%3D15282/ UNHCRIMOleafletpersonsrescuedatsea.pdf.

[177] SOLAS Convention, Chapter V, Regulation 33(1) and 33(1.1).

[178] See Chapter 8, section 2.7.

[179] *Australian Senate Report*, p. 482 (Minority Report of Government Members); DIMIA (2005), p. iii.

[180] P. Matthew, 'Australian refugee protection in the wake of the *Tampa*', (2002) 96 AJIL 661; and see Migration Act 1958 (No.62 of 1958), ss. 46A and 198A, as inserted by the Migration Amendment (Excision from Migration Zone) Act 2001 (No. 127 of 2001) and Migration Amendment (Excision from Migration Zone) (Consequential Provisions) Act 2001 (No. 128 of 2001), respectively. These provisions remained in force as at 24 June 2008.

('the Pacific Solution'). It was said by members of the then government that the Pacific Solution aimed

to ensure that those arrivals not found to be refugees do not have access to lengthy appeal processes in the Australian Courts.... Moreover, even those asylum seekers who are successful in their claim for refugee status have no presumed right to resettlement in Australia.[181]

Whether this violated the duty to grant asylum-seekers access to national courts is beyond the scope of this book.[182] The Pacific Solution was abandoned as formal policy following a change of government in 2007, with the few remaining detainees on Nauru being removed to Australia in 2008.[183] However, the Pacific Solution clearly provided part of the rationale for Australian interdiction practice in the period 2001–7.

The long title to the Border Protection (Validation and Enforcement Powers) Act 2001 (Border Protection Act)[184] declares it '[a]n Act to validate the actions of the Commonwealth and others in relation to the MV *Tampa* and other vessels, and to provide increased powers to protect Australia's borders'.

The Act has retroactive and prospective components, expressly validating certain actions between 27 August and 27 September 2001 ('the validation period')[185] and providing specific national law powers to deal with irregular migration thereafter. The Border Protection Act declares 'any action' taken by the Commonwealth against any vessel or persons aboard during the validation period to have been legal, provided there were 'reasonable grounds for believing that ... [the passengers'] intention was to enter Australia unlawfully'.[186] This validation effectively acknowledges that the Australian government acted unlawfully during the *Tampa* episode.[187] The Act also amends the Customs and Migration Acts, granting in substantially identical terms powers to detain a ship and bring it into a port or other place 'including ... a place within the territorial sea or the contiguous zone'.[188]

---

[181] *Australian Senate Report*, p. 482 (Minority Report).

[182] M. White, '*Tampa* incident: some subsequent legal issues' (2004) 78 ALJ 249 at 260; see also Refugee Convention, Article 16, and Vienna Convention on the Law of Treaties, Article 26.

[183] K. Marks, 'The island that had (and lost) everything', *Independent*, 21 February 2008, p. 24.

[184] No. 126 of 2001 (Australia).   [185] Border Protection Act 2001, s. 4.

[186] *Ibid.*, s. 5.   [187] White, '*Tampa* incident: some subsequent legal issues', 257.

[188] Amendments to Customs Act 1901 (No.6 of 1901), s. 185(3) and Migration Act 1958 (No. 62 of 1958) s. 245F(8), in Border Protection Act 2001, Schedule 1.

This power may be exercised against Australian vessels, ships 'in Australia', and foreign ships 'outside Australia', where officials reasonably suspect that 'the ship is, will be or has been involved in a contravention' of the Customs Act, Migration Act, Division 307 of the Criminal Code (concerning the illegal importation of drugs and plants) or an act prescribed consistently with UNCLOS (including EEZ regulations).[189] The term 'in Australia' is defined to include the territorial sea.[190] Interdiction of foreign vessels upon the high seas remains limited to situations where there would be a general right at international law or a right under a bilateral treaty to board the vessel.[191] These broad powers are conferred without prejudice to 'any executive power ... to protect Australia's borders, including, where necessary, by ejecting persons who have crossed those borders'.[192] The Border Protection Act allows the detention and movement of suspect vessels to a port or 'another place'. Nothing in either the Customs or Migration Act suggests that 'another place' means only a place within Australia or Australian waters. It was certainly Australian practice in 2001 to attempt to return interdicted migrant vessels to the high seas or to escort them back to Indonesian waters.

Given the declining, and now negligible, number of irregular migrants arriving in Australian waters, Australian interdiction practice since 2001 has been limited.[193] Some twelve vessels were interdicted in the course of the navy's 'Operation Relex' between 7 September and 16 December 2001, and these incidents are usually referred to by the acronym SIEV (suspected illegal entry vessel) and a number (SIEV 1, SIEV 2, etc.). The Australian policy on naval interdictions of SIEVs underwent several changes in the course of Operation Relex. Initially, interdiction followed several steps:

- 'detection and interception ... through a combination of air and sea surveillance';

---

[189] Customs Act 1901, s. 185(3); Migration Act 1958, s. 245F(8).
[190] Acts Interpretation Act 1901, s. 15B.
[191] Migration Act 1958, s. 245B; on 'hovering' mother ships, as provided for in s. 245B(5)(c), see discussion in Chapter 2, section 2.3, at n. 30.
[192] Migration Act 1958, s. 7A; on the existence of such an executive power see *Ruddock v. Vardalis* (2001) 183 ALR 1 at 50–3, per French J, and 7–12, per Black CJ (Dissenting Opinion).
[193] There were five such interdictions in late 2008: P. Mercer, 'Australia stops "asylum vessel"', BBC News, 4 December 2008: http://news.bbc.co.uk/2/hi/asia-pacific/7764092.stm.

- deploying rigid hulled inflatable boats (RHIBs) to warn the SIEV's crew of the 'penalties under Australian law for people smuggling … in [both] English and Bahasa', while keeping naval frigates 'over the horizon' and out of sight;
- if (as usually happened) warnings were ignored, waiting for vessels to enter the contiguous zone, on the basis that the navy lacked authority to board suspect vessels in international waters;
- boarding the vessel in the contiguous zone following approval by an interdepartmental process; and
- then either steaming the vessel out 'under its own power' or, if it had been sabotaged by those aboard, towing it out into international waters and releasing it there (again on the basis that Australia lacked jurisdiction in international waters).[194]

This strategy posed several problems. The first was that those aboard a SIEV would often attempt to sabotage it in order to generate a safety of life at sea incident, forcing a naval rescue.[195] This is why the initial warning was made from RHIBs with rescue-capable frigates kept beyond visual range. The second was that, upon being released in international waters, vessels could and did simply re-enter the contiguous zone, prompting repeated interdictions.[196] Alternately, even where a SIEV did turn back towards Indonesia it could have been rendered unfit to sail through the passengers' sabotage, again forcing a rescue.[197] Where a SIEV re-entered the contiguous zone several times the Australian policy was to 'board [the SIEV] and hold the UAs [unauthorized arrivals] for shipment' by sea to a designated country.[198] Following the experience with SIEVs 1–4, interdiction policy changed.

From 12 October 2001 the navy was instructed to escort interdicted SIEVs 'from the Australian contiguous zone to the edge of Indonesian waters'.[199] Warnings were no longer given in international waters, interdepartmental approval was no longer required, and only one boarding within the contiguous zone now had to be effected.[200] This minimised opportunities for suspected smugglers to sabotage their vessels.[201] Once interdicted, irregular migrants were 'kept aboard their own vessels as long as they were even "marginally seaworthy"'.[202] When rescued and taken aboard a navy vessel, irregular migrants would be taken to offshore processing centres. This approach, however, could

---

[194] *Australian Senate Report*, pp. 25–6.   [195] *Ibid.*, p. 25.   [196] *Ibid.*, p. 26.
[197] *Ibid.*, pp. 33–8.   [198] *Ibid.*, p. 26.   [199] *Ibid.*, p. 18.   [200] *Ibid.*, p. 27.
[201] *Ibid.*   [202] *Ibid.*, references omitted.

clearly come into tension with safety of life at sea obligations and result in 'brinkmanship' between SIEVs and naval vessels.[203] In the event,

SIEVs 5, 7, 11 and 12 were escorted back to Indonesia. SIEVs 4, 6 and 10 sank at some point during the interception or tow-back process. Their passengers were rescued, with the loss of two lives on SIEV 10, and transported ... [to offshore processing centres].[204]

The loss of life in the towing-back of SIEV 10 raises serious questions as to the policy's compatibility with ensuring safety of life at sea. Arguably, where vessels are only marginally seaworthy and an Australian officer goes aboard, SOLAS obligations to prevent the vessel taking to the open sea are engaged. While these obligations only strictly apply to inspections in port, it seems contrary to the policy of securing the safety of life at sea, let alone elementary principles of humanity, to return marginally seaworthy and grossly overcrowded vessels to international waters.

Australia's apparent change in view as to its authority over vessels in international waters is noteworthy. No legal justification was offered for the navy's practice of escorting vessels back to the edge of Indonesian waters, especially given the obvious prior concern that Australia lacked the authority to keep a foreign vessel under its control in international waters. Certainly, the Border Protection Act seemingly allows, under Australian law, a vessel to be taken to 'a place' just outside Indonesian waters to prevent an offence that 'will' otherwise occur. However, unless these vessels were somehow considered stateless it is difficult to see the basis of Australian authority over them in international waters.

There is also a notable contrast in Australian and US attitudes to rescuing migrants at sea. Australian practice in 2001 emphasised rescuing persons in distress only when strictly necessary, in order to avoid incurring even offshore processing obligations.[205] The US experience suggests that rescuing vessels in distress in international waters may allow, as it were, collateral interdiction and considerable leeway in the disposition of rescuees.

---

[203] Ibid., p. 38.   [204] Ibid., pp. 27–8.
[205] Cf. apparent Foreign Office advice to the Royal Navy that there is 'a risk that captured pirates could claim asylum in Britain': M. Woolf, 'Pirates can claim UK asylum', Sunday Times, 13 April 2008, www.timesonline.co.uk/tol/news/uk/article3736239.ece.

2.6 Mediterranean practice: Italy, Spain and Malta

2.6.1 Introduction

Irregular migration across the Mediterranean is a rapidly changing phenomenon. In the 1990s, the principal route for irregular maritime migration into Europe was from Albania into Italy. This route is now of less significance, given the explosion in illicit migration from north Africa. Irregular African migrants tend to arrive in Italy on the islands of Sicily or Lampedusa, in Spain on the Canary Islands (or the mainland after crossing the Gibraltar strait), or in Malta when mischance diverts those bound for Spain and Italy. These three states have all requested EU assistance to deal with a perceived, mounting 'migration crisis'.[206] Italy and Spain have entered repatriation arrangements with the most frequent states of departure. These arrangements, however, have attracted criticism or even broken down entirely. Maritime patrols of the Mediterranean or off west Africa to deter irregular migrant vessels have been conducted. There have also been several *Tampa*-like episodes with disputes as to responsibility for assessing refugee claims and resettling or repatriating intercepted migrants. These are often disputes about burden sharing, as the states of first entry into Europe are often not migrants' desired destination. 'Front line' states thus consider that in conducting refugee assessments or repatriations they are protecting the interests of destination States such as Germany and the United Kingdom.[207]

2.6.2 Italy

Italy, once 'a staging post' for migrants transiting 'towards more desirable destinations', has become itself a major destination for irregular migration.[208] As early as 1997, Italy negotiated a ship-rider agreement with Albania to interdict migrant smuggling vessels. Only 70 n.m. of

---

[206] 'Malta migrant crisis deal reached', BBC News, 20 July 2006, http://news.bbc.co.uk/go/pr/fr/-/1/hi/world/europe/5197590.stm; 'Bid to solve Malta migrant crisis', BBC News, 19 July 2006, http://news.bbc.co.uk/go/pr/fr/-/1/hi/world/europe/5194836.stm; F. Kennedy, 'Italy rocked by arrival of 1,000 Kurdish migrants', *Independent*, 20 March 2002, p. 16.

[207] M.-T. Gil-Bazo, 'The practice of Mediterranean states in the context of the European Union's justice and home affairs external dimension' (2006) 18 IJRL 571, 578.

[208] Office of the United Nations High Commissioner for Refugees, 'UNHCR Country Operations Plans 2003 – Italy', 1 September 2002, 1, www.unhcr.org/home/RSDCOI/3d941f5d24.pdf; cf. UNHCR, 'UNHCR Country Operations Plans 2006 – Italy', undated, 1–2, www.unhcr.org/home/RSDCOI/4332cd9f2.pdf.

the Adriatic Sea separate southern Italy from Albania; the Albanian government's 1997 collapse thus prompted a wave of irregular migration into Italy. Italy subsequently played a leading role in restoring order in Albania.[209] Concluded against this backdrop, the Italy–Albania ship-rider agreement was 'enacted by an exchange of letters … [on 25] March 1997 and supplemented by an Implementing Protocol of [2] April 1997'.[210] In fact, it was the Protocol that settled the precise 'modalités d'exécution' of the exchange of letters and there was not a complete interdiction arrangement giving authority to board until that time.[211]

Under this Agreement Albanian officials were placed aboard two Italian naval vessels, which could then stop Albanian vessels in international waters or *any* vessel in Albanian waters.[212] The Agreement further allowed Italian warships, either in Albanian waters or upon the high seas, to

- demand information from Albanian vessels regarding their passengers' nationality, their port of departure and their destination;
- board and inspect the vessels to verify information received; and
- order any vessel back to an Albanian port if its crew refused boarding and inspection or if irregularities were detected during such boarding.[213]

In practice, Italian authorities would escort into Italian waters Albanian vessels which refused boarding or an order to return to port, whereupon they could 'detain, arrest and repatriate the unauthorized

---

[209] P. Acconci *et al.*, 'Italian practice relating to international law: legislation' (1999) 9 IYBIL 311 at 360–2.

[210] G. Andreone, 'Cemil Panuk and others' (2001) 11 IYBIL 273 at 275; Protocol Between Italy and Albania to Prevent Certain Illegal Acts and Render Humanitarian Assistance to those Leaving Albania, 2 April 1997, text in *Gazzetta Ufficiale della Republica Italia*, No. 163, 15.07.1997 (Italian–Albanian Agreement) (copy on file with author).

[211] *Xhavara et Quinze Autres c. l'Italie et l'Albanie,* Décision sur la Recevabilité de la requête no.39473/98 (11 January 2001), at B(c) (*Xhavara Case*), www.rettsveven.info/Content/Menneskerett/CaseLaw/Judgments/98_039473.html.

[212] M. Pugh, 'Europe's boat people: maritime cooperation in the Mediterranean', Institute for Security Studies, Western European Union, Chaillot Paper 41, July 2000, 16 n. 17, www.iss-eu.org/chaillot/chai41e.pdf, quoting Divisione Assistenza ai Profughi, 'Richiedenti asilo dal 1990 al 1998' (Department for Assistance to Refugees (Italy), 'Applicants for political asylum from 1990 to 1998'), Rome, 11 March 1999.

[213] Italian–Albanian Agreement, Article 4.

aliens'.[214] The Agreement was a temporary measure, entering into force for an initial period of thirty days.[215]

The *Xhavara* case concerned a maritime tragedy in the period between the exchange of letters and the implementing protocol being concluded. On 28 March 1997, an Albanian migrant-smuggling vessel bound for Italy, the *Kater I Rades*, sank 35 n.m. from the Italian coast after colliding with the Italian warship *Sibilla*, killing fifty-eight persons.[216] The Italian account of events indicates that the *Kater I Rades* was first approached by a military vessel, the *Zeffiro*, ignored warnings to stop and carried out evasive manoeuvres in order to continue towards Italy.[217] When the *Sibilla* approached it, the Italian military's and Albanian survivors' accounts diverge as to whether the smuggling vessel's or the military vessel's aggressive manoeuvring caused the collision.[218]

While the European Court of Human Rights ultimately found against the Albanian survivor plaintiffs on other grounds, it made several relevant observations about state responsibility. First, it found that there could be no complaint against Albania relating to the shipwreck merely because it had entered bilateral agreements with Italy permitting such action (irrespective of the implementing agreement not being in force). The Court found it significant, regarding claims that the interdiction programme generally and the *Sibilla*'s actions in particular violated human rights, that there was no evidence of any *intent* to provoke a collision. The Court also referred to states' well-established right at international law, subject to their treaty obligations, to control non-nationals' entry into their territory.[219] The Court did not comment on the plaintiffs' contention that diverting persons at sea without any assessment of their possible refugee status breached human rights. The Court also did not comment on Italy's lack of jurisdiction to compel a foreign vessel to heave to in international waters, absent an in-force boarding agreement. Italy clearly had no right to prevent infringement of its immigration laws 35 miles (or approximately 30 n.m.) from its coasts. While it could have taken limited preventative action within a 24-n.m. contiguous zone, it has not claimed

---

[214] Andreone, 'Cemil Panuk and others', 276.
[215] Italian–Albanian Agreement, Article 13.
[216] *Xhavara* case, at A(1).
[217] Scovazzi, 'La tutela della vita umana in mare', 110.
[218] *Ibid.*, 111; *Xhavara* case, at A(2).   [219] *Xhavara* case, at 'En droit', (1).

one to date.[220] Further, under Italian law Italian authorities can 'only interfere onboard foreign ships that are inside ... Italian territorial waters'.[221] Without a treaty arrangement in force it is very difficult to see a legal basis for the *Sibilla*'s doing anything more than approaching and warning the suspected smuggling vessel that it would be arrested if it entered territorial waters.

This tragedy did not deter other irregular migrants. As recently as 2002 it was reported that 'every night smugglers with high-speed boats, capable of reaching 80 mph, cross the sea with drugs and migrants'.[222] The difficulty of intercepting 'go-fast' vessels at night has been noted regarding US practice. Nonetheless, the interdiction agreement has been credited with a more than 40 per cent decline in irregular arrivals from Albania (dropping from 38,200 persons in 1998 to 23,700 in 2002 and down again to 8,881 for the first six months of 2003), leaving migration from north Africa a far greater concern.[223]

Migrant smuggling by sea from Libya has become especially worrying.

Libya appears to be a transit point for thousands of Africans resorting to illegal immigration between Africa and Europe. A growing number of departures has been seen (in 2002–2003) ... crossing to the Italian island of Lampedusa, some 275 km away.... Their frequency is such that standardisation is detectable in these frail boats (charging $800–$1200 per person) approximately 12 metres long and equipped with a dilapidated motor often resulting in shipwrecks.[224]

---

[220] See the table of European maritime claims as of 30 June 2006 on the UN Division for Ocean Affairs and the Law of the Sea website, www.un.org/Depts/los/ LEGISLATIONANDTREATIES/europe.htm; cf. the CIA, *World Factbook 2008*, www. cia.gov/library/publications/index.html. However, the US Department of Defense's *Maritime Claims Manual 2005* lists Italy as having claimed a 24-n.m. contiguous zone in 1940, www.dtic.mil/whs/directives/corres/20051m_062305/Italy.doc.

[221] Andreone, 'Cemil Panuk and others', 275.

[222] *Migration News*, September 2002, http://migration.ucdavis.edu/mn/more. php?id=2796_0_4_0.

[223] P. Popham, 'Strewn with corpses, another refugee ship offloads its cargo', *Independent*, 21 October 2003, p. 2; *Migration News*, October 2003, http://migration. ucdavis.edu/mn/more.php?id=2955_0_4_0.

[224] Author's translation, footnotes omitted. 'La Libye semble être un point de passage de milliers d'Africains ayant recours à l'immigration illégale entre l'Afrique et l'Europe. On a assisté à un nombre croissant de départs (2002–2003) de ce pays pour rejoindre l'île italienne de Lampedusa distante de 275km. ... La fréquence est telle qu'on peut y déceler une forme de standardisation de ces frêles embarcations ($800–$1200 par personnes) d'environ 12 mètres de long

There is similar evidence that frequent smuggling vessel departures from Turkey to Italy, and fierce competition among smuggling gangs, result in price standardisation for 'smugglees'.[225] Lampedusa, only 70 n.m. from Tunisia, has become the major point of entry for irregular migrants, overtaking the sea route from Albania to Apulia.[226] In one incident in September 2001, Italian authorities intercepted a '115-foot fishing boat carrying 463 illegal migrants'.[227] Such overloaded vessels frequently capsize with attendant loss of life, or drift without power until passengers die of dehydration.[228] In 1997, 1999 and 2002 Italy declared states of emergency allowing, under national law, 'expedite[d] asylum requests and expulsion procedures'.[229] In 2002, the Italian navy was reported as having been given national legal authority to 'forcibly board vessels in the open sea ... believed to be carrying migrants headed to Italy'.[230] It is not clear how many, if any, interdictions occurred under this law. In 2002, the Italian navy was involved in bringing into port the *Monica*, a vessel carrying 928 Kurdish asylum seekers.[231] In 2003 it was similarly reported that 'Italian coastal patrols have been told to turn back ... immigrants if their vessels are capable of making the return journey'.[232] This appears similar to Australian practice. Again, as in Australia, those rescued at sea are taken to the mainland for medical assistance and processing.[233] The number of irregular migrants arriving on Lampedusa has been high: 6,350

équipés d'un moteur vétuste souvent responsable des naufrages.' G. Giacca, 'Clandestini: ou le problème de la politique migratoire en Italie', New Issues In Refugee Research, UNHCR Evaluation and Policy Analysis Unit, Working Paper No. 101, March 2004, 6, www.unhcr.org.

[225] Jones, 'Turkey's booming people trade', n. 11 above.

[226] *Migration News*, September 2002, http://migration.ucdavis.edu/mn/more. php?id=2796_0_4_0.

[227] *Migration News*, October 2001, http://migration.ucdavis.edu/mn/more. php?id=2474_0_4_0.

[228] Popham, 'Strewn with corpses', n. 223 above.

[229] *Migration News*, April 2002, http://migration.ucdavis.edu/mn/more. php?id=2603_0_4_0.

[230] *Ibid.*

[231] I. Thomas, 'L'affaire du "Monica" et l'immigration clandestine en Europe' (2002) 106 RGDIP 391; 'Kurdish migrants taken to Sicily', *Independent*, 19 March 2002, p. 17.

[232] P. Popham, 'Workers for Italian vineyards dry up in migrant crackdown', *Independent*, 28 July 2003, p. 8.

[233] 'Migrants die on voyage to Italy', BBC News, 29 July 2006, http://news.bbc.co.uk/1/hi/world/europe/5227436.stm.

in 2002, approximately 10,000 in 2004 and an astonishing 23,000 in 2005.[234] On one estimate some 70,000 migrants arrived in Lampedusa between 2002 and 2007.[235]

Italian policy, at least between October 2004 and March 2005, appears to have been to exclude such arrivals – with the exception of persons from Eritrea, Somalia and Ethiopia – from the Italian refugee screening processes and to return them to Libya or Egypt by air.[236] An Italian–Libyan deal was apparently struck at a heads of state meeting on 25 August 2004, which included joint patrols in Libya's territorial waters to prevent irregular migrants departing.[237] While Libya is a party to the Protocol against the Smuggling of Migrants, the Protocol only entered into force for Italy on 2 August 2006.[238] It is not clear if the Protocol has been used as the basis for interdictions since that time. The Italian government is now apparently co-operating with the UNHCR and other international agencies in processing irregular migrants arriving on Lampedusa.[239]

Numerous Mediterranean migrant vessels are unseaworthy and require rescue. The 2004 *Cap Anamur* incident especially recalls the Australian *Tampa* episode. The German-flagged *Cap Anamur* was owned by an eponymous German organisation long concerned with rescuing 'boat people'. On 20 June 2004 the vessel discovered a rubber dinghy in the Mediterranean containing thirty-seven African men, claiming to be 'fleeing the crisis in Darfur, Sudan' or Sierra Leone.[240] The aid group said that it found them 'purely by chance … 100 miles from …

---

[234] D. Rennie, 'Emergency EU squads to tackle waves of migrants', *Daily Telegraph*, 14 January 2006, p. 10; B. Johnston, 'Island overrun by "refugees"', *Daily Telegraph*, 16 March 2005, p. 14; 'EU sends border aid to Lampedusa', BBC News, 4 August 2006, http://news.bbc.co.uk/1/hi/world/europe/5244796.stm.

[235] *Migration News*, October 2007, http://migration.ucdavis.edu/mn/more. php?id=3326_0_4_0.

[236] United Nations High Commission for Refugees, 'UNHCR deeply concerned over returns from Italy', UNHCR press release, 4 October 2004, www.unhcr.org; United Nations High Commission for Refugees, 'UNHCR calls for access, transparency after Lampedusa deportations', UNHCR press release, 21 March 2005, www. unhcr.org; *Migration News*, October 2004, http://migration.ucdavis.edu/mn/more. php?id=3051_0_4_0.

[237] B. Johnston, 'Berlusconi's migrant summit with Gaddafi', *Daily Telegraph*, 26 August 2004, p. 15. See also Gil-Bazo, 'Practice of Mediterranean states', 591–2.

[238] See www.unodc.org/unodc/en/treaties/CTOC/countrylist.html.

[239] F. Williams, 'Interview transcript: Antonio Guterres, UN High Commissioner for Refugees', *Financial Times*, 2 January 2008, www.ft.com.

[240] J. Fowler, 'Let refugees land, UN tells Italy', *Guardian*, 10 July 2004, p. 21.

Lampedusa and 180 miles from Malta'.[241] The dinghy was described as totally unseaworthy:

The motor had failed, and one of the air chambers was already half-empty. These were people in a life-threatening situation. ... Some were suffering from hypothermia.[242]

Three days later the *Cap Anamur* responded to a fisherman's report that another migrant boat was in danger within Maltese territorial waters.[243] The *Cap Anamur* found eleven people aboard a 'rusty boat' and escorted it to the nearest Maltese port, Marsaxlokk.[244] The first-rescued group, wishing to apply for asylum in Germany, did not disembark.[245]

Cap Anamur then headed back towards Italy ... [and] was told to head for Porto Empedocle on the southern coast of Sicily.
    But on arriving 12 nautical miles off the port on 1 July, ... [it] was denied permission to enter. The fact that ... [its] last port of call had been Malta, and that the Africans on board were asking for asylum in Germany, gave Italy's Interior Ministry two excellent reasons to stall.[246]

Italian coast guard and police vessels also reportedly prevented the *Cap Anamur* from entering port.[247] Italy asserted that the vessel 'had first passed through Maltese waters and [those aboard] should apply for asylum there. Germany backed that view.'[248] This stalemate continued until 12 July 2004, ending only when the captain signalled that he was unable 'to guarantee control of the ship and command of the crew', as the rescued migrants were highly stressed and 'threatening to jump overboard'.[249] Simultaneously, Germany rejected any possibility that it might process the migrants' refugee claims.[250] Italy then allowed them to disembark on 'humanitarian grounds'.[251] Police rapidly identified the men as probably not Sudanese, but Nigerians and Ghanaians.[252] Subsequently, the vessel's master and aid organisation officials 'were charged [in Italy] with

[241] 'Italy agrees to take in Africans rescued at sea', *Guardian*, 13 July 2004, p. 9.
[242] P. Popham, 'Judge frees crew of ship that saved migrants', *Independent*, 17 July 2004, p. 26.
[243] P. Popham, 'Africa's boat people finally allowed to dock in Italy', *Independent*, 13 July 2004, p. 15.
[244] *Ibid.*   [245] Popham, 'Judge frees crew'.   [246] Popham, 'Africa's boat people'.
[247] 'Italy agrees to take in Africans', above.   [248] *Ibid.*   [249] *Ibid.*
[250] Popham, 'Africa's boat people'.   [251] *Ibid.*
[252] A. Lewis, 'Aid worker held as Italy lets refugees land', *Guardian*, 13 July 2004, p. 9.

abetting illegal migration' and were arrested.[253] Within days almost all the migrants were deported to Ghana.[254] After several days the arrested aid officials and master were released.[255] The *Cap Anamur* itself was detained for seven months and only released upon a bank guarantee.[256]

The analysis here follows the *Tampa* incident. Unless the *Cap Anamur* was in distress (and it may not have been before the master signalled his need for urgent assistance) there was no duty to admit it to port. If Italian authorities used coast guard vessels to block its entry, that action was probably legal. However, to arrest the rescuers for migrant smuggling merely because those rescued seemingly lacked genuine asylum claims is manifestly wrong. Unless evidence indicated that the *Cap Anamur* crew had transported migrants for profit, they could not have committed migrant smuggling at international law. Nonetheless, Italian authorities repeated this approach in late 2007, charging Tunisian fishermen who rescued a group of migrants off Lampedusa before bringing them into an Italian port with 'facilitating illegal migration'.[257] The fear is that this evidences a deliberate policy to deter fisherman from carrying out their duties of rescue. Rather more humanity was shown by the Italian navy earlier that year in rescuing twenty-seven men left on a Maltese fishing vessel's lowered walkway for three days while the captain refused to allow them to board and Malta refused to take responsibility.[258]

2.6.3 Spain

Irregular migration into Spain has traditionally transited Morocco in order to enter Spanish enclaves in north Africa or cross the Gibraltar Strait to mainland Spain. The Spanish government's heavy patrolling of, and satellite monitoring of small boats in, the Gibraltar Strait

---

[253] *Migration News*, October 2004, http://migration.ucdavis.edu/mn/more. php?id=3051_0_4_0; K. Berkenkopf, 'Italy releases Cap Anamur crew', *Lloyd's List*, 20 July 2004, p. 3.

[254] P. Popham, 'Italy told to explain why "sea beggars" were expelled', *Independent*, 24 July 2004, p. 26.

[255] Berkenkopf, 'Italy releases Cap Anamur crew'.

[256] B. Erdogan, 'Mercy group to sell vessel', *Lloyd's List*, 30 March 2005, p. 5; 'Business briefs', *Lloyd's List*, 26 April 2005, 'Business & Insurance', p. 2.

[257] P. Popham, 'Tunisian fishermen face 15 years' jail in Italy for saving migrants from rough seas', *Independent*, 20 September 2007, p. 30.

[258] 'African migrants are dying because no one wants to do anything about it', *Independent*, 28 May 2007.

has now prompted irregular migrants to attempt to make landfall in the Spanish Canary Islands, given that 10,400 irregular migrants were stopped in the Gibraltar Strait in 2004 alone.[259] 'The Canaries lie about 910 miles north of Senegal ... and the trip ... takes about 10 days'.[260] Many die making the dangerous crossing, but despite the hazards arrivals have been increasing. In 2005 some 7,500 irregular African migrants arrived in the Canary Islands.[261] In 2006 that number was 31,000, of whom the Spanish coast guard intercepted fewer than 5,000 at sea.[262] An estimated 6,000 died or went missing making the crossing in 2006.[263] In 2007, some 13,000 irregular migrants arrived by boat.[264] This change in irregular migration routes has found a ready supply of smugglers; some Senegalese fishermen have turned to smuggling following increased competition from 'foreign industrial trawlers'.[265]

Spain's response has been to call for EU assistance in maritime patrols and refugee claim processing,[266] and to launch a diplomatic campaign to secure African states' co-operation in deterring irregular departures and accepting repatriated migrants.

Spain approved an 'Africa Plan' in May 2006 to cope with migration from Senegal as well as from Cape Verde, Gambia, Guinea, Liberia, Mali, Mauritania and Sierra Leone. Under pressure and with aid from Spain, the Senegalese Navy began to stop fishing boats loaded with migrants from setting off for the Canaries. The European Union's external border security agency, ... Frontex, sent two emergency coordination teams to the Canary Islands in May 2006.[267]

---

[259] A. Browne, 'Looking to halt the tide from the sea', *The Times*, 11 July 2006, p. 33; Gil-Bazo, 'Practice of Mediterranean States', 577.

[260] *Migration News*, 17 July 2006, http://migration.ucdavis.edu/mn/comments. php?id=3210_0_4_0.

[261] 'Spain to get migrant patrol help', BBC News, 30 May 2006, http://news.bbc. co.uk/go/pr/fr/-/1/hi/world/europe/5028506.stm; 'Countries agree migration plans', BBC News, 11 July 2006, http://news.bbc.co.uk/go/pr/fr/-/1/hi/world/ africa/5169736.stm.

[262] 'Canaries migrant death toll soars', BBC News, 28 December 2006, http://news.bbc. co.uk/1/hi/world/europe/6213495.stm.

[263] *Ibid*.

[264] 'African migrant boat in disaster', BBC News, 25 October 2007, http://news.bbc. co.uk/go/pr/fr/-/2/hi/africa/7062200.stm.

[265] S. Lafraniere, 'Europe takes Africa's fish, and migrants follow', *International Herald Tribune*, 14 January 2008, www.iht.com/articles/2008/01/14/ africa/14fishing.php.

[266] See www.frontex.europa.eu/examples_of_accomplished_operati/art5.html.

[267] 'Canaries migrant death toll soars', n. 262 above.

Simultaneously Spain declared that it needed EU assistance to deploy an 'additional five patrol boats, five helicopters and a surveillance plane to track' irregular migrants arriving in the Canaries.[268]

It appears that Frontex has patrolled the Senegalese 24-n.m. customs and migration zone, presumably with Senegal's consent, and returned to shore any migrant vessels found within that zone (returning 1,243 people in three months in 2006 and 1,167 in two months in 2007).[269] Remarkably, where 'found outside that zone, the boats ... [were] escorted the extra 2,300 km' to the Canaries for migration processing.[270] Elsewhere, EU members agreed to 'deploy coastguard patrols and helicopter surveillance units off the coasts of Senegal, Mauritania, Cape Verde, and The Gambia'.[271] These patrols started as a nine-week measure in 2006, but the operation was extended until 15 December 2006, and further patrols off the Senegalese coast were carried out using assets from 'Spain, Italy, Luxembourg and France' in February–April 2007.[272] It appears that those migrants who reach dry land or are taken aboard patrol vessels receive expert assistance,[273] although press releases mention only the role of experts in gathering information relevant to repatriations and law enforcement intelligence to target African migrant-smugglers.[274]

It appears that Spanish interdiction measures aim at redirecting seaworthy craft to their country of departure. On 3 February 2007 the Spanish navy towed the *Marine I*, a migrant vessel broken down at sea, back to a position outside the territorial waters of its state of departure, Mauritania. Mauritania and neighbouring Senegal both refused permission for the vessel to enter harbour, asserting that they had neither the responsibility nor the resources to deal with the 200 predominantly Pakistani persons aboard.[275] Mauritania finally allowed docking

---

[268] 'Spain to get migrant patrol help', BBC News, 30 May 2006, http://news.bbc.co.uk/go/pr/fr/-/1/hi/world/europe/5028506.stm.

[269] D. Bailey, 'Stemming the immigration wave', BBC News, 10 September 2006, http://news.bbc.co.uk/1/hi/world/europe/5331896.stm; Frontex Press Release, 13 April 2007, www.frontex.europa.eu/newsroom/news_releases/art21.html; on Hera II operations in the 'territorial waters of Senegal and Mauritania', see *Frontex Annual Report 2006*, p. 12, www.frontex.europa.eu/annual_report.

[270] *Ibid.*   [271] 'Spain to get migrant patrol help', above.

[272] See 'Canary Islands – Hera', 19 December 2006, www.frontex.europa.eu/examples_of_accomplished_operati/art5.html; and Frontex press release, 15 February 2007, www.frontex.europa.eu/newsroom/news_releases/art13.html.

[273] Frontex press release, 15 February 2007.   [274] *Ibid.*

[275] 'Mauritania rejects migrant boat', BBC News, 6 February 2007, http://news.bbc.co.uk/1/hi/world/africa/6352623.stm.

and disembarkation on 12 February 2007 after Spain agreed to finance medical treatment and repatriation costs.[276] It would appear that Spain and Mauritania subsequently agreed a memorandum of understanding on migrant interdiction operations in October 2007.[277] While this agreement contemplates the systematic return of Mauritanian-flagged irregular migrant vessels found within the Mauritanian EEZ back to Mauritanian ports, it only expressly appears to contemplate the possibility of Spanish ship-riders aboard Mauritanian government vessels to help achieve this end.[278] An associated technical agreement provides for Spanish military assistance through aerial surveillance of Mauritanian waters.[279] In November 2007 the two states concluded a bilateral agreement on temporary labour migration, concluded with the object of curbing irregular migration.[280]

As noted, Spain has attempted to conclude repatriation agreements with African states of departure.[281] However, Senegal agreed only to co-operate in repatriating any Senegalese nationals wishing to return.[282] In June 2006 Senegal 'temporarily' ceased such co-operation.[283] This

---

[276] 'Migrant ship docks in Mauritania', BBC News, 12 February 2007, http://news.bbc.co.uk/2/hi/africa/6352623.stm.

[277] Memorando de Entendimiento entre le Gobierno del Reino de España y el Gobierno de la República Islámica de Mauritania sobre la coordinación y colaboración operativas en el marco de la lucha contra la migración clandestina por via marítima y para el salvamento de vidas humanas en el mar (16 October 2007) (copy on file with author).

[278] *Ibid.*

[279] Acuerdo Técnico entre el Ministerio de Defensa del Reino de España y el Ministerio de Defensa de la República Islámica de Mauritania sobre la colaboración en materia de formación militar, búsqueda y rescate (S.A.R.) y vigilancia marítima con medios aéreos (16 October 2007) (copy on file with author).

[280] Acuerdo entre el Reino de España y la República Islámica de Mauritania relativo a la regulación y ordenación de los flujos migratorios laborales entre ambos Estados (25 July 2007), www.senado.es/legis8/publicaciones/html/maestro/index_CG_A452.html. This built on an earlier bilateral repatriation agreement: Acuerdo entre el Reino de España y la República Islámica de Mauritania en materia de inmigración (1 July 2003), www.congreso.es/public_oficiales/L7/CORT/BOCG/A/CG_A483.

[281] 'Spain halts Senegal deportations', BBC News, 1 June 2006, http://news.bbc.co.uk/go/pr/fr/-/1/hi/world/africa/5037808.stm.

[282] 'EU to help Spain block migrants', BBC News, 24 May 2006, http://news.bbc.co.uk/go/pr/fr/-/1/hi/world/europe/5011746.stm. In fact, it appears that Senegal only concluded a formal treaty with Spain regarding the repatriation of unaccompanied minors: Acuerdo Entre la República de Senegal y el Reino de España sobre cooperación en el ámbito de la prevención de la emigración de menores de edad senegaleses no acompañados, su protección, repatriación y reinserción (5 December 2006), www.congreso.es/public_oficiales/L8/CORT/BOCG/A/CG_A371.

[283] 'Spain halts Senegal deportations', above.

followed reports that a group of migrants returned to Dakar by air had been handcuffed and deceived by Spanish authorities regarding their destination; Senegal expressed concern at the lack of dignity in their treatment.[284] When irregular migrants are unwilling to return voluntarily, tensions clearly arise between the basic norms of humane treatment and a state's right to control migration to its territory.[285] In December 2006, Spain agreed to 'give 4,000 Senegalese temporary work permits over the [following] two years'.[286]

2.6.4 Malta

Malta views itself as besieged by irregular migration. With a population of only 400,000, Malta received 1,800 migrants by sea in 2006 and over 1,500 in 2005.[287] As noted, these are usually accidental arrivals wishing to make landfall in Spain or Italy.[288] Malta detains irregular migrants for refugee claim processing for eighteen months in rudimentary camps.[289]

On 15 July 2006, Malta refused the Spanish fishing trawler *Francisco Catalina* permission to disembark fifty-one persons rescued in the Mediterranean, mostly Eritreans.[290] Malta contended that the rescued migrants 'were the responsibility of Spain or Libya since the [rescue] boat was Spanish and the migrants were picked up in Libya's search-and-rescue

[284] *Ibid.*

[285] On dignity as a principle of return see Action Plan, Ministerial Conference on Euro-African Migration and Development, 10–11 July 2006, www.maec.gov.ma/migration/Doc/PA%20final%20EN.pdf; Commission of the European Communities, 'Communication from the Commission on policy priorities in the fight against illegal immigration of third-country nationals', 19 July 2006, COM(2006) 402, paras. 8 and 42, http://eur-lex.europa.eu/LexUriServ/site/en/com/2006/com2006_0402en01.pdf; UN Economic and Social Council, Recommended Principles on Human Rights and Human Trafficking (20 May 2002), UN Doc E/2002/68/Add.1, para. 3.

[286] 'Timeline: Senegal', BBC News, 4 March 2008, http://news.bbc.co.uk/2/hi/africa/country_profiles/2988226.stm.

[287] M. Donkin, 'Malta faces African emigrant flood', BBC News, 29 September 2006, http://news.bbc.co.uk/1/hi/world/europe/5382456.stm; F. Schmid and S. Laitner, 'Malta pleads for help with illegal migrants', *Financial Times*, 4 July 2007, www.ft.com/cms/s/0/bff35d4a-2a24–11dc-9208–000b5df10621.html. No figures for later periods appear to be available.

[288] D. Sandford, 'Immigrant frustration for Malta', BBC News, 21 October 2005, http://news.bbc.co.uk/go/pr/fr/-/1/hi/world/europe/4365030.stm.

[289] M. Buchanan, 'Malta alarmed by migrant influx', BBC News, 4 July 2006, http://news.bbc.co.uk/go/pr/fr/-/1/hi/world/europe/5145168.stm.

[290] J. Pagonis, 'Malta: Spanish trawler waits offshore, UNHCR calls for EU burden-sharing', UNHCR Briefing Notes, 18 July 2006, www.unhcr.org; UNHCR, 'UNHCR welcomes positive outcome for 51 boat people off Malta', press release, 21 July 2006, www.unhcr.org.

zone', a stance echoing Australia's initial assertions during the *Tampa* incident.[291] Following calls by Malta and the UNHCR for increased burden-sharing, the EU negotiated a solution whereby Malta would take three migrants, Spain the majority and Italy and Andorra the rest for refugee processing.[292] Malta was clearly under no duty to allow the rescued migrants to disembark and does not appear to have compromised safety of life at sea obligations by insisting that the vessel should sail on. As in the *Tampa* case, it illustrates the difficulty posed by the 'incomplete' duty of rescue.[293] In a similar incident on 28 May 2007, Malta refused the tug *Mont Falco* permission to disembark twenty-six rescued North African migrants.[294]

In June and July 2007 Malta received EU assistance in dealing with migrant flows co-ordinated by Frontex in 'Operation Nautilus'.[295] During the operation some 464 migrants were detected, '166 migrants were rescued... and 316 migrants arrived' in Malta, coming mainly from 'Eritrea, Somalia, Ethiopia and Nigeria'.[296] Operation Nautilus 2007 also provided another example of the difficulties caused by the incomplete nature of search and rescue obligations:

The mission [initially had to be placed] on hold due to the difference of opinion concerning the responsibility [for] migrants saved at sea. After discussions rules regarding the disembarkation of persons rescued at sea during the operation will remain the same as in last year's operation. Migrants saved in the Libyan Search and Rescue Area (SAR) will be taken to Libya, [and] when [that is] not possible to [the] closest safe haven.[297]

In 2008 Operation Nautilus ran again and saw an astonishing 2,321 migrants arriving in Malta and 16,098 in Italy. FRONTEX has not publicised the numbers intercepted at sea, although it seems clear that none were diverted back at sea.[298]

---

[291] 'Malta migrants allowed on shore', BBC News, 21 July 2006, http://news.bbc.co.uk/go/pr/fr/-/1/hi/world/europe/5205084.stm.

[292] *Ibid.* [293] See text accompanying n. 170, above.

[294] 'Migrant rescue "a legal must"', *Lloyd's List*, 30 May 2007, p. 1.

[295] This was preceded by a pilot exercise in October 2006: Frontex press release, 26 October 2006, www.frontex.europa.eu/newsroom/news_releases/art4.html; *Frontex Annual Report 2006*, p. 13.

[296] Frontex press release, 6 August 2007, www.frontex.europa.eu/newsroom/news_releases/art28.html.

[297] Frontex press release, 7 May 2008, www.frontex.europa.eu/newsroom/news_releases/art36.html.

[298] Frontex press release, 17 February 2009, www.frontex.europa.eu/newsroom/news_releases/art40.html.

2.7 *Returning asylum-seekers interdicted at sea and* non-refoulement

It is common state practice to apply migration law only to those arriving on dry land. International law certainly allows states to take all reasonable measures in the territorial sea to prevent the entry into port of a vessel carrying illegal immigrants, and to require such a vessel to leave the territorial sea.[299]

This should be understood in the light of the law of distress, discussed above,[300] and Refugee Convention obligations. While state parties to the Refugee Convention are not obliged to admit those claiming refugee status to their territory, could returning a vessel to the high seas constitute *refoulement* (the prohibited returning of a refugee to a place where he or she will face persecution)?[301]

A brief discussion of refugee law is thus necessary. In order to be a refugee under the Refugee Convention a person must have a 'well-founded' fear of persecution on a relevant ground ('race, religion, nationality, membership of a particular social group or political opinion'), be unable or unwilling to avail themselves of the protection of his or her state of nationality, and be 'outside' that state.[302] The common judicial shorthand that a refugee is someone who has already arrived in a Refugee Convention state is thus plainly wrong;[303] one can only say that someone who has not yet left their own state cannot be a refugee.[304] Similarly, the Convention provision on *non-refoulement* contains no geographical limitation. Under Article 33(1),

No Contracting State shall expel or return ('*refouler*') a refugee *in any manner whatsoever* to the frontiers of territories where his life or freedom would be threatened on account of [a relevant ground of persecution].[305]

Further, Article 1(3) of the Refugee Protocol provides that Articles 2–34 of the Refugee Convention 'shall be applied by the States Parties

---

[299] Goodwin-Gill, *Refugee in International Law*, p. 164.

[300] Text accompanying n. 160, above.

[301] M. Pallis, 'Obligations of states towards asylum seekers at sea: interactions and conflicts between legal regimes' (2002) 14 IJRL 329 at 344; but note Goodwin-Gill, *Refugee in International Law*, pp. 155–67.

[302] Refugee Convention, Article 1, as modified by Protocol Relating to the Status of Refugees 1967, 606 UNTS 267, Article 1(2).

[303] E.g. *Khawar*, 15, per McHugh and Gummow JJ; cf. *European Roma Rights Centre*, 542–3 and 551.

[304] *European Roma Rights Centre*, 546–7.

[305] Refugee Convention, Article 33(1) (emphasis added).

hereto without any geographic limitation'. Australia, Italy, Malta, Spain and the United States are all parties to the Protocol. It is thus clear that the physical location of an asylum seeker is irrelevant to whether *refoulement* has occurred.[306] If in a boatload of several dozen irregular migrants there is one person with a genuine claim to refugee status ('the refugee') then there will be *refoulement* where the refugee is involuntarily repatriated to the state he is fleeing after being interdicted at sea, or where removing a vessel to the high seas leaves it with no option but to return to a place where the refugee will face persecution. Unless individual refugee status determinations are conducted, interdiction followed by either involuntary repatriation or simply turning boats back risks breaching the Protocol. To give effect to their *non-refoulement* obligations parties to the Protocol should, at a minimum, conduct some form of individual refugee screening process at sea in such cases.

It might be thought that returning a vessel to the high seas was not likely to result in *refoulement*, as the vessel could theoretically, if seaworthy and adequately supplied, travel to any coastal state in the world. One must, however, look to practical consequences: if an action has the effect of returning a refugee to a place of persecution it constitutes *refoulement* or, where the effect is to force the vessel into a third state that will so return the refugee, 'chain *refoulement*'.[307] Indeed, as international responsibility 'is analogous to joint and several responsibility',[308] if the combined effect of multiple states expelling the same vessel from their waters is that a refugee must return to a place of persecution, then this, too, constitutes 'chain', or 'collective', *refoulement*.

On their plain words Convention obligations have more than merely territorial application. Despite this, the *Sale* majority interpreted *non-refoulement* obligations as applying only within US territory as Article 33(2) provides that

The benefit of the present provision may not ... be claimed by a refugee whom there are reasonable grounds for regarding as a danger to the security of the country *in which he is* ... (emphasis added)

---

[306] E. Lauterpacht and D. Bethlehem, 'The scope and content of the principle of *non-refoulement*: opinion' in E. Feller, V. Turk and F. Nicholson (eds.), *Refugee Protection in International Law: UNHCR's Global Consultations on International Protection* (Cambridge University Press, 2003), pp. 110–15, 159–60.

[307] Pallis, 'Obligations of states', 349.

[308] J. Crawford and P. Hyndman, 'Three heresies in the application of the Refugee Convention' (1989) 1 IJRL 155 at 171.

That is, if Article 33(2) permits the expulsion of 'dangerous' asylum seekers only once *within* a state's territory, it would seem anomalous if Article 33(1) is not similarly limited, as such dangerous persons could not then be repatriated directly from the high seas.[309] Dissenting, Blackmun J observed,

The signatories' understandable decision to allow nations to deport criminal aliens who have entered their territory hardly suggests an intent to permit the apprehension and return of noncriminal (sic) aliens who have not entered their territory ...[310]

This is convincing. *Non-refoulement* 'becomes a hollow promise if nations can circumvent it by stopping ... refugees before arrival'.[311]

Nonetheless, the United States and Australia appear to have taken the view that returning irregular migrant vessels to the high seas or involuntarily repatriating those interdicted is permissible at international law. There are also reports of a similarly 'indiscriminate' Greek policy of repulsing irregular migrant vessels in the Aegean Sea into Turkish waters.[312] Three possibilities arise. First, this might constitute practice subsequent to the treaty capable of 'establishing the agreement of the parties regarding its interpretation'.[313] Second, it could evidence state practice on the part of specially affected states supporting a rule of *lex specialis* modifying the application at sea of the *lex generalis* of refugee law, assuming that a subsequent rule of customary law may modify a prior rule of treaty law.[314] Or, third, it could simply be regarded as conduct breaching an international obligation in any case where individual refugees are subjected to *refoulement* as a result. Does the practice evidence a breach of obligations, or the emergence of an exception? The ICJ in *Nicaragua* reasoned that state conduct inconsistent with a rule will not constitute practice supporting the emergence of a new rule or exception where it has generally been treated as a breach of the existing rule.[315] The most persuasive evidence that conduct is not

---

[309] *Sale*, 179–80.   [310] *Ibid.*, 193.

[311] A. Helton, 'The United States government program of intercepting and forcibly returning Haitian boat people to Haiti' (1993) 10 *New York Law School Journal of Human Rights* 325 at 341; cf. Legomsky, 'USA and the Caribbean Interdiction Program', 688–93.

[312] Galpin, 'Migrants run Greek gauntlet'.

[313] VCLT, Article 31(3)(b); A. McNair, *The Law of Treaties* (Oxford: Clarendon Press, 1961), pp. 424–31.

[314] *Brownlie*, p. 5; Michael Akehurst, 'The hierarchy of the sources of international law' (1974–5) 47 BYIL 273 at 275; cf. VCLT, Article 53.

[315] *Nicaragua Case*, [1986] ICJ Rep. 14 at 98.

rule-creating, rule-interpreting or rule-modifying would be evidence of its condemnation as rule-breaching. While this approach was posited concerning the development of customary law, it is also sensible when assessing 'interpretative' treaty practice. The Kennebunkport order and *Sale* judgment might be considered as a state's executive and judicial branches defending its conduct by reference to a purported exception to the international rule (the strictly territorial application of Article 33). However, the result in *Sale* has been criticised by international bodies (including the Inter-American Commission on Human Rights) and state organs (including the UK House of Lords).[316] UNHCR has also expressed its concern, in reference to Australian, US and Mediterranean practice, that '[maritime] interception measures that effectively deny refugees access to international protection, or which result in them being returned to the countries where their security is at risk' 'may' violate the Refugee Convention.[317] If UNHCR refers here to those with genuine refugee claims, 'may' is too gentle a word. Norway was certainly strongly critical of Australia's stance in the *Tampa* crisis, but otherwise there has been little state-to-state condemnation of such policies. It is unlikely that protests by international entities and commentators can remedy this basic deficiency. This makes assessment difficult. Maritime interdiction of irregular migrants without providing some form of refugee screening process is strictly incompatible with the Refugee Convention and Protocol. However, as irregular migration by sea increases worldwide there appears a growing perception among 'point of entry' states that they are unable to cope with the numbers arriving and preventative maritime patrols are a legally permissible response. It could well be that European practice is beginning to follow the US and Australian approach of turning seaworthy vessels back to their point of departure. One could argue that such interdiction practice, coupled with other parties' acquiescence, 'establish[es] the agreement of the parties' that such acts are compatible with the Convention.[318] It is certainly possible that treaty revision may be brought about 'by practice or conduct, rather

---

[316] Inter-American Commission on Human Rights Report No. 51/96, Decision of the Commission as to the Merits of Case 10.675 (United States), 13 March 1997, at paras. 155 ff., www.cidh.org/annualrep/96eng/USA10675.htm; *European Roma Rights Centre*, 547.

[317] See UNHCR, *The State of the World's Refugees* (Oxford University Press, 2006), p. 40, www.unhcr.org; cf. UNHCR, Conclusion on Protection Safeguards in Interception Measures, Executive Committee 54th Session, Executive Committee Doc. No. 97 (LIV) – 2003, www.unhcr.org.

[318] VCLT, Article 31(3)(b).

than effected by and recorded in writing'.[319] If there is a strong trend in the practice of the only relevantly affected states, generally *unprotested* by other state parties, it makes a case that such an exception – however undesirable on humanitarian grounds – may become, or already be, established in international law.

It is occasionally argued in the alternative that, if the Refugee Convention is territorially limited, *non-refoulement* obligations should still apply in a state's sovereign territorial sea on the basis that it forms part of the state's territory either for Refugee Convention purposes or more generally, given the close connection between sovereignty and territory.[320] While sovereignty certainly follows from a state's possession of territory, the exercise of sovereignty or sovereign rights over a space or object does not make it territory. The classic example is the general rejection of the 'floating island' theory of a state's sovereign jurisdiction over its flag vessels.[321] The argument that territorially limited international obligations would necessarily apply in the territorial sea in the same manner as on land is thus unconvincing.

3 Human trafficking

3.1 Introduction

Practices similar to slavery, in the form of human trafficking, remain with us today.[322] The relationship between slavery and similar practices is, however, not always clear. The UNTOC Human Trafficking Protocol targets the exploitation of vulnerable people (principally women and children).

'Trafficking in persons' shall mean the recruitment, transportation, transfer, harbouring or receipt of persons, by means of the threat or use of force or other forms of coercion, of abduction, of fraud, of deception, of the abuse of power or of a position of vulnerability ... for the purpose of exploitation. Exploitation shall include, at a minimum, ... sexual exploitation, forced labour or services, slavery ..., servitude or the removal of organs.[323]

---

[319] G. Fitzmaurice, 'The law and procedure of the International Court of Justice 1951–4: treaty interpretation and other treaty points' (1957) 33 BYIL 203 at 223–5.

[320] Pallis, 'Obligations of States', 343.

[321] O'Connell, pp. 733–5.

[322] On 'traditional' slavery practices in Mauritania, Niger, Sudan and Haiti, see US Department of State, *Trafficking in Persons Report* (2005), pp. 66, 70, 78 and 250, www.state.gov/g/tip/rls/tiprpt/2005/.

[323] Human Trafficking Protocol, Article 3(a).

Slavery is thus listed as one exploitative practice among many relevant to whether a person has been trafficked. The majority of trafficked persons are women or girls, trafficked for sexual exploitation or, to a lesser extent, forced labour.[324] Finding reliable data on the extent of human trafficking is difficult; the first effort at a global analysis based on systematically collected information came only in 2006.[325] One estimate suggests that annually 600,000–800,000 persons are trafficked worldwide.[326] Most trafficking operations are conducted by hierarchically organised criminal syndicates, although the looser 'enterprise model' found in Chinese–US migrant smuggling is not unknown.[327] Further, significant amounts of *internal* trafficking may occur in many states in the forms of forced labour, forced prostitution or forced marriage.[328]

Like previous human trafficking conventions,[329] the Human Trafficking Protocol does not provide for high-seas interdiction, perhaps because trafficking victims are seldom moved in large numbers in vessels solely used for that purpose. While there is little data on transportation methods,[330] victims trafficked internationally seem more likely to be moved individually or in small groups by scheduled international flights and/or by land rather than sea.[331] Further, trafficked persons often enter a country legally either on 'tourist visas or their own passports'.[332] Cases where persons initially volunteer to be smuggled by sea and are subsequently exploited upon arrival will, however, constitute migrant smuggling. This could provide a high-seas right of visit and search not available under the Human Trafficking Protocol.

---

[324] Forced labour may be under-reported: UNODC (2006), 33 and 65–66; contra, Obokata, 'Trafficking of human beings', 447, and D. Hughes, 'The "Natasha" trade: the transnational shadow market of trafficking in women' (2000) 53 *Journal of International Affairs* 625 at 628.

[325] UNODC (2006), 37; cf. Department of State (2005), 15.

[326] Department of State (2005), 15 and 23.

[327] UNODC (2006), 69; cf. Department of State (2005), 96; AIC Report, 13 and 27; Hughes, '"Natasha" trade', 642.

[328] Department of State (2005), 40 ff.

[329] See International Agreement for the Suppression of the White Slave Traffic 1904, 1 LNTS 83; International Convention for the Suppression of the White Slave Traffic 1910 (as amended), 98 UNTS 101; International Convention for the Suppression of the Traffic in Women and Children 1921, 9 LNTS 415 (as amended); Convention for the Suppression of the Traffic in Women of Full Age 1933, 150 LNTS 431 (as amended); and Convention for the Suppression of the Traffic in Persons and the Exploitation of the Prostitution of Others 21 March 1950, 96 UNTS 271.

[330] See UNODC (2006), 61.   [331] *Ibid.*, 63, 70.

[332] *Ibid.*, 62; Obokata, 'Trafficking of human beings', 448; cf. DIMIA (2005), p. 64.

If a person is being trafficked into slavery, then limited, but universal, rights of visit and search will arise under UNCLOS Article 110. Determining when trafficking will constitute the slave trade, however, requires further examination of relevant international definitions.

3.2 Human trafficking and the slave trade

As noted above, slavery involves the exercise of rights of ownership over a person,[333] while 'practices similar to slavery' include debt bondage, serfdom, forced marriage and child labour.[334] Under the Supplementary Convention on the Abolition of Slavery parties must abolish these 'similar' practices 'whether or not they are covered by the definition of slavery' under the Slavery Convention. This makes it difficult to directly equate these practices with slavery under conventional or customary law. How the international crime of 'enslavement' relates to these various practices and definitions provides a further complication. 'Enslavement' is defined under the ICC Statute as

the exercise of any or all of the powers attaching to the right of ownership over a person and includes the exercise of such power in the course of trafficking in persons, in particular women and children.[335]

Clearly, though, this only goes to say that a person may be enslaved in the course of being trafficked, not that all forms of exploitation constituting trafficking are slavery. It is 'rights of ownership' that are critical. The ICC Elements of Crimes specify that exercising rights of ownership includes 'purchasing, selling, lending or bartering such a person or persons, or by imposing on them a similar deprivation of liberty'.[336]

Further, 'deprivation of liberty may, in some circumstances, include exacting forced labour or otherwise reducing a person to a servile status as defined in the [Supplementary Slavery Convention]'.[337]

These definitions were considered in the *Kunarac* case. In *Kunarac* two young women abducted by Serb soldiers were kept in a locked apartment, threatened with murder if they left, and were 'obliged to cook, clean and wash clothes' and repeatedly sexually assaulted before

---

[333] See Chapter 4, section 2.
[334] Slavery Convention, Article 1; Supplementary Slavery Convention, Article 1.
[335] ICC Statute, Article 7(2)(c).
[336] www.icc-cpi.int/library/about/officialJournal/Element_of_Crimes_English.pdf.
[337] *Ibid.*

being sold to other soldiers.[338] The International Criminal Tribunal for the former Yugoslavia (ICTY) trial chamber found that these facts constituted enslavement, but cautiously noted that 'enslavement' might have a broader meaning than 'slavery' at general international law.[339] Initially, the Chamber found that

enslavement as a crime against humanity in customary international law consist[s] of the exercise of any or all of the powers attaching to the right of ownership over a person.[340]

This obviously, *mutatis mutandis*, mirrors the definition of slavery and one might think the two coextensive. The Chamber's indicia of enslavement, however, were considerably broader:

indications of enslavement include elements of control and ownership; the restriction or control of an individual's autonomy, freedom of choice or free-dom of movement; and, often, the accruing of some gain to the perpetrator. The consent or free will of the victim is absent. It is often rendered impossible or irrelevant by, for example, the threat or use of force or other forms of coer-cion; the fear of violence, deception or false promises; the abuse of power; the victim's position of vulnerability; detention or captivity, psychological oppres-sion or socio-economic conditions. Further indications of enslavement include exploitation; the exaction of forced or compulsory labour or service, often without remuneration and often, though not necessarily, involving physical hardship; sex; prostitution; and human trafficking.[341]

This is, effectively, an undigested compendium of all available defini-tions of slavery, servitude and exploitation. The buying or selling of a person was held not to be a necessary element; but control of movement (including 'measures taken to prevent or deter escape'), psychological control (including 'force, threat of force or coercion'), the duration of control, 'assertion of exclusivity' and 'subjection to cruel treatment and abuse, control of sexuality and forced labour' may all be relevant indica-tions of enslavement.[342] Unfortunately, a shopping list of relevant indi-cia does not provide a legal test of when a crime has been committed.

Two views could be taken of this approach. The broad view would be that one could look to the indicia listed for guidance as to when a person is subject to 'the exercise of ... powers ... of ownership'. This would tend to assimilate practices similar to slavery into the general

---

[338] *Prosecutor v. Kunarac*, para. 68 and cf. paras. 75, 587, 747–782.
[339] *Ibid.*, paras. 541 and 781.　　[340] *Ibid.*, para. 539.　　[341] *Ibid.*, para. 542.
[342] *Ibid.*, paras. 542–543.

definition of enslavement, suggesting that while the 'similar practices' are not necessarily slavery, they may be taken together to amount to slavery in many cases. The stricter view is that the compendious list of indicia suggests that practices punishable as 'enslavement' may include those lacking 'the ownership features characteristic of slavery';[343] thus a broader range of crimes may be punished as 'enslavement' than would traditionally have constituted slavery. On the latter view, the chamber was correct to suggest that enslavement is broader than the general definition of slavery.

Debt bondage, a 'similar practice' to slavery, is the most prevalent form of human exploitation involved in modern human trafficking. It is common for trafficked persons to be told that they have incurred a debt for visas, transport or other 'services' rendered by their exploiters to be repaid by providing labour or prostitution.[344] In line with the Supplementary Slavery Convention definition, there is often no specified length of service or their labour's reasonable value is not applied to reduce the debt, leaving the trafficked person in indefinite servitude. Such servitude is not, however, likely to constitute slavery. The European Commission of Human Rights has taken 'servitude' to mean much the same thing as serfdom under the Supplementary Slavery Convention, namely 'having to live and work on another person's property and perform certain services for them, whether paid or unpaid, together with being unable to alter one's condition' ('ECHR servitude').[345] ECHR servitude has been considered as lacking 'the ownership features characteristic of slavery', although it might be thought of as 'differing from [slavery] less in character ... than in degree'.[346] US case law also suggests that servitude practices resting on psychological subordination or indentured labour, while related to slavery, constitute a broader and distinct category.[347] It thus seems unlikely that debt-bonded servitude legally constitutes slavery.

[343] Council of Europe, Council of Europe Convention on Action against Trafficking in Human Beings and its Explanatory Report (Warsaw, 2005), para. 95, www.coe.int/ trafficking (Council of Europe Explanatory Report).

[344] See Department of State (2005), pp. 9, 10, 13, 14, 19, 20, 86, 92, 103, 115, 190, 194, 196, 208, 210, 225, 239, 244, 247, 251 and 253; UNODC (2006), pp. 51, 66, 70, 71 and 74.

[345] See Report of the Commission, *Van Droogenbroeck Case*, European Court of Human Rights, Series B, No. 44, 30; cf. definition of 'serfdom' under Supplementary Slavery Convention, Article 1.

[346] Council of Europe Explanatory Report, para. 95.

[347] See *Slaughter-House Cases* 83 US 36 (1872) at 69, per Miller J, and 90, per Field J (Dissenting Opinion); as discussed in *US v. Shackney*, 333 F.2d 475 (C.A.Conn. 1964), 485–8.

While in popular usage, even among government agencies, trafficking victims are commonly referred to as slaves,[348] there remain real difficulties in concluding that debt bondage, child labour and other slavery-like practices lacking ownership features can be treated as assimilated to slavery. This being the case, the rights of maritime interdiction pertaining to the slave trade will seldom apply where a person is being trafficked into exploitative slavery-like practices.

4 Conclusions

While there are bilateral and multilateral migrant interdiction arrangements which function in a manner similar to the drug interdiction treaties, the practice of migrant interdiction at sea goes considerably further. States seem increasingly willing to tow seaworthy interdicted craft back to a position outside the territorial waters of the departure state, irrespective of the agreement of the flag state. While states must admit vessels in distress to their ports, some states have asserted a right to close even their territorial sea to vessels in distress carrying smuggled migrants. This seriously compromises the comity required to give effect to obligations regarding rescue and safety of life at sea. The obligation to rescue those in peril at sea if pursued aggressively, however, may allow a collateral form of interdiction to take place. Once persons are removed from an unseaworthy craft onto a state vessel, their disposition is essentially a question for the rescuing State. Contrary to the plain words of the Refugee Protocol, several states have at times taken the view that there is no obligation to provide any screening of refugee claims made by those interdicted at sea in order to prevent prohibited *refoulement*. Australian and Spanish practice appears to suggest that at the least such an obligation will still arise in cases where persons are removed onto a government vessel. The United States, however, appears only to provide such screenings – and then only of a preliminary character – when an interdicted migrant directly makes a refugee status claim.

Turning to trafficking, while there might be extreme cases where human trafficking would amount to the slave trade it will more usually also constitute migrant smuggling. This would make interdiction possible under Migrant Smuggling Protocol procedures. Such practice under the Protocol, however, appears rare or non-existent.

---

[348] E.g. State Department (2004), 5–13, 18–20.

9 Maritime counter-proliferation of weapons of mass destruction

1 Introduction

This chapter examines current multilateral and bilateral efforts to interdict the trade in nuclear, radiological, chemical and biological weapons of mass destruction (WMD), related 'precursors' used in their construction and their potential delivery systems (collectively, 'WMD materiel'). These include recent US bilateral treaties closely modelled on drug interdiction treaties and a new Protocol to the Convention for the Suppression of Unlawful Acts against the Safety of Maritime Navigation (SUA Protocol 2005) which was concluded at the IMO in October 2005.[1] However, some current state practice in interdicting WMD materiel does not follow the treaty-based law enforcement model. Also relevant for present purposes are the efforts of the Proliferation Security Initiative (PSI) and the UN Security Council which are not premised upon establishing new treaties. While the PSI seeks to utilise existing laws to effect interdictions, Security Council Resolution 1540 imposes new obligations upon states to take steps to suppress transfers of WMD materiel to non-state actors. Although UNSCR 1540 does not expressly contemplate interdiction it is not without consequences for maritime jurisdiction.

[1] See Convention for the Suppression of Unlawful Acts against the Safety of Maritime Navigation, 1988 (1988) 27 ILM 672 (SUA Convention); and Protocol of 2005 to the Convention for the Suppression of Unlawful Acts Against the Safety of Maritime Navigation, IMO Doc. LEG/CONF.15/21, 1 November 2005 (SUA Protocol 2005), not in force. At 7 May 2008 it had eighteen signatories and two ratifications: P. McNerney, Testimony before the Senate Foreign Relations Committee, Washington, DC, 7 May 2008, www.state.gov/t/isn/rls/rm/104477.htm. The signatories are Australia, Austria, Bulgaria, Denmark, Estonia, Finland, France, Greece, Italy, Netherlands, New Zealand, Norway, Portugal, Spain, Sweden, Turkey, United Kingdom and United States (information provided by IMO Secretariat).

One difference between WMD interdiction and a more established field such as narcotics interdiction is the undoubted underlying illegality of drug trafficking. As the 183 state parties to the UN Narcotics Convention have agreed, such traffic is a crime of international concern, and its 'eradication ... is a collective responsibility',[2] thus seizing drugs as evidence of a crime is uncontroversial. There is nowhere near such widespread consensus as to the inherent illegality of trade in WMD materiel. Absent a relevant treaty obligation, there is no customary law prohibition on possessing WMD, and the existing WMD treaties, while they may contain obligations to reduce or destroy weapon stockpiles, do not criminalise trade in WMD materiel.[3] A largely unexplored consequence of this is the potential impact of interdictions on third-party states. Is there any international wrong committed when state A boards a flag-vessel of state B (with its consent) and removes legally purchased WMD materiel bound for state C? A related question is, even with flag-state consent, what principle of jurisdiction can an interdicting state invoke in such a case to justify the application of its national law to such an interdicted cargo? General theories of jurisdiction to prescribe often emphasise doubts about the legitimacy of national laws directed at extraterritorial conduct not intended to have an effect against a prescribing state's nationals or ultimately within its territory.[4] UNSCR 1540 and the SUA Protocol 2005 constitute steps towards criminalisation at international law, and the extent to which they justify maritime WMD interdiction will be considered.

This chapter begins by surveying recent counter-proliferation efforts, including shipping interdiction practice, declarations of 'principles' and the passage of UNSCR 1540. The WMD interdiction treaties (at present, US bilateral treaties and the SUA Protocol 2005) are then discussed. It concludes by addressing some practical and state responsibility problems that may arise.

2 Statements of political intent

In 1992 the Security Council identified the 'proliferation of all weapons of mass destruction' as a 'threat to international peace and security'.[5]

---

[2] UN Narcotics Convention, Preamble.
[3] R. Wedgwood, 'The fall of Saddam Hussein: Security Council mandates and preemptive self-defense' (2003) 97 AJIL 576 at 579, 585.
[4] Other than cases of universal jurisdiction: Lowe, 'Jurisdiction', pp. 341–2.
[5] UN Doc. S/23500, 31 January 1992.

The 11 September 2001 terrorist attacks gave the issue renewed urgency, raising concerns among industrialised states that terrorist groups might obtain WMD.[6]

In June 2002 the Group of Eight (G8) most highly industrialised states committed themselves to six principles to 'prevent terrorists ... from acquiring or developing' WMD materiel (the Kananaskis Principles).[7] Principles 4 and 6 call on all states to:

Develop and maintain effective border controls, law enforcement efforts and international cooperation to detect, deter and interdict ... illicit trafficking in such items ... [and to] provide assistance to states lacking sufficient expertise or resources to strengthen their capacity to detect, deter and interdict ... illicit trafficking ...; [and] Adopt and strengthen efforts to manage and dispose of stocks of fissile materials designated as no longer required for defence purposes, eliminate all chemical weapons, and minimize holdings of dangerous biological pathogens and toxins, ... [recognising] that the threat of terrorist acquisition is reduced as the overall quantity of such items is reduced.

The Kananaskis Principles thus emphasise co-operative and capacity-building measures to allow interdiction (the term here not being limited to at-sea measures) of trafficked WMD materiel, and the concomitant value of reducing stockpiles of WMD. The accusation made against major nuclear-weapon-holding states has, however, been that in their subsequent actions, especially in the Security Council, the emphasis on counter-proliferation has been at the expense of disarmament or stockpile reduction.[8]

The first such co-operative effort at interdicting WMD materiel soon followed. On 9 December 2002 the Spanish navy, acting on US intelligence, boarded the *So San*, a vessel that had left North Korea with a concealed cargo of Scud missiles and dual-use chemicals.[9] When Yemen claimed to have purchased these weapons legally, both vessel and cargo were released. The White House nonetheless saw the incident as focusing international attention upon enhancing anti-proliferation measures.[10]

---

6 Statement by G8 leaders, The G8 Global Partnership Against the Spread of Weapons and Materials of Mass Destruction, Kananaskis Summit, Canada, 26–27 June 2002, www.g8.gc.ca/2002Kananaskis/gp_stat-en.pdf.

7 *Ibid.*

8 UN Doc. S/PV.4950 (22 April 2004), 7 (Spain), 10 (Chile), 15 (Pakistan), 20 (Peru), 22 (South Africa), 23–24 (India), 32 (Iran); UN Doc. S/PV.4950 (Resumption 1), 4 (Malaysia), 11 (Jordan), 16 (Namibia).

9 Discussed further at section 4, below.

10 A. Fleischer, White House Press Secretary, Press Briefing, 11 December 2002, www.whitehouse.gov/news/releases/2002/12/20021211–5.html#2.

The next day, on 10 December 2002, the United States released its National Strategy to Combat Weapons of Mass Destruction.[11] Despite references to the importance of 'interdiction' and 'pre-emptive action' to 'destroy an adversary's WMD assets' before their use, it also refers to the role of multilateral treaties and international co-operation.[12]

President Bush subsequently announced the Proliferation Security Initiative (PSI) on 31 May 2003,[13] and PSI participants later announced a 'Statement of Interdiction Principles'.[14] The Interdiction Principles represent a political commitment to co-operate to interdict transfers of WMD materiel and secure such materiel where present in national jurisdiction. This co-operation is to include participants giving serious consideration to authorising other states to interdict their flag vessels, if reasonably suspected of transporting WMD materiel (paragraph 1). The PSI targets WMD materiel transfers to state or non-state actors of 'proliferation concern'. These actors are, somewhat circularly, defined as those 'countries or entities that the PSI participants involved establish should be subject to interdiction activities because they are engaged in proliferation' (paragraph 1). No list of such actors has ever been published, although one chairman's statement from a PSI meeting specifically referred to North Korea and Iran.[15] It is not likely that the PSI, a non-organisation whose participants have agreed to consider case-by-case co-operation, will publish general lists of 'contraband' materiel or targeted states.[16] In practice all this 'definition' will require is that those states actually involved in any given interdiction consider it desirable (given available intelligence) and permissible under existing law.

---

[11] White House, National Strategy to Combat Weapons of Mass Destruction, Washington DC, December 2002, www.state.gov/documents/organization/16092.pdf.

[12] Ibid., pp. 2–3.

[13] Bureau of Nonproliferation, 'The Proliferation Security Initiative', Washington DC, 26 May 2005, www.state.gov/t/isn/rls/fs/46839.htm.

[14] www.state.gov/t/isn/rls/fs/23764.htm.

[15] Chairman's Statement, Proliferation Security Initiative, Brisbane Meeting, 9–10 July 2003, www.dfat.gov.au/globalissues/psi/chair_statement_0603.html; cf. SC Res. 1718 (14 October 2006); SC Res. 1737 (27 December 2006). One should also note that the United States lists Cuba, Iran, North Korea, Sudan and Syria as sponsors of terrorism, although it may be about to 'de-list' North Korea: US State Department, 'State sponsors of terrorism', www.state.gov/s/ct/c14151.htm; N. Onishi and E. Wong, 'US to remove North Korea from terror list', International Herald Tribune, 26 June 2008, www.iht.com/articles/2008/06/26/asia/nuclear.php.

[16] Contra, M. Becker, 'The shifting order of the oceans: freedom of navigation and the interdiction of ships at sea' (2005) 46 HILJ 131 at 225–6; cf. Valencia, Proliferation Security Initiative, pp. 73–4.

The PSI regularly conducts high-level 'plenary' meetings, meetings of operational experts and joint training exercises including mock interdictions at sea.[17] The point of such activities is to improve the lines of communications and the interoperability of systems, personnel and assets that underpin co-operative interdictions.

States learn through PSI conferences, exercises, and real-world interdictions how to share information, communicate more effectively, and improve their national legal authorities and operational capabilities.[18]

Those involved commonly describe the PSI as 'an activity, not an organization', emphasising its flexible, non-institutional character.[19] Active participants now include Australia, Canada, Denmark, France, Germany, Italy, Japan, Netherlands, New Zealand, Norway, Poland, Portugal, Russia, Singapore, Spain, Turkey, the United Kingdom and the United States.[20] These participants also probably form part of the twenty-state membership of the PSI 'Operational Experts Group', an

expanding network of military, law enforcement, intelligence, legal and diplomatic expertise … [that meets] periodically to develop new operational concepts, organize an interdiction exercise program, share information about national legal authorities, and pursue cooperation with key industry sectors.[21]

Statements refer to ninety-one countries which support the Interdiction Principles.[22] This figure may include public references to Argentina,

[17] Y.-H. Song, 'The US-led Proliferation Security Initiative and UNCLOS: legality, implementation, and an assessment' (2007) 38 ODIL 101 at 107–9; F. Spadi, 'Bolstering the Proliferation Security Initiative at sea: a comparative analysis of ship-boarding as a bilateral and multilateral implementing mechanism' (2006) 75 NJIL 249 at 252 n. 8; Valencia, *The Proliferation Security Initiative*, pp. 30 ff.

[18] W. Sharp, 'Proliferation Security Initiative: the legacy of Operation Socotora' (2006–7) 16 TLCP 991 at 1003.

[19] J. Bolton, 'The Bush administration's forward strategy for nonproliferation' (2004–5) 5 CJIL 395 at 400.

[20] Song, 'US-led Proliferation Security Initiative', 102. The issue of PSI membership is confused by its very flexibility. Initially there was talk of 11–15 core members and a wider group of supporting states. The idea of a 'core group' was apparently abandoned in August 2005: Valencia, *Proliferation Security Initiative*, p. 29.

[21] Sharp, 'Proliferation Security Initiative', 1005, quoting a defunct State Department website.

[22] Washington Declaration for PSI 5th Anniversary Senior-Level Meeting, 28 May 2008, www.state.gov/r/pa/prs/ps/2008/may/105268.htm; cf. Proliferation Security Initiative: Chairman's Statement at the Fifth Meeting, 5 March 2004, www.state.gov/t/isn/rls/other/30960.htm; Chairman's Statement at the 1st Anniversary PSI Meeting, Krakow, Poland, 1 June 2004, www.state.gov/t/isn/rls/other/33208.htm.

Iraq and Georgia as PSI members and Pakistan's publicly claimed membership.[23]

Paragraph 4(d) of the Interdiction Principles contemplates that participants, to the extent consistent with their national law and international legal obligations, will:

- 'stop and/or search in their internal waters, territorial seas, or contiguous zones' vessels reasonably suspected of carrying WMD materiel and seize any such cargoes; and
- 'enforce conditions on vessels entering or leaving their ports, internal waters or territorial seas that are reasonably suspected of carrying such cargoes' including making 'boarding, search, and seizure of such cargoes' a condition of entry.

This statement obviously expresses a view that participants may interdict in their territorial waters and contiguous zones vessels suspected of transporting WMD materiel. As previously observed, there is some support for the view that states have a general right to enforce their customs laws out to the 24-n.m. limit,[24] but the better view must be that 'foreign-flagged vessels merely sailing through a coastal State's contiguous zone may not be intercepted on the basis of national customs laws'.[25] PSI treaty practice on contiguous zone interdictions is discussed below.

It is occasionally questioned whether the PSI is consistent with international law or UNCLOS. To ask if the PSI is legal is as redundant as asking if diplomatic and military co-operation is legal. The legality of PSI interdictions will turn on an assessment of individual interdictions. Nothing on the face of the interdiction principles suggests that extra-legal action is contemplated. Claims that 'the PSI Principles, in practice, will represent a Potemkin Village behind whose facades the United States will undertake a broad campaign of interdiction' and that the PSI will inevitably undermine customary law by 'blurring' jurisdictional boundaries are premature and contrary to the available evidence, discussed below.[26] The public position of those involved remains that '[the]

---

[23] See C. Rice, US Secretary of State, 'Remarks on the second anniversary of the Proliferation Security Initiative', Washington, DC, 31 May 2005, www.state.gov/secretary/rm/2005/46951.htm; Byers, 'Policing the high seas', 528; UN Doc. S/PV.4956, 5.

[24] See Chapter 2, section 2.3.

[25] Song, 'US-led Proliferation Security Initiative', 117.

[26] T. Perry, 'Blurring the ocean zones: the effect of the Proliferation Security Initiative on the customary international law of the sea' (2006) 37 ODIL 33 at 40, 47.

PSI does not create a new enforcement mechanism. It uses existing enforcement capabilities effectively, co-operatively, and in a timely manner.'[27] It is perhaps easier to criticise the PSI on the basis that its emphasis on co-operative action means that it risks being ineffectual and that its secrecy makes it impossible to measure results.[28]

The PSI Interdiction Principles and the Kananaskis Principles form the background to UNSCR 1540.[29]

3 UNSCR 1540 (28 April 2004)

3.1 Content and adoption of the resolution

In UNSCR 1540, the Security Council, acting under Chapter VII, required all states to prohibit and criminalise the transfer of WMD materiel to non-state actors.[30] The resolution does not affect state-to-state transfers, but is nonetheless an extraordinary exercise in law-making, having much in common with UNSCR 1373.[31] Both resolutions impose wide-ranging obligations upon UN members that are unconstrained as to time and apply to an abstract class of persons, whereas previous compulsory measures obliged members to impose sanctions only upon a specified state or group of persons.[32] Both resolutions can thus be described as legislative.

The constitutional implications of Chapter VII 'legislation' have been discussed elsewhere.[33] The present chapter considers only the

[27] White House, Remarks by National Security Advisor Stephen J. Hadley at the Proliferation Security Initiative Fifth Anniversary Senior Level Meeting, Washington, DC, 28 May 2008, www.whitehouse.gov/news/releases/2008/05/20080528–3.html.

[28] Song, 'US-led Proliferation Security Initiative', 101–2.

[29] Note also European Council, Basic Principles for an EU Strategy against Proliferation of Weapons of Mass Destruction (16 June 2003), Principle 4, Doc. 10352/03, http://ue.eu.int/ueDocs/cms_Data/docs/pressdata/en/reports/76328.pdf.

[30] SC Res. 1540 (28 April 2004). Certain reporting requirements have been extended by SC Res. 1673 (2006) and SC Res. 1810 (2008).

[31] SC Res. 1373 (2001).

[32] R. Lavalle, 'A novel, if awkward exercise in international law-making: Security Council Resolution 1540 (28 April 2004)' (2004) 51 NILR 413; S. Sur, 'La résolution 1540 du conseil de sécurité (28 avril 2004): entre la prolifération des armes de destruction massive, le terrorisme et les acteurs non étatiques' (2004) 108 RGDIP 855 at 861, 864.

[33] Ibid.; S. Talmon, 'The Security Council as world legislature' (2005) 99 AJIL 175; D. Joyner, 'Non-proliferation law and the United Nations system: Resolution 1540 and the limits of the power of the Security Council' (2007) 20 LJIL 489.

effectiveness of creating treaty-like obligations by Security Council 'fiat'[34] and the interaction of UNSCR 1540 with the law of the sea. Both require an examination of the substantive obligations the resolution creates. UNSCR 1540 applies principally to nuclear, chemical and biological weapons, and their means of delivery. The resolution, in operative paragraph 2, requires that

all States … shall adopt and enforce appropriate effective laws which prohibit any non-State actor to manufacture, acquire, possess, develop, transport, transfer or use nuclear, chemical or biological weapons and their means of delivery …

It further requires in operative paragraph 3(c) and (d) that states

[d]evelop and maintain appropriate effective border controls and law enforcement efforts to detect, deter, prevent and combat, including through international cooperation when necessary, the illicit trafficking and brokering in such items in accordance with their national legal authorities and legislation and consistent with international law

and

[e]stablish … appropriate effective national export and trans-shipment controls over such items, including appropriate laws … [and] establishing and enforcing appropriate criminal or civil penalties for violations of such export control[s] …

The fact that UNSCR 1540 was preceded by five months of informal consultations both within the Security Council and between Security Council members and other states,[35] and by an open debate in the Security Council in which some forty-nine member states participated, represented an acknowledgement that consensus-building was needed to enhance the resolution's legitimacy.[36]

The resolution's genealogy is apparent on its face: the text of operative paragraph 3 reproduces, in some cases word for word, Kananaskis Principles 2–5. Kananaskis Principle 1 is also substantially reproduced in operative paragraph 8. This comparison draws attention to two points. First, at China's request,[37] in the translation

---

[34] UN Doc. S/PV.4950 (Resumption 1), 14 (Nepal).
[35] Lavalle, 'A novel, if awkward exercise', 425–6; Sur, 'La résolution 1540', 856 ff.
[36] Concerns were still expressed about the process; see UN Doc. S/PV.4950, 6 (China), 21 (New Zealand), 29 (Switzerland), 30 (Cuba), 31 (Indonesia), 32 (Iran); S/PV.4950 (Resumption 1), 14 (Nepal).
[37] UN Doc. S/PV.4950, 6.

of Kananaskis Principle 4 to operative paragraph 3(c), all references to 'interdiction' were removed. Second, Resolution 1540 contains no equivalent to Kananaskis Principle 6 on reducing stockpiles of WMD precursor materiel 'based on the recognition that the threat of terrorist acquisition is reduced' thereby.

From the perspective of smaller states, by omitting any equivalent to Principle 6 the resolution may appear to be a stick without a carrot. As the majority of the world's states have 'nothing to proliferate',[38] UNSCR 1540 imposes significant obligations on smaller states to police leakages from states with larger militaries, especially the nuclear states. The point, while valid, assumes an irony when made by India, Pakistan and Iran.[39]

3.2 UNSCR 1540 and criminal jurisdiction over the territorial sea

It has been said that one, essentially US, objective of UNSCR 1540 was to increase the international legitimacy of the PSI, but its lack of any reference to 'interdiction' sets back the search for broader legal justification for the PSI's coercive actions.[40] Is this necessarily the case? UNSCR 1540 does not expressly override any existing obligations. Nor does it purport to enlarge member states' domestic jurisdiction.[41] Thus there should be no conflict between its implementation and obligations under UNCLOS incapable of resolution by applying Articles 25 and 103 of the UN Charter (obliging members to implement Security Council decisions and providing that Charter obligations prevail over other obligations). Rather, the resolution imposes duties to exercise existing jurisdiction in a certain manner in certain cases. Under it all states must 'adopt and enforce ... effective laws' prohibiting non-state actors from, *inter alia*, acquiring, possessing or transporting WMD materiel.[42] The question for present purposes becomes the extent of enforcement jurisdiction over the territorial sea and contiguous zone.

The territorial sea has been characterised as a 'sovereignty minus' jurisdiction: full sovereign power, as qualified by innocent passage.[43]

---

[38] UN Doc. S/PV.4950, 2 (Philippines).
[39] UN Doc. S/PV.4950, 15 (Pakistan), 24 (India), 32 (Iran).
[40] Sur, 'La résolution 1540', 862, 872–3; Becker, 'The Shifting Order of the Oceans', 218.
[41] D. Joyner, 'The Proliferation Security Initiative: nonproliferation, counterproliferation and international law' (2005) 30 YJIL 507 at 540–1.
[42] SC Res. 1540 (28 April 2004), para 2.
[43] R. McLaughlin, 'United Nations mandated naval interdiction operations in the territorial sea?' (2002) 51 ICLQ 249 at 268; cf. Meyers, pp. 77–80.

However, while Part II, Section 3 of UNCLOS is entitled 'Innocent Passage in the Territorial Sea', not all provisions therein are necessarily predicated upon innocent passage as elaborated in Articles 17–26. Nevertheless, innocent passage remains a useful starting point.

Does UNSCR 1540 deprive vessels transporting WMD materiel of the right of innocent passage? When passage is not innocent, the 'coastal State may take the necessary steps in its territorial sea to prevent' it.[44] While common sense tempts the conclusion that no activity that the Security Council has declared prejudicial to international peace and security could be 'innocent', closer analysis is warranted.

'Passage' involves traversing the territorial sea without entering internal waters. Under Article 19(1) this lateral transit is innocent 'so long as it is not prejudicial to the peace, good order or security of the coastal State. Such passage shall take place in conformity with this Convention and with other rules of international law.' The first sentence raises an apparently direct nexus between the transit and 'prejudice' to the coastal state. The second concerns the passage's conformity with 'other rules of international law'.

Regarding the first sentence, arguably, if an activity threatens international peace and security by definition it also affects national security. But this approach seems unsatisfactory, relying on an indirect threat to meet a direct nexus requirement. While 'prejudice' might comprehend inchoate threats to the coastal state, if a shipment of WMD materiel intended for use against a distant state is only temporarily present in territorial waters it is hard to see how this accident inherently prejudices coastal-state interests. This is especially so if the shipment consists only of delivery system components. An unassembled Scud missile without a payload is not, in itself, threatening. The 'prejudice' it may represent to (some state's) security is heavily contingent on its intended end use: a 'non-state actor' could be interested in it for scrap metal or as an exhibit. The same logic applies to arguments that a coastal state could straightforwardly justify seizure by characterising such shipments through its territorial waters as a threat to both its security and that of other states.[45] One cannot bootstrap oneself into jurisdiction.

---

[44] UNCLOS, Article 25(1); cf. Chapter 8, section 2.5, text accompanying n. 153.
[45] D. Joyner, 'The PSI and international law' (2004) 10 *The Monitor* 7 at 8;
W. Heintschel von Heinegg, 'The Proliferation Security Initiative: security vs freedom of navigation?' (2005) 35 IYBHR 181 at 195.

Arguing that transporting WMD materiel is not innocent as it is contrary to 'other rules of international law' also encounters difficulties. 'Other rules of international law' could obviously include obligations arising under Security Council resolutions.[46] The reference, however, in Article 19(2) of UNCLOS to 'passage shall take place' coupled with the illustrative list of acts not regarded as 'innocent' indicates a focus on the character of the passage itself. The assumption is that it is the external acts of a vessel engaged in innocent passage, not its internal economy, which may prejudice a coastal state's security. It is hard to see that a latent threat in the vessel's hold, destined elsewhere, has any 'external' manifestation capable of affecting the character of passage.[47]

By contrast, UNCLOS Article 27 is concerned with the vessel's internal economy. Article 27 deals with the assertion by a coastal state of criminal jurisdiction over a vessel in its territorial sea, and such action does not require a prior determination that the vessel's passage per se is non-innocent.[48] Article 27(1) provides that '[t]he criminal jurisdiction of the coastal State should not be exercised on board a foreign ship passing through the territorial sea … save only in the following cases'. As noted previously, the formulation 'jurisdiction … *should not* be exercised' is hortatory.[49] The contrast with prohibitions on national legislation ('shall not') in the same section is apparent.[50] Thus states have criminal jurisdiction over ships within their territorial sea which they generally should not exercise for purposes outside Article 27, but nonetheless may. In the context of WMD shipments passing through the territorial sea, it is exactly that capacity to act which becomes an *obligation* to act under UNSCR 1540.

What of the Article 27(5) exclusion of enforcement jurisdiction over crimes committed aboard a ship simply passing through territorial waters 'before the ship entered the territorial sea'? Some crimes, such as a murder committed on the high seas, are self-evidently complete before the vessel enters territorial waters. However, under UNSCR

---

[46] Talmon, 'Security Council as world legislature', 179.
[47] This objection also covers arguments based on UNCLOS, Article 301; see Song, 'US-led Proliferation Security Initiative', 117.
[48] Contra, Joyner, 'Proliferation Security Initiative', 535–6; cf. J. Garvey, 'The international institutional imperative for countering the spread of weapons of mass destruction: assessing the Proliferation Security Initiative' (2005) 10 JCSL 125 at 130–1.
[49] See Chapter 2, section 2.2.   [50] UNCLOS, Articles 21(2) and 24(1).

1540 transporting, transferring and possession of WMD materiel must all be prohibited under effective laws. These are continuous acts, breaches of the prohibition occurring as much within territorial waters as without. The Article 27(5) exclusion therefore does not apply. While it might be argued that Article 27(5) could also exclude jurisdiction over continuous acts (as they are partly or equally committed before entering the territorial sea), the narrower reading is more consistent with the intent to preserve state jurisdiction expressed in Article 27(1).[51]

The case of the contiguous zone is less straightforward. Enforcement jurisdiction between 12 and 24 n.m. from coastal-state baselines only applies to punish crimes committed (or having effect) on shore or within the 12-n.m. territorial sea, or to prevent crimes threatened to be committed within those jurisdictions. 'Prevention' would probably not extend to seizure of a vessel for violation of customs laws such as the transport of WMD materiel listed on export control lists, but merely to measures such as inspection and warning.[52] Nonetheless, such limited action might still serve a valuable intelligence-gathering function. The contiguous zone issue is, however, further complicated by the US bilateral PSI agreements discussed below.

Despite coercive or legislative overtones, UNSCR 1540 leaves a great deal of flexibility to national law in its implementation, especially given its lack of precise definitions.[53] It would clearly be legitimate for national legislatures to hold that compliance requires exercise of criminal jurisdiction in the territorial sea, much as that might alarm those who hold the exceptions to innocent passage to be exhaustively codified by Articles 19 and 27 of UNCLOS.[54]

4 WMD-related interdiction in state practice

States are undoubtedly already stopping and searching at sea vessels considered to be security risks. There are credible reports that numerous high-seas interdictions have been conducted since 11 September

---

[51] See Chapter 2, section 2.2.   [52] See Chapter 2, section 2.3.

[53] Sur, 'La résolution 1540', 869.

[54] On the similar conclusion, by different reasoning, that SC Res. 1540 may *permit* territorial sea enforcement, see Song, ' US-led Proliferation Security Initiative', 116–17; Joyner, 'Proliferation Security Initiative', 535–6; and Heintschel von Heinegg, 'Proliferation Security Initiative', 193–5. The present author considers that SC Res. 1540, however, *requires* such action.

2001 by PSI member states, all with flag-state consent.[55] Many of these operations may never be publicly reported or discussed:[56] it may not be in the interests of boarding states, flag states or shipping owners to publicise these operations, even when successful.

The highly public mistake in December 2001 when British authorities interdicted the MV *Nisha* may have been a salutary lesson in the consequences of prematurely publicising interdictions. Inevitably, some actions based on intelligence and risk assessments will prove unwarranted. The *Nisha* was suspected of carrying explosives for terrorist purposes, but held only 26,000 tons of sugar.[57] It would also appear that the vessel was intercepted outside the UK territorial sea, with the flag state's consent[58] although no public statement was made as to the legal basis for this action.

One heavily reported interdiction was, as noted above, the *So San* incident. On 9 December 2002 the MV *So San*, transporting fifteen Scud missiles from North Korea to Yemen, was interdicted 960 km from its destination by a Spanish frigate, acting on US intelligence.[59] The *So San* had been tracked by the United States for some weeks. It displayed no flag or identifying markings.[60] Responding to radio queries, its master identified his cargo as concrete before attempting to 'speed away'; warning shots were then fired before special forces troops boarded it by helicopter.[61] The missiles were discovered under sacks of concrete.[62]

[55] Royal Institute of International Affairs (Chatham House), 'The Proliferation Security Initiative: is it legal? Are we more secure?', summary of a discussion at Chatham House, London, 24 February 2005, www.chathamhouse.org.uk/files/3248_ilp250205. pdf; and cf. Rice, 'Remarks'; Song, 'US-led Proliferation Security Initiative'.

[56] Rice, 'Remarks'.

[57] S. Carrell, 'Did they stop the wrong ship?' *Independent on Sunday*, 23 December 2001, p. 2; N. North and J. Edwards, 'Terror cargo alert', *Daily Record*, 22 December 2001, pp. 6–7.

[58] *Ibid.*; N. Brown, 'Panel III Commentary – Maritime & Coalition Operations' (2003) 79 *International Law Studies* 305, quoted in P. Jiminez Kwast, 'Maritime interdiction of weapons of mass destruction in an international legal perspective' (2007) 38 *Netherlands Yearbook of International Law* 163 at 237.

[59] 'US lets Scud ship sail to Yemen', CNN, 12 December 2002, http://archives.cnn. com/2002/WORLD/asiapcf/east/12/11/us.missile.ship/index.html; 'Spanish official details high seas drama', CNN, 11 December 2002, http://archives.cnn.com/2002/ WORLD/europe/12/11/missile.ship.spain/index.html.

[60] 'US lets Scud ship sail to Yemen'; Fleischer, Press Briefing at n. 10 above.

[61] 'Scud missiles are ours, says Yemen', CNN, 11 December 2002, http://archives.cnn. com/2002/WORLD/asiapcf/east/12/11/scud.ship/index.html.

[62] J. Goodman, 'Official: Spain perplexed by Scud decision', CNN, 11 December 2002, http://archives.cnn.com/2002/WORLD/europe/12/11/spain.ship.reax/index.html.

The interdiction has widely been presumed, as the *So San* flew no flag and had obscured its name and home port, to have been justified by a suspicion of statelessness under UNCLOS Article 110.[63] While Article 110 would certainly have permitted boarding to ascertain its nationality, it appears that prior to boarding flag-state authorisation was sought and received from Cambodia after the master 'had attempted to declare it ... a Cambodian vessel'.[64] Inspection confirmed its Cambodian registration.[65] The declaration of cargo aboard listed neither the Scud missiles nor Yemen as a destination.[66] Yemen, however, asserted that it had purchased the missiles legally and guaranteed the United States that they were intended only for defence. Consequently, the *So San* was released, the White House citing the lack of any international law allowing seizure of otherwise legal weapons.[67] The incident, and this outcome, brought world attention to bear upon the potential traffic in WMD and may have helped prompt the PSI's formation.[68]

In 2003, the widely publicised interception of the *BBC China*, carrying centrifuge components produced by part of the Khan network in Malaysia to Libya, has been credited with causing Libya to abandon its WMD programme.[69] The events are concisely summarised by Roach:

The *BBC China* was a German-owned ship (flagged in Antigua and Barbuda) that the UK and US had information was carrying uranium centrifuge parts to Libya. In early October 2003 a request was made to the German government to search the ship. The German government agreed and had the owner ... bring the ship in to the Italian port of Taranto where centrifuge parts were removed by Italian customs before permitting the ship to continue.[70]

This exemplifies the PSI's probable practical operation: it was an action by some PSI participants, based on intelligence sharing and

---

[63] Byers, 'Policing the high seas', 526; Becker, 'Shifting order of the oceans', 152–3; Guilfoyle, 'Proliferation Security Initiative', 740–1.

[64] Byers, 'Policing the high seas', 526 n. 5.   [65] *Ibid.*

[66] 'Spain: US apologises over Scud ship', CNN, 11 December 2002, http://archives.cnn. com/2002/WORLD/asiapcf/east/12/12/missile.ship/index.html.

[67] Fleischer, Press Briefing, at n. 10, above; on other possible considerations see Guilfoyle, 'Proliferation Security Initiative', 736.

[68] Byers, 'Policing the high seas', 528.

[69] *Ibid.*, 529; W. Hawkins, 'Interdict WMD smugglers at sea', US Naval Institute Proceedings, December 2004, www.military.com/NewContent/0%2C13190% 2CNI_1204_Sea-P1%2C00.html.

[70] Roach, 'Proliferation Security Initiative', p. 357.

creative use of existing national and international law.[71] Flag-state consent was not required as the ship owner was amenable to directing the vessel into a port where national customs law enforcement, presumably through export control lists, could prevent the transhipment of WMD materiel. A similar port-state interdiction occurred in April 2003, when Egypt intercepted a French vessel, the *Ville de Virgo*, carrying a German cargo of aluminium tubes capable of use in uranium enrichment destined for North Korea.[72] The vessel was intercepted within the Suez Canal on the basis of French and German intelligence. The unresolved issue is whether Libya or North Korea would have been entitled to claim compensation for the components. Trade in such materiel is not a crime at international law, although it will be criminalised under the SUA Protocol 2005, when it enters into force and as between the states parties. The issue has not gone unnoticed by PSI participants, who resolved in a 2008 statement to 'work together to seek solutions to outstanding legal questions, such as the disposition of detained cargo, that may result from interdiction actions'.[73]

5 The US bilateral WMD interdiction agreements

The United States has concluded bilateral PSI ship-boarding agreements with Liberia,[74] Panama[75] and the Marshall Islands[76] in 2004 and

---

[71] *Ibid.*, 358; Rice, 'Remarks', at n. 23, above.

[72] Valencia, *Proliferation Security Initiative*, p. 36. Flag states now have specific duties regarding transfers of WMD materiel to North Korea and Iran; see references at n. 154, below.

[73] Washington Declaration, at n. 22, above.

[74] Agreement between the US and the Republic of Liberia concerning Cooperation to Suppress the Proliferation of Weapons of Mass Destruction, Their Delivery Systems, and Related Materials by Sea 2004 (entered into force 9 December 2004), www.state.gov/t/isn/trty/32403.htm (Liberian PSI Agreement).

[75] Amendment to the Supplementary Arrangement between the US and the Republic of Panama to the Arrangement between the US and Panama for Support and Assistance from the United States Coast Guard for the National Maritime Service of the Ministry of Government and Justice 2004 (entered into force 1 December 2004), www.state.gov/t/isn/trty/32858.htm (Panamanian PSI Agreement).

[76] Agreement between the US and the Republic of the Marshall Islands concerning Cooperation to Suppress the Proliferation of Weapons of Mass Destruction, Their Delivery Systems, and Related Materials by Sea 2004 (entered into force 24 November 2004), www.state.gov/t/isn/trty/35237.htm (Marshall Islands PSI Agreement).

with Croatia,[77] Cyprus,[78] Belize,[79] Malta[80] and Mongolia[81] in 2005–7. On 11 August 2008 it announced the conclusion of a PSI ship-boarding agreement with the Bahamas, but at the time of writing no treaty text was as yet available. The United States appears to be the only PSI participant that has so far concluded such agreements. While Belize reported to the Security Council that it is 'actively considering' entering such an arrangement with the United Kingdom,[82] the latter has not concluded any such arrangements yet.[83] These agreements all work within the framework of flag-state consent, upholding the requirement of flag-state permission to board a vessel in international waters and the primacy of its jurisdiction to prosecute offences discovered aboard. The agreements define those vessels which may be interdicted in international waters, provide a procedure for obtaining consent to interdict and contain 'safeguards' governing boarding state conduct and claims provisions on any loss or damage arising.

By number of vessels, Panama, Liberia and Malta are among the world's four largest shipping registries, while Cyprus ranks twelfth.[84] This gives these agreements considerable reach and indicates US use of

[77] Agreement between the US and the Republic of Croatia concerning Cooperation to Suppress the Proliferation of Weapons of Mass Destruction, Their Delivery Systems, and Related Materials 2005 (entered into force 5 March 2007), www.state.gov/t/isn/trty/47086.htm (Croatian PSI Agreement).

[78] Agreement between the US and the Republic of Cyprus concerning Cooperation to Suppress the Proliferation of Weapons of Mass Destruction, Their Delivery Systems, and Related Materials by Sea 2005 (entered into force 12 January 2006), www.state.gov/t/isn/trty/50274.htm (Cypriot PSI Agreement).

[79] Agreement between the US and Belize concerning Cooperation to Suppress the Proliferation of Weapons of Mass Destruction, Their Delivery Systems, and Related Materials by Sea 2005 (entered into force 19 October 2005), www.state.gov/t/isn/trty/50809.htm (Belizean PSI Agreement).

[80] Agreement between the US and Malta concerning Cooperation to Suppress the Proliferation of Weapons of Mass Destruction, Their Delivery Systems, and Related Materials by Sea 2007 (entered into force 19 December 2007), www.state.gov/t/isn/trty/81883.htm (Maltese PSI Agreement).

[81] Agreement between the US and Mongolia concerning Cooperation to Suppress the Proliferation of Weapons of Mass Destruction, Their Delivery Systems, and Related Materials by Sea 2007 (not yet in force), www.state.gov/t/isn/trty/94626.htm (Mongolian PSI Agreement).

[82] UN Doc. S/AC.44/2004/(02)/7/Add.1 (10 August 2005); cf. Roach, 'Proliferation Security Initiative', 354.

[83] Personal communications with Abda Sharif, Foreign and Commonwealth Office, 22 February 2006, and Annabelle Bolt, Her Majesty's Revenue and Customs, 17 May 2005.

[84] See CIA, *World Factbook* (2008), www.cia.gov/library/publications/the-world-factbook/rankorder/2108rank.html.

its comparative advantage in diplomatic and legal resources to build a negotiated framework for WMD-materiel interdictions.[85] It has been said that any interdiction occurring under these arrangements will simply reflect the United States' 'inordinate leverage'.[86] It is, of course, unlikely that many of these treaty partners would decline a US request to board and inspect a vessel; and it is improbable that, say, Liberia would ever seek to interdict consensually a US vessel.[87] However, another view can be taken: that this may represent a means for a small state to externalise some of its security or reputation costs. Officials in Liberia and Panama have described these agreements as bringing their flag vessels under the US 'security umbrella' and as assuring the world of their determination to prevent WMD trafficking aboard their vessels.[88]

All bilateral PSI agreements target 'proliferation by sea', commonly defined as 'the transportation by ship of weapons of mass destruction, their delivery systems, and related materials to or from States and non-State actors of proliferation concern'.[89] As discussed, this is a PSI concept of flexible content, subject simply to the ad hoc agreement of the states involved in an interdiction. The only real constraint upon action is the necessity of convincing another government that interdiction is warranted.[90] While this may allow states to sidestep the widely noted problems in defining what will constitute WMD materiel, especially so-called 'dual use' items, it may also aggravate existing criticisms that PSI interdictions lack stable criteria.[91]

Under these agreements, where one party encounters a suspect vessel on the high seas which is flying the flag or bearing marks of nationality of the other party it may request that it confirm the vessel's nationality and, if confirmed, request permission to board.[92] Reference

---

[85] Notably, the United States has not been able to conclude such agreements with important but better-resourced flag states such as China and Greece, the third- and thirteenth-largest merchant marine registries respectively.

[86] Garvey, 'International institutional imperative', 137.

[87] Spadi, 'Bolstering the Proliferation Security Initiative', 256.

[88] Becker, 'Shifting order of the oceans', 183 n. 244.

[89] Panamanian PSI Agreement, Article 1(2); Marshall Islands PSI Agreement, Article 1(3); Liberian PSI Agreement, Article 1(1); Belizean PSI Agreement, Article 1(1); Cypriot PSI Agreement, Article 1(1); Croatian PSI Agreement, Article 1(1); Maltese PSI Agreement, Article 2(1).

[90] Which may not be much of a restraint: Garvey, 'International institutional imperative', 137.

[91] Becker, 'Shifting order of the oceans', 225–6.

[92] Belizean PSI Agreement, Article 4(1); Cypriot PSI Agreement, Article 4(1); Croatian PSI Agreement, Article 4(2); Maltese PSI Agreement, Article 5(1).

to a registry check is conspicuously absent.[93] It thus rests with the requested flag state to decide whether the vessel has a valid claim of nationality. If the requested state refutes the claim of nationality, the vessel will be rendered constructively stateless and will be subject to boarding in any event.

Four of the five PSI treaties concluded in 2005–7 condition the grant of permission to board upon the requesting state providing 'information ... [that] is sufficiently reliable' to substantiate its suspicions justifying boarding, and all expressly allow the flag state to require more information before granting permission to interdict.[94]

Most of the agreements also provide for deemed consent in certain circumstances. The three 2004 treaties are cast in similar terms. The Liberian agreement grants deemed consent to boarding in international waters if there is no response to an *acknowledged* request within two hours; the Marshall Islands agreement grants similar deemed consent after four hours.[95] As the Panamanian agreement is an amendment to a 2002 treaty on illicit traffic, the two-hour deemed consent provision in that treaty applies.[96] The easily overlooked point is that these time-limit provisions only apply where the request has been acknowledged *and* there has been no response. As noted previously, any reply, even one stating that more time is required, will 'stop the clock'.[97] Each of the 2005–7 treaties takes a slightly different position on deemed consent. The Mongolian PSI agreement provides that where the competent authority does not respond to a 'received' request within the time limit the requesting party will have deemed authorisation to board and search the vessel and question persons on board.[98] The

---

[93] See Chapter 5, section 7. Some agreements make provision for competent authorities, where 'nationality is not verified' within the time limits, nonetheless authorising boarding (or stating their non-objection to boarding) or refuting registration, presumably to cover situations where national registry checks take too long: Cypriot PSI Agreement, Article 4(3)(c); Maltese PSI Agreement, Article 5(3)(c); Mongolian PSI Agreement, Article 4(3)(c).

[94] See Belizean PSI Agreement, Article 4(3); Cypriot PSI Agreement, Article 4(3); Croatian PSI Agreement, Article 4(4); Maltese PSI Agreement, Article 5(3); note the variant drafting in Mongolian PSI Agreement, Article 4(3). Cf. SUA Protocol 2005, Article 8*bis*(7).

[95] Liberian PSI Agreement, Article 4(3)(b); Marshall Islands PSI Agreement, Article 4(3)(b).

[96] Panama Supplementary Agreement, Article 10(6) (see Chapter 4, section 5).

[97] Roach, 'Proliferation Security Initiative', 391; see also Chapter 5, section 6.1. See also Belizean PSI Agreement, Article 4(3)(d); Maltese PSI Agreement, Article 5(3)(b).

[98] Marshall Islands PSI Agreement, Article 4(3)(d); Mongolian PSI Agreement, Article 4(3)(d).

stipulation that time runs from when a request is 'received' rather than 'acknowledged' (as in the 2004 treaties) is unlikely to create substantive differences. There is no indication that time should run from when the request is *sent*. The Belizean treaty is quite procedural. It requires a response two hours after a boarding request is acknowledged, even if it is only a request for more time.[99] If a timely response is not received, the requesting state must attempt to contact the requested state once more. If no contact can then be made, the requesting state may board the suspect vessel and inspect its documents to verify its nationality. If the vessel is confirmed as having the nationality of the requested party, there is deemed consent 'to question persons on board and to search the vessel to determine if it is so engaged in proliferation by sea'.[100] The Cypriot and Maltese agreements do not directly provide for deemed consent, but rather the time-limit clauses provide that if 'nationality is not verified or verifiable within … four hours' then the requested party *shall* either (i) 'stipulate that it does not object to the boarding and search by … the requesting Party', or (ii) 'refute the claim of the suspect vessel to its nationality'.[101] The concern appears to be to avoid positive authorisation but to achieve the same result as deemed consent. A statement of non-objection or refutation of nationality would certainly preclude any boarding being wrongful as between the United States and Cyprus or Malta.[102] Notably, the Croatian agreement contains no deemed consent provision. While it obliges the requested state to reply within four hours, no consequences follow from exceeding this time as the requesting party may not board the vessel without 'express written authorization'.[103]

Critics of the time-limit provisions suggest that they are either inherently unworkable or lack credibility. It has been suggested that four hours is ample time to dispose of any WMD materiel overboard,[104] or that four hours provides no genuine opportunity for a state to assess

[99] Belizean PSI Agreement, Article 4(3).   [100] *Ibid.*

[101] Cypriot PSI Agreement, Article 4(3)(b) and (c); Maltese PSI Agreement, Article 5(3)(b) and (c).

[102] As to whether this is sufficient to grant positive authorisation to interdict, see Chapter 5, section 2. Extraordinarily, the Mongolian agreement expressly provides that failure to verify nationality within the time limit is no obstacle to the requested state granting positive permission authorisation for boarding and search: Mongolian PSI Agreement, Article 4(3)(c).

[103] Croatian PSI Agreement, Article 4(4)(b) and (d).

[104] Chatham House, 'Ship-boarding: an effective measure against terrorism and WMD proliferation?', summary of discussion at Chatham House, 24 November 2005, www.chathamhouse.org.uk/pdf/research/il/ILP241105.doc.

the information said to justify interdiction.[105] However, fisheries prosecutions routinely proceed on the basis that evidence was witnessed being dumped overboard;[106] and in a counter-proliferation context a PSI party (subject to environmental concerns) might not be entirely unhappy with WMD materiel being dumped into the sea. The view that the agreements will result in parties being given only two to four hours to consider material is also mistaken. As the *So San* incident illustrates, a suspect vessel may be tracked at sea for weeks before an interdiction, providing ample opportunity for intelligence sharing. Four-hour deemed consent is a mechanism that is likely to be the last, not first, resort.

The treaties also contain a 'lukewarm' provision allowing automatic boarding and inspection of vessels not flying the flag or showing marks of registry of a party but verbally claiming registry in a party, to prove or disprove that claim.[107] This is either simply a restatement of the right to board vessels suspected of being stateless, or an example of jurisdiction to prevent abuse of claims of nationality.[108]

Regarding jurisdiction over any proliferation activities discovered, all the PSI bilateral treaties provide for a primary right of flag-state enforcement jurisdiction ('including seizure, forfeiture, arrest, and prosecution'), but allow the flag state either to waive that right or to 'consent to the exercise of jurisdiction by the other [boarding] Party'.[109] This is a familiar mechanism in drug interdiction treaties; however, the narcotics treaties ordinarily require that parties establish national jurisdiction over offences discovered when acting as boarding states, so that they may effectively exercise jurisdiction if the flag state relinquishes it.[110] The PSI bilateral arrangements contain no such provision.

---

[105] Garvey, 'International institutional imperative', 133.

[106] E.g. the *Camouco Case (Panama v. France)* (2000) 39 ILM 666 at 672.

[107] Spadi, 'Bolstering the Proliferation Security Initiative', 262; see Belizean PSI Agreement, Article 4(4); Croatian PSI Agreement, Article 4(6); Cypriot PSI Agreement, Article 4(4); Liberian PSI Agreement, Article 4(4); Maltese PSI Agreement, Article 5(4); Marshall Islands PSI Agreement, Article 4(4); Mongolian PSI Agreement, Article 4(4).

[108] See Chapter 5, section 7.

[109] Panamanian PSI Agreement, Article 11; Marshall Islands PSI Agreement, Article 5; Liberian PSI Agreement, Article 5; Belizean PSI Agreement, Article 5(1); Cypriot PSI Agreement, Article 5(1); Croatian PSI Agreement, Article 5(1); Maltese PSI Agreement, Article 6(2); Mongolian PSI Agreement, Article 5(1).

[110] See UN Narcotics Convention, Article 4(1)(b)(ii); Council of Europe Agreement, Article 3, as discussed in Gilmore, 'Narcotics interdiction at sea: the 1995 Council of Europe Agreement', 11; cf. Chapter 3, section 5.

This may not be a significant issue if there are already adequate national laws in place, a point addressed below regarding the SUA Protocol 2005.

The PSI bilateral treaties also contain a series of provisions on enforcement action in the contiguous zone.[111] These provisions apply to situations 'involving the vessel of one Party that arise in the contiguous zone of the other Party and in which both Parties have authority to board in accordance with their respective jurisdictions',[112] thus assuming that there could be simultaneously valid enforcement jurisdiction on the basis of flag-state jurisdiction and coastal-state authority to prevent the infringement of its customs laws in the contiguous zone. As discussed in Chapter 2, this would only be the case where a vessel of state A, by its actions in the contiguous zone of state B, infringes customs laws in the territorial sea of B, and where these acts also constitute a crime in A. The usual example would be a mother ship offloading prohibited goods to smaller vessels to smuggle them ashore. Generally, the PSI treaties confer the primary right to exercise enforcement jurisdiction upon the party that actually conducts the boarding within the contiguous zone,[113] although the agreement with Belize upholds the primacy of flag-state jurisdiction in such cases. In the case of vessels fleeing the territorial sea into the contiguous zone, coastal-state jurisdiction generally takes primacy.[114]

All the PSI bilateral boarding agreements – except that with Panama – contain a relatively uniform article on 'safeguards' (drawn from earlier drafts of the SUA Protocol, the UN Narcotics Convention and the UNTOC Migrant Smuggling Protocol).[115] The common safeguards article requires that the boarding state shall take account of matters of human safety, the security of vessel and cargo, and environmental protection during the interdiction; shall allow the master to contact

---

[111] Panamanian PSI Agreement, Article 11(3); Marshall Islands PSI Agreement, Article 5(2); Liberian PSI Agreement, Article 5(2); Cypriot PSI Agreement, Article 5(2); Croatian PSI Agreement, Article 5(2); Maltese PSI Agreement, Article 6(3); Mongolian PSI Agreement, Article 5(2).

[112] See, e.g., Maltese PSI Treaty, Article 6(2).   [113] *Ibid.*

[114] *Ibid.*, thus taking the narrow Fitzmaurice view of jurisdiction to enforce in the contiguous zone; see Chapter 2, section 2.3.

[115] See Roach, 'Proliferation Security Initiative', 401; SUA Protocol 2005, Article 8*bis*(10)(a); Migrant Smuggling Protocol, Article 9; Marshall Islands PSI Agreement, Article 8; Liberian PSI Agreement, Article 8; Belizean PSI Agreement, Article 8; Cypriot PSI Agreement, Article 8; Croatian PSI Agreement, Article 8; Maltese PSI Agreement, Article 10; Mongolian PSI Agreement, Article 8; cf. Panamanian PSI Agreement, Article 15.

the vessel's owner, manager or flag state; shall ensure that 'persons on board are afforded the protections, rights and guarantees provided by international law and the boarding State's law and regulations' and must 'not prejudice the commercial or legal interests of the Flag State'. Such provisions are discussed further in Chapter 10.

In the event of an unwarranted boarding (or wrongful acts committed during boarding), all the PSI agreements contain a claims provision. This provides, with minor variations, that any 'claim[s] submitted for damage, harm, injury, death or loss resulting from an operation carried out by a Party under this Agreement shall be resolved in accordance with the domestic law' of the boarding party and 'in a manner consistent with international law'.[116] 'Harm' and 'injury' probably refer to physical damage, while 'loss' and 'damage' appear broad enough to encompass economic loss, including delay.[117] This claims provision is not predicated upon the boarding being in any sense in breach of the treaty. It clearly envisages claims made by foreign nationals or corporations and would not appear to address any claims the flag state might have in respect of a breach of the treaty itself. If this is its intent, while it may provide a useful compensation mechanism, it cannot bind the nationals of third-party states.[118] The most recent PSI agreements also contain a separate provision for consultations where boarding-state officials are alleged to have acted *ultra vires* by taking action 'in contravention' of the PSI agreement, including 'improper, disproportionate or unreasonable' actions or action 'taken on unfounded suspicions'.[119] These clauses are, however, only a consultation mechanism and are expressly 'without prejudice' to other legal recourse.

In the case of claims by affected individuals or corporations, the US Coast Guard – the agency most likely to conduct interdictions under

---

[116] Marshall Islands PSI Agreement, Article 13(2); Liberian PSI Agreement, Article 13(2); Belizean PSI Agreement, Article 13(2); Cypriot PSI Agreement, Article 13(2); Croatian PSI Agreement, Article 13(2); Maltese PSI Agreement, Article 16(2); Mongolian PSI Agreement, Article 13(2). See also Spadi, 'Bolstering the Proliferation Security Initiative', 266–7, on drafting variations.

[117] See the comments at the IMO Legal Committee, IMO Doc. LEG 90/15 (9 May 2005), paras. 94–95.

[118] See further Chapter 12, section 2.

[119] Cypriot PSI Agreement, Article 13(3); Croatian PSI Agreement, Article 13(3); Maltese PSI Agreement, Article 16(3); Mongolian PSI Agreement, Article 13(3); slightly different language, omitting 'disproportionate' and 'unfounded suspicions', is found in Marshall Islands PSI Agreement, Article 13(3); Liberian PSI Agreement, Article 13(3).

a PSI bilateral agreement – can pay out meritorious claims through an administrative procedure as an alternative to litigation.[120] There is obviously concern about the economic impact of interdictions and fear in some quarters that PSI members might be unwilling to pay for their mistakes.[121] Pragmatically, it seems unlikely that PSI states would not seek to avert adverse publicity and negative reactions from the shipping industry by simply paying out such claims promptly, including compensating for loss and delay in cases where WMD materiel is actually found but there is no evidence of wrongdoing by vessel operators. It is perhaps suggestive that while the MV *Nisha*'s owners publicly stated that they would consider suing British authorities, there was no report that court proceedings were ever commenced.[122]

As noted above, the common safeguards provision requires those aboard an interdicted vessel to be accorded both international 'protections, rights and guarantees' and those applicable under the law of the *boarding* state. This is sensible, as it would be clearly impractical to require the boarding state to apply the procedural law of the flag state. However, neither the safeguard nor claims provision addresses possible joint liability for substantive human rights violations, especially if agents of the boarding state were to act *ultra vires* in the execution of their duties.[123] This point is discussed further in relation to the SUA Protocol 2005.

6 The SUA Protocol 2005

The SUA Protocol 2005 was adopted at an IMO diplomatic conference on 14 October 2005.[124] The Protocol, upon entry into force, will be the first international instrument creating crimes of transporting WMD materiel by sea and providing for the suppression of such crimes through high-seas interdictions.[125] It might be said of the SUA Protocol, as of UNSCR 1540, that it represents an attempt to universalise PSI activities – an attempt heavily inscribed with US predominance.[126] Such conclusions should be ventured with caution.

---

[120] Roach, 'Proliferation Security Initiative', 408.

[121] Chatham House, 'Proliferation Security Initiative'.

[122] D. Brown, 'Campaign against terrorism: owners of ship seized in Channel consider suing police', *Independent*, 28 December 2001, p. 5.

[123] See the discussion of the *Transdnistria* case, accompanying n. 140, below.

[124] See the text adopted by the conference: IMO Doc. LEG/CONF.15/21 (1 November 2005) (SUA Protocol 2005).

[125] Not in force: see n. 1, above.   [126] Sur, 'La résolution 1540', 872–3.

The SUA Protocol 2005 is an ambitious instrument – at once an effort to create a new international crime of proliferation, a ship-boarding regime and a method of strengthening the Treaty on the Non-Proliferation of Nuclear Weapons – negotiated within a large multilateral forum, the IMO Legal Committee. If the resulting draft-ing can be called 'sloppy',[127] this principally reflects the difficulty of achieving an acceptable package solution balancing the competing interests at play.[128] It is no secret that the negotiations were long and that the final text embodies extensive compromises.[129] The result is, perhaps, overburdened with verbiage and minor inconsistencies, but the real task is to assess how it might operate in practice.

Before addressing the boarding provisions, several observations need to be made about the underlying criminal offence of prolifer-ation created by the Protocol and the requirement to exercise national prescriptive jurisdiction (elements absent from the PSI bilateral agreements). The new Article 3*bis*(1) creates the substantive terror-ist offences of intentionally using a ship in an action 'likely to cause death or serious injury or damage' in order to 'intimidate a popula-tion, or to compel a government ... to do or to abstain from doing any act', whether that act involves using WMD or not. Article 3*bis*(2) cre-ates further offences of intentionally transporting aboard a ship any biological, chemical or nuclear (BCN) weapon, any special fissionable material with knowledge of its intended use in an activity not subject to International Atomic Energy Agency safeguards, or 'dual use' mate-rials. The latter is defined as 'any equipment, materials or software or related technology that significantly contributes to the design, manu-facture or delivery of a BCN weapon, with the intention that it will be used for such purpose.'[130]

This 'largely functional and, in part, indeterminate definition'[131] of dual-use materials drew criticism at the drafting stage, the IMO Legal Committee only approving the wording by a majority.[132] It clearly turns on a mixed question of fact ('significantly contributes') and subjective

---

[127] Chatham House, 'Ship-boarding', at n. 104, above.
[128] See the US Statement to the SUA Protocol Conference, IMO Doc. LEG/CONF.15/14 (20 September 2005), para. 12.
[129] See comments in IMO Doc. LEG 90/15, paras. 30–31.
[130] Article 3*bis*(1)(b)(4); see SUA Protocol 2005, Article 4.
[131] Author's translation: 'une définition largement fonctile et en partie indéterminée', Sur, 'La résolution 1540', 871, referring to SC Res. 1540.
[132] IMO Doc. LEG 90/15, paras. 33–41.

intent. Once again, like UNSCR 1540 and the PSI principles, this leaves a great deal to ad hoc bilateral agreement as to whether a given shipment warrants interdiction. In practice, a boarding state seeking to persuade a flag state to permit interdiction under the Protocol is likely to refer not to its own national standards, such as export control lists, but to the guidelines of multilateral co-operative forums such as the Wassenaar Arrangement on dual-use technologies.[133] Framing adequate definitions for the purposes of national criminal implementing legislation may be another issue entirely.

Critically, since it is a protocol to amend the SUA Convention, parties must establish jurisdiction over these offences on the same basis as under the SUA Convention itself. The SUA Convention in Article 6 specifies that each party must establish certain categories of jurisdiction and may establish others. Parties must exercise prescriptive jurisdiction over offences committed by their nationals, on their vessels or when the offender is subsequently found upon their territory. In addition parties *may* exercise prescriptive jurisdiction to criminalise conduct committed against their nationals or in order to coerce or threaten that state party. However, like the PSI bilateral agreements, the Protocol lacks any requirement to establish jurisdiction over offences committed aboard a vessel interdicted with flag-state consent. This is unsurprising, given that there were originally no boarding provisions in the SUA Convention, but problematic following the addition of Article 8*bis*.

Article 8*bis*(8), provides that the flag state retains exclusive enforcement jurisdiction over any offences discovered during an interdiction; however, it may, 'subject to its constitution and laws, consent to the exercise of jurisdiction by another State having jurisdiction under Article 6'. The narrow reading would be that the flag state could only relinquish jurisdiction to the boarding state if the latter could prosecute on the basis of either the offender's nationality or because the offence was intended to intimidate the boarding state. But Article 6 is arguably not a provision *creating* jurisdiction, but one *obliging* states to provide for it. Thus the question is not whether interdiction per se somehow falls within Article 6, but whether the boarding state will be able to prosecute an offence under its domestic law. That result should clearly follow once a suspect is removed into its territory. Admittedly, this requires reading paragraph 8 as referring to a flag state 'consent[ing]

[133] See www.wassenaar.org.

to the [future] exercise of jurisdiction' by a state which has adequately provided for 'jurisdiction under Article 6'. This may be necessary, however, to give the provision practical effect, and seems perfectly consistent with other provisions requiring parties either to extradite or prosecute those suspected of Convention offences.[134]

The high-seas boarding provisions are found in Article 8*bis*, which contains further similarities to and differences from the PSI bilateral agreements.

1. It refers to flag states confirming a vessel's 'nationality' not 'registry', thus not strictly requiring registry checks and permitting presumptive flag-state authorisation.
2. Flag-state consent is critical to any boarding: no measures may be taken without express flag-state authorisation, and that authorisation may be subjected to such conditions as the flag state thinks fit.
3. Consent to board does not imply consent to exercise enforcement jurisdiction, which must be sought separately and will be subject to the flag state agreeing to relinquish it.
4. While no time-limit is set after which deemed consent arises (although flag states are to respond to requests 'as expeditiously as possible'), parties may upon ratification declare that they will either permit boarding on the basis of four-hour deemed consent or grant comprehensive permission in advance to other parties to board and search their vessels (although not to exercise enforcement jurisdiction).[135]
5. It contains a safeguards provision limiting the use of force to the minimum necessary and containing requirements as to safety at sea, respect for human rights, environmental protection and efforts to avoid prejudicing the flag state's commercial interests or unduly delaying the vessel.[136]
6. It exhorts parties to work towards developing harmonised procedures for joint operations (a key PSI objective).
7. It contemplates the conclusion of further 'agreements or arrangements to facilitate law enforcement', opening the door to further PSI bilateral agreements.

---

[134] SUA Convention, Articles 7 and 10. For a reading requiring a strict 'jurisdictional nexus' under Article 6, see Klein, 'Right of visit', 327.

[135] SUA Protocol 2005, Article 8*bis*(1) and (5)(d)–(e).

[136] Article 8*bis*(10)(a); the listed safeguards seem largely drawn from provisions such as UN Narcotics Convention, Articles 15 and 17(5), and UNTOC Migrant Smuggling Protocol, Article 9, as discussed in Chapter 9. State responsibility and safeguard provisions are discussed in Chapter 10.

Article 8*bis* (10)(a) also contains a provision on state responsibility:

Provided that authorisation to board by a flag State shall not per se give rise to liability, States Parties shall be liable for any damage, harm or loss attributable to them arising from measures taken … when … the grounds for such measures prove to be unfounded … or … such measures are unlawful or exceed that reasonably required.

Parties must 'provide effective recourse' in such cases. The reference to 'States Parties' clearly does not rule out possible joint liability of both boarding and flag states.[137] The choice of words is best construed as displacing any presumption that authorisation creates a relationship of agency between the boarding state and flag state and thus joint liability for *all* acts committed by the boarding state.[138] Obviously, the actions of the boarding state's forces would not ordinarily be 'attributable' to the flag state unless they were placed at the flag state's disposal.[139] The exception might be cases where there are non-derogable duties to prevent wrongful acts occurring within a state's jurisdiction, as with certain human rights. The drafting would not seem inconsistent with the reasoning in the *Transdnistria* case that states (or at least parties to the European Convention on Human Rights) are not relieved of all responsibility for human rights breaches occurring within their jurisdiction committed by military forces outside their control.[140] The state of formal jurisdiction should still take 'appropriate and sufficient' measures, using all 'legal and diplomatic means available', to endeavour to ensure compliance with applicable human rights obligations.[141] The concept of jurisdiction considered in *Transdnistria* was not *necessarily* territorially limited and could possibly apply in cases of the exclusive jurisdiction of states over their flag vessels.[142] The point is, however, far from certain. Such issues are discussed in greater detail in Chapter 10.

As to compensation for mistaken or wrongfully conducted boardings, parties must 'provide effective [means of] recourse' for 'any damage, harm or loss attributable to them'.[143] The IMO Legal Committee took the words 'damage, harm or loss' to cover physical harm or injury

---

[137] A proposal to refer only to the boarding state was defeated: IMO Doc. LEG 90/15, para. 97.
[138] See Chapter 12, section 2.   [139] ILC Articles on State Responsibility, Article 6.
[140] *Case of Ilaşcu and Others v. Moldova and Russia* (2005) 40 EHRR 46.
[141] *Ibid.*, paras. 333–334.   [142] *Ibid.*, paras. 314–319.
[143] SUA Protocol 2005, Article 8*bis*(10)(a).

and economic loss, including loss attendant upon delay.[144] As the injuries contemplated would principally be to natural persons or commercial interests, the Protocol should be read as requiring the creation of effective local remedies under each party's national law. As noted above, the United States has an administrative procedure for settling maritime tort claims. However, despite the usual rule on the exhaustion of local remedies, injured parties might have direct recourse to diplomatic protection on the theory that there must be some voluntary connection between the injured individual and the respondent state for the rule to apply.[145] It is hard to see how such a voluntary connection – what might ordinarily be thought of as an open-eyed submission to the respondent state's territorial jurisdiction and law – could arise in the course of a high–seas interdiction. Issues of state responsibility are considered further in Chapters 10–12.

7 Conclusion: criminalisation, liability and implementation

The three critical elements of any international counter-proliferation regime involving interdiction will be adequate criminalisation at the national and international level, effective mechanisms for dealing with claims arising from wrongful boardings and genuine political will to implement measures such as UNSCR 1540. As regards criminalisation, the SUA Protocol 2005 upon entering into force will establish a series of proliferation and WMD terrorist crimes and provide for interdiction as an enforcement measure. The US bilateral PSI agreements rely on the underlying criminality of the conduct in both implicated jurisdictions at national law. While their national reports to the UNSCR 1540 Committee indicate that the United States, the Marshall Islands, Cyprus, Panama and Malta all have national criminal laws against WMD proliferation,[146] the position of other states party to PSI

---

[144] IMO Doc. LEG 90/15, paras. 94–95.
[145] P. Okawa, 'Issues of admissibility and the law on international responsibility', in Malcolm Evans (ed.), *International Law*, 2nd edn (Oxford University Press, 2006), p. 479 at p. 503.
[146] See UN Doc. S/AC.44/2004/(02)/5, 12 October 2004 (National Report of the United States of America); UN Doc. S/AC.44/2004/(02)/82, 23 November 2004 (National Report of the Marshall Islands); UN Doc. S/AC.44/2004/(02)/85, 30 November 2004 (National Report of Cyprus); UN Doc. S/AC.44/2004/(02)/6, 22 October 2004 (National Report of Malta), cf. Criminal Code 1854 (Malta), ss. 5(1)(b) and 328A(2)(f), as amended, http://docs.justice.gov.mt/lom/legislation/english/leg/vol_1/chapt9.pdf, and Nuclear Safety and Radiation Protection Regulations No.44 of 2003 (Malta), s. 7,

bilateral agreements is less clear. Article 163 of the Croatian Penal Code 1997 makes it an offence to 'transfer[] or transport[] chemical or biological weapons or any other military equipment which is prohibited by international law'.[147] This reference back to international law may severely hamper the exercise of Croatian jurisdiction other than in cases falling within UNSCR 1540.[148] In August 2005 Belize could only report that it was in the process of passing national laws criminalising the development, production or use of chemical weapons only.[149] It is also not clear if this law, once passed, will prohibit transport of relevant precursor technologies. Liberia has not yet submitted the report required by UNSCR 1540. Mongolia has national laws criminalising 'acquisition, production or proliferation of chemical, biological, and other weapons of mass destruction prohibited by' treaties binding upon Mongolia and 'stockpiling, using or transferring toxic chemicals to be used as chemical weapons'.[150] Again, it is not entirely clear, however, that Mongolia's laws prohibit transport of precursor technologies or WMD materiel, other than those intended for use as chemical weapons.

Irrespective of national law considerations, it may remain relevant to ask if the activity in question is internationally prohibited where the interdiction has an impact upon third parties. If acquiring WMD materiel is not internationally unlawful one would ordinarily expect seizure of such materiel legally owned by a third state or individual to give rise to a right of compensation, even if carried out under national criminal law or for defence purposes.[151]

Issues of procedural justice might also arise. It would appear contrary to basic principles of justice (*nullem crimen sine lege*) to allow someone to

---

http://docs.justice.gov.mt/lom/Legislation/English/SubLeg/365/15.pdf; and UN Doc. S/AC.44/2004/(02)/120/Add.1, 8 March 2006 (National Report of Panama).

[147] http://disarmament2.un.org/Committee1540/Legislative%20DB/Croatia%20Legislation%20DB.doc.

[148] As of May 2008, Croatia was not a party to the SUA Protocol 2005, and so will not be bound by it upon its entry into force. See n. 1, above.

[149] UN Doc. S/AC.44/2004/(02)/7, 22 October 2004 (National Report of Belize); see also UN Doc. S/AC.44/2004/(02)/7/Add.1. Belizean law prohibits the import or export of nuclear material by sea, but seemingly not its mere passage through territorial waters or its transport on any Belizean vessel on the high seas: War Material Act 2000, ss. 10–12, www.belizelaw.org/lawadmin/PDF%20files/cap146.pdf.

[150] UN Doc. S/AC.44/2004/(02)/119, 31 May 2005 (national report of Mongolia).

[151] Brownlie, p. 511; cf. United Nations Convention on Jurisdictional Immunities of States and Their Property, GA Res 59/39 (2005) (not yet in force), Articles 19 and 21(1)(b).

be punished for an act not an offence in the jurisdiction to which they are subject at the time of an extradition request.[152] Such concerns may arise under some of the US bilateral PSI agreements, if US interdictions of PSI partners' flag vessels result in prosecutions under US criminal laws which lack a clear counterpart in the flag state. This could be a risk in the case of any consensual interdiction of Croatian, Belizean, Liberian or Mongolian vessels under relevant PSI agreements.

Such concerns would be less apparent if there were an underlying international crime or prohibition in place. The proposed SUA Protocol will not be a solution, at least in the short term. Even if it rapidly comes into force, many states may never become parties. There are also certain international crimes (both existing and proposed) dealing with the possession of nuclear material by individuals.[153] UNSCR 1540 may close the gap more broadly as regards transferring WMD materiel to non-state actors only. The very specific regimes prohibiting WMD transfers to North Korea and Iran do impose duties upon states to prevent the use of their flag vessels in such transfers, but do not contemplate interdiction as the term is used here.[154] Gaps in the criminalisation or general prohibition of proliferation activity at the international level thus remain.

The real effectiveness of measures such as the SUA Protocol and UNSCR 1540 will ultimately depend upon the willingness of PSI and G8 states to engage in capacity building and intelligence sharing,[155] and the willingness of developing states to accept purpose-tied aid and to collaborate in law enforcement. Security Council 'legislation' cannot, of itself, create either effective law or its enforcement. This requires national laws, international co-operation, and considerable will and resources. Realistically, a variety of jurisdictional bases will continue to be used to effect interdictions of WMD materiel for the conceivable

---

[152] International Covenant on Civil and Political Rights 1966, 999 UNTS 171, Article 15(1).

[153] Convention on the Physical Protection of Nuclear Material 1980, Article 7, 1456 UNTS 101, entered into force 8 February 1987, 136 parties at 23 May 2008. Cf. International Convention for the Suppression of Acts of Nuclear Terrorism 2005, untreaty.un.org/English/Terrorism/English_18_15.pdf, entered into force 7 July 2007, 29 parties at 2 October 2007.

[154] SC Res. 1696 (31 July 2006), para. 4; SC Res. 1718 (14 October 2006), paras. 8(a) and (b); SC Res. 1737 (27 December 2006), paras. 3, 4 and 7; SC Res. 1803 (3 March 2008), para. 8. See also SC Res. 1747 (24 March 2007), para. 5; and SC Res. 1540 (28 April 2004), para. 2.

[155] See the comments of both India and South Africa in UN Doc. S/PV.4950, 23.

future. The combined effect of UNSCR 1540 and the entry into force of the SUA Protocol 2005 is unlikely to be the withering away of the PSI. On the contrary, the PSI may well remain the best 'political' forum for the effective co-ordination of interdictions within existing legal frameworks. The PSI may not be an organisation, but it is certainly a means of organisation: it has proven a continually evolving strategy for the co-ordination of existing jurisdictional bases for interdiction and the creation of new ones. This mere 'activity' has already had legal effects: harnessing the compulsory powers of the Security Council to its aims, and prompting a major multilateral shipping interdiction treaty. While not an institution, the PSI appears to be generating increasingly organised and formal legal structures.

The contribution of the SUA Protocol 2005 and the PSI treaties to our understanding of the law applicable during interdictions is taken up in the following chapters.

PART III
The general law of interdiction

10 Interdiction: modalities and international law standards

1 The structure of Part III

This book has examined the international law rules permitting one state to operate within another's sphere of jurisdiction ('jurisdictional rules') and governing the conduct of such operations ('operational rules'). This chapter focuses upon the operational rules of maritime interdiction at general international law, while the following chapters deal with the consequences of their breach under the rules of state immunity and state responsibility. This chapter commences by discussing the emergence of increasingly standard safeguard provisions applicable to interdictions before discussing in detail the law on the use of force during interdictions. These safeguard provisions constitute the essential primary obligations during an interdiction, breach of which gives rise to issues of state immunity and responsibility.

Allegations of wrongdoing, especially under flag-state law, raise questions of whether boarding-party officials enjoy state immunity for their acts aboard foreign vessels. As seen in NAFO practice, disgruntled vessel masters may undermine inspection regimes by bringing proceedings against individual inspectors for their official acts. The immunity of boarding parties is thus a practical issue in maritime policing and is considered in Chapter 11.

Issues of state responsibility may arise from interdictions in three principal cases: alleged breaches of public international law (including rules on the use of force), wrongs to private parties and breaches of flag-state law. These may overlap. The use of excessive force during an interdiction may constitute a public wrong against the flag state and a violation of individual rights of those aboard. The most common question, however, will be boarding-state liability to the shipowner, charter party, crew or passengers in the event of delay, loss or injury arising from an unwarranted boarding. These issues, consequent upon a finding that primary obligations have been breached, are discussed in Chapter 12.

2 Applicable safeguards in interdicting foreign vessels, including human rights law

The most obvious constraint upon interdictions is that they must be carried out by a warship or duly authorised government vessel 'clearly marked and identifiable as being on government service'.[1] One can also discern over time an emerging consensus on minimum safeguard provisions for interdiction operations in the SUA Protocol, the UNTOC Migrant Smuggling Protocol, the US PSI bilateral treaties and, to a lesser extent, the earlier FSA.[2] There are effectively three sets of duties.

1. Boarding states must take due account of the need not to endanger the safety of life at sea, the safety and security of the ship and its cargo, and the need not to prejudice the commercial or legal interests of the flag state.[3]
2. Boarding states must take reasonable steps to avoid unduly detaining or delaying the vessel.[4]
3. Boarding states must ensure that boarding and search is conducted in accordance with applicable international law; all persons aboard are treated in a manner consistent with their basic human dignity and international human rights law (and the boarding state's law and regulations); anyone against whom proceedings are commenced is afforded fair treatment at all stages of the proceedings; within

---

[1] UNCLOS, Articles 107, 110(5) and 111(5); UN Narcotics Agreement, Article 17(10); Council of Europe Agreement, Article 11(2); Caribbean Area Agreement, Article 1(e); FSA, Article 21(4); Marshall Islands, Liberian, Belizean, Cypriot and Croatian PSI Agreements, Article 1; SUA Protocol 2005, Article 8bis(10)(d); Migrant Smuggling Protocol, Article 9(4). Most RFMOs provide for the display of a special pennant: e.g., NAFO Scheme 2008, Article 32(2); NEAFC Scheme 2007, Article 16.

[2] See Caribbean Area Agreement, Article 20(4); SUA Protocol 2005, Article 8bis(10)(a); and Maltese PSI Agreement, Article 10; or Marshall Islands, Liberian, Belizean, Cypriot or Croatian PSI Agreements, Article 8. Cf. FSA, Articles 21(10) and 22(1).

[3] *Ibid.* See also Migrant Smuggling Protocol, Article 9(1); UN Narcotics Agreement, Article 17(5); and Official Records: Narcotics Convention Conference, 28th meeting, UN Doc E/CONF.82/C.2/SR.28, para. 9; Council of Europe Agreement, Article 12; Spanish–Italian Treaty, Article 5(4).

[4] Council of Europe Agreement, Article 12(1); Caribbean Area Agreement, Article 20(4); SUA Protocol 2005 and PSI Agreements, at n. 2, above. Cf. NAFO Scheme 2007, Article 25(9); NEAFC Scheme 2007, Article 25(3).

available means, any measures taken are environmentally sound; and the ship's master is advised of the intention to board and is afforded the earliest opportunity to contact the ship's owner and the flag state.[5]

These relatively common safeguards will be discussed in only limited detail principally because they are variously not controversial, are of uncertain content or are redundant. The question of applicable national law and human rights law will be addressed in slightly more detail, although the former is ultimately a question more for national courts and constitutional orders than international law.

Regarding the first set of mild duties to 'take due account of' various matters, it is difficult to see how anything short of grossly excessive action or the endangerment of human life would breach them. The safety of life at sea is scarcely a new principle and has been discussed in Chapter 8. The SUA Protocol 2005 additionally requires the boarding state to take due account of the 'need not to interfere with or to affect … the rights and obligations and the exercise of jurisdiction of coastal states' under the law of the sea.[6] This appears to be a gloss on the controversy surrounding interdictions in a third state's EEZ, discussed above.[7]

The second duty, to take steps to avoid undue delay, is not obviously a separate duty from the duty to take due account of the flag state's commercial interests. Insofar as it implies a duty to compensate for undue delay, it is discussed in Chapter 12.

The third set of duties, to 'ensure' various outcomes, should not be controversial. Admittedly, only the SUA Protocol 2005 and PSI Agreements contain all of these 'duties to ensure', although the humane treatment and environmental obligations appear in the Migrant Smuggling Protocol,[8] the specific obligations towards vessel masters are also found in the FSA[9] and a savings clause on individual rights in legal proceedings appears in the Caribbean Area Agreement.[10]

---

[5] SUA Protocol 2005 and PSI Agreements as at n. 2, above.

[6] Article 8*bis*(10)(c); Klein, 'Right of visit', 320.

[7] See Chapter 5, section 3, text accompanying nn. 26–29.

[8] Migrant Smuggling Protocol, Article 9(1).

[9] FSA, Article 22(1)(b) and (c); cf. NEAFC Scheme 2007, Article 15(4).

[10] Caribbean Area Agreement, Article 29(1). At the time of writing, the application of the ECHR to extraterritorial maritime law enforcement had been upheld in *Medvedyev v. France* (Application No. 3394/03), European Court of Human Rights, Judgment of 10 July 2008, para. 50. On the specific facts, the court found that the deprivation of liberty following arrest at sea and a thirteen-day journey to port did

To require respect for 'applicable' international law is redundant. It is perhaps useful to state clearly the right of the ship's master to communicate with the vessel's flag state and owner, but the point should be beyond dispute. The most fundamental issue relating to matters of safety of life at sea, respect for human rights and not causing undue damage and delay is the rules governing the use of force by the boarding party, which are discussed further below.

Questions going to applicable human rights law, however, merit some consideration at this stage. Principles of fair treatment and respect for human rights are universal. In terms of more concrete rules, the International Convenant on Civil and Political Rights (ICCPR) is extremely widely ratified[11] and its standards are prima facie applicable to the extraterritorial conduct of state organs, at least where those organs exercise 'effective control of an area outside ... national territory'.[12] There is also an established line of European Convention on Human Rights (ECHR) cases holding that, even though the Convention is ordinarily territorially limited, it nonetheless applies extraterritorially where a member state's police take a person into custody abroad even where they act with the permission of the local state.[13] On either view, an armed boarding party, even one with its law enforcement powers circumscribed by flag-state-imposed conditions, exercises a very high degree of effective control over an interdicted vessel. The boarding party will thus be bound by the ICCPR and possibly other human rights instruments to which the boarding state is a party.

not violate ECHR Article 5(3), but the legal basis of the subsequent prosecutions failed to satisfy ECHR Article 5(1) due in part to a defect in French law.

[11] There were 161 parties at 18 April 2008, including those states with the most capacity to conduct maritime interdictions: Australia, Canada, United States and the United Kingdom and the other EU states. China is not a party.

[12] Dominic McGoldrick, 'The extra-territorial application of the International Covenant on Civil and Political Rights' in Menno T. Kamminga and Fons Coomans (eds.), *Extra-territorial Application of Human Rights Treaties* (Oxford: Intersentia, 2004), p. 41 at pp. 69–71, arguing that this conclusion is consistent with *Bankovic v. Belgium* (2002) 41 ILM 517. See generally *Legal Consequences of the Construction of a Wall in the Occupied Palestinian Territory*, Advisory Opinion, [2004] ICJ Rep. 136 at 179–80; *López v. Uruguay* (UN Human Rights Committee) (1981) 68 ILR 29 at 38; *Celeberti de Casariego v. Uruguay* (UN Human Rights Committee) (1981) 68 ILR 41 at 45–6; UN Human Rights Committee, General Comment 31 on Article 2 of the ICCPR, UN Doc. CCPR/C/21/Rev.1/Add.13 (29 March 2004), para. 10; cf. Committee Against Torture, Concluding Observations: United States of America, UN Doc. CAT/C/USA/CO/2 (25 July 2006), para. 15.

[13] See the cases discussed in *Al-Skeini v. Secretary of State for Defence* [2007] UKHL 26, paras. 118–120, per Lord Brown, and *Medvedyev v. France*, at n. 10, above.

The 'duties to ensure', however, extend beyond universal or regional human rights instruments to requiring treatment in conformity with the boarding state's law and regulations. The question of the extra-territorial applicability of boarding-state laws, especially in respect of national human rights law, may pose some practical difficulties and invite theoretical controversy. Strictly, this is not a question for international law but one for each national legal system to resolve. Nonetheless, relevant national cases frequently refer to the inter-national law of jurisdiction, sometimes with confused results. Two decisions on the extraterritorial application of national human rights standards may usefully be contrasted.

In *R v. Hape* the Canadian Supreme Court held that section 8 of the Canadian Charter of Rights and Freedoms, which *inter alia* imposes a procedural requirement upon powers to conduct both perimeter searches and covert entry by law enforcement officials, did not have extraterritorial effect.[14] The reasoning of the majority was that such acts were an exercise of enforcement jurisdiction, which could only be exercised extraterritorially with the territorial state's consent. Here, Canadian officials had not obtained warrants for such activities while acting 'under the authority' of Turks and Caicos Islands officials either for the reason that no such requirement applied locally or, in cases where it did, they believed it had been complied with.[15] To require warrants in cases where no such procedure exists under local law, in the majority's view, would involve requiring the Turks and Caicos legal system 'to develop a procedure for issuing a warrant ... simply to com-ply with' the Charter, constituting a 'blatant interference with Turks and Caicos sovereignty'.[16]

This approach is profoundly misguided. Any rule requiring a state organ to refrain from act A unless condition B is met is a purely internal restraint, having no impact on a foreign state's sovereignty. Such a rule does not require the foreign state to modify its law to satisfy condition B, it simply requires the state organ to refrain from act A. So much was, in fact, conceded by the *Hape* majority.[17] If this consequence stymies police co-operation,[18] the fault is not with international law but with Canadian law, for failing to have a constitutionally valid mechanism

---

[14] *R v. Hape* (2007) 46 ILM 815. 'Perimeter search' involves examining a building from the exterior, e.g. to observe its locks and security: para. 5. 'Covert entry' is effected to conduct a search without notifying the suspect: para. 9.

[15] *Ibid.*, paras. 86, 116, 120.   [16] *Ibid.*, para. 86.

[17] *Ibid.*, para. 97.   [18] *Ibid.*, paras. 86, 96–100.

for authorising such action. The preferable approach would have been to hold, as the concurring minority did, that there is no inherent problem with Canadian law applying to Canadian officials wherever they are, and that such extraterritorial application of the Charter does not 'automatically result in an interference with the sovereign authority of foreign states'.[19] From the perspective of international law the case could readily be characterised as one involving concurrent jurisdiction over the acts of Canadian officers present in a foreign state with the territorial sovereign's consent, thus 'subjecting the Canadian agents to both Turks and Caicos law and Canadian law – including the Charter'.[20] Practical difficulties arising from this outcome are for national law to resolve. The concurring minority in *Hape*, for example, would have found that Charter requirements were satisfied where Canadian officials abroad followed local legal requirements after having satisfied themselves that those local standards were 'consistent with fundamental human rights norms'.[21]

Al-Skeini v. Secretary of State for Defence concerned, in part, whether the actions of British troops in causing the death of a civilian detained in a UK military base in occupied Iraq were subject to the UK Human Rights Act. In finding that the Act could apply extraterritorially, the majority of the House of Lords took a similar view to the minority in *Hape*, that such laws are prima facie directed at 'public authorities' irrespective of their location.[22] The Human Rights Act incorporates into UK law rights protected by the European Convention on Human Rights, which apply only when a person is within a state party's 'jurisdiction'. This was a relevant factor, as national courts should not find a government responsible for securing an individual's Convention rights in circumstances where the European Court of Human Rights would not. As the European Court's judgments do not obviously 'speak with one voice' on the extent of 'jurisdiction' for Convention purposes,[23] the majority chose to apply the more conservative test available. Under this approach application of Convention rights outside the collective

---

[19] *Ibid.*, paras. 160–162.   [20] P.-H. Verdier, 'R v. Hape' (2008) 102 AJIL 143 at 147.

[21] *R. v. Hape*, para. 169.

[22] [2007] UKHL 26, paras. 38–59, especially para. 53, per Lord Rodger; 86–88, per Baroness Hale; 96–97, per Lord Carswell; and 139–140, per Lord Brown.

[23] *Ibid.*, para. 67, per Lord Rodger. Note that the meaning of jurisdiction in human rights law is perhaps different from that in general international law: R. Wilde, 'Triggering state obligations extraterritorially: the spatial test in certain human rights treaties' (2007) 40 *Israel Law Review* 503 at 514.

territories of the state parties is the exceptional case, one such exception being situations 'where a state exercised effective control of an area outside its national territory'.[24] The UK Secretary of State for Defence conceded that the relevant military base fell within UK jurisdiction for Convention purposes and on this basis the majority found that the Human Rights Act applied within that space.[25]

As noted above, where an armed boarding party with powers of arrest is aboard a foreign flag-state vessel it will be hard to argue that it is not exercising a high degree of effective control over a limited space. If *Al-Skeini* is correct, this would appear enough to trigger ECHR obligations and the applicability of the UK Human Rights Act. Even more broadly, on the minority view in *Hape*, there is no obstacle arising from the international law of jurisdiction to the extraterritorial application of national human rights laws to the conduct of state organs – at least where those laws operate as a restraint on government power. As explained above, the minority view in *Hape* must be correct. Whether a given national legal system does extend such laws extraterritorially, however, is a question for each national system.

3 The use of force in interdicting foreign vessels

3.1 Introduction

After reviewing the limited case law (the *I'm Alone* case,[26] the *Red Crusader* case[27] and *MV Saiga (No. 2)*) commentators usually conclude that under customary international law using force is a 'measure of last resort'[28] and that any force must be 'reasonable and necessary in the circumstances'.[29] Such general statements offer decision-makers little guidance, a difficulty compounded by the fact that the available cases generally concern instances of clearly *disproportionate* force. Sinking a vessel to prevent its escape in the *I'm Alone* case or firing live, large-calibre rounds into a slow-moving merchant vessel in *MV Saiga (No. 2)* were scarcely reasonable or necessary actions. Thus the US delegation

---

[24] *Loizidou v. Turkey* (Preliminary Objections), (1995) 310 Eur Ct HR (Ser. A), para. 62.
[25] *Al-Skeini*, para. 61, per Lord Rodger; paras. 90–92, per Baroness Hale; para. 97, per Lord Carswell; and para. 132, per Lord Brown. Lords Carswell and Brown relied, peculiarly, on an analogy with control over embassies abroad.
[26] (1935) 3 RIAA 1609; (1935) 29 AJIL 326.
[27] (1962) 35 ILR 485 at 499.   [28] O'Connell, p. 1073.
[29] *MV 'Saiga' Case (No. 2)*, (1999) 38 ILM 1323 at 1355; cf. FSA, Article 22(1)(f).

took the view during SUA Protocol 2005 negotiations that, '[s]imply put, there is almost no specific guidance regarding the use of force while conducting a boarding pursuant to treaty or customary international law.'[30] Further guidance nonetheless may be derived from the general international law on the use of force and its codification in specific contexts. Given the special status of UN Charter obligations, the Charter is the appropriate place to begin.

3.2 The UN Charter

There is a general consensus that high-seas maritime interdiction operations, at least in those cases authorised by UNCLOS Article 110, are not prohibited by the UN Charter law on the use of force.[31] However, one's choice of theory explaining this result may have consequences in other cases. Countermeasures may not involve the use of force. Therefore if maritime interdiction generally involves a use of force prohibited under the UN Charter it may not be used as a countermeasure.[32] The question of the relationship between Article 110 and the UN Charter is thus an important one.

Irrespective of whether the prohibition on the use or threat of force in international relations is *jus cogens*,[33] the rule as embodied in Article 2(4) of the UN Charter prevails over other international obligations as a consequence of Charter Article 103. Article 2(4) states that all UN members 'shall refrain *in their international relations* from the threat or use of force against the territorial integrity or political independence of any state' (emphasis added). These words are reproduced verbatim in UNCLOS Article 301, and the prohibition might logically be thought to extend to maritime interdictions. Boarding a foreign vessel on the high

---

[30] See United States IMO Delegation, White Paper on Article 8*bis*, 22 December 2003, at para. 2.9.2, www.ccaimo.mar.mil.br/SecIMO/Outros/outros_assuntos/ SUA8bisWP0621.doc; cf. Spadi, 'Bolstering the Proliferation Security Initiative', 276.

[31] A. Randelzhofer, 'Article 2(4)' in Bruno Simma (ed.), *The Charter of the United Nations: A Commentary,* 2nd edn (Oxford University Press, 2002), I, pp. 112, 124.

[32] Arguments suggesting that interdiction could be used as a countermeasure to enforce collective interest obligations in a fisheries context were addressed in Chapter 6.

[33] Compare A. Orakhelashvili, 'The impact of peremptory norms on the interpretation and application of United Nations Security Council resolutions' (2005) 16 EJIL 59, at 63 (asserting that the prohibition on the use of force is *jus cogens*) with the ILC commentary to its Articles on State Responsibility: [2001] II(2) YBILC, 85 at (5). ILC Rapporteur Robert Ago distinguished uses of force constituting aggression (prohibited by *jus cogens*) from 'less serious' (but still prohibited) uses of force: [1980] II YBILC, 39–40.

seas falls within the sphere of 'international relations'. At the least, non-compliant (resisted) boardings will be preceded by firing warning shots across the bow. This is an obvious *threat* of armed force. However, is the position affected by the words 'against the territorial integrity or political independence of any state'? Two views may be taken.

The first is that interdiction is permissible as, forceful or not, it is not an act *against* the territory or political independence of a state. As flag states have only 'exclusive' (not 'territorial') jurisdiction over their vessels, interdiction cannot constitute force used against the flag state's territorial integrity and any temporary exercise of enforcement jurisdiction cannot be said to affect the flag state's political independence.[34] The simple answer to such an approach is that the prohibition upon 'the threat or use of force' is not qualified or reduced in scope by the subsequent words 'against the territorial integrity or political independence of any state'. These words were added as a result of an Australian proposal further to guarantee the prohibition's comprehensive nature, not to introduce exceptions.[35]

The second, preferable view therefore is that the prohibition is absolute and not subject to exceptions. On this view, an interdiction not otherwise authorised by international law would be prohibited as involving a threat or use of force.[36] This approach may draw some further support by analogy with the rules governing self-defence at sea. Under Article 51 of the UN Charter it is widely accepted that the right to self-defence extends to protecting flagged vessels – even merchant vessels – against armed attacks.[37] This orthodoxy of the law of armed conflict at sea may startle the general international lawyer. After all, a

---

[34] S. Kaye, 'The Proliferation Security Initiative in the maritime domain' (2005) 35 IYBHR 205 at 218; cf. D. Bowett, *Self-Defence in International Law* (Manchester University Press, 1958), p. 152.

[35] Thomas Franck, *Recourse to Force: State Action against Threats and Armed Attacks* (Cambridge University Press, 2002), p. 12; Ian Brownlie, *International Law and the Use of Force by States* (Oxford: Clarendon Press, 1963), pp. 265–8.

[36] McLaughlin holds that 'active' naval enforcement of UN embargoes requires an authorisation to use force, at least in respect of non-compliant boarding: 'United Nations mandated naval interdiction operations', 252–6.

[37] See Dieter Fleck (ed.), *The Handbook of Humanitarian Law in Armed Conflicts* (Oxford University Press, 1995), p. 2; D. Raab, '"Armed Attack" after the *Oil Platforms* Case' (2004) 17 LJIL 719 at 727; C. Gray, 'The British position with regard to the Gulf conflict (Iran–Iraq): part 2' (1991) 40 ICLQ 464 at 469; V. Lowe, 'Self-defence at sea', in W. E. Butler (ed.), *The Non-use of Force in International Law* (Dordrecht: Martinus Nijhoff, 1989), p. 185 at p. 189; P. Bowett, *Self-Defence in International Law*, p. 71; cf. *Case Concerning Oil Platforms (Islamic Republic of Iran v. United States of America)*, Judgment, [2003] ICJ Rep. 161 at 191, and North Atlantic Treaty 1949, 34 UNTS 243, as amended

flagged merchant vessel might be thought to enjoy no closer connection with its state of nationality than a naturalised citizen. Any suggestion that there is a right to defend nationals abroad is clearly controversial. Lowe has noted that '[t]his right to defend merchant ships is generally acknowledged, but writers have avoided explaining its basis'; concluding that 'the only sound basis' for this 'extension of ... self defence ... is that international law contains a specific rule to this effect' which may not be generalised to other cases such as defence of nationals abroad.[38] In the present author's view, no such analogy could be made in any event. Protecting a vessel on the high seas requires no incursion into another state's territory as is invariably the case regarding protection or rescue of nationals abroad. This is simply a case of *lex specialis*. Turning to Article 2(4), it is clear that the range of conduct Article 2(4) prohibits is *wider* than 'armed attacks' of sufficient 'scale and effects' to permit Article 51 self-defence.[39] It would be startling, then, if international law held that national merchant vessels are objects protected from an 'armed attack' under Article 51 but are not protected from lesser unlawful uses of force under Article 2(4).

It might be thought relevant that in *Guyana v. Suriname* a threat of unspecified 'consequences' made by a Surinamese government patrol boat in disputed waters against a mobile drilling platform licensed by Guyana was held to be a 'threat of the use of force [by Suriname] in contravention of the Convention, the UN Charter and general international law'.[40] The arbitral tribunal did not expose its reasoning on this point. The platform was not itself registered in Guyana, but was located within an EEZ area awarded to Guyana and attached to the seabed therein. This fact might be thought to have given Guyana exclusive jurisdiction, analogous to flag-state jurisdiction, over the platform under UNCLOS Article 60(2). However, Article 60(2) was not referred to by the tribunal. Perhaps of more significance was Guyana's submission that 'the duty to refrain from the threat or use of force ... as a means of solving international disputes, including

---

by Protocol to the North Atlantic Treaty on the Accession of Greece and Turkey 1951, 126 UNTS 350, Article 6.

[38] Lowe, 'Self-defence at sea', pp. 188, 193.

[39] *Nicaragua Case*, 103–4; *Oil Platforms Case*, 161. Cf. C. Gray, *International Law and the Use of Force*, 2nd edn (Oxford University Press, 2004), pp. 140, 145; A. Randelzhofer, 'Article 51' in Bruno Simma (ed.), *The Charter of the United Nations: A Commentary*, 2nd edn (Oxford University Press, 2002), I, p. 788 at p. 796; and R. Macdonald, 'The *Nicaragua Case*: new answers to old questions?' (1986) 24 CYBIL 127, 154.

[40] *Guyana v. Suriname* (2008) 47 ILM 164, para. 445.

territorial disputes and problems concerning frontiers' articulated in the Friendly Relations Declaration constituted an authoritative interpretation of Article 2(4).[41] Thus the threat of force may have been held wrongful as it clearly occurred in the course of a boundary dispute, even if the relationship between the object of the threat and Guyana was unclear. Two views of the case may be taken: either that it stands for a broad interpretation of the prohibition in Article 2(4), or that it concerns only the effect of that prohibition in boundary disputes and is constrained to its facts.

If one accepts the broad view of the conduct prohibited by Article 2(4), it nonetheless does contain one important exception: where a state *invites* military intervention, there is no breach of the norm against the use of force.[42] That is, state A may consent to state B's use of force within the sphere of A's exclusive jurisdiction.[43] States commonly authorise law enforcement action upon their vessels by foreign officials under the multilateral or bilateral treaties discussed in this book, and Article 2(4) is irrelevant in that context.

However, co-operative interdiction arrangements do not support the alternative argument that 'police actions' conducted by a state outside its own territory are not uses of force. This argument runs that as UNCLOS expressly contemplates such enforcement action in limited cases, and as UNCLOS provisions cannot be presumed to be contrary to the UN Charter prohibition, it must then follow that such 'police actions' are not prohibited.[44] Supporters of this view could now refer to *Guyana v. Suriname*, where the tribunal found 'that the action mounted by Suriname ... seemed more akin to a threat of military action rather than a mere law enforcement activity', suggesting that it endorses the force/police action distinction. The case is, however, ultimately ambiguous on this point, as the tribunal also accepted that 'force may be used in law enforcement activities provided that such force is unavoidable, reasonable and necessary'.[45] This would appear to suggest that it is a

---

[41] *Ibid.*; The Declaration on Principles of International Law Concerning Friendly Relations and Co-operation among States in Accordance with the Charter of the United Nations, GA Res. 2625 (XXV), UN GAOR, 25th Session, UN Doc. A/8082 (1970).

[42] Shaw, pp. 1042–3; Gray, *International Law and the Use of Force*, p. 68; Brownlie, *International Law and the Use of Force by States*, p. 317.

[43] Cf. *Arrest Warrant Case*, 169, per Judge ad hoc Van Den Wyngaert (Dissenting Opinion).

[44] Rayfuse, 'Countermeasures and high seas fisheries enforcement', 74.

[45] *Guyana v. Suriname*, para. 445. The requirement that force be 'unavoidable' may be, in context, a reference to duties to make every effort to enter provisional

consideration of all relevant circumstances that allows a tribunal to categorise force as either lawful (a police action) or unlawful (a breach of Article 2(4)). In other words, 'police action' may only describe a legal characterisation of a given use of force after the fact, not a general a priori category.

The correct starting point must be that the exclusive jurisdiction principle renders a vessel immune from foreign interference unless there is either a permissive rule of international law allowing the interference or the flag state itself consents to the interdiction.[46] Article 110 of UNCLOS provides the sole grounds – absent the flag state's consent – when an interdicting state may ignore the flag state's exclusive jurisdiction. Of the grounds listed in Article 110, only those of piracy, being stateless, or having the same nationality as the interdicting warship reflect customary international law. It is difficult to imagine that the practice of a handful of European states in suppressing high-seas 'pirate radio' broadcasts, principally in the period 1958–67, created binding general international law.[47] A general right to board vessels at sea suspected of slaving was also not widely accepted prior to UNCLOS.[48] Article 110, then, is partially a codification of prior general law and the creation, as among parties, of new treaty-based rights. These are not examples of a general rule relating to 'policing', but are discrete and individually agreed rules. One cannot, therefore, create new categories of permissible interdiction action by analogy. Article 110 represents the prior consent of states to their vessels being interdicted in certain cases, not a non-exhaustive list of police powers. A 'police action' is not something other than a use of force; consent may simply render it not a *prohibited* use of force. The same may be said of the use of reasonable force within the EEZ for EEZ-related purposes; such a use of force is encompassed within the grant of sovereign rights within the EEZ and is analogous to police action within state territory. The *excessive* use of force in the EEZ against a foreign vessel may still constitute an internationally recognised wrong, but only under ordinary principles of diplomatic protection.[49]

---

arrangements and negotiations pending settlement of delimitation disputes under UNCLOS, Articles 74(3) and 83(3).

[46] *Lotus Case*, 25; High Seas Convention, Article 6(1); UNCLOS, Article 92(1).

[47] See Chapter 7.

[48] McDougal and Burke, pp. 881 ff.; Reuland, 'Interference with non-national ships', 1190; and see Chapter 4, section 2.

[49] See Chapter 12.

This approach necessarily prohibits recourse to interdiction in other cases, even as a countermeasure following another state's unlawful conduct at sea. If there is not flag-state consent given in advance to interdicting a flag vessel in international waters, or a specific exception allowing the interdiction, it will be prohibited as a use of force. The argument that states might resort to unilateral interdictions as a form of 'countermeasure in the collective interest' to enforce fisheries obligations against delinquent states was examined in Chapter 6. It was dismissed on the basis that RFMO members cannot generally be considered 'specially affected' states entitled to take countermeasures against such conduct.[50] The countermeasures argument must also fail as such actions would necessarily violate the prohibition on the use of force which also prohibits forceful countermeasures.[51] The next question, then, pertains to the rules governing force during permissible interdictions.

3.3 Customary international law and codification: the Caribbean Area Agreement rules

ITLOS restated the general international law on the use of force to affect interdictions in MV 'Saiga' (No. 2). Noting the lack of specific UNCLOS provisions, it found that general international law

> requires that the use of force must be avoided as far as possible and, where ... unavoidable, it must not go beyond what is reasonable and necessary in the circumstances. Considerations of humanity must apply...
>
> The normal practice ... is first to give an auditory or visual signal to stop, using internationally recognized signals. Where this does not succeed, a variety of actions may be taken, including the firing of shots across the bows of the ship. It is only after the appropriate actions fail that the pursuing vessel may, as a last resort, use force. Even then, appropriate warning must be issued ... and all efforts should be made to ensure that life is not endangered.[52]

The tribunal referred to the I'm Alone and Red Crusader cases and to FSA Article 22(1)(f) as having 'reaffirmed' the 'basic principle'.[53] This was an interesting elision, as the cases dealt only with use of force against a vessel while the FSA deals with the use of force aboard a vessel. The tribunal clearly treated the use of force in 'arresting' a vessel as one

---

[50] See Chapter 6, section 6.3.
[51] See ILC Articles on State Responsibility, Article 50(1)(a); D. Guilfoyle, 'Interdicting vessels to enforce the common interest: maritime countermeasures and the use of force' (2007) 56 ICLQ 69 at 78–81; Guyana v. Suriname, para. 446.
[52] MV 'Saiga' (No. 2), 1355.   [53] Ibid.

standard applicable in both cases and viewed the applicable rules as preceding, not arising from, relevant case and treaty law. The relevant FSA provision requires that inspectors

avoid the use of force except when and to the degree necessary to ensure the[ir] safety ... and where the inspectors are obstructed in the execution of their duties. The degree of force used shall not exceed that reasonably required in the circumstances.

Almost the same language is used in Article 8*bis*(9) of the SUA Protocol 2005, which limits force to 'the minimum degree ... necessary and reasonable in the circumstances'. This language appears stricter but may only reflect the fact that officers seeking WMD aboard foreign vessels will more likely be armed than fisheries inspectors.

The question is whether these general formulations are usefully supplemented by the more detailed provisions found in drug interdiction treaties, and whether the latter may provide some guidance regarding the applicable general international law. The majority of bilateral drug interdiction treaties have been concluded between the United States and Caribbean states. Such a treaty network may reflect 'hub and spoke' bilateralism, where a disproportionately powerful player may achieve greater concessions in bilateral negotiations than it could in multilateral negotiations.[54] Bilateral arrangements may then more likely reflect a 'deal' than consensus on the general law. It is preferable to focus on the multilateral Caribbean Regional Arrangement on drug interdiction, as it resulted from negotiations between nineteen states.[55] Participants in its drafting included the United States and Caribbean states as well as the United Kingdom, France and the Netherlands (all significant maritime powers) representing overseas territories or associated states.[56] Not only are the Regional Arrangement's provisions on the use of force detailed, but 'great care' was taken in their drafting 'to reflect the essence of pre-existing customary law'.[57] The results merit close attention. Article 22 of the Caribbean Regional Arrangement states:

[54] E.g. S. Cho, 'Breaking the barrier between regionalism and multilateralism: a new perspective on trade regionalism' (2001) 42 HILJ 419 at 432; cf. Klein, 'The right of visit', 313–14, commenting that 'a multilateral negotiating context ... considerably undermined' US leverage in the negotiation of the SUA Protocol 2005.

[55] Gilmore, *Agreement Concerning Co-operation*, p. 7.

[56] *Ibid.*, p. 44. Only France, the United States, Jamaica and Belize had ratified the Agreement as of March 2008: US State Department, *International Narcotics Control Strategy Report* (2008), www.state.gov/p/inl/rls/nrcrpt/2008/vol1/html/100778.htm.

[57] Gilmore, *Agreement Concerning Co-operation*, p. 36.

(1) Force may only be used if no other feasible means of resolving the situation can be applied.

(2) Any force used shall be proportional to the objective for which it is employed.

(3) All use of force pursuant to this Agreement shall in all cases be the minimum reasonably necessary under the circumstances.

(4) A warning shot shall be issued prior to any use of force except when force is being used in self-defence.

(5) In the event that the use of force is authorized and necessary in the waters of a Party, law enforcement officials shall respect the laws of the Party.

(6) In the event that the use of force is authorized and necessary during a boarding and search seaward of the territorial sea of any Party, the law enforcement officials shall comply with their domestic laws and procedures and the directions of the flag State.

(7) The discharge of firearms against or on a suspect vessel shall be reported as soon as practicable to the flag State Party.

(8) Parties shall not use force against civil aircraft in flight.

(9) The use of force in reprisal or punishment is prohibited.

(10) Nothing in this Agreement shall impair the exercise of the inherent right of self-defence by law enforcement or other officials of either Party.

While still relatively general, this provision usefully attempts to disaggregate the general customary international law into ten more specific rules. The question is whether, as the drafters apparently intended, these rules codify pre-existing customary law. It might be thought, on the basis of the usual approach to the relationship between treaty law and customary law, that this would be difficult to achieve in the present case. After all, the principal evidence consists of bilateral treaty practice and three multilateral conventions – the FSA, the SUA Protocol 2005 and the Caribbean Area Agreement – the last two of which are not in force.[58] The mere existence of the same rule in a variety of bilateral treaties is, of course, not necessarily evidence of its customary status.[59] Further, the ICJ in the *North Sea Continental Shelf* cases found that a low level of ratification of a multilateral treaty might weigh against its provisions having entered customary law.[60] One could set against this the argument that treaty-making nonetheless remains a form of state practice relevant to the assessment of customary international

---

[58] See Chapter 6, n. 29, Chapter 9, n. 1, and n. 56 above for ratification information.

[59] Michael Akehurst, 'Custom as a source of international law' (1974–5) 47 BYIL 1 at 43; *Lotus Case*, 27.

[60] *North Sea Continental Shelf Cases*, para. 73.

law, and relatively little state practice may be required to establish the existence of a rule, provided that 'there is no practice which conflicts with the rule' and the proposed rule does not attempt to 'overturn' a prior rule or attempts to modify it only slightly.[61] The present situation is precisely such a case of a 'blank slate' with no established rule to displace and little evidence of contradictory state practice. One might also attempt to attach some significance to the 'votes and views of states' during debates on the SUA Protocol 2005 in the IMO Legal Committee as 'evidence of customary law'.[62] However, such an approach may not be entirely helpful.

It is not obvious that all of the ten rules posited here are new rules. Many of these 'rules' actually represent *conclusions* as to which rules of general international law apply in the interdiction context and how they do so. Alternatively, they might be treated as examples of 'subsequent practice in the application' of UNCLOS obligations which 'establishes the agreement of the parties regarding [the] interpretation' of UNCLOS.[63] What is thus required is an assessment of whether the posited rules are best treated as accurately reflecting established, pre-existing rules of international law, or as providing evidence of an emerging customary rule; or whether they can be treated, at the least, as evidence of how a limited number of state parties to UNCLOS interpret UNCLOS in its application *inter se*.

3.3.1 Rules 1–4 and 8: the proportionate use of force as a last resort, warning shots and aircraft

The first principle, that force 'may only be used if no other feasible means of resolving the situation can be applied', obviously embodies the *MV 'Saiga' (No. 2)* standard that force is a measure of last resort. It should be understood to apply both to boarding a vessel and to 'situations' arising once aboard, including obstructing officials carrying out authorised actions.

The second and third principles, that force shall be proportional to the objective in sight and the minimum reasonably necessary, may be treated together. The formula that force shall be 'the minimum

---

[61] Akehurst, 'Custom as a source of international law', 19 and 53.

[62] Rosalyn Higgins, *The Development of International Law through the Political Organs of the United Nations* (London: Oxford University Press, 1963), p. 2; cf. Brownlie, p. 6; J. Cavenagh (ed.), 'Australian practice in international law 2004' (2006) 25 AYBIL 463 at 693.

[63] VCLT, Article 31(3)(b).

reasonably necessary' is found in almost every US bilateral drug interdiction treaty,[64] as well as in *MV 'Saiga' (No. 2)*. Its repetition in the SUA Protocol, after the Caribbean Area Agreement's conclusion, is therefore unsurprising.[65] However, the introduction of proportionality as a further constraint is relatively rare. Only two US bilateral treaties refer to force being the 'minimum reasonably necessary and proportionate'.[66] Is there any difference between the terms 'the minimum reasonably necessary' and 'proportionate'?

In some situations *any* force, even as a last resort, might be disproportionate to the goal in sight. A master's refusal to open a locked document cupboard would not justify compelling him to do so at gunpoint, especially if the cupboard could be levered open by the boarding party. However, this is giving 'proportionality' unnecessary work to do. The situation is already covered by the first principle – requiring that force may only be used after all other methods have been exhausted. Further, the 'minimum reasonably necessary force' should always fall within what is 'proportionate'. If force is the last resort, and the force used is the minimum necessary, it is hard to see how such use could ever be disproportionate. It is difficult to give both provisions a separate meaning.

The better question is what defines appropriate 'objectives', the ends to which force must be proportionate/reasonably necessary. The test must be that force has been used to secure a permitted goal, being an action either authorised directly by international law or an action falling within the scope of flag-state authorisation. It must be correct to say that force is acceptable where, as a last resort, it is the minimum reasonably necessary to achieve an authorised end. One might ask three questions. Was force used only after other means were exhausted (rule 1)? Was force used to achieve an authorised end (rule 2)? Was the force actually used the minimum reasonably necessary to achieve that end (rules 2 and 3)?

---

[64] Antigua and Barbuda Agreement, Article 16; Barbados Agreement, Article 13; Colombia Agreement, Article 12; Costa Rica Agreement, Article 7(6); Dominica Agreement, Article 16; Dominican Republic Agreement (as amended), Article 16; Grenada Agreement, Article 16; Guatemala Agreement, Article 13; Haiti Agreement, Article 21; Jamaica Agreement (as amended), Articles 3(8) and 17; Nicaragua Agreement, Article 15; Panama Supplementary Agreement, Article 17; Saint Kitts and Nevis Agreement, Article 16; Saint Lucia Agreement, Article 16; Suriname Agreement, Article 16.

[65] SUA Protocol 2005, Article 8*bis*(9).

[66] Colombia Agreement, Article 12; Jamaica Agreement (as amended), Articles 3(8) and 17(2).

The fourth rule, that warning shots shall be used in cases other than self-defence, is universally accepted. As noted, warning shots will normally be fired across the bow of a vessel which is resisting boarding, and then only after it has ignored signals to stop.

The eighth rule, prohibiting the use of force against civilian aircraft in flight, is found in several US bilateral agreements[67] and Article 3*bis* of the Chicago Convention.[68] It may be considered to be a case where using force will always be disproportionate to the risk to human safety or contrary to elementary considerations of humanity.

Collectively these rules appear to be no more than a restatement or reformulation of the basic principle proclaimed as customary international law in *MV 'Saiga' (No. 2)*.

3.3.2 Rule 5: respect for local law

The fifth rule states that where using force is 'authorized and necessary' in another state's territorial sea, 'law enforcement officials shall respect' coastal state law. This requires careful disaggregation. That using force in another state's territory must be 'authorised' follows from the rule that enforcement action may generally only be undertaken in another state's territory with its consent.[69] Reference to necessity merely restates the first rule, that force must be a last resort. This leaves for consideration the question of respect for local law.

There would appear to be a generally applicable rule that foreign state organs voluntarily admitted to a receiving state should respect local law. The oldest customary law examples relate to ambassadors and foreign warships in port. Article 41 of the Vienna Convention on Diplomatic Relations 1961 provides that diplomatic agents, '[w]ithout prejudice to their privileges and immunities', have a 'duty … to respect the laws and regulations of the receiving State'. This is a customary and long-established rule. In 1758 Vattel expressed it as a duty upon ambassadors to conform in matters of their external conduct with the local law.[70] The case of foreign warships in port is discussed in more detail in the next chapter, but the basic rule is similarly that

---

[67] Guatemala Agreement, Article 13(1); Jamaica Agreement (as amended), Article 17; Nicaragua Agreement, Article 15; Panama Agreement, Article 17(1); Dominican Republic Agreement (as amended), Article 16.

[68] Gilmore, *Agreement Concerning Co-operation*, p. 36; Convention on International Civil Aviation 1944, 15 UNTS 295 (as amended), www.icao.int/icaonet/dcs/7300.html.

[69] *Lotus Case*, 25.   [70] Vattel, *Law of Nations*, III, p. 377.

they are 'expected to comply voluntarily' with local law but remain immune from local jurisdiction.[71] In both cases, the remedy for the receiving state for any failure to observe local law would appear to be the right of expulsion. The NATO Status of Forces Agreement (SOFA) also provides that visiting armed forces must 'respect the law of the receiving state'.[72] The rule appears to be one commonly applied in cases where foreign state organs are admitted to the jurisdiction of a receiving state.

What then, does such a duty to respect entail? One, largely unhelpful, view is that this standard requires 'substantial rather than literal compliance', being compliance with local law's 'purposes' though not its exact 'procedural requirements'.[73] This suggestion arises under the NATO SOFA and principally in administrative law contexts, such as licences to draw water or discharge effluent within a visiting force's base, and provides little assistance for present purposes.[74] The preferable view is thus that a boarding state's officials must comply voluntarily with any *applicable* local law when conducting operations in foreign territorial waters. As a matter of general principle, once such officials have entered a foreign state's jurisdiction, they are 'subject as a matter of legal substance to the laws of the receiving state' and should obey them even if they benefit from an immunity from local enforcement and adjudicative jurisdiction.[75] They will certainly be liable for any infringements of local law, should that immunity be waived.

The question of what local law is applicable is complex and can only be answered by reference to local law.

While there may be local laws on the use of force by private citizens, national armed services and private law bodies such as companies, a visiting force may, 'as an emanation of a foreign state', not be regarded

---

[71] *Oppenheim*, 9th edn, p. 1169.

[72] Agreement Between the Parties to the North Atlantic Treaty Regarding the Status of Their Forces 1951, 199 UNTS 67 (NATO SOFA), Article 2; cf. Vienna Convention on Diplomatic Relations 1961, 500 UNTS 95, Article 41(1).

[73] E. Schwenk, 'Jurisdiction of the receiving state over forces of the sending state under the NATO Status of Forces Agreement' (1972) 6 *International Lawyer* 525 at 530; R. Batstone, 'Respect for the law of the receiving state' in Dieter Fleck (ed.), *The Handbook of the Law of Visiting Forces* (Oxford University Press, 2001), p. 61 at p. 62.

[74] Batstone, 'Respect for the law of the receiving state', p. 64.

[75] Eileen Denza, *Diplomatic Law: Commentary on the Vienna Convention on Diplomatic Relations*, 3rd edn (Oxford University Press, 2008), p. 461. Similarly, in 1764 Wolff regarded ambassadors as being, in principle, in the same position as other 'foreigners living in alien territory', but protected in practice by special rules of 'sanctity': *Jus gentium*, pp. 534 ff.

as any of these things.[76] Local law is therefore liable 'to require adaptation' to accommodate the actions of boarding parties.[77] Unless appropriately adapted, there is a risk that local law could treat foreign officials as having no right to use force other than in self-defence. The ordinary principle that treaties be implemented in good faith requires that a foreign force 'should be able to carry out the purposes for which it' was admitted into local territory.[78] Implementing a treaty allowing foreign law enforcement operations in territorial waters will require that the officers of a foreign boarding state should (within the scope of their permission to act) be treated as having the same powers as coastal-state officials. Reaching a different conclusion would defeat a law enforcement treaty's object and purpose. This would not follow if these treaties envisaged that all enforcement action was being under-taken by a ship-riding officer of the local state. The majority of agree-ments, including the Regional Agreement, do contemplate foreign officials taking enforcement action. National implementation is thus critical, especially as most such treaties contemplate that the coastal state may ultimately assert jurisdiction to prosecute. Prosecutions could well fail if foreign agents, lacking police powers in local law, arrest a person subsequently prosecuted before local courts.[79] As Fox notes, 'lack of proper attachment to the local police force can result in the visiting [officials] committing [local] offences out of ignorance … and their evidence being dismissed'.[80] US bilateral treaty practice on the point has used several formulas. Only the US–Barbados Agreement specifically requires that any use of force in territorial waters must strictly accord with local law.[81] Agreements with Nicaragua and Jamaica provide that all territorial-sea operations are 'subject to the [coastal state's] authority and jurisdiction',[82] which may imply the same result. Others more ambiguously provide that territorial-sea operations are the coastal state's 'responsibility' and 'subject to [its] authority'.[83] In all

---

[76] Batstone, 'Respect for the law of the receiving state', p. 64.

[77] *Ibid.*, p. 66.   [78] *Ibid.*, p. 65; VCLT, Article 26; and cf. *Schooner Exchange*, 139.

[79] As has happened in a non-maritime context: *Ministère Public v. Saelens* (Court Martial of Ypres, Belgium) (1945) 13 ILR 85.

[80] Hazel Fox, *The Law of State Immunity* (Oxford University Press, 2004), p. 359.

[81] Barbados Agreement, Article 13(2).

[82] Nicaragua Agreement, Article 3; Jamaica Agreement (as amended), Article 4.

[83] Belize Agreement, Article 2; Costa Rica Agreement, Article 3; Dominica Agreement, Article 2; Dominican Republic Agreement, Article 2; Grenada Agreement, Article 8; Guatemala Agreement, Article 3; Haiti Agreement, Article 3; Saint Kitts and Nevis Agreement, Article 2; Saint Lucia Agreement,

cases, and especially Barbados's strictly phrased provision, one would anticipate national implementing legislation. The relevant minister in Barbados or Grenada may authorise a 'person' to stop, board and arrest a vessel within the territorial sea if it is engaged in offences against national law, including 'taking on board or off-loading' cargo contrary to local customs law.[84] This, however, would not appear to cover smuggling vessels pursued from the high seas into Barbadian or Grenadian waters and not actually unloading cargo there. A similar situation prevails under Saint Kitts and Nevis's and Saint Lucia's legislation.[85] Jamaica has, admirably, passed a law expressly allowing a foreign state to pursue suspected smuggling vessels into its waters and to board and search such a vessel 'in accordance with the laws of Jamaica'.[86] The legislation of several other Caribbean states appears entirely silent on such delegated enforcement jurisdiction.[87]

Many ship-rider treaties omit reference to this issue altogether, perhaps presuming (optimistically) that in all but exceptional cases a ship-rider would be available to enforce the coastal state's laws in its territorial waters. It might be that the lack of implementing legislation has never been a practical issue, or that local legislatures are unwilling to facilitate such US operations. Nonetheless, the issue has now been squarely raised by Article 20 of the Caribbean Area Agreement, which expressly requires parties to take

> such measures as may be necessary under … domestic law to ensure that foreign law enforcement officials, when conducting actions in [territorial] waters

Article 2; Suriname Agreement, Article 3. Wendel argues that this provision may have the result of excluding US responsibility for wrongful acts in the course of such interdictions: *State Responsibility for Interferences with the Freedom of Navigation*, p. 225. It is not obvious why an applicable law clause would have this result.

[84] Barbados Territorial Waters Act 1979, CAP 386, ss. 7 and 8, www.caricomlaw.org/laws.php; Grenada Territorial Waters Act, No.17 of 1978, ss. 7 and 8, www.un.org/Depts/los/LEGISLATIONANDTREATIES/PDFFILES/GRD_1978_Act17.pdf.

[85] The Maritime Areas Act (Act No.3 of 1984) (Saint Kitts and Nevis), ss. 23(2)(a) and 23(11), www.un.org/Depts/los/LEGISLATIONANDTREATIES/PDFFILES/KNA_1984_Act.pdf; The Maritime Areas Act (Act No.6 of 1984) (Saint Lucia), ss. 23(2)(a) and 23(11), www.un.org/Depts/los/LEGISLATIONANDTREATIES/PDFFILES/LCA_1984_Act.pdf.

[86] Maritime Drug Trafficking (Suppression) Act 1998 (Act 1 of 1998, Jamaica), s. 18, www.caricomlaw.org/laws.php.

[87] See Maritime Areas Act 1992, CAP 11 (Belize); Archipelagic Waters and Maritime Jurisdiction Act 1993 (No.37 of 1993) (Bahamas); and cf. para. 2(a), US–Bahamas Exchange of Notes: Cooperative Ship-rider and Overflight Drug Interdiction Program 1996, KAV 4743. All legislation available at www.un.org/Depts/los/LEGISLATIONANDTREATIES/latinamerica.htm.

under this Agreement, are deemed to have like powers to those of domestic law enforcement officials.

Given the general lack of adequate national implementation, it is perhaps unsurprising that the Agreement has not yet entered into force.

Where necessary adaptations to local law have been made, what follows? Are boarding parties in territorial-sea operations required to follow local law or merely required not to breach it? To some extent it will turn on the treaty arrangements and national laws in force. At the least the obligation to respect local law will require a boarding party not to breach it, irrespective of whether it is obliged to follow local law. Any breach, or at least any serious breach, of applicable local law by a foreign state organ will constitute a clear breach of the international obligation to respect it.[88] To say that a failure to respect local law may breach an international obligation is, of course, quite different from saying that a state is bound by local law and amenable to local jurisdiction.

To conclude, the fifth rule upholds a coastal state's right to exercise, subject to limited qualifications, plenary enforcement jurisdiction over its territorial sea.[89] This rule reflects pre-existing customary international law, being only a specific application of two more general rules. First, the national law of a state will apply throughout the entirety of its territory and may apply throughout its territorial sea, subject to any exceptions established by national or international law.[90] Second, following from the first, where a foreign force 'is granted the right to do something' within another state's territory this does not necessarily imply that the territorial state has renounced its power to regulate the foreign force's conduct.[91] If a state has passed national laws applicable to foreign officials conducting territorial-sea law enforcement operations (for example, by deeming them local officials or 'authorised persons'), then foreign officials covered by such laws will be bound to respect them.

---

[88] Batstone, 'Respect for the law of the receiving state', p. 69; cf. international responsibility arising from government vessels breaching local navigational laws in the territorial sea: UNCLOS, Article 31.

[89] See Caribbean Area Agreement, Article 1(h); UNCLOS, Articles 2(1) and 49; Churchill and Lowe, pp. 61 and 127.

[90] Batstone, 'Respect for the law of the receiving state', p. 63; Brownlie, p. 299; *The Schooner Exchange v. McFaddon* 11 US (7 Cranch) 116 (1813) at 136; *Wright v. Cantrell*, 12 ILR 133 at 134–5; *Wilson v. Girard* (1956) 354 US 524 at 545.

[91] Batstone, 'Respect for the law of the receiving state', p. 65.

In such cases foreign officials should be conversant with local laws and procedures. In practice, many bilateral and multilateral drug inter-diction treaties provide for the exchange of information on national law enforcement procedure.[92] In the event of ad hoc authorisation, the boarding state should try to secure specific confirmation that its pro-posed course of action accords with local law.

In summary, if the coastal state has passed national laws binding upon territorial sea interdictions conducted by foreign officials and that law is breached, two consequences follow. First, an international wrong will have been committed. Where the acts of a state organ in a receiving state are attributable to their sending state, it will not matter that the international obligation to respect local law is given specific content by local law. A breach of local law may constitute an interna-tionally wrongful act attributable to the sending state,[93] as breaching an applicable law would be the clearest case of a failure to respect it. Second, that breach may involve the individual criminal liability of a sending-state official under the receiving state's law. This raises issues of state immunity, discussed in Chapter 11. If the coastal state has not made any necessary adjustments to its internal laws allowing foreign law-enforcement operations within its territory, local courts will likely conclude that any use of force, other than in self-defence, is illegal.

3.3.3 Rule 6: applicable national law on the use of force

The sixth rule addresses one practical consequence of concurrent juris-diction on the high seas, stating that where 'the use of force is author-ized and necessary during ... [an interdiction], the law enforcement officials shall comply with their [own] domestic laws and procedures and the directions of the flag State'. The second part of the rule, requir-ing compliance with flag-state directions, should be uncontroversial. That the primacy of flag-state jurisdiction entails the ability to impose conditions upon the boarding state's conduct, including limits as to the

---

[92] See Caribbean Area Agreement, Article 25(1); Antigua and Barbuda Agreement, Article 17; US–Barbados Agreement, Article 16; Costa Rica Agreement, Article 7(8); US–Grenada Agreement, Article 17; Guatemala Agreement, Article 14; Haiti Agreement, Article 22; Honduras Agreement, Article 8; Saint Lucia Agreement, Article 17; Suriname Agreement, Article 17; Dominica Agreement, Article 17; Dominican Republic Agreement, Article 17.

[93] *Zafiro Case* (1925) 6 RIAA 160–165 (looting by the crew of a merchant vessel in government service was wrongful conduct attributable to the US despite being unauthorised).

use of force, is self-evident and well attested in treaty practice.[94] Our focus here should thus be on the first part of the rule. The formulation that boarding-state officials shall comply with their own 'domestic laws and procedures' is the only practical one. It would be impossibly onerous to require every interdiction (especially under a multilateral treaty) to be conducted strictly under flag-state law.

While practical, the limited relevant practice provides slender evidence as to whether this rule is a rule of general international law.[95] The applicable national law on the use of force during high-seas boardings is not addressed in any bilateral US treaty. The United States has also contended in multilateral negotiations that there are effectively no specific international law standards governing interdictions (other than respect for human rights).[96] The 1990 Spanish–Italian Interdiction Treaty provides that '[o]n ships sailing under national flags, police powers granted by the respective legal systems remain valid.'[97] As discussed in chapter 5, section 4 this provides for the non-displacement of the flag state's law of police powers while the vessel is under another state's effective control. It does not require that the interdicting state's officers act in accordance with anything other than their national law. Thus it might be thought to be consistent with a proposition that they are bound to follow their national law. However, only the 1995 Council of Europe Agreement expressly provides that enforcement action taken aboard a vessel, presumably including any use of force, 'shall be governed by the law of the intervening State'.[98] The treaty practice is thus limited and not necessarily consistent. It provides no secure basis from which to begin inferring customary rules.

However, this is not necessarily a question that international law must answer. Aboard the flag vessel, the flag state's law will apply. The conduct of the boarding party, as an organ of a foreign state, will be governed by the law of that state. Setting aside questions of respect for the flag state's law or immunity from its courts for breaches of that law, the mere fact of being within another state's jurisdiction does not invalidate the boarding state's control over its forces.[99] The final test

---

[94] SUA Protocol 2005, Article 8*bis*(5)(c) and (7); Migrant Smuggling Protocol, Article 8(5); UN Narcotics Convention, Article 17(6); Council of Europe Agreement, Article 8(1).

[95] Although in certain cases little practice might be needed: Cheng, 'United Nations resolutions on outer space', 35 ff. Shaw, pp. 74–5.

[96] See references at n. 30, above.   [97] Article 5(1).   [98] Article 11(1).

[99] *Schooner Exchange*, 139 ff.

of the legality of any individual use of force will be the international standard found in the first, second and third rules. If the force officers actually use is disproportionate, or more than the minimum necessary, it will be no defence that they acted in accordance with (their or the flag state's) national law.[100] Conversely, use of force in a manner which breached the flag or boarding state's law but was proportionate and the minimum necessary would seldom give rise to an international wrong, other than possibly breaching the duty to respect local law. It is thus difficult to see why public international law would be directly concerned with this issue.

The most obvious reason for including applicable law provisions in treaty arrangements is to prevent a dispute between parties as to the proper conduct of an interdiction. It is perhaps helpful to stipulate that boarding officers may follow their national law on using force and need not attempt to implement flag-state procedures (unless directed to), but there is no reason that international law should so provide. The question, from a national constitutional perspective, of what national law applies may be more complicated, as is illustrated by previous discussion of *R v. Hape* and *Al-Skeini*.

3.3.4 Rule 7: firearms

The seventh rule, a reporting requirement on the discharge of firearms, presumes the prior issue of their *permissible* use in interdictions. Where their use is permitted, accountability, mutual respect and comity would strongly suggest a reporting requirement. This does not, however, answer the prior question.

Article 10(3) of the Caribbean Area Agreement (and many other narcotics treaties) permits boarding parties to carry small arms.[101] The carrying of firearms in other interdiction contexts may be controversial. The relevant FSA provision, largely replicated in the SUA Protocol, contains no express reference to firearms. Article 15(4) of the NEAFC Scheme expressly prohibits fishery inspectors carrying firearms. There has been some dispute in CCAMLR as to whether inspectors may carry 'personal safety equipment' including firearms under the existing Scheme, and proposed amendments addressing the lacuna failed in 2007.[102] One

---

[100] See ILC Articles on State Responsibility, Article 3, and commentary in [2001] II(2) YBILC, pp. 36–8.

[101] E.g. Council of Europe Agreement, Article 12(2).

[102] CCAMLR XXVI, 67 (Australia on the necessity of inspectors carrying 'personal safety equipment'), 167 (Argentina asserting firearms are impermissible).

stumbling block in negotiating an enforcement scheme in the WCPFC was exactly this issue. The 2005 draft scheme's provisions stated that

> inspectors are not authorized to carry firearms ... and force shall not be used for the purpose of stopping, slowing or boarding a vessel or once on board a vessel for carrying out inspection activities or for gaining access to any portion of the vessel.[103]

The draft Scheme permitted only the 'minimum necessary' force to relieve a 'real and imminent threat to the safety of the enforcement vessel, its crew or to the boarding party'.[104] In September 2006 this was curiously reformulated as

> The use of force shall be avoided except when and to the degree necessary to ensure the safety of the inspectors and where the inspectors are obstructed in the execution of their duties. The degree of force used shall not exceed that reasonably required in the circumstances.[105]

This wording, taken directly from FSA Article 22(1)(f), was criticised for not specifically prohibiting the use of force to conduct 'hostile' interdictions of 'non-compliant' vessels.[106] This was, however, the text finally adopted by the WCPFC.[107]

This debate reflects a common perception that IUU fishing is not as 'serious' as drug smuggling and that self-employed fishermen should not be treated as dangerous criminals.[108] This view ignores the ecological and human food-security consequences of overfishing and the real involvement of corporate (and organised criminal) elements in much high-seas IUU fishing.[109] It also ignores the real risks faced by law-enforcement officials dealing with some IUU fishermen. The

---

[103] Boarding and Inspection Procedures (Secretariat Paper), 10 November 2005, WCPFC/TCC1/15 (Rev.1), para. 25 and 26, www.wcpfc.int/tcc1/pdf/ WCPFC-TCC1-15.pdf.

[104] *Ibid.*

[105] See WCPFC/TCC2/2006/12, Attachment 2: Secretariat's Commentary on the WCPFC Boarding and Inspection Procedures, undated, at Article 26, www.wcpfc.int/tcc2/ index.htm#info.

[106] *Ibid.*, and cf. EU Comments in Attachment 2, cover note and p. 7.

[107] WCPFC, Summary Report: Third Regular Session of the Commission for the Conservation and Management of Highly Migratory Fish Stocks in the Western and Central Pacific Ocean, 11–15 December 2006, para. 156, www.wcpfc.int/wcpfc3/ index.htm.

[108] Personal communication with Joao Neves, NEAFC, 17 May 2006.

[109] French submissions in the *Monte Confurco* case: ITLOS/PV.00/6/Rev.1 (7 December 2000), 6.

Australian experience of illegal, principally Indonesian, IUU fishing in its northern waters is telling. There has been a shift from 'village crews seeking subsistence catches' to professionally crewed and well equipped 'larger blue-water [fishing] vessels', where the 'expense involved … indicate[s] that large international cartels are backing them'.[110] With this has come '[a]n alarming increasing tendency for active resistance to boarding and search', 'many of the boarding parties hav[ing] been put at risk of serious injury'.[111] Compared with subsistence illegal fisherman, these professional IUU fishing crews

[are] more aggressive with machetes and large knives being waved at boarding parties, iron spikes being inserted in rubber strakes to deter boarding boats getting alongside and missiles being hurled at boarding personnel … Australian courts have [given] jail sentences for assault and other offences when boarding parties are actively opposed… As a result of the increased violence offered over recent years against customs and navy personnel all boarding personnel now carry personal arms and even the customs department patrol vessels have deck-mounted machine guns.[112]

There is no reason to believe that these risks are confined to the Australian experience in confronting IUU vessels. The Australian navy has since revised its rules of engagement to allow 'direct disabling fire upon [illegal fishing] vessels that are seeking to escape capture' and has fired into one foreign vessel after giving auditory warnings and firing shots across its bow.[113] Presumably the rules of engagement must now also allow the use of firearms by the boarding party once aboard the suspect vessel.

Overall, it is difficult to suggest that there is a generally accepted rule on firearms. Where the matter is not specifically addressed, it is obviously one regarding which the flag state could impose conditions. Pirate and stateless vessels will be at the mercy of the boarding state's national law.

---

[110] White and Forrest, 'Australian maritime law update: 2005', 300.

[111] M. White, 'Australian maritime law update: 2006 – Part I' (2007) 38 JMLC 293, 294.

[112] White and Forrest, 'Australian maritime law update: 2005', 300–1; see also White, 'Australian maritime law update: 2006 – Part I', 297–8 for the dramatic facts in *Jamaludin v. Commonwealth DPP* [2006] SASC 104.

[113] Quoting Dr Brendan Nelson, Australian Defence Minister: 'New rules allow navy to fire on illegal fishing boats', ABC News, 6 December 2006, www.abc.net.au/news/stories/2006/12/06/1805232.htm; 'Navy fires on "illegal" foreign fishing boat', ABC News, 23 August 2007, www.radioaustralia.net.au/programguide/stories/200708/s2012783.htm.

3.3.5 Rule 9: the prohibition on reprisals

The prohibition on the use of force in a reprisal is certainly a rule found in general international law.[114] The more difficult question is what constitutes a reprisal. A reprisal may be defined as a use of force carried out for punitive or deterrent motives, or it may be used as a shorthand term for a use of force rendered unlawful for its failure to comply with requirements of necessity and proportionality. There is, obviously, room for overlap between these categories as a purely punitive use of force is unlikely to satisfy standards of necessity and proportionality.

While there is a lively debate as to what distinguishes a reprisal from legitimate self-defence under UN Charter Article 51,[115] that debate is irrelevant for present purposes. As *authorised* uses of force, the legal limits of action during a permissive interdiction are set not by the general law of self-defence in interstate relations but by the scope of the flag state's consent. While the general international law of self-defence in interstate relations rejects any subjective test in favour of a strictly objective assessment of whether action in self-defence was warranted,[116] that approach need not necessarily apply in the interdiction context. Once that is appreciated, there is no compelling reason not to test whether a use of force was a 'reprisal' by reference to the actors' intentions and subjective appreciation of the facts. Further, a subjective intent to engage in a punitive use of force could be inferred where the use of force is manifestly disproportionate or resorted to before the exhaustion of other means. For example, the facts in *MV 'Saiga' (No. 2)* looked very much like an effort by Guinean authorities to punish foreign vessels breaching local (extraterritorial) laws against the at-sea refuelling of vessels fishing in Guinean waters. In the interdiction context, the gap between objective and subjective theories of reprisals might be narrower than is perceived in other debates.

3.3.6 Rule 10: individual self-defence

The foregoing rules are without prejudice to the right of self-defence of any boarding party or law-enforcement vessel. The tenth rule refers to

---

[114] See Declaration on Principles of International Law Concerning Friendly Relations and Co-Operation among States in Accordance with the Charter of the United Nations.

[115] Gray, *International Law and the Use of Force*, pp. 163–4.

[116] D. Kaye, 'Adjudicating self-defense: discretion, perception, and the resort to force in international law' (2005–6) 44 CJTL 134; cf. *Oil Platforms (Merits)*, 195 ff.

law-enforcement officials' or vessels' individual right of self-defence and is obviously not subject to the same constraints as a state's right of self-defence. A number of drug interdiction treaties, fisheries inspection schemes and the SUA Protocol expressly recognise the right[117] and it is undoubtedly a generally applicable rule.

4 Conclusion

The primary rules of police action applicable in any interdiction may be summarised as consisting of, first, a duty on the part of a boarding state to take due account of safety of life at sea, the ship and its cargo; and the need not to prejudice the commercial or legal interests of the flag state, including taking reasonable steps to avoid unduly delaying the vessel. Second, boarding parties must comply with applicable international human rights law, inform the master of their intention to board, and afford the master the earliest opportunity to contact the ship's owner and flag state. Third, the basic rule relating to the use of force is that it is acceptable where, as a last resort, the force used is the minimum reasonably necessary to achieve an authorised end. This rule applies both as regards using force against a vessel to force it to accept a boarding party, and by a boarding party once aboard the vessel. The only difference is that, in the first case, it would generally be a requirement to first give an auditory or visual signal to stop, followed by firing warning shots across the bow, before resorting to force directly against the vessel. Firing live, large-calibre, solid rounds into the body of a vessel to force it to come to a halt will almost always constitute an unacceptable risk to human life.[118]

On the use of force to board a vessel, the conclusion has been that any interdiction constitutes a prohibited threat of the use of force in international relations unless justified under UNCLOS Article 110 or permitted by flag-state consent, including consent given by treaty arrangements. As regards the use of force by boarding-state law-enforcement officials once aboard, the following additional rules have been offered:

- if a state has passed national laws applicable to foreign officials conducting territorial-sea law-enforcement operations, those foreign

---

[117] Antigua and Barbuda Agreement, Article 16; Belize Agreement, Article 16; Caribbean Area Agreement, Article 22(10); FSA, Article 22(1)(f), as discussed above; NEAFC Scheme 2007, Article 15(4); SUA Protocol 2005, Article 8*bis*(9).

[118] *M/V 'Saiga' (No. 2)*; *I'm Alone* (1935) 3 RIAA 1609; *Red Crusader* (1962) 35 ILR 485.

officials must voluntarily comply with them, and failure to respect local law may constitute an international wrong;

- the use of firearms during interdictions will be governed by the basic rule on the use of force and any conditions imposed upon permission to interdict by a relevant flag or coastal state; and
- purely punitive uses of force (reprisals) are prohibited.

No applicable rule deprives a boarding party or interdicting vessel of its right of individual self-defence.

Irrespective of any international liability for breaching these rules, any action by the boarding party in conducting a police investigation and especially any action using force may bring individual officers into conflict with applicable flag-state law. This raises issues of immunity, discussed in the next chapter.

11 National jurisdiction and immunities during interdictions

1 Introduction

What happens if during an interdiction a boarding party member breaches the criminal law of the flag state? The question is more than hypothetical. In Chapter 6 it was noted that within NAFO at least one Portuguese master had laid a criminal complaint alleging that a Canadian inspector's actions in searching for logbooks aboard a Portuguese vessel breached Portuguese law. To resolve such situations one must first determine the law governing state organs' extraterritorial conduct. Ordinarily a state may place law-enforcement officials aboard a foreign vessel in two scenarios: either upon the high seas with flag-state consent (unless a permissive rule allows interdiction); or within another state's territorial sea with that territorial sovereign's consent. In either case the consent of the state having otherwise exclusive criminal enforcement jurisdiction ('the receiving state') is required to extend any jurisdictional competence to the boarding state. Three questions follow. First, is the boarding state entitled at international law to apply its own law to conduct discovered aboard? Second, what are the boarding state's obligations under the receiving state's law? That is, must the boarding state follow or implement receiving-state law and are boarding-state officials subject to or immune from that law? Third, what are the boarding state's obligations regarding any breach of the receiving state's law by its boarding party? Some interdiction treaties address these matters, but often in a partial or incomplete manner. One must therefore examine applicable rules of general international law. In discussing analogous authorities on the position of foreign-state organs invited to enter territorial jurisdiction the terms 'sending' and 'receiving' state are used instead of 'boarding' and 'flag' state.

2 Enforcement of boarding-state law against interdicted vessels

As regards high-seas interdictions, previous chapters amply illustrate that states believe that they may arrest, detain and ultimately try in their own courts and under their own national law offences discovered aboard foreign vessels boarded with flag-state consent. Considerable state practice supports a rule of general international law that flag-state consent is sufficient to permit this exercise of extraterritorial enforcement jurisdiction and vest a parallel jurisdiction in the boarding state. A state may go further and waive part of its jurisdiction in favour of another state, and a limited waiver may be implied simply from inviting a foreign state organ to enter a receiving state's territory.[1]

Practice regarding stateless vessels is instructive. The proposition that in international waters a vessel not flagged by (or registered in) any state 'enjoys no protection whatever' from interference by warships[2] assumes a *general* power in states to exercise jurisdiction on the high seas. If states can exercise control over stateless vessels there cannot be a general prohibition against states exercising extraterritorial enforcement jurisdiction on the high seas. Rather, there must be a rule regarding flag vessels' immunity from such foreign interference.

[J]urisdiction over a stateless vessel ... flows from the nature of the high seas regime; the high seas are subject to the concurrent jurisdiction of all States, rather than the jurisdiction of no State. Thus, a State does not have exclusive jurisdiction over a ship simply because the vessel has its nationality; rather, but for such nationality all other states would have jurisdiction as well.[3]

---

[1] *The Schooner Exchange v. McFaddon* (1813) 11 US (7 Cranch) 116 at 136–7 and 139 ff., per Marshall CJ; *Chung Chi Cheung v. The King* [1939] AC 160, 176; *Reference re Exemption of United States Forces from Canadian Criminal Law*, [1943] 4 DLR 11 at 39, per Taschereau J; *Chow Hung Ching v. The King* (1949) 77 CLR 449 at 465, per Latham CJ, 472, per Starke J, 481–2, per Dixon J, 487–8, per McTiernan J. See also *Wright v. Cantrell* (Australia, Supreme Court of New South Wales), (1943) 12 ILR 133, discussed at n. 58, below; I. A. Shearer, *Starke's International Law*, 11th edn (London: Butterworth, 1994), p. 207 and cf. p. 192.

[2] *Molvan v. Attorney-General for Palestine*, 124 quoting L. Oppenheim, *International Law: A Treatise*, 6th edn, ed. H. Lauterpacht (London: Longman, 1947), I, p. 546. Oppenheim's Editors cited no authority for this proposition until the ninth edition, which refers, quixotically, to *Molvan* (at p. 731, n. 4).

[3] D. Carson, 'Ships, nationality and status' in R. Bernhardt (ed.), *Encyclopedia of Public International Law*, Vol. 4 (Amsterdam: North-Holland, 2000), p. 404; the view is consistent with Gidel, I, pp. 229–33, and Meyers, pp. 318–21.

This underlying concurrent jurisdiction allows a boarding state to assert jurisdiction over a vessel once the flag state has (completely or partially) waived its immunity.

Territorial sea interdictions may concern three states: the territorial/coastal state, the boarding state and a third-party flag state. The argument has been made that UNCLOS Article 19 only contemplates the coastal state exercising enforcement jurisdiction within the territorial sea, the inference being that a third-party flag state might be immunised from interdiction by a state other than the coastal state through the *pacta tertiis* principle.[4] International law, however, clearly allows a state to: authorise another to act within its sphere of jurisdiction,[5] delegate the exercise of its jurisdiction to another state, or use the organ of another state placed at its disposal to conduct enforcement action.[6] It would be strange if a territorial state's sovereign right, valid against the world, could not be exercised by delegation due to the *pacta tertiis* principle.

Flag and coastal states ('receiving states') may authorise boarding states to act aboard their vessels or within their waters. Once a foreign boarding party is aboard a vessel, the question arises as to its relationship with the receiving state's law.

3 Boarding-state obligations under receiving-state law

A receiving state *could* entirely waive its jurisdiction over any crimes discovered aboard an interdicted vessel in advance. This, however, will generally be the exception. Most treaties provide for parallel or concurrent enforcement jurisdiction over discovered criminal activity and make provision for determining which jurisdiction will take priority ('primary jurisdiction').[7] Primary enforcement jurisdiction is generally

---

[4] Kathy-Ann Brown, *The Shiprider Model: An Analysis of the US Proposed Agreement Concerning Maritime Counter-Drug Operations in its Wider Legal Context*, Contemporary Caribbean Legal Issues, 1 (Bridgetown, Barbados: Faculty of Law, University of the West Indies, 1997), pp. 39–41.

[5] Apart from treaty arrangements discussed throughout this book, see also Convention Applying the Schengen Agreement 1990, Articles 40–43; Convention on Mutual Assistance in Criminal Matters between the Member states of the European Union 2000 (entered into force 23 August 2005), Official Journal of the European Communities C 197/3 (its Explanatory Report is in the Official Journal C 379/7 of 29 December 2000), Articles 12–16.

[6] See ILC Articles on State Responsibility, Article 6 and commentary in [2001] II(2) YBILC, 43–45.

[7] Cf. Meyers, pp. 41–52; contra, Gidel, I, p. 229.

held by the receiving state, and is seldom waived simply by granting permission to board. The receiving state's substantive criminal law (i.e. prescriptive and enforcement jurisdiction) clearly remains applicable aboard the vessel and is not displaced by the jurisdiction granted to the boarding state. The boarding party will, as a state organ, additionally remain subject to the boarding state's law of police procedure unless its national law provides otherwise.[8]

What follows from this simultaneous validity of two national legal systems? While questions of state immunity are raised, the first question must be the boarding party's duties under local law. Within the territorial sea, boarding-state officials must respect the receiving state's laws. This was discussed in Chapter 10, where it was suggested that this is a customary rule.[9] The obligation to respect local law was explained as a duty not to breach it, any breach being an internationally wrongful act.

The point is well illustrated by analogy with the status of warships in port.

[Warships] are expected to *comply voluntarily* with the [territorial sovereign's] laws ... regard[ing] ... order in the ports, the places for casting anchor, sanitation and quarantine, customs and the like. A warship which refuses to do so can be expelled, and ... steps may be taken against her... However, even in that case a warship does not fall under the jurisdiction of the littoral state.[10]

The duty of voluntary compliance is an implied term of the warship's general permission to enter port and the immunity from local jurisdiction granted by the receiving state. As the immunities accorded warships generally extend to foreign public vessels engaged in 'only government non-commercial service',[11] it would seem sensible to hold that they are bound by the same correlative duty. If the principle of voluntary compliance with local law applies in the territorial sea and within ports, there appears to be no reason to presume that it does not also apply, as an implied term of the authorisation under which they are acting, to forces voluntarily admitted to a vessel subject to receiving-state law.

---

[8] On the extraterritorial application of national law, as determined by national courts, see Chapter 10, section 2.

[9] See Chapter 10, section 3.3.2; cf. UNCLOS, Articles 30 and 31.

[10] *Oppenheim*, 9th edn, p. 1169 (emphasis added, footnotes omitted); cf. UNCLOS, Article 30.

[11] Anthony Aust, *Handbook of International Law* (Cambridge University Press, 2005), p. 172 (emphasis in original); cf. UNCLOS, Article 32.

4 Boarding-state immunity from flag-state criminal jurisdiction

4.1 Introduction

Flag-state or coastal-state jurisdiction applies, in principle, to boarding-state officers' conduct during consensual interdictions. The question is whether boarding-state officers are protected from the exercise of local *criminal* enforcement and adjudicative jurisdiction. For example, if boarding-state officers use force occasioning death or injury to a person aboard a foreign vessel, under what circumstances (if any) will they be liable to criminal prosecution in the flag state's territory? Civil (tortious) actions against the boarding state for the same conduct are considered below.

Analogies might be drawn with either the immunity of foreign law-enforcement officials before local courts or the jurisdiction of a territorial sovereign over another state's visiting military forces. Either analogy involves basic principles of state immunity. The historic approach to state immunity was of course the doctrine of absolute immunity, based on the principle that no state should subject a juridically equal sovereign to the adjudicative and enforcement jurisdiction of its courts (*par in parem non habet imperium*).[12] Under this rule the only relevant question was whether a foreign state organ or individual officer was acting in an official capacity at the time. This approach began to shift from about the time of the Second World War in favour of allowing foreign states to be subjected to the processes of local courts, at least in respect of commercial transactions and acts 'which a private person may perform'.[13] The generally accepted rule is now 'restrictive' state immunity, which holds that an organ of a foreign state may not be subjected to the adjudicative or enforcement jurisdiction of local courts in respect of acts having an inherently sovereign character (*acta iure imperii* or 'sovereign acts') but that state acts of a character which any private person could perform (*acta jure gestionis*) enjoy no such procedural immunity. The test is twofold: a person or entity of a certain

---

[12] Other rationales may be suggested: Shearer, *Starke's International Law*, p. 192. A range of objections may also be made to arguments grounded solely in sovereign equality: Fox, *State Immunity*, pp. 32–6.

[13] *Canada v. Employment Appeals Tribunal* (High Court, Ireland, 1991) 95 ILR 467 at 477–81, per O'Flaherty J, refers to case law and practice preceding the statutes and treaties which emerged in the period 1972–86 (see n. 21, below). A 1942 Irish case, *Zarine v. Owners of SS Ramava* [1942] IR 148, may have been among the first to apply such a doctrine.

status (an organ of state) must carry out a certain function (a sovereign act) to benefit from state immunity. The trend of jurisprudence has been to focus 'more upon the act than the actor'.[14] It is the act's governmental character that attracts immunity.[15] The exact contours and application of this approach vary between jurisdictions.

Conceptually, restrictive immunity can be characterised as being either an immunity *ratione materiae* attaching to official acts or a general immunity *ratione personae* attaching to state organs, but subject to certain exceptions. The generally accepted view of restrictive immunity may be considered one of an immunity *ratione materiae*, as it turns on a distinction between 'official', 'governmental' or 'sovereign' acts (*acta iure imperii*, which only a state may undertake) and 'ordinary' or 'commercial' acts (*acta jure gestionis*, which a private person could perform).[16]

An alternative view points to the fact that there is no generally accepted means of distinguishing between governmental/sovereign and commercial/ordinary acts.[17] International law provides no relevant definitions, and in the absence of such agreement the distinction is easily manipulated to a party's desired result.[18] Nor is the dichotomy itself inherently convincing or coherent: distinguishing the scope of 'government' activity necessarily involves policy judgements about 'the proper sphere of state activity'.[19] On this understanding, it is better to treat state immunity as applying to all organs of state by virtue of their status as such (*ratione personae*), but then to define acknowledged exceptions such as 'commercial or trading activity'.[20] This approach, commencing from a general rule of immunity and then defining the

---

[14] Fox, *State Immunity*, p. 4; cf. Hazel Fox, 'Restraints on the exercise of jurisdiction by national courts' in M. Evans (ed.), *International Law*, 2nd edn (Oxford University Press, 2006), p. 361 at p. 372.

[15] Cf. the definition of 'State' as including 'agencies ... of the State ... to the extent that they are entitled to perform and are actually performing *acts in the exercise of sovereign authority*' and 'representatives of the state *acting in that capacity*' (emphasis added) in United Nations Convention on Jurisdictional Immunities of States and their Property, Annexed to UNGA Res 59/38 (2 December 2004), http://untreaty. un.org/English/notpubl/English_3_13.pdf (not yet in force), Article 2(1)(b)(iii) and (iv).

[16] Fox, *State Immunity*, p. 367.

[17] J. Crawford, 'International law and foreign sovereigns: distinguishing immune transactions' (1983) 54 BYIL 75 at 89; see also critical theoretical approaches summarised in Fox, *State Immunity*, pp. 42–5.

[18] Crawford, 'International law', pp. 89–91.

[19] Ian Brownlie, *Principles of Public International Law*, 3rd edn (Oxford: Clarendon, 1979), pp. 330–1.

[20] Crawford, 'International law and foreign sovereigns', p. 91.

exceptions, has found favour in the structure of numerous relevant conventions and statute law.[21] While descriptively accurate at the level of international law, it is municipal courts which must make decisions on immunity in concrete cases, and it is at this level that the immunity *ratione materiae* approach with its focus on identifying distinctively sovereign acts prevails.

How is the law of state immunity applied in criminal cases concerning a sending state's law-enforcement or military organs? This is a surprisingly difficult question. The relevant treaties and statutes on the general law of immunity normally do not apply in cases of local criminal jurisdiction or to foreign military organs, leaving these issues to be regulated by general international law. We also derive limited assistance from agreements on the status of visiting military forces. While such agreements have proliferated following the Second World War, the consensus is that they do not represent customary law. We are thus left in search of case law governing situations where the immunities of foreign law-enforcement officials or military personnel have not been expressly determined in advance and the issue has had to be resolved under general international law.

As discussed below, the most useful case law is that furnished by the Mixed Courts of Egypt, which had to resolve questions of the immunity from local criminal jurisdiction (or the lack of it) enjoyed by the soldiers and sailors of visiting military forces in Egypt in the 1940s. Superficially, this presents a difficulty in that such cases were determined when *absolute* immunity was the generally accepted rule. Nonetheless, we can detect in these cases a clear movement towards a doctrine of restrictive state immunity. The Mixed Courts only accorded foreign servicemen immunity when they were acting *as part of* a foreign military force. This was resolved by a twofold question: was the individual in question on duty at the relevant time and, if so, were his acts within the scope of his duties?[22] Taken as a whole, this test might be thought of as being a test of whether an individual benefited from an

---

[21] European Convention on State Immunity 1972, (1972) 11 ILM 470; United Nations Convention on Jurisdictional Immunities of States and their Property, n. 15, above; State Immunity Act (United Kingdom) 1978, 1978 Chapter 33, (1978) 17 ILM 1123; Foreign Sovereign Immunities Act 1976 (US), 28 USCA §1602, (1976) 15 ILM 1388, and see Congressional Committee Report (1976) 15 ILM 1398, 1407; Foreign States Immunities Act 1985 (Australia) (No. 196 of 1985), (1986) 25 ILM 715; State Immunity Act 1982 (Canada), 1980–83, c. 95; (1982) 21 ILM 798.

[22] The male pronoun is used as these cases never concerned female service personnel.

immunity *ratione personae* due to their status. However, the focus upon whether an individual's actions fell within the proper scope of their duty is clearly compatible with the modern focus upon the act rather than the actor. Nonetheless, before turning to the law governing foreign military forces, the more obviously apt analogy for the purposes of maritime interdiction is the status of foreign police officers operating within local jurisdiction.

4.2 The immunity from local criminal jurisdiction of visiting police organs: an unanswered question?

Law-enforcement activity is an obvious exercise of sovereign author-ity.[23] It is hard to imagine how the exercise of police authority, especially when exercised in the course of foreign affairs in boarding foreign-flag vessels (or, indeed, firing into them),[24] could be anything but a sovereign act. The same considerations apply to fisheries inspectors, who, although performing activities mandated by international law, generally remain within their nominating state's employ and com-mand.[25] Any applicable immunity regarding such sovereign functions would be rendered illusory if 'officers … could be sued as individuals for matters of state conduct regarding which the state they were serv-ing had immunity'.[26] As a consequence, 'it is generally recognized that a suit against an individual acting in his official capacity is the prac-tical equivalent of a suit against the sovereign directly' and individual

---

[23] Fox, *State Immunity*, p. 374; *Claim against the Empire of Iran Case* (Germany, Constitutional Court, 1963) 45 ILR 57 at 81; *Church of Scientology Case* (Germany, Federal Supreme Court, 1978) 65 ILR 193 at 197–8; *Propend Finance v. Sing* (England, Court of Appeal, 1997) 111 ILR 611 at 669; *McElhinney v. Williams* (Ireland, Supreme Court, 1995) 104 ILR 691, 699–700. See also ILC Commentary in [2001] II(2) YBILC, 42 at (11). Nor is sovereign immunity lost through a state's abuse of police powers: *Saudi Arabia v. Nelson* (United States Supreme Court, 1993) 100 ILR 545 at 553–4; *Bouzari v. Iran* (Canada, Ontario Superior Court of Justice, 2002) 124 ILR 428 at 434 ff.

[24] See *Perez v. The Bahamas* (US District Court of Columbia, 1980) 63 ILR 350, upheld on appeal 63 ILR 601. The facts occurred within the Bahamian territorial sea, and so strictly raise issues less of immunity *ratione materiae* than non-justiciability under the act of state doctrine.

[25] See NAFO Scheme 2008, Article 32(2); NEAFC Scheme 2006, Article 15(2) (omitted from later NEAFC schemes); CCAMLR Scheme, Article I(c); ICCAT Scheme 1975, Article 7.

[26] *Propend Finance v. Sing*, 669; *Church of Scientology Case*, 198; cf. *Zoernsch v. Waldock*, [1964] 1 WLR 675 at 692 per Lord Diplock, quoted in Fox, *State Immunity*, p. 353; *Hénon v. Egyptian Government and British Admiralty* (Egypt, Civil Tribunal of the Mixed Courts, 1947) 14 ILR 78 at 78–9.

officers will in principle be protected by immunity *ratione materiae* for their official acts.[27] Thus, policing officials operating within a foreign jurisdiction should be treated as state organs capable of benefiting from state immunity for their official acts.[28]

As noted above, if foreign police officers are not treated as authorised law-enforcement officials by local law, their actions may be regarded as crimes by local courts.[29] Restrictive state immunity could play an important role in such cases. It has been observed, however, that 'there do not appear to be cases where a [visiting] state official has ... resist[ed] criminal jurisdiction by the invocation of state immunity *per se*'.[30] If one excludes the case law dealing with visiting armed forces abroad and cases dealing with the immunity of serving heads of state and high officials, this may be strictly true.[31] Equally, however, there do not appear to have been *any* cases in which foreign law-enforcement officials were prosecuted under local criminal law for their official conduct. Many cases upholding state immunity have involved citizens bringing *civil* actions alleging that foreign officials have engaged in illegal entry, search and seizure operations;[32] illegal confiscation of property;[33]

---

[27] *Chiudian v. Philippine National Bank* (US Court of Appeals, Ninth Circuit, 1990) 92 ILR 486–8; cf. *Church of Scientology in the Netherlands Foundation v. Herold and Heinrich Bauer Verlag* (District Court of Amsterdam, 1980) 65 ILR 380; *Kline v. Kaneo* (US District Court, New York, 1988) 101 ILR 497; *Schmidt v. Home Secretary* (Ireland, High Court, 1994) 103 ILR 322; *Jones v. Saudi Arabia* [2006] 2 WLR 1424 at 1430; see also the cases discussed in M. Tomonori, 'The individual as beneficiary of state immunity: problems of the attribution of *ultra vires* conduct' (2001) 29 DJILP 261 at 269–73.

[28] Fox, *State Immunity*, p. 354; *Carrato v. US* (Ontario High Court, 1982) 90 ILR 229; *Tritt v. US* (Ontario High Court, 1989) 94 ILR 260; *Jaffe v. Miller* (Ontario Court of Appeal, 1993) 95 ILR 446; *Propend Finance v. Sing*, 669–72; *US v. Guitno* (Philippines, Supreme Court, 1990) 102 ILR 132 at 142–4 (immunity of foreign military police upheld in tort claim).

[29] Chapter 10, section 3.3.2, at n. 80. Some treaties give other parties' police the same status before local courts as national police officers: Convention Applying the Schengen Agreement 1990, Article 42; Convention on Mutual Assistance in Criminal Matters between the Member States of the European Union 2000, Article 15. This may represent a lower standard of immunity than at general international law.

[30] Chanaka Wickremasinghe, 'Immunity of officials and international organisations' in M. Evans (ed.), *International Law*, 2nd edn (Oxford University Press, 2006), p. 395 at p. 410.

[31] See *Arrest Warrant Case*, 21–2; *Re Mofaz* (Bow Street Magistrates' Court, UK, 2004) 128 ILR 709; *Re Bo Xilai* (Bow Street Magistrates' Court, UK, 2004) 128 ILR 713; cf. *R v. Bow Street Stipendiary Magistrate. Ex Parte Pinochet (No. 3)* [2000] 1 AC 147 at 201–3, per Lord Browne-Wilkinson, 249–50, per Lord Hutton, 265, per Lord Saville, 268–9, per Lord Millet, 285, per Lord Phillips.

[32] *Tritt v. US*.

[33] *Carrato v. US*.

breaches of a court order;[34] or unlawful detention.[35] Such alleged acts – if lacking local statutory authority – would also amount to *criminal* offences such as burglary, theft, contempt of court and kidnapping. It is difficult to see logically why a court would find immunity to exist or not depending on the identity of the party bringing the action (a private litigant or a state prosecutor) when the acts alleged constitute both civil and criminal wrongs. However, absent clear statements of *opinio juris*, it is difficult to conclude that states' general failure to prosecute such conduct evidences a rule going beyond civil immunity and extending to the prohibition of criminal prosecutions.[36] Other examples must be sought in support of an applicable rule. One must thus return to the case of visiting military forces.

4.3 The jurisdictional immunities of visiting armed forces

4.3.1 Introduction

The extent of any immunity from local jurisdiction enjoyed by visiting forces under general international law is often thought uncertain, principally due to a failure to distinguish the separate contexts in which immunity arises. The category of state practice to examine in determining the question of any boarding state immunity must, therefore, be selected with care. Three relevant contexts may be suggested:

- immunity from local criminal enforcement and adjudicative jurisdiction in matters of discipline and internal administration ('supervisory jurisdiction');
- immunity from local criminal jurisdiction when mingling with the general population, a branch of law now largely governed by SOFAs; and
- immunity from local criminal jurisdiction 'within lines' when foreign forces are admitted to a defined area such as a base or zone of operations.

The argument presented here will be that the third category of state practice is the most relevant to the present study.

The still-definitive survey of the immunities of foreign armed forces at general international law is found in three articles written by Barton between 1949 and 1954, in which he generally denied that visiting forces could enjoy any immunity not granted to them by

---

[34] *Propend Finance v. Sing.*   [35] *Jaffe v. Miller.*
[36] *Lotus Case*, 28; *North Sea Continental Shelf Cases*, [1969] ICJ Rep. 3 at 44; cf. Brownlie, pp. 8–9.

local law.[37] One of Barton's principal concerns was to demolish the ill-founded contention that visiting forces, even in times of peace, were entitled to complete immunity from local criminal jurisdiction.[38] Foreign forces might well enjoy complete immunity from local jurisdiction during an occupation,[39] but attempts to extend the rule to other situations usually rest on a misreading of Marshall CJ's dictum in *Schooner Exchange*:[40]

The grant of a free passage … implies a waiver of all jurisdiction over the [foreign] troops during their passage, and permits the foreign general to use that discipline, and to inflict those punishments which the government of his army may require.[41]

This dictum deals only with the temporary passage of an organised body of foreign troops through another state's territory with the territorial sovereign's consent.[42] It may be thought of as applying the rule regarding warships to an analogous 'sealed unit' in passage (on the presumption that a disciplined force in transit will have limited interaction with the local population).[43] That is,

The immunity of the foreign vessel of war is frequently said to apply in respect of members of the crew while on shore and 'on duty'. This has undoubtedly furnished the concept applied … to an army. Based on the theory of exterritoriality [now generally rejected], the latter is a 'body' and immunity beyond its 'lines' is confined to members on duty. In the case of [foreign] troops [stationed] in [a receiving state], however, there is no defined area: they are here generally and available wherever they may be required.[44]

---

[37] G. Barton, 'Foreign armed forces: immunity from supervisory jurisdiction' (1949) 26 BYIL 380; 'Foreign armed forces: immunity from criminal jurisdiction' (1950) 27 BYIL 186; 'Foreign armed forces: qualified jurisdictional immunity' (1954) 31 BYIL 341.

[38] Barton, 'Foreign armed forces: immunity from criminal jurisdiction', 192–3, 207, 210.

[39] See *Leban v. Alexandria Water Co.* (Egyptian Mixed Court of Appeal, 1929), 5 ILR 485; *Manuel v. Ministère Public* (Egyptian Mixed Court of Cassation, 1943) 12 ILR 154 at 157–60; *French Occupation Forces Case* (Austria, Court of Appeal of Vienna, 1949) 16 ILR 144; *Belgian State v. Botte* (Belgium, Court of Cassation, 1953) 21 ILR 634; contra, result in *In re Besednjak* (Court of Assize, Trieste, 1948) 15 ILR 106.

[40] R. Baxter, 'Criminal jurisdiction in the NATO Status of Forces Agreement' (1958) 7 ICLQ 72 at 72.

[41] *Schooner Exchange*, 140.   [42] Brownlie, 6th edn, p. 362.   [43] *Ibid.*, pp. 362–3.

[44] *Reference re Exemption of US Forces from Canadian Criminal Law* [1943] 4 DLR 11 at 47 per Rand J.

The limited context in which the original rule arose has not prevented some writers contending that *Schooner Exchange* supported a rule of absolute immunity in all cases.[45]

The rule propounded by Marshall CJ was subtler, however, resting on an express or implied licence.[46]

One sovereign being in no respect amenable to ... the jurisdiction of another, can be supposed to enter a foreign territory only under an express license, or in the confidence that the immunities belonging to his independent sovereign station, though not expressly stipulated, are reserved by implication, and will be extended to him.[47]

What Marshall CJ 'had in mind' was to prohibit the 'exercise of jurisdiction which would prevent the troops from acting as a force ... not exercise of jurisdiction over individual soldiers in respect of liabilities incurred or wrongs done perhaps out of all connection with their military duties'.[48]

The receiving state's waiver of jurisdiction must be taken to extend, *at the minimum*, to laws relating to immigration and carrying arms and to allowing the foreign force's service courts to enforce military discipline including by means (for example, imprisonment) which would otherwise breach local law.[49] This may be referred to as immunity from *supervisory* jurisdiction, a generally admitted principle of customary law that is not directly relevant to present discussion.[50] More importantly, *Schooner Exchange* stands for the broader proposition that, absent express agreement to the contrary, 'the bare fact of admission' of visiting forces to a receiving state's territory 'produces certain generally recognised consequences of international law', including an *implicit* concession of those immunities from local jurisdiction necessary to maintain an effective force.[51] That is, quite apart from the general law of state immunity, there is a specific rule applying in cases where a

---

[45] A. King, 'Jurisdiction over friendly foreign armed forces' (1942) 36 AJIL 539 at 540–2 and 559 ff. and 'Further developments concerning jurisdiction over friendly foreign armed forces' (1946) 40 AJIL 257; criticised in J. Brinton, 'The Egyptian Mixed Courts and foreign armed forces' (1946) 40 AJIL 737 and Barton, 'Foreign armed forces: immunity from criminal jurisdiction', 216–18.

[46] Fox, *State Immunity*, p. 365; Crawford, 'International law and foreign sovereigns', 87.

[47] *Schooner Exchange*, 137.

[48] *Wright v. Cantrell*, 136, per Jordan CJ.   [49] *Ibid.*, 140.

[50] See Barton, 'Foreign armed forces: immunity from supervisory jurisdiction'; cf. *Schooner Exchange*, 140, and *Chow Hung Ching v. The King* (High Court of Australia, 1948) 15 ILR 147 at 168 and 171, per Dixon J.

[51] Shearer, *Starke's International Law*, p. 207, and cf. p. 192.

foreign military force is invited to enter the territory of a receiving state. The difficulties of applying this general principle in particular cases are best illustrated by first considering the legal position of members of a foreign force when mingling with the general population and then turning to their position when 'within lines' or a defined area of operations.

4.3.2 Immunity from local criminal law when among the general population: the general law

The broad issue of the immunity from criminal jurisdiction (if any) of a serviceperson when ashore from a warship or when outside a zone of operations or the lines of a military base is a rich and fascinating one. While of limited relevance for present purposes, it nonetheless requires brief discussion to illustrate applicable principles of characterisation. It is an area dominated since 1951 by the rise of SOFAs, discussed further below. Pre-existing case law is limited, and often confused. One frequently cited authority is the 1943 *Exemption of US Forces* case in which the Supreme Court of Canada was asked to consider whether US military personnel consensually present in Canada were 'exempt from [Canadian] criminal proceedings … and, if so, to what extent'.[52] The controversy arose from the tension between the sending state's interest in having its personnel available reliably and on short notice for duty on the one hand and the receiving state's interest in maintaining order and safety when visiting forces were mingling or interacting with the general population on the other. The former considerations led the United States to advocate a doctrine of absolute immunity for foreign service personnel in all cases, even when off duty, throughout the Second World War[53] and as late as the negotiation of the 1951 NATO SOFA.[54] In *Exemption of US Forces* three approaches were taken. Two judges considered that visiting forces were in principle subject to the substantive local criminal law, but found that Canadian courts in practice would decline to exercise jurisdiction over events occurring 'within … lines … in cases in which the act or offence does not affect the person or property of a Canadian subject'.[55] Two judges favoured complete immunity for the visiting forces based on a literal reading

---

[52] [1943] 4 DLR 11.
[53] S. Lepper, '*Short v. The Kingdom of the Netherlands*: is it time to renegotiate the NATO Status of Force Agreement?', (1991) 24 VJTL 867, at 883 and 911–12.
[54] Conference Doc. MS-R(51) 4, *NATO Travaux Préparatoires*, p. 64.
[55] *Exemption of US Forces*, 24–25, per Duff CJ and Hudson J.

of *Schooner Exchange*.[56] One proposed a division of jurisdiction between the service courts of the visiting force and local courts, granting jurisdiction over offences against persons not from the visiting force to the latter.[57] While the case is sometimes taken as authoritative evidence of the lack of settled law on the point, the various opinions converge to a surprising extent. All agree that under certain circumstances, local courts will decline to exercise jurisdiction over a visiting force. Two judges found in favour of immunity in all cases based solely on the identity of the defendant (immunity *ratione personae*). Two judges favoured immunity *ratione personae*, but restricted its application to cases 'within lines' and not involving Canadian subjects. The final view similarly held that immunity *ratione personae* was restricted, but abandoned the geographical 'within lines' criterion in favour of focusing upon the nationality of the victim. The entire court could agree that they were starting from a proposition of immunity *ratione personae* – the question was its limits. All five judgments focus on the identity of the *parties* involved, not the legal *character* of their acts. The case is thus unlikely to assist modern courts used to approaching these issues by characterising the acts involved.

A more coherent view based on distinctions *ratione materiae* was taken in the same year by the New South Wales Supreme Court in *Wright v. Cantrell*. Chief Justice Jordan held that

A State which admits to its territory an armed force of a foreign friendly Power impliedly undertakes not to exercise any jurisdiction over the force collectively or its members individually which would be inconsistent with its continuing to exist as an efficient force available for the service of its sovereign.[58]

This did not extend to immunity in respect of civil 'liabilities incurred or wrongs done ... out of all connection with ... military duties'.[59]

Outside these limited cases, by far the best and most frequent attention given to the issue was by the Mixed Courts of Egypt.[60] The Mixed Courts were a remarkable institution having jurisdiction between 1876 and 1949 over Egyptian cases involving foreigners, and

---

[56] *Ibid.*, 33, per Kerwin J, and 39 per Taschereau J.
[57] *Ibid.*, 51 per Rand J.   [58] *Wright v. Cantrell*, 140.
[59] *Ibid.*, 136. Criminal jurisdiction over visiting US forces was covered by national regulations.
[60] J. Brinton, 'Jurisdiction over members of allied forces in Egypt' (1944) 38 AJIL 375; Barton, 'Foreign armed forces: qualified jurisdictional immunity', 351.

were staffed in large part by foreign judges.[61] British troops remained in Egypt long after the end of formal British occupation and it was not until 1936 that their status under domestic Egyptian law was regulated by treaty.[62] Further, during the Second World War considerable numbers of foreign troops were stationed in Egyptian territory with Egypt's consent but without formal arrangements being concluded with the sending states. Inevitably, some members of these visiting forces breached local criminal law and the cases fell to be determined in accordance with general international law.[63] The Mixed Courts applied a rule of immunity for acts committed while on a 'mission under orders' or '*service commandé*'. Barton tends to dismiss the Mixed Courts' jurisprudence on the basis that it applied a merely temporal test, looking only to whether at the time a force member was 'on duty' and not whether the acts complained of fell within the scope of the serviceman's duty.[64] This was certainly the rule applied in *Ministère Public v. Triandafilou*.[65] However, subsequent cases qualified or distinguished *Triandafilou*. The test that emerged was that a serviceperson's act had to be 'dictated by military requirements' to be immune.[66] Any strict temporal test was decisively rejected in *Cambouras v. Ministère Public*.[67] In *Cambouras* a Greek sentry, technically on duty for a continuous 24-hour period, left his post at 11 am

[61] On their history see Brinton, 'Jurisdiction over members of allied forces', 'Egyptian Mixed Courts and foreign armed forces', and *The Mixed Courts of Egypt*, rev. edn (New Haven: Yale University Press, 1986); S. Messina, 'Les Tribunaux Mixtes et les rapports interjurisdictionnels en Égypte' (1932-III) 41 *Recueil des Cours* 367; and M. Hoyle, 'The Mixed Courts of Egypt 1938–1949' (1988) 3 *Arab Law Quarterly* 83. Hoyle wrote nine other articles on the Mixed Courts (see vols. 1–3 of the *Arab Law Quarterly*). See also *Salem Case (US v. Egypt)* (1932) 6 ILR 188 at 193–5.

[62] See Convention Concerning the Immunities and Privileges to be Enjoyed by the British Forces in Egypt, 26 August 1936, UKTS (1937), No. 6, Cmnd 5360, p. 23.

[63] See Hoyle, 'Mixed Courts of Egypt 1938–1949', 94–95, 99 ff.; Brinton, 'Jurisdiction over members of allied forces in Egypt'.

[64] Barton, 'Foreign armed forces: qualified jurisdictional immunity', 351–8.

[65] (Egypt, Tribunal of Alexandria (Chambre du Conseil), 1942), 11 ILR 169.

[66] *Ministère Public v. Tsoukharis* (Egyptian Mixed Court of Cassation, 1943) 12 ILR 150 at 151–2. See also the emphasis placed on whether a soldier was acting as an 'integral part of the force' or within 'the limits of ... effective command' at the relevant time in *Manuel v. Ministère Public* (1943) 12 ILR 154 at 161. These tests were, ultimately, very similar to the reasoning applied at first instance in *Ministère Public v. Triandafilou*: (1942) 11 ILR 165 at 166–7.

[67] For an account see Barton, 'Foreign armed forces: qualified jurisdictional immunity', 354–5 quoting *Journal des Tribunaux Mixtes*, 26–27 January 1944, No. 3259, 2–4.

to spend four hours drinking. On his return, he became involved in a brawl. The court was not concerned that at the relevant time he was theoretically continuously 'on duty', and affirmed that service personnel could not abuse the doctrine of mission under orders. In substance, immunity was denied because the accused was engaged on a spree of his own and not official conduct dictated by military requirements. Much the same principle has been upheld in Japan. *Japan v. Smith and Stinner*[68] concerned two British sailors ashore who had assaulted and robbed a taxi driver. The Japanese constitution incorporated international law within Japan's supreme law and the court had no difficulty in holding that

it is a principle agreed that if a sailor belonging to a foreign warship goes ashore on official business and, while on that business, commits a crime, his home state has [exclusive] jurisdiction over him.[69]

However, that immunity did not obtain here as the sailors were 'ashore for their own purposes'.[70]

4.3.3 Immunity from local criminal law when among the general population: Status of Forces Agreements

The widespread adoption of SOFAs introduced considerably greater consistency to this field. In particular, Article 7 of the NATO SOFA 1951 has formed the general model for many subsequent agreements on the allocation of jurisdiction over visiting forces.[71] Modern SOFAs represented a considerable innovation, and it is evident that the NATO SOFA's drafters did not believe themselves to be codifying pre-existing customary international law. Rather, they saw themselves as shaping a new compromise to govern a new situation: the semi-permanent stationing of state forces in a foreign jurisdiction during times of peace.[72] While it is

---

[68] (District Court of Kobe, Japan, 1952), 19 ILR 221.   [69] *Ibid.*, 122.   [70] *Ibid.*

[71] *Oppenheim*, 9th edn, pp. 1162–4; and see Agreement regarding the treatment of United States armed forces visiting the Philippines (entered force 1 June 1999), KAV 5493, Article 5(3)(b)(2); Protocol to Amend Article XVII of the Administrative Agreement under Article III of the Security Treaty between the USA and Japan 1953, 4 UST 1847; Agreement under Article IV of the Mutual Defense Treaty regarding facilities and areas and the status of United States Armed Forces in the Republic of Korea, 1966 (entered into force 9 February 1967), 674 UNTS 163, Article 22(3)(a)(ii).

[72] K. Priest-Hamilton, 'Who really should have exercised jurisdiction over the military pilots implicated in the 1998 Italy gondola accident?' (1999–2000) 65 JALC 605 at 617–19; cf. Baxter, 'Criminal jurisdiction in the NATO Status of Forces Agreement', 73–4.

doubtful whether Article 7 now represents customary law, its application in practice illustrates relevant issues.

The customary international law prior to, and the state practice during, the Second World War had all concerned the *temporary* presence of visiting forces within a receiving state not itself under occupation during a war of limited duration. Collective self-defence agreements during the Cold War contemplated something novel: the *indefinite*, if not permanent, stationing of allied forces within receiving states. While states had been prepared to concede absolute immunity to US and sometimes UK troops as the price of their participation in particularconflicts, such treatment was less acceptable in peacetime.[73] It was widely thought that in peacetime the underlying jurisdiction of the territorial sovereign should prevail in all cases other than the immunity from supervisory jurisdiction discussed above. This approach was codified in Article 7 of the treaty on the status of Members of the Armed Forces of the Brussels Treaty Powers.[74] Tellingly, this treaty never entered into force, its territorial supremacy approach failing principally due to opposition from the largest 'exporter' of visiting forces, the United States.[75]

Article 7 of the NATO SOFA instead provides that the sending state shall have 'criminal and disciplinary' jurisdiction over those *persons* subject to its military law present within the sending state, and provides that the receiving state will have jurisdiction over *offences* against its law committed by the force inside its territory.[76] Generally this will result in concurrent jurisdiction, as most cases will involve a person subject to foreign military law committing an offence against local law. Only in cases of purely military offences or acts which are criminalin only one of the two states will an offender be subject to either party's exclusive jurisdiction.[77] However, the range of offences which may be subject to concurrent jurisdiction is expanded by Article 134

[73] Baxter, 'Criminal jurisdiction in the NATO Status of Forces Agreement', 74; Barton, 'Foreign armed forces: immunity from criminal jurisdiction', 199–204; D. Wijewardane, 'Criminal jurisdiction over visiting forces with special reference to international forces' (1965–6) 41 BYIL 122 at 125–8.

[74] Cmd. 7868, reproduced in *NATO Travaux Préparatoires*, p. 331 (never entered into force).

[75] R. Stanger, *Criminal Jurisdiction over Visiting Armed Forces*, International Law Studies, 1957–8 (Newport: Naval War College, 1965), pp. 224–5 and nn. 26–28.

[76] NATO SOFA, Article 7(1).

[77] *Ibid.*, Article 7(2); see Serge Lazareff, *Status of Military Forces under Current International Law* (Leyden: Sijthoff, 1971), pp. 151 ff.

of the US Uniform Code of Military Justice, under which a violation of local law might also give rise to the sending-state offence of bringing the military into disrepute.[78] The SOFA's creation of concurrent jurisdiction was not without controversy[79] and was clearly a compromise balancing the interests of receiving and sending states.[80]

In cases of concurrent jurisdiction, Article 7(3)(a) provides that

> The military authorities of the sending State shall have the primary right to exercise jurisdiction over a member of a [visiting] force ... in relation to ... offences arising out of any act or omission done in the performance of official duty.

What scope is to be given to the terms 'primary right' and 'performance of official duty'? The first point to consider is whether this 'primary right' creates something similar to the regimes of preferential jurisdiction discussed elsewhere in this book.[81] That is, will a primary *right* to exercise jurisdiction always bar the exercise of local jurisdiction unless it is waived? The SOFA text may be open to interpretation on this point. Article 7(3)(c) reads,

> If the State having the primary right decides not to exercise jurisdiction, it shall notify the authorities of the other State as soon as practicable. The ... State having the primary right shall give sympathetic consideration to a request from the ... other State for a waiver of its right ...

One strained view of this provision is that primary jurisdiction is waived either *implicitly* by deciding not to exercise jurisdiction or *expressly* in response to a request. This construction effectively creates an 'extradite or prosecute' obligation and follows from the view that the NAFO SOFA was designed to 'assure that wrongdoers were brought to trial'.[82]

---

[78] J. Rouse, 'The exercise of criminal jurisdiction under the NATO Status of Forces Agreement' (1957) 51 AJIL 29 at 38–9; E. Schuck, 'Concurrent jurisdiction under the NATO Status of Forces Agreement' (1957) 57 *Columbia Law Review* 355 at 356; Lepper, 'Short v. The Kingdom of the Netherlands', 892.

[79] Stanger, *Criminal Jurisdiction over Visiting Armed Forces*, pp. 224–5 and nn. 26–28.

[80] Conference Doc. MS-R(51) 4, *NATO Travaux Préparatoires*, p. 66.

[81] Chapter 5, sections 4 and 5; Chapter 8, section 2.3.

[82] Lazareff, *Status of Military Forces*, p. 206; cf. the reasoning of Rand J in *Reference re Exemption of US Forces*, 49–50.

Alternatively, and more naturally, the paragraph may require that primary jurisdiction always be waived expressly; the notification provision may thus exist only to allow the state of concurrent jurisdiction to request such a waiver more effectively. This view gives clearer effect to the textual distinction between the existence of the 'primary right' of jurisdiction and its 'exercise'. A state does not have a diminished right to prosecute someone following an administrative decision not to prosecute them *now*. It retains the right to do so later. This interpretation also seems to better accord with treaty practice. French courts have rejected the proposition that local authorities may prosecute acts covered by Article 7 if the state having primary jurisdiction fails to do so.[83] Functionally, then, there is no difference between a 'primary right to exercise jurisdiction' and a general immunity from local jurisdiction.

The second matter to consider is the scope of acts or omissions arising from the 'performance of official duty' that attracts immunity. Obviously, where the acts in question fall outside these official acts, no immunity applies. This qualifies the otherwise expansive immunity of the primary jurisdiction regime, creating on its face a system of immunity *ratione materiae* where the most important question would appear to be the character of the act, not the identity of the actor. How is this test applied in practice? There are surprisingly few cases on the point. The SOFA practice has generally been that where a member of a visiting force is charged with a local offence his or her sending state will submit a certificate evidencing its view as to whether the offence arose from conduct in the course of duty. Many states, including France, Germany, Turkey and Hungary, accept the sending state's certificate as conclusive.[84] Italian authorities have also tended to defer to the sending state's characterisation of the facts.[85] In the light of the general practice of giving effect to the sending state's determination, there are few reported cases available from which one might establish a legal test as applied by local courts. Despite the fact that the United Kingdom has expressly reserved the right for its courts to determine as 'a jurisdictional fact' whether an act giving rise to an offence was committed in the course of duty, no reported cases have been decided on this basis.[86]

---

[83] *Re Gadois Deceased* (Court of Appeal of Paris, 1953) 20 ILR 186.

[84] P. Conderman, 'Jurisdiction' in Dieter Fleck (ed.), *The Handbook of Humanitarian Law in Armed Conflicts* (Oxford University Press, 1995), p. 99 at pp. 111–12.

[85] Priest-Hamilton, 'Who really should have exercised jurisdiction?', 627.

[86] Lazareff, *Status of Military Forces*, pp. 179–80; Visiting Forces Act (UK), 1952 (c. 67), s. 11(4).

The Japanese- and South Korean-agreed understandings as to the operation of SOFAs may offer a standard. Both provide that 'a substantial departure from the acts a person is required to do in a particular duty usually will indicate an act outside of his "official duty"'.[87] However, as between South Korea and the United States, a certificate from the commanding officer is *conclusive* as to duty status unless the two governments agree otherwise, thus removing the question from the realm of judicial determination.[88] Under the Japanese SOFA a commanding officer's certificate stating that acts were committed in performance of official duty will 'be sufficient evidence of the fact unless the contrary is proved' in judicial proceedings.[89] Despite this, the point does not appear to have been decided directly. The indirect consideration of the issue in *Japan v. Girard* is discussed below. Importantly, though, the 'substantial departure' principle confirms that not all acts committed during periods of duty are necessarily immune.[90]

4.3.4 The immunity of visiting forces 'within lines': barracks, bases and areas of operation

The key cases on the degree of immunity enjoyed by consensually present visiting forces when within reserved military areas may not initially appear consistent. However, principles may be extracted which are consistent with Marshall CJ's theory of an implied licence accompanying an invitation to a foreign-state organ to enter a receiving state's territory. Indeed, it may be that the terms of such a licence are easier to infer when the admission is to a specified area and members of the force are not mingling with the general population.

The most important case is *In re Gilbert*. The case concerned the fatal shooting by the perimeter guard of a US military base of a Brazilian civilian who, despite the guard's efforts, had persistently attempted to enter the camp to reclaim a debt from another soldier stationed there.[91] The US forces were present with Brazil's consent, but the issue of immunity was not regulated by treaty. The Court said,

---

[87] Facilities and areas and the status of United States Armed Forces in Korea agreement, 9 July 1966, 17 UST 1677 and 1816 (Agreed Minute re Article XXII) (US–Korea SOFA and US–Korea Agreed Minute); Protocol to Amend Article XVII of the Administrative Agreement under Article III of the Security Treaty between the USA and Japan, 29 September 1953, 4 UST 1847 and 1851 (Agreed Minute re Paragraph 3) (US–Japan SOFA and US–Japan Agreed Minute).
[88] US–Korea Agreed Minute.   [89] US–Japan Agreed Minute.
[90] *Wilson v. Girard* (1956) 354 US 524 at 542.
[91] (Brazil, Supreme Federal Court, 1944) 13 ILR 86.

In general the jurisdiction of the national courts cannot be questioned in regard to crimes committed on national territory, whether the offenders be nationals or aliens. ... [Following an 1846 incident between US sailors and Brazilian policemen] the United States Government ... [recognized] the right of the Brazilian authorities to try and punish crimes ... committed within this territory by sailors, citizens or subjects of any State whatever. But in those cases the offences were common offences committed by members of foreign armed forces who were present on Brazilian soil but not on duty at the time ... [In this case] the said marine committed the offence *in the exercise of his specific duty* as a sentry at the camp.[92]

The court rejected the notion that the camp was somehow extra-territorial space and spoke of 'immunity from jurisdiction' as the governing theory.[93] That immunity was accorded in this case not because the accused had been (temporally) on duty but because the impugned act had been 'in the exercise of his specific duty'. The connection between his act and his duty was not severed by his excessive use of force. One could readily suggest that shooting a civilian was not 'dictated by military necessity' or involved a 'substantial departure' from what was necessary to carry out his orders. However, a perimeter guard's very function is to use force, if necessary, to secure the perimeter of a camp. He was thus an organ of state (as he was on duty at the time), which was present with the territorial sovereign's consent (so an immunity must be implied) and was carrying out a duty under orders (an immune act).

Whether limits could or should be placed on the broad scope of offences committed in the course of official duty proved a difficult issue in the course of NATO SOFA negotiations.[94] Suggested words of limitation included that orders should be carried out 'within the limits of duty' or 'according to the tenor thereof'.[95] The fact that such amendments were not included in the final text tends to suggest that a broad view of the scope of official duty was intended. Generally, one can suggest that carrying out an authorised act in an unauthorised manner (as opposed to acts unconnected with authorised duty or solely for personal motives) will not deprive a serviceperson of 'on duty' immunity. One example of this principle might be the 1998 incident in which a US jet on manoeuvres in Italy flew off-course and 3,300 feet below altitude restrictions, resulting in it severing a ski gondola cable and killing twenty people. An Italian prosecutor sought to indict the pilots. The United States

[92] *Ibid.*, 87–88 (emphasis added).   [93] *Ibid.*, 88.
[94] *NATO Travaux Préparatoires*, pp. 172–3 and pp. 454 ff.   [95] *Ibid.*

argued that the 'jet was flying under the auspices of the alliance when the incident occurred' and therefore it had primary jurisdiction over any negligent homicide.[96] The Italian prosecutor argued that deviation from 'mandated flight patterns' meant that the aircraft was no longer acting within its mission, and therefore Italy had primary jurisdiction. An Italian judge properly found that local courts lacked jurisdiction.[97] A mistake in the performance of orders, resulting in them being carried out in an unauthorised manner, cannot render them unconnected with official duty. A wrong has been committed, but by the sending state and not the pilots as individuals. A similar approach has been taken in other Italian cases concerning accidents involving foreign military aircraft.[98]

A case sometimes quoted for the proposition that there is not necessarily any immunity 'within lines' is *R v. Navratil*.[99] The defendant was a Czechoslovakian soldier stationed in England who unsuccessfully attempted suicide by shooting himself inside Czechoslovakian barracks. The bullet passed through him, and the wall of his hut, and a fragment killed a Czechoslovakian subject sweeping outside. Navratil was charged with attempted suicide and manslaughter. The defence argued, quoting Oppenheim, that the court lacked jurisdiction because foreign barracks enjoyed extraterritorial immunity.[100] Justice Cassels held that Oppenheim's proposition was limited to excluding jurisdiction over disciplinary measures that might otherwise constitute local crimes.[101] However, the case is not relevant for present purposes as there is no suggestion that Navratil was on duty at the time and so acting as an organ of state. Even if he had been on duty, his acts would still not have been protected as his attempted suicide was not part of any 'mission under orders' or official function. Quite apart from this, the United Kingdom's consent to the presence of Czechoslovakian forces was governed by express treaty conditions placing 'the offence of manslaughter ... within the exclusive jurisdiction of the English courts'.[102]

---

[96] Priest-Hamilton, 'Who really should have exercised jurisdiction?', 607.

[97] *Ibid.*, 606.

[98] *FILT-CGIL Trento v. USA (Decision No 530/2000)* (Court of Cassation, Italy, 2000) 128 ILR 644 (training flights of visiting forces unquestionably acts *jure imperii*, even if posing risks to local civilian life and safety).

[99] (High Court of England, 1942) 11 ILR 161.

[100] L. Oppenheim, *International Law: A Treatise*, 5th edn, ed. H. Lauterpacht (London: Longman, 1937), I, pp. 662–3.

[101] 11 ILR 161, 164–5. Oppenheim's 'within lines' immunity was also discussed in the *Exemption of US Forces Case* as noted above.

[102] Wijewardane, 'Criminal jurisdiction over visiting forces', 136.

A more difficult case is *Japan v. Girard*. Girard, a US serviceman stationed in Japan, killed a local woman, Mrs Saki. Saki had been trespassing on an artillery range to scavenge scrap metal during the course of military exercises.[103] Girard was under orders to guard a machine gun (an object not directly threatened by scavenging). Despite not having authority to use his grenade launcher to fire objects other than grenades,[104] Girard used his to fire a spent cartridge at Saki, which struck and killed her. The applicable SOFA was discussed above, and granted the US primary jurisdiction over acts arising out of official duties, on an understanding that 'substantial departures' from what was required to fulfil such duties would ordinarily indicate that an act was not official.

Girard was on duty as a member of a visiting force at the time, and was not 'outside lines' on personal business or recreation. He was therefore an organ of state and his acts were prima facie immune, unless an exception applied. There are two possible characterisations of Girard's act. He was either performing an authorised act in an unauthorised manner, or he acted to abuse his function for personal gratification. Although surrendering Girard to Japan, the United States never abandoned its claim that these events arose 'out of the performance ... of official duty'. The United States characterised the act as an unlawful use of force, which offence 'arose out of an act (firing a weapon to repel a trespasser)' done 'in the performance of official duty (guarding the machine gun)'.[105] On this analysis the facts are analogous to those in *In re Gilbert*. The only two ways to overcome the conclusion that the same result should follow are either to split hairs (he acted to repel a trespasser but was only authorised to guard a machine gun) or demonstrate that further facts existed severing the connection between Girard's acts and his duty.

The local court took both routes. Strictly, Girard's immunity was not in question as the United States had waived it by surrendering him. The court nonetheless indicated that it considered that no such immunity would have applied. The court held that Girard's use of his grenade launcher to fire blank cartridges was forbidden by US military regulations, and could therefore not be part of his official duty. The

---

[103] On the history and facts, see Lazareff, *Status of Military Forces*, p. 173; and the affidavit as to facts in the related US Supreme Court case, reproduced at (1956) 354 US 524 at 530 ff. Girard was convicted but his sentence suspended.

[104] (1956) 354 US 524 at 545.

[105] W. Carroll, 'Official duty cases under Status of Forces Agreements: modest guidelines toward a definition' (1970) 12 *United States Air Force JAG Law Review* 284, 286.

argument is unconvincing. Minor violations of military regulations do not mean that an act has not arisen from the performance of duty, and accepting the argument would involve oppressively strict scrutiny of the actions of voluntarily admitted foreign forces.

The court, however, also accepted allegations that Girard had encouraged Saki to approach by indicating scrap metal nearer his position. Indeed, there was some suggestion in the evidence that Girard was in a habit of luring scavengers towards him, in order to chase them off. The court found that shooting at Saki was an action gratifying Girard's 'momentary caprice' and could 'only be regarded as excessive mischief, completely irrelevant to the performance of the duty of guarding light machine guns ... and as having no subjective or objective relationship [with that duty]'.[106]

Any finding that firing at metal scavengers could have no 'objective' relation with guarding a machine gun is probably wrong. Keeping civilian trespassers at bay is consonant with such a duty. However, if one accepts that Girard encouraged Mrs Saki to approach, in order to have an excuse to fire at her, such an act is clearly an abuse of duty which should not be protected by immunity. Even here, though, the court may have been wrong to focus on Girard's *subjective* purpose or gratification. If Girard was a sadist or violent racist it might have gratified him to shoot a civilian when it was militarily necessary or permissible (*In re Gilbert*). However, such an act would still be immune: it would have been done for an objective military purpose. Deliberately encouraging Mrs Saki to approach his position, however, was an act entirely outside the scope of his duties or the military necessities of the case.

5 Conclusion: distinguishing immune and non-immune police acts

Despite assertions in the literature that the criminal liability of individual officers is a difficult issue, there is no reason why it should not be susceptible to much the same rules of state immunity as apply in civil cases. Indeed, civil cases arising from obviously criminal acts have often been barred by state immunity.[107] It would be curious if the foreign state was *civilly* immune for acts in respect of which its individual agents were *criminally* liable. This would defeat the widely acknowledged

---

[106] 26 ILR 203 at 207.
[107] Cases cited in notes 32–35 above.

principle that immunity regarding sovereign functions would be rendered illusory if officers could be sued individually for matters regarding which their sending state would be immune.[108] Quite apart from considerations of the general law of immunity, there is a specific rule of general international law in cases where foreign forces are invited into a receiving state's territory implying – absent specific agreement on the point – such immunity as is necessary for the force to operate effectively and carry out its functions.[109] Such an implied immunity may well be easier to discern and uphold where the admission is to a limited area for a limited purpose, as occurs during an interdiction.

Either under the general law of state immunity or the specific rule regarding visiting forces, during a period of duty a serviceperson is, prima facie, an organ of state. Not all his or her acts, however, during that period are necessarily immune. A theory or test to distinguish immune and non-immune acts is required. Under SOFA law there is some indication that immunity extends to 'offences arising out of any act or omission done in the performance of official duty' but excludes acts involving a 'substantial departure' from 'the acts a person is required to do in a particular duty'. Under general international law the test may be that acts committed under orders, or 'service commandé', are immune, but acts not 'dictated by military requirements' will not be. Despite the more restrictive tone of the *service commandé* test, it is doubtful that there is a real difference of principle involved.[110] The Egyptian Mixed Court of Cassation said in *Tsoukharis* that 'mission under orders'

> means a mission *dictated by military requirements* ... The person giving the order is interested in the report of the person sent, whereas the latter is interested in prolonging the duration of the mission ... [A] soldier who abuses his mission to prolong his leave will cease to be covered by immunity from jurisdiction ... [T]he alleged mission should be defined with due regard to the facts.[111]

This seems consonant with the idea of a flexible test, looking for acts which constitute a substantial departure from the acts required by a particular duty. It has been suggested above that the correct test is whether the acts involved fulfilled a military purpose and that this should not be construed overly narrowly.

---

[108] *Propend Finance v. Sing*, 669.

[109] Shearer, *Starke's International Law*, p. 208. See the cases cited above at notes 1, 67 and 69.

[110] Wijewardane, 'Criminal jurisdiction over visiting forces', 141–3.

[111] 12 ILR 150 at 151–2 (emphasis added).

Analysis in such cases is not assisted by simple recourse to claims about a state agent's individual motives (i.e. the agent's *subjective* purpose) any more than claims about an act's supposed nature – that is, a general assertion that acts such as guarding machine guns and repelling trespassers are inherently military acts. While analysis may remain difficult, the approach required is what has been called in another context 'individuation', or 'identify[ing] with precision' the 'act or series of acts' that falls for classification.[112] This is an essential precursor to classification, which will have to proceed by reference to some notion of purpose.[113] The relevant purpose here is whether the act serves a military end for which the force was admitted to the jurisdiction. This is obviously an objective test of 'purpose' in the sense of function. The immunity of a visiting force in an interdiction context will be of this type: an immunity arising from an implied licence that a foreign force will be allowed to fulfil the purpose (in the sense of function, not subjective intention) for which it was admitted to the jurisdiction. The correct test focuses upon identifying the objective military purpose for which a force was admitted, and examining whether identified acts are reasonably capable of serving that end. In the context of law-enforcement interdictions, where a boarding party has temporarily been admitted to a defined space, this should be reasonably straightforward. A boarding party official should be held personally immune for any act referable to a law-enforcement function unless it involves a substantial departure from the acts necessary to fulfil that function. Generally, the use of excessive force when authorised to use force will not result in a loss of immunity to the civil and criminal processes of the local courts. This position might, of course, be altered by specific agreements concluded to the contrary.

Two final questions should briefly be addressed regarding, first, the applicable law where state agents enter a foreign sovereign's jurisdiction unbidden and, second, the relationship between immunity and state responsibility (if any). The situation where a state agent enters foreign territory uninvited is obviously not covered by the specific *Schooner Exchange* rule regarding the implied licence granted to visiting

---

[112] Crawford, 'International law and foreign sovereigns', 94; cf. Wijewardane, 'Criminal jurisdiction over visiting forces', 141–3.
[113] *Ibid.*, 95.

forces. One might suggest that a similar rule should follow simply from the principle *par in parem non imperium habet* and the application of general rules of state immunity.[114] After all, even an illegally conducted policing or military operation remains a sovereign function. The question has not fallen often for determination. In the McLeod incident it was conceded that a state agent who entered foreign territory uninvited to commit acts *jure imperii* and contrary to local law should have been held immune to local adjudicative and enforcement jurisdiction in respect of those acts.[115] In New York in 1840 McLeod had unwisely boasted he had been part of the British raiding party that entered US territory to destroy the *Caroline* during the 1837 Canadian rebellion. The United States never expressly conceded that the *Caroline*'s destruction was justified by the law of self-defence, possibly suggesting that immunity could extend to acts *jure imperii* that are wrongful at international law. The obvious modern case is the bombing in 1985 of the *Rainbow Warrior* by French agents in Auckland Harbour, New Zealand, resulting in one death and the loss of the vessel. Two agents involved were subsequently arrested. Once the French government had admitted responsibility it took the position that '[t]hose who simply carried out the deed must obviously be exonerated since it would not be acceptable to expose [to prosecution] these military men who simply obeyed orders'.[116] However, for whatever reason, France did not assert any immunity from local jurisdiction in respect of its agents in the criminal proceedings against them in New Zealand.[117] The officers themselves pleaded guilty, although they did plead the fact of their being on a mission under orders in mitigation of sentence.[118] When New Zealand and France approached the UN Secretary-General for a ruling on their respective differences, France submitted that following its acceptance of responsibility an 'equitable

---

[114] Possible objections to a theory of state immunity based solely on this principle are noted at n. 12, above.

[115] R. Jennings, 'The *Caroline* and *McLeod* cases' (1938) 32 AJIL 82 at 93.

[116] *Rainbow Warrior (New Zealand v. France)* (United Nations, Ruling of the Secretary General, 1986) 74 ILR 241 at 261.

[117] See *R v. Mafart and Prieur* (New Zealand High Court, 1985) 74 ILR 241 and cf. the prosecution of Indonesian soldiers in *In re BPZS* (Netherlands New Guinea Court of Justice, 1955) 22 ILR 208. On implicit waiver of state immunity through failure to protest proceedings, see *Gounaris v. Ministère Public* (Egypt, Mixed Court of Cassation, 1943), 12 ILR 152 at 152–4.

[118] *Ibid.*, 250–1.

and principled' settlement necessarily 'implies the immediate release' of the convicted agents, and that 'for reasons of law and in order to restore the traditional friendly relations between the two countries, it behoves the New Zealand Government to release the two offenders'.[119] France did not explain the relevant reasons of law justifying this conclusion, beyond New Zealand's ability under national law to deport sentenced prisoners and France's inability to hold them in custody absent a treaty arrangement on transfer of prisoners. The Secretary-General did not accept this argument, at least insofar as it suggested that the only acceptable result was the agents' unconditional release. Instead he ruled that they should be transferred into French custody and confined to a military base outside France for three years. It is not clear that *Rainbow Warrior* is in conflict with McLeod's case, as France did not directly assert state immunity before either the courts of New Zealand or the Secretary-General. In any event, this practice has limited value in the context of consensual interdiction arrangements, as it concerns the rule applicable to state agents present within a 'receiving' state's jurisdiction *without* its consent.

Second, some have suggested that guidance as to the scope of state *immunity* might be provided by the rules on state *responsibility*.[120] Indeed, this seems to be the substance of the French position in *Rainbow Warrior*: that once responsibility was admitted, local adjudicative and enforcement jurisdiction over the relevant acts of individuals was precluded. While state responsibility and immunity might coincide in some cases, the suggestion is ultimately without merit, as it would potentially widen the scope of state immunity beyond that which is currently recognised. State responsibility attaches in cases where a state official commits a wrongful act using the ostensible authority of his or her position or means placed at his or her disposal by the state.[121] State responsibility may even extend to acts which were in no way sovereign or related to the carrying out of an official duty, but where the state failed to take reasonable measures to supervise its agents or prevent such conduct.[122] To extend state immunity to cover all cases of state responsibility would

---

[119] *Rainbow Warrior*, 268–9.
[120] Tomonori, 'Individual as beneficiary of state immunity', 275; C. Whomersley, 'Some reflections on the immunity of individuals for official acts' (1992) 41 ICLQ 848 at 857.
[121] *Caire Case* (1929) 5 RIAA 516; cf. ILC Articles on State Responsibility and Commentary in [2001] II(2) YBILC, 45–47, Article 7.
[122] *Zafiro Case* (1925) 6 RIAA 160.

be to cover many instances of wrongful personal conduct of individual officers contrary to the policy in *Tsoukharis* and the 'substantial departure' rule under some SOFA arrangements. Conversely, it is also obvious that the existence of state immunity at the national level does not preclude international responsibility. It is to the applicable rules of international responsibility and claim settlement that this book now turns.

12 International responsibility and settlement of claims

1 Liability: applicable standards and diplomatic protection

Under general international law an interdicting state is obliged to compensate a boarded vessel for any loss, damage, injury or delay arising from wrongful boarding and inspection.[1] This is a separate obligation from any responsibility to the flag state for unjustified interference with a vessel bearing its nationality.[2] The procedure to be followed and the standard of assessment and quantification of loss to be applied might be thought to be more controversial. SOFAs usually embody a claims procedure under which the receiving state will process claims for compensation arising out of acts committed by visiting forces and will then receive a partial indemnity from the sending state under a cost-sharing formula. A similar approach is taken under European treaties dealing with cross-border police activities.[3] It would be hard to say, however, that any such pre-agreed formula evidenced a general rule that responsibility lies with the receiving (or flag) state to settle claims arising from consensual interdictions. Such rules are better

---

[1] See *The Jessie, The Thomas F. Bayard and The Pescawa*, (1921) 6 RIAA 57 at 58–9; *The Marianna Flora*, (1826) 11 Wheaton 1, 42; O'Connell, p. 808. The principle also covers destruction of the vessel: *Red Crusader*, (1962) 35 ILR 485; *Amerada Hess Shipping v. Argentine Republic*, (US Court of Appeals, 1987) 79 ILR 1 at 9–10.

[2] Such injury may be purely moral and not monetarily compensable: see the refused claim for both 1 franc's nominal damage for interference with the flag state's rights and 100,000 francs in 'moral and political' damages arising from a failure to observe the law of the sea in *The Manouba* (1913) 11 RIAA 463 at 475. Note, however, UNCLOS, Article 106, providing a direct right of compensation to the flag state for unwarranted interference on suspicion of piracy.

[3] The receiving state is entitled to a full indemnity from the pursuing state: Convention Applying the Schengen Agreement 1990, Article 43; Convention on Mutual Assistance in Criminal Matters between the Member States of the European Union 2000, Article 16.

considered a *lex specialis* displacing the ordinary rules of diplomatic protection or state immunity which might apply in such cases. In any event, there is no need to turn to analogies regarding visiting forces or cross-border policing when there are applicable rules of the law of the sea dealing with losses incurred during an interdiction.

Where an interdiction has been conducted upon the suspicion that one of the legal grounds under UNCLOS Article 110(1) exists, Article 110(3) further provides:

If the suspicions prove to be unfounded, and provided that the ship boarded has not committed any act justifying them, it shall be compensated for any loss or damage that may have been sustained.

This wording was first used in the High Seas Convention, and similar language is used in the Migrant Smuggling Protocol and the Council of Europe Agreement.[4] A similar obligation also applies in cases of wrongful hot pursuit.[5] Notably, the requirement to compensate 'the ship' (namely the *interests* in the ship) may well extend to natural persons aboard, the owner and the bareboat charterer, although it might not extend to the owners of cargo.[6] These provisions reflect a general agreement that under either customary law or Article 110 a state interdicts at its own risk, and is liable to pay compensation if its suspicion proves unfounded, strict liability being justified in order to deter abuse of the 'privilege' of visit and inspection.[7] On its face, however, this formula does not specify by what standard such compensation is to be judged or even who is to pay. It does, however, indicate that no compensation is due where the vessel has committed acts justifying suspicion. This was the result in the *Marianna Flora* case, where the US cruiser *Alligator* had approached the *Marianna Flora* on suspicion of piracy and then been fired upon by that vessel, its master fearing the *Alligator* to be a pirate craft itself.[8] The *Alligator* subdued and seized the *Marianna Flora* and took it to port for adjudication. On a final and objective analysis, the grounds for the *Alligator*'s boarding were mistaken: the *Marianna*

---

[4] See High Seas Convention, Article 22(3), and cf. Article 20; Migrant Smuggling Protocol, Article 9(2); Council of Europe Agreement, Article 26(2). Note also UNCLOS, Article 106 (unwarranted interference on suspicion of piracy).

[5] See UNCLOS, Article 111(8). This may apply even where there has been no boarding.

[6] Wendel, *State Responsibility for Interferences with the Freedom of Navigation*, p. 93; cf. MV *'Saiga' (No. 2)*, paras. 106–107.

[7] Brownlie, p. 234; Oppenheim, p. 738; *The Marianna Flora* (1826) 11 Wheaton 1, 42; [1951] II YBILC, 82–3; [1956] II YBILC, 284, contra, the position of Yugoslavia at 97.

[8] *The Marianna Flora.*

Flora was not a pirate vessel. Liability did not follow, however, because the *Marianna Flora* had fired first and without provocation, a voluntary and positive act justifying the suspicion. The Article 110(3) rule is, perhaps, simply a *lex specialis* application of the general principle of state responsibility that in determining any reparation due 'account shall be taken of the contribution to the injury by wilful or negligent action or omission of the injured state or any person or entity in relation to whom reparation is sought.'[9]

A similar, but differently phrased obligation arises in relation to unwarranted enforcement action to prevent marine pollution by flag, port or coastal states under Part XII of UNCLOS. Article 232 provides in such cases:

States shall be liable for damage or loss attributable to them arising from measures taken pursuant to [UNCLOS Articles 213–22] ... when such measures are unlawful or exceed those reasonably required in the light of available information. States shall provide for recourse in their courts for actions in respect of such damage or loss.

The SUA Protocol 2005 in Article 8*bis*(10)(b) largely adopts this more detailed formulation, but includes elements of Article 110(3) in its drafting (see section 2, below). The first sentence of Article 232, but not the second, is reproduced verbatim as Article 21(18) of the FSA.

The legal effect of the Article 110(3) and Article 232 formulas and their respective variants may vary.[10] Both certainly provide that natural and legal persons have a right of compensation, seemingly separate from any right in respect of the flag state, against intervening states for any losses incurred in the case of unwarranted or otherwise wrongful interdictions.[11] One minor difference is the clear requirement to make provision for domestic remedies under Article 232 of UNCLOS and Article 8*bis* of the SUA Protocol 2005. While the Article 232 formula identifies 'states' as the parties responsible for compensating vessels, like Article 110(3) it does not identify with any precision which of several potentially involved states bears liability. More significantly, Article 232 suggests that an obligation to compensate arises where measures taken 'exceed those reasonably required in the light

---

[9] ILC Articles on State Responsibility, Article 39; cf. Wendel, *State Responsibility for Interferences with the Freedom of Navigation*, pp. 162–5.

[10] Contra, Wendel, *State Responsibility for Interferences with the Freedom of Navigation*, pp. 94–112.

[11] *Ibid.* and authorities cited at n. 1, above.

of available information'. This suggests that some latitude is given to the boarding state, as interdiction per se is not necessarily wrongful if 'available information' warrants it; however, it subjects the acts undertaken by the boarding state to more scrutiny, as they may be wrongful if they go beyond what is 'reasonably required' given the information to hand. This is clearly different from the strict liability standard found in Article 110(3), which has little to say about the measures taken during interdiction. The point is considered further below, where it is suggested that Article 232 is a consensual variation by treaty of the strict liability standard that would otherwise apply under general international law.[12]

It is sometimes suggested that such provisions constitute a rare example of state responsibility arising from lawful acts and are an exception to the general rule that state responsibility follows only from an internationally wrongful act.[13] This unnecessarily confuses the issue. One could more simply observe that the relevant international wrong – unwarranted interdiction – is defined variously by an objective standard (the suspicion justifying interdiction proves to be unfounded), a reasonableness or proportionality standard (where measures taken exceed those reasonably required) or a requirement that legally permissible acts are nonetheless carried out by lawful means.

There may, nonetheless, be a question as to what measures in the course of an interdiction are justified in the light of a boarding state's suspicion, under UNCLOS Article 110. Frequently the justification for an interdiction may be the suspicion of statelessness. For example, in the *So San* incident the vessel involved displayed no flag or identifying markings.[14] This alone may have justified boarding and inspection on grounds of suspected statelessness. Wendel argues, however, that the right to verify nationality in such cases cannot justify inspection of the hold or cargo and that the only relevant material will be the vessel's papers.[15] If satisfactory papers are presented, no further search should be undertaken. This in Wendel's view raises questions regarding the legality of searching the hold in the *So San* incident. Setting aside the fact that the *So San* interdiction had flag-state consent, the terms of

[12] Text accompanying nn. 47–48.
[13] Wendel, *State Responsibility for Interferences with the Freedom of Navigation*, pp. 112–26.
[14] See Chapter 9, section 4.
[15] Wendel, *State Responsibility for Interferences with the Freedom of Navigation*, p. 51.

which may have authorised such a search,[16] the general point is a fair one. It only serves, however, to bring us back to the text of Article 110(2), stating that '[i]f suspicion remains after the documents have been checked, [the boarding state] may proceed to a further examination on board the ship, which must be carried out with all possible consideration.'[17] This right of 'further examination' appears to be general and possibly wide-ranging. Even if narrowly construed by reference to the original suspicion, where inadequate papers have been presented and the relevant suspicion is one of statelessness, inspection of the hold may reveal information such as a 'main beam number' capable of assisting in the vessel's identification.[18]

Looking to other treaties, the drug interdiction treaty practice is instructive. While the UN Narcotics Convention contains no specific reference to compensation for unwarranted boarding, interdictions under Article 17 must be 'in conformity with the law of the sea' and must take account of the need not to prejudice the flag state's commercial interests. This would incorporate by reference, as part of the law of the sea, the specific obligation to compensate a wrongfully interdicted vessel.[19] Although a number of US bilateral narcotics interdiction treaties include express claims provisions, many are far from detailed. They commonly provide that the parties will either consult to resolve such disputes or that disputes will be settled under the boarding state's law in a manner consistent with international law.[20] The latter approach is generally taken in the US bilateral PSI treaties.[21] The Maltese PSI Agreement refers to such claims being resolved, in the first instance, under 'the domestic law of the Party to [sic] which the claim is brought'.[22] The Caribbean Area Agreement might be taken to reject the primacy of boarding-state claims procedures, as its Article 28 simply provides that claims

---

[16] See Chapter 9, section 4, text accompanying n. 64.
[17] Cf. *Oppenheim*, 9th edn, p. 738 on the correct procedure.
[18] *United States v. Cortes*, 588 F.2d 106, 110 (1979). The introduction, however, of the IMO ship identification number scheme in 1987 may have reduced the need for such searches.
[19] See n. 1, above.
[20] Antigua and Barbuda Agreement, Article 20; Barbados Agreement, Article 19; Costa Rica Agreement, 1999, Article 7(11); Dominica Agreement, Article 20; Grenada Agreement, Article 20; Guatemala Agreement, Article 17; Haiti Agreement, Article 25; Saint Kitts and Nevis Agreement, Article 20; Venezuela Agreement, Article 4.
[21] Belizean, Croatian, Cypriot, Liberian and Marshall Islands PSI treaties, Article 13(2).
[22] Article 16(2).

against a Party for damage, injury or loss resulting from law enforcement operations pursuant to this Agreement, including claims against its law enforcement officials, shall be resolved in accordance with international law.

But this wording is unlikely to have an appreciably different effect from that contained in other agreements. At general international law, any claim against the boarding state brought by a person aboard an interdicted vessel (or by its owner or bareboat charterer) will involve the ordinary rules of diplomatic protection. The boarding state will be immune before the courts of the flag state, and in the first instance a wronged individual or corporation will need to seek compensation under the national law of the boarding state. Once local remedies have been exhausted, or have proven inadequate, a claim may be agitated at the international level.[23] This will be the case for affected individuals notwithstanding that the obligation breached is contained in an interdiction treaty or UNCLOS.[24] Indeed, UNCLOS itself requires the exhaustion of local remedies unless the question is one of 'prompt release'.[25] Thus, despite the potential availability of UNCLOS compulsory dispute resolution in many interdiction scenarios,[26] the first question will be the applicable standard of compensation that international law requires of domestic tribunals. This does not admit an easy answer: the reasoning of arbitral tribunals is often obscure on the quantification of damages.[27] While any rules on quantification of damage are beyond the scope of the present study, a number of relevant observations can be made. The best, although still quite abstract, conclusion is that under both treaty arrangements and the general law of state responsibility a boarding state should be responsible for those losses that would typically arise from and could reasonably be foreseen prior to an interdiction, but not for more 'remote' damages.[28] The most obvious categories

---

[23] Brownlie, pp. 472–81; Shaw, pp. 730–2; ILC Draft Articles on Diplomatic Protection, Articles 14 and 15, http://untreaty.un.org/ilc/texts/instruments/english/draft%20 articles/9_8_2006.pdf.

[24] *ELSI Case*, [1989] ICJ Rep. 15; J. Crawford and S. Olleson, 'The nature and forms of international responsibility' in M. Evans (ed.), *International Law*, 2nd edn (Oxford University Press, 2006), p. 451 at p. 464.

[25] UNCLOS, Articles 292 and 295; *Camouco Case*, para. 55.

[26] N. Klein, *Dispute Settlement in the UN Convention on the Law of the Sea* (Cambridge University Press, 2005), pp. 308–13.

[27] E.g. *The Coquitlam* (1920) 6 RIAA 45, 47 (tribunal acting on report of experts without commenting on methodology); cf. nn. 33–34, below.

[28] Wendel, *State Responsibility for Interferences with the Freedom of Navigation*, pp. 171–2.

of award on this approach would be for[29] delay,[30] loss of profits,[31] the value of the vessel and cargo (where destroyed or confiscated),[32] injury to the persons aboard[33] and interest.[34] In the United States, at least, the Coast Guard and the Navy have the ability 'to consider and pay meritorious claims for [for death, personal injury, damage to or loss of] … property arising from maritime law enforcement operations' made by affected foreign nationals or corporations through an administrative procedure.[35] Reparation for direct injury to the rights of the flag state, for example interference with its right to freedom of navigation, is likely to be satisfied by any finding (or admission) of wrongful conduct by the boarding state.[36] Only unjustified *seizure* on suspicion of piracy results in an obligation materially to compensate the flag state in its own right.[37]

Rules of diplomatic protection may not apply where the act complained of can be brought within relevant foreign-state immunities legislation. Under section 5 of the UK State Immunity Act[38] a foreign

[29] *Ibid.*, pp. 179 ff.

[30] Delays following at-sea interdiction may cost shipping companies up to $40,000 per hour: T. Egan, 'Some ships get Coast Guard tip before searches', *New York Times*, 20 May 2006, www.nytimes.com/2006/05/20/us/20ships.html.

[31] On assessing the loss of a season's fishing, see *Horace B. Parker,* (1925) 6 RIAA 153 and the cases at n. 54, below.

[32] *Red Crusader* case; *Amerada Hess Shipping v. Argentine Republic,* (US Court of Appeals, 1987) 79 ILR 1 at 9–10.

[33] Extending to compensation for 'unlawful arrest, detention or other forms of ill-treatment': *MV 'Saiga' (No. 2)*, para. 172. In making such awards, ITLOS appears implicitly to have taken into account the practice of the United Nations Compensation Commission on assessment of damages for false imprisonment: Wendel, *State Responsibility for Interferences with the Freedom of Navigation*, pp. 187–8. See United Nations Compensation Commission, Governing Council Decision No. 8, UN Doc. S/AC.26/1992/8 (27 January 1992), (1992) 31 ILM 1036–7.

[34] See interest calculations in *MV 'Saiga' (No. 2)*, paras. 173, 175; and analysis in Wendel, *State Responsibility for Interferences with the Freedom of Navigation*, pp. 193–6. Cf. [2001] II(2) YBILC, 107–9.

[35] Roach, 'Proliferation Security Initiative', 407, and see 33 CFR §25.503. Cf. Wendel, *State Responsibility for Interferences with the Freedom of Navigation*, p. 228. Studies of this mechanism's use have been conducted within the US defence community, but are not publicly available. Personal communication: Professor Dennis Mandsager, US Naval War College, 6 June 2006.

[36] *MV 'Saiga' (No. 2)*, para. 176; cf. *Manouba Case,* 475 (finding that a state has breached its international obligations itself constitutes a serious sanction) and comments at n. 2 above.

[37] UNCLOS, Article 106. It is not clear whether this is to the exclusion of duties of compensation that would ordinarily be owed the vessel itself under general international law or under UNCLOS, Article 110.

[38] 1978 Chapter 33, (1978) 17 ILM 1123.

state 'is not immune as respects proceedings in respect of – (a) death or personal injury; or (b) damage to or loss of tangible property, caused by an act or omission in the United Kingdom'. This provision has no application to criminal cases, and so does not affect the position regarding the criminal liability of individual officers. It does, however, mean that the boarding state could be civilly liable under UK law for personal injury or property damage caused within the United Kingdom. This would apply if the boarding state conducted a consensual interdiction within the United Kingdom's territorial sea. The application of the UK Act, however, only extends to territorial waters and designated continental shelf areas, and does not include UK flag vessels on the high seas.[39] In construing a similar statutory exception to state immunity, US courts have held that injuries aboard a US vessel caused by foreign law-enforcement action within that foreign state's territorial sea cannot be considered as having occurred within the United States.[40] The result should have been no different had the vessel been upon the high seas.[41]

2 The flag or coastal state: issues of individual and joint liability

Very few treaties address the possibility that there might be flag-state liability for interdictions conducted by a foreign boarding state. Assuming that a particular case implicated flag-state responsibility, third-state nationals or corporations adversely affected by an interdiction would not be bound by any agreement between flag and boarding states as to responsibility. Such third-party nationals might thus have a choice of defendant in any diplomatic protection claim brought. Once the possibility of flag-state liability is contemplated, a basic question of classification arises under the law of state responsibility. If a boarding party is considered to be solely the organ of its sending state, its wrongful acts entail only the boarding state's responsibility. If it is considered an organ acting 'on joint behalf' of the boarding and flag state, it might incur their joint responsibility.[42] If it is considered to be an organ placed 'at the disposal of' the flag

---

[39] *Ibid.*, s. 17(4).
[40] *Perez v. The Bahamas* (US District Court of Columbia) (1980) 63 ILR 350.
[41] While the plaintiffs cited 18 USC §7(1) on the territorial status of flag vessels on the high seas, this only applies in criminal cases and not actions for civil damages.
[42] 'Joint responsibility' is not a term appearing on the face of the ILC Articles on State Responsibility. The concept is discussed further below.

state, the flag state will bear sole responsibility for its acts.[43] The correct classification will depend upon the treaty arrangements in place and the facts of the case.

The initial presumption must be that the boarding state is liable for the conduct of its organ, the boarding party. Joint liability of the flag state should not be presumed to arise simply because absent its permission to interdict the boarding party could not have committed any wrongful acts aboard its vessel. Nor will mere permission to interdict normally constitute aiding or assisting any subsequent wrongful conduct of the boarding party. The general international standard for responsibility for aiding or assisting an internationally wrongful act is that (i) the aid must have been given 'with a view to facilitating the commission' of the specific act in question; (ii) it must have been given with an awareness of the circumstances making the act wrongful; and (iii) 'the completed act must be such that it would have been wrongful had it been committed by the assisting state itself'.[44] Where the wrongful act, for example, is the excessive use of force in arresting a suspect, the flag state would not necessarily have knowledge of those specific circumstances or have permitted interdiction with a view to facilitating that abuse.[45] To proceed beyond generalities requires examining the relevant treaties. These are not, however, always of great assistance.

The SUA Protocol 2005 states that

[p]rovided that authorization to board by a flag State shall not *per se* give rise to its liability, States Parties shall be liable for any damage, harm or loss attributable to them arising from measures taken pursuant to this article when:

(i)   the grounds for such measures prove to be unfounded, provided that the ship has not committed any act justifying the measures taken; or

---

[43] ILC Articles on State Responsibility and commentary, Article 6 in [2001] II(2) YBILC, 44 at (3).

[44] [2001] II(2) YBIL, 66 at (3). Such aid and assistance may also be termed 'complicity': J. Quigley, 'Complicity in international law: a new direction in the law of state responsibility', (1986) 57 BYIL 77.

[45] Although if the boarding state in question was known to perpetrate such abuses routinely, flag-state complicity might arise regarding any abuse committed: Quigley, 'Complicity in international law', 92–5, 112–13 (arguing that knowledge of a high likelihood of the assistance being used to commit a wrong is sufficient); cf. [2001] II(2) YBILC, 67 at (9).

(ii)   such measures are unlawful or exceed those reasonably required in light of available information to implement the provisions of this article.[46]

This formulation assists us little. Sub-paragraph (i) simply restates the rule of strict liability in UNCLOS Article 110(3) described above. The reference to unlawful measures in sub-paragraph (ii) merely embodies the general principle that a state must make reparation for its internationally wrongful acts. The further requirement to compensate where measures taken 'exceed those reasonably required in light of available information' – language taken directly from Article 232 of UNCLOS and FSA Article 21(18) – is less likely to reflect general international law.[47] Not every unreasonable use of a police power is necessarily internationally wrongful. Certainly any use of force going beyond that 'reasonably required' will exceed the strict tests for lawfulness outlined in Chapter 10,[48] but other cases may be different.[49] The rule in sub-paragraph (ii) is perhaps best thought of as a treaty standard that may be somewhat stricter than the general rule of international law. Otherwise, the provision makes the obvious point that the fact of the flag state granting authorisation to board, in response to a boarding state's request, does not per se create a situation of joint or exclusive liability on the part of the flag state. This does not indicate what 'damage, harm or loss' might be attributable to a flag state and under what conditions.

Article 26(3) of the Council of Europe Agreement provides that liability for any damage resulting from action requested by the flag state – that is, where it has requested other parties' intervention to suppress crimes aboard its own flag vessel – 'shall rest with the requesting state, which may seek compensation from the requested [i.e. boarding] state where the damage was a result of negligence or some other fault attributable to that state'.

This is a sensible rule, reflecting two more basic propositions. The first is the rule that the acts of a state organ 'placed at the disposal' of,

---

[46] SUA Protocol 2005, Article 8*bis*(10)(b); see also the discussion of the *Xhavara* Case in Chapter 8, section 2.6 (no form of joint responsibility per se arises from merely entering treaty interdiction arrangements).

[47] See Chapter 5, section 5 for similar language in Council of Europe Agreement, Article 26.

[48] See Chapter 10, section 3.3.

[49] See text accompanying nn. 14–18, above, on arguments that the scope of powers exercisable in an interdiction under UNCLOS, Article 110, are limited by reference to the interdicting state's suspicions justifying boarding.

and exercising elements of the 'governmental authority' of, a foreign state are attributable to that latter state.[50] Second, the state placing a boarding party at the flag state's disposal might nonetheless incur some degree of liability if it fails to take steps to prevent foreseeable abuses by agents within its effective control.[51] The division of responsibility should largely follow the degree of effective control exercised. This rule could logically extend not only to situations where a boarding state intervenes at a flag state's express invitation,[52] but to situations such as the Spanish–Italian Treaty on drug interdiction where each party grants the other permission in advance to interdict its flag vessels on the express theory that 'each party recognizes the other's right to intervene [aboard] *as its agent*'.[53] While this result has certainly followed in older case law determined on theories of agency,[54] it is precluded in the Spanish–Italian Treaty by an express provision that if a party 'intervenes without adequate grounds for suspicion, it may be held liable for any loss or damage incurred' unless acting on the flag state's request.[55] In any event, as noted above, such provisions are only binding as between the parties and do not affect a claim brought by a third-party national.

Cases of express invitation and relationships of agency are likely to be the only ones in which the flag state may bear principal responsibility for acts undertaken by the boarding party. The mere assertion of preferential jurisdiction by a flag state will not of itself show that it has adopted the conduct – including any wrongful conduct – of the boarding state as its own.[56] This might, however, be the case where it expressly approved of the wrongful act after the event, or 'was at least aware of, and consented to' the wrongful act's commission in the first place.[57]

An interdiction might also involve liability of both the flag and boarding states arising from their collaborative conduct, or the

---

[50] ILC Articles on State Responsibility, Article 6.   [51] *Zafiro* case, above.

[52] As under UN Narcotics Convention, Article 17(2); Migrant Smuggling Protocol, Article 8(1).

[53] Spanish–Italian Treaty, Article 5(1) (emphasis added).

[54] *Wanderer* (1921) 6 RIAA 68; *Kate* (1921) 6 RIAA 77; and *Favourite* (1921) 6 RIAA 82 (United States Navy acting on behalf of British government in enforcing sealing treaty aboard British vessels, United States remains liable for naval officers' mistake of law).

[55] Spanish–Italian Treaty, Article 5(4).

[56] ILC Articles on State Responsibility, Article 10.

[57] Cf. Israel's conduct regarding the abduction of Adolf Eichmann: [2001] II(2) YBILC, 53 at (5). Cases of consent in advance could significantly overlap with liability for aiding or assisting wrongful acts.

simultaneous liability of each state arising from the one interdiction but in respect of different legal obligations. Such situations are often referred to as matters of 'joint' liability. Joint liability could perhaps arise in circumstances analogous to the *Nauru* case, where the boarding party performs acts on the 'joint behalf' of boarding and flag states.[58] This might be thought to follow in any situation where the boarding state has been permitted to board and search a vessel pending instructions from the flag state as to which will ultimately exercise jurisdiction over any crimes discovered.[59] The boarding party could be considered as acting at all times, until such a decision is made, on behalf of both potential prosecuting states. This analysis might seem attractive if one accepted the theory that the only jurisdiction a boarding state could exercise over a foreign flag vessel was one somehow 'loaned' by the flag state.[60] Such reasoning might suggest that either state could be held internationally responsible for the conduct of the boarding prior to disposition being determined and diplomatic protection proceedings could be commenced against one, even in the absence of the other, in respect of this joint conduct.[61] The very limited case law, however, suggests that such an analysis would be mistaken.

The *Nauru* case can be analysed in terms of either joint organs or joint obligations giving rise to joint responsibility. Prior to independence, the Administering Authority of Nauru was formally the three governments of Australia, New Zealand and the United Kingdom acting together under a 1947 UN trusteeship, although in practice 'Australia played a very special role' in the administration of the territory.[62] The exploitation of Nauru's natural phosphate resources was conducted by 'an enterprise managed by three "British Phosphate Commissioners" appointed by the three Governments'.[63]

---

[58] *Certain Phosphate Lands in Nauru (Nauru v. Australia)*, Preliminary Objections, [1992] ICJ Rep. 240 at 258; [2001] II(2) YBILC, 64 at (3). On joint responsibility and maritime interdiction, see Wendel, *State Responsibility for Interferences with the Freedom of Navigation*, pp. 135 ff.

[59] See, among many examples, Caribbean Area Agreement, Article 12; UN Narcotics Convention, Article 17; Haiti Agreement, Article 14; Dominican Republic Migrant Interdiction Agreement, Article 8; Migrant Smuggling Protocol, Article 8.

[60] See Chapter 5, section 5, and Chapter 13.

[61] *Certain Phosphate Lands in Nauru*, 258–9 at para. 48. The question whether in such a case the respondent state is liable to make full restitution or only a 'proportionate share' was not determined: [2001] II(2) YBILC, 124 at (4).

[62] *Certain Phosphate Lands in Nauru*, 258 at para. 47.

[63] Ibid., 256.

Their joint responsibility in respect of environmental damage result-ing from phosphate mining might thus be thought to flow from their conscious choice to act through a common organ.[64] Judge Shahabuddeen, however, pointed out that the determination of whether the obligation involved was joint or not could be readily made on 'the terms of the Trusteeship Agreement and those terms alone. Previous or subsequent facts could not make the obligation joint if it was not joint under the … Agreement.'[65] The formal source of rights and obligations involved must be the starting point for deter-mining if joint responsibility exists, despite the possibility of joint responsibility arising simply from a common course of conduct.[66] For example, ship-rider agreements are commonly described in the relevant treaties as establishing 'joint', 'co-operative' or 'combined' drug interdiction programmes. In practice, however, they operate by allowing a ship-riding flag-state officer to authorise or request the assistance of the foreign officers of the vessel upon which she or he is embarked in enforcing flag-state law against a vessel of the ship-rider's nationality.[67] Formally, then, the boarding party is akin to an organ placed at the ship-rider's disposal; however, it is scarcely 'under the complete direction and authority' of the ship-rider or flag state in the sense of being a mere 'loaned servant'.[68] While assistance must be rendered within the terms of the request, there remains the dis-cretion not to assist at all and any assistance rendered must usually be compatible with the laws and procedures of both the flag and the boarding state. This implies that a large degree of judgement and con-trol rests with the commanding officer of the boarding party acting as an organ of his state. The ship-rider may be requested to assist the state officials of the vessel upon which she or he is embarked under similar conditions. The ship-rider and boarding state officials aboard

---

[64] Cf. *Anglo-Chinese Shipping Company v. US* (US Court of Claims, 1955) 22 ILR 982, an attempt to sue the United States for acts of the Supreme Commander for the Allied Powers, which office was a joint organ of the occupying powers in Japan from 1945 to 1952. The court discusses, *obiter*, theories of agency, but the claim failed on other grounds.

[65] *Certain Phosphate Lands in Nauru*, 274 per Shahabuddeen J (Separate Opinion).

[66] J. Noyes and B. Smith, 'State responsibility and the principle of joint and several liability' (1988) 13 YJIL 225 at 242 ff.

[67] For example, Haiti Agreement, Articles 5–6 and 8; Belize Agreement, Articles 5(e), 6(d) and 7; Barbados Agreement, Articles 3(6)(c), 3(7)(c) and 4; Bahamas Agreement, para 2; cf. Caribbean Area Agreement, Articles 9(3)(e) and 9(4).

[68] Noyes and Smith, 'State responsibility', 246.

a single vessel are thus not under any unified command or *obligation* to assist each other unconditionally in particular operations. If wrongful conduct occurs under a ship-riding agreement, it is more likely to be a case of the ship-rider or boarding party assisting in the other's wrongful conduct than their acting as a joint organ. In such cases of assisting wrongful conduct, the assisting state 'will only be responsible to the extent that its own conduct has caused or contributed to the internationally wrongful act'.[69]

Further, this book has suggested that certain non-derogable human rights may continue to bind states (or at least state parties to the European Convention on Human Rights) in respect of areas within their jurisdiction but under the actual control of foreign forces.[70] If the principle applies to a broader concept of state jurisdiction, it could raise the possibility of joint liability on the part of the flag state for *any* human rights violations (including the excessive use of force) committed by a boarding party on the high seas. However, the situation is far from certain and the obligation imposed on the state having formal jurisdiction but lacking effective control is at most one of due diligence.[71] Responsibility for extra-territorial human rights abuses committed by a boarding state will generally rest, in the first instance, with the boarding state.[72] This may even apply to invited intervention aboard a foreign vessel, as the boarding state is likely to remain in the best position to supervise effectively the boarding party's conduct, unlike many other cases in which a state organ is placed at the disposal of another state.

3 Conclusion

This chapter has suggested that there is a general duty to compensate for any loss or damage sustained in the case where the suspicions justifying an interdiction prove to be unfounded and the vessel itself did nothing to justify such suspicions. While this obligation arises under general international law, it will fall in the first instance to be resolved under the boarding state's national law as a consequence of

---

[69] See [2001] II(2) YBILC, 67 at (11) and 124 at (1). As noted by the ILC, any case against an assisting state might be prevented from proceeding before an international tribunal where the state committing the wrong assisted is not present: *Monetary Gold Removed from Rome in 1943*, [1954] ICJ Rep. 19 at 32–4.

[70] See Chapter 9, section 6.   [71] *Ibid.*

[72] See cases and reports cited in Chapter 10, section 2, n. 12.

the ordinary rules of diplomatic protection applying to claims brought by individuals against a foreign state. The same situation will generally obtain regarding claims for personal injury. The possible exception is where the interdiction has occurred in a state's territorial sea, where there may be an exception to boarding-state immunity allowing an action to be brought in the coastal state's courts. The joint, or principal, liability for wrongful conduct committed in the course of an interdiction of the flag or coastal state permitting interdiction will be the exception, rather than the rule. It is most likely to arise where the flag or coastal state has specifically invited interdiction on terms suggesting that the foreign boarding party is acting in the exercise of flag-or coastal-state government functions and has been placed at that state's disposal.

13 General conclusions: a law of interdiction?

This book has examined law enforcement at sea and in particular those situations where a state's public vessel, being a warship or vessel clearly marked as on government service, may take action either against vessels on the high seas not having the interdicting vessel's nationality or vessels located in the territorial waters of another state. The focus has been upon interdiction regimes where interdiction is understood to involve, first, the boarding, inspection and search of a ship at sea suspected of prohibited conduct ('search'), and, second, where such suspicions prove justified, taking measures including any combination of arresting the vessel, arresting persons aboard or seizing cargo ('seizure'). Analysis commenced from a consideration of basic principles of maritime jurisdiction, principally jurisdiction in the territorial sea and over vessels on the high seas.

A state's public vessels may interdict a non-national vessel on the high seas in one of three cases:

- where the flag state consents;
- where a permissive rule of general international law allows the interdiction; or
- where the vessel is without nationality (i.e. stateless).

Where a boarding state seeks to effect an interdiction with flag-state consent, two initial issues arise: the determination of which state is the flag state (the question of how a vessel acquires nationality); and the authority enjoyed by the flag state over the vessel (the question of jurisdiction). As has been noted, a vessel acquires nationality either through registration or a separate right to fly a state's flag, the latter usually being the case as regards small, private craft. A vessel, in effect, makes an ostensible claim to nationality through its external markings of home port or registration, through flying a flag, or directly through the master's verbal assertion in response to being hailed by a public vessel.[1] Some treaties condition granting a request for permission to interdict upon the requested flag state confirming registry.[2] Clearly this is problematic, as not all national craft must be registered. The United States, in particular, avoids the need for registry checks through the doctrine of presumptive flag-state authority. That is, it takes the view that it may grant permission to interdict as regards any vessel ostensibly claiming its nationality. This is both practical and gives effect to a presumption that states must have a power to prevent abuse of claims of nationality.[3] The presumptive nationality approach has often been followed within consent-based interdiction regimes. This approach is presumed in any treaty allowing a national vessel to be boarded, even for limited purposes, prior to the flag state being contacted. Such an outcome can only be rationalised on the basis that the flag state must have the capacity to consent to the boarding of any vessel ostensibly claiming its nationality. The approach is also perhaps tacitly adopted in treaties requiring confirmation of nationality rather than registration.

The second question in consent-based interdiction is the jurisdiction enjoyed by the flag state over a national vessel. This is said to be an 'exclusive jurisdiction', which has two important elements. First, it confers immunity upon such national vessels – while they are upon the high seas – from acts of boarding, search or seizure by foreign public vessels. This has been called the 'excluding jurisdiction' of the flag state.[4] Second, the criminal law and enforcement jurisdiction of the flag state is applicable aboard the vessel while it is upon the high seas. This means that when a foreign state is given consent to interdict, that consent may be given upon conditions and the prescriptive and enforcement jurisdiction of the flag state over its vessel continues uninterrupted. The boarding state will enjoy a concurrent or parallel jurisdiction over the vessel only to the extent of the permission granted by the flag state. Commonly, permission to search does not encompass permission to seize, and if evidence of prohibited conduct is found further disposition instructions must be sought from the flag state before further enforcement action is taken against the vessel, its

---

[1] See Chapter 5, section 7.
[2] UN Narcotics Convention, Article 17(3); Migrant Smuggling Protocol, Article 8(2).
[3] See Chapter 5, section 7.   [4] *Harvard Research*, 810.

cargo or persons aboard. That said, the state practice amply illustrates that flag states are competent to relinquish their 'primary' jurisdiction and allow a boarding state to prosecute conduct discovered aboard a flag vessel on the high seas and that boarding states may conduct such prosecutions under their own national law.

Where a general permissive rule allows the interdiction of foreign-flagged vessels, the same concerns do not obtain, and boarding states may proceed irrespective of flag-state consent. But exceptions allowing unilateral action are few and, in many cases, subject to limitations. The oldest and most obvious exception to the exclusive jurisdiction of the flag state is that of piracy. Where the elements of piracy are made out – an act of violence not sanctioned by state authority, committed on the high seas, from one vessel against another – a public vessel may interdict the pirate craft, irrespective of its nationality, and try those aboard under the law of the boarding state. The only other case in which a general right of both search and seizure of foreign-flagged vessels is conferred is unauthorised broadcasting.[5] However, before this right of interdiction can be exercised, the interdicting state must satisfy a special jurisdictional nexus. The unauthorised broadcasts must be capable of being received, or causing interference, in the interdicting state's territory, or one of the offenders aboard must be of its nationality. The only other case where there is a general permissive rule allowing interdiction – ships suspected of slave-trading – permits only the exercise of search, not seizure, jurisdiction.

The third case where high-seas interdiction of non-national vessels is permitted is in the case of stateless vessels. The category of stateless vessels has occasioned some uncertainty. A vessel suspected of statelessness is certainly subject to visit, inspection of its papers and further search if doubts as to its status remain. Whether such a vessel can be seized either on account of its statelessness per se or only for participation in other impugned conduct with a connection to the interdicting state is less clear.[6] Many law-enforcement treaties providing for the search of stateless vessels are silent on the question of their seizure or use formulas capable of accommodating divergent views such as providing that the interdicting state 'may take such action as may be

---

[5] It is not clear that this is a rule of custom (see Chapter 10, section 3.2, text accompanying n. 47); it is described here as a 'general' rule on the basis of the large number of parties to UNCLOS.

[6] For contrasting views, see Churchill and Lowe, p. 214; McDougal and Burke, pp. 1084–5; cf. the 'legal vacuum' theory discussed in Chapter 7, section 2.

appropriate in accordance with international law.'[7] Some states, most notably the United States, do take the view that they may assert jurisdiction over stateless vessels, and this practice has gone unprotested, even by the state (or states) of nationality of the crews involved.[8]

The category of stateless vessels can only be conceptualised in one of two ways, both starting from a consideration of consent-based interdiction of flag vessels enjoying nationality. One view of consensual interdiction is that the jurisdiction exercised by the boarding state is one 'loaned' by the flag state. That is, the only jurisdiction applicable to the vessel is that enjoyed by the flag state and it is indivisible and incompatible with any concurrent jurisdiction existing. This makes interdiction simply a delegation of power. On this view, jurisdiction over stateless vessels is simply an exception to the ordinary rule that a state may only exercise jurisdiction to enforce within its territory, along with the exception made for the existence of jurisdiction over its own vessels upon the high seas. The preferable view is that the boarding state exercises its own enforcement jurisdiction, the immunity of the flag vessel from interference having been waived. This implies an underlying concurrent jurisdiction of all states over the high seas: the consequence of it being a commons is that it is a space where all have jurisdiction, not where all have no jurisdiction.[9] This view is preferable if only because it is more coherent: it requires less exception-finding than the approach commencing from a presumption that jurisdiction to enforce is strictly territorial, and better accounts for the ability of a state to enforce its own law against both consensually interdicted foreign vessels and stateless vessels.

Of these three models, the one most widely adopted has been that of consent-based interdiction, examined in relation to drug smuggling, fisheries management, transnational crime and countering WMD proliferation. It is in these policing contexts that the general law relating to the conduct of interdictions has developed. This law concerns the primary rules of international law applicable during any interdiction, the position of the boarding state in relation to the national law of the flag state, including questions of immunity, and how any claims for compensation arising from a boarding are to be resolved under the secondary rules of international law.

---

[7] FSA, Article 21(17).

[8] See Chapter 6, section 5.2 (text accompanying n. 113) and cases such as *US v. Bravo*, 489 F.3d 1 (2007) and *US v. Tinoco*, 304 F.3d 1088 (2002).

[9] Carson, 'Ships, nationality and status', 404, as discussed in Chapter 11, section 2.

Under the primary rules of police action applicable to all interdictions, the boarding state must take due account of the safety of life at sea, the ship and its cargo and the need not to prejudice the commercial or legal interests of the flag state. In addition, boarding parties must comply with relevant human rights law and must inform the master of the intention to board and should afford him or her the earliest opportunity to contact the ship's owner and flag state. In the course of a legally permitted interdiction, the basic rule relating to the use of force is that force is acceptable where, as a last resort, the force used is the minimum reasonably necessary to achieve an authorised end, such ends being defined by applicable international law or the scope of flag- or coastal-state consent. None of these principles deprives a boarding party or interdicting vessel of its right of individual self-defence.

As regards the relationship of the boarding state with local law, if a state has passed national laws applicable to foreign officials conducting territorial-sea law-enforcement operations then those foreign officials must voluntarily comply with them. Failure to respect applicable local law will constitute an international wrong. As a practical matter, especially as regards interdictions conducted in the territorial sea, it is desirable that the receiving state passes laws deeming boarding-state officers to have local police powers and that boarding-state officers are made aware of the constraints of local law. Irrespective of this duty of voluntary compliance, the ordinary principles of state immunity apply to the actions of a boarding party during an interdiction. Officers of the boarding state will be individually immune from the enforcement of local criminal law in respect of acts undertaken in performance of the function for which they were admitted to the vessel. Excessive use of force in carrying out an authorised function – let alone minor breaches of the receiving state's law of police procedure – will not, per se, render their actions non-immune. Only acts involving a substantial departure from those necessary to fulfilling their function will not be immune. Ultimately, however, the courts of the receiving state have jurisdiction to determine whether immunity applies. In the course of interdictions in another state's territorial sea, the boarding state may not enjoy immunity in civil proceedings regarding death, injury or damage to goods arising from the interdiction under some states' national legislation.

Under general international law states are obliged to make reparation for their internationally wrongful acts. Under the law of the sea, this extends to a duty to compensate a vessel for loss or delay arising from an interdiction where the suspicions justifying interdiction prove unfounded and the vessel, by its own conduct, has done nothing to provoke such suspicions. As a consequence of the ordinary rules of diplomatic protection, such claims will fall for resolution – in the first instance – before national courts or procedures. Under limited circumstances the flag state might also be liable for a wrongful interdiction, or wrongful acts committed during an interdiction. This will principally occur in cases where the flag state itself has requested assistance in suppressing the use of one of its vessels for an illicit purpose and the boarding party has been effectively placed at the flag state's disposal. Flag states might also in certain cases be subject to a duty of due diligence to take steps to ensure the observance of certain fundamental human rights standards by the boarding party.

As a consequence of the widespread use of the consent model in designing interdiction regimes, it cannot be said that there is a single unified theory which will indicate when interdictions are *permitted*, in the sense of vesting unilateral rights in a boarding state. With a few exceptions, interdiction will only be permitted when the flag state consents; indeed, unless permitted by the flag state or an exceptional rule interdiction will be prohibited as a use of force.[10] What this book has demonstrated, however, is that there may be a law that is generally applicable to how interdictions are *conducted* and to the consequences of wrongfully conducted interdictions before national tribunals.

---

[10] See Chapter 10, section 3.2.

Select bibliography

BOOKS, ARTICLES AND MONOGRAPHS

Acconci, Pia *et al.* (eds.), 'Italian practice relating to international law: legislation' (1999) 9 *IYBIL* 311–65.

Akehurst, M., 'Custom as a source of international law' (1974–5) 47 *BYIL* 1–53.
'The hierarchy of the sources of international law' (1974–5) 47 *BYIL* 273–85.

Akiba, Okon, 'International law of the sea: the legality of Canadian seizure of the Spanish trawler (*Estai*)' (1997) 37 *Natural Resources Journal* 809–28.

American Law Institute, *Restatement of the Law Third: The Foreign Relations Law of the United States* (St. Paul, Minn.: American Law Institute, 1987).

Andreone, Gemma, 'Cemil Panuk and Others' (2001) 11 *IYBIL* 273.

Aust, Antony, *Handbook of International Law* (Cambridge University Press, 2005).
Modern Treaty Law and Practice (Cambridge University Press, 2000).

Baird, Rachel, 'CCAMLR initiatives to counter flag state non-enforcement in Southern Ocean fisheries' (2006) *Victoria University of Wellington Law Review* 733–55.
'Coastal state fisheries management: a review of Australian enforcement action in the Heard and McDonald Islands Australian fishing zone' (2004) 9 *DLR* 91–118.
'Illegal, unreported and unregulated fishing: an analysis of the legal, economic and historical factors relevant to its development and persistence' (2004) 5 *MJIL* 299–334.

Balkin, Rosalie, 'The International Maritime Organization and maritime security' (2006) 30 *TMLJ* 1–34.

Balton, David A., 'The Bering Sea Doughnut Hole Convention: regional solution, global implications' in Olav Schramm Stokke (ed.), *Governing High Seas Fisheries: The Interplay of Global and Regional Regimes* (Oxford University Press, 2001), pp. 143–77.
'Strengthening the law of the sea: the new agreement on straddling fish stocks and highly migratory fish stocks' (1996) 27 *ODIL* 125–51.

Bantz, Vincent P., 'Views from Hamburg: *The Juno Trader case* or how to make sense of the coastal state's rights in the light of its duty of prompt release' (2005) 24 *UQLJ* 415–44.

Barnes, Richard, 'Refugee law at sea' (2004) 53 *ICLQ* 47–77.

Barrios, Erik, 'Casting a wider net: addressing the maritime piracy problem in Southeast Asia' (2005) 28 *BCICLR* 149–63.

Barston, Ronald, 'The law of the sea and regional fisheries organisations' (1999) 14 *IJMCL* 333–52.

Barton, G. P., 'Foreign armed forces: immunity from supervisory jurisdiction' (1949) 26 *BYIL* 380–413.
  'Foreign armed forces: immunity from criminal jurisdiction' (1950) 27 *BYIL* 186–234.
  'Foreign armed forces: qualified jurisdictional immunity' (1954) 31 *BYIL* 341–70.

Batstone, Rodney, 'Respect for the law of the receiving state' in D. Fleck (ed.), *The Handbook of the Law of Visiting Forces* (Oxford University Press, 2001), pp. 61–70.

Baxter, R. R., 'Criminal jurisdiction in the NATO Status of Forces Agreement' (1958) 7 *ICLQ* 72–81.

Becker, Michael A., 'The shifting order of the oceans: freedom of navigation and the interdiction of ships at sea' (2005) 46 *HILJ* 131–230.

Beckman, Robert C., 'Issues of public international law relating to piracy and armed robbery against ships in the Malacca and Singapore straits' (1999) 3 *SJICL* 512–23.

Bederman, David J., 'Counterintuiting countermeasures' (2002) 96 *AJIL* 817–32.

Bingham, Joseph W. *et al.*, *Harvard Research in International Law: Draft Convention on Piracy*, (1932) 26 *AJIL* Supp. 739–886.

Bockley, Kathryn M., 'A historical overview of refugee legislation: the deception of foreign policy in the land of promise' (1995) 21 *North Carolina Journal of International Law and Commercial Regulation* 253–92.

Boister, Neil, 'Transnational criminal law?' (2003) 14 *EJIL* 953–76.

Bolton, John R., 'The Bush administration's forward strategy for nonproliferation' (2004–5) 5 *CJIL* 395–404.

Bos, Maarten, 'La liberté de la haute mer: quelques problèmes d'actualité' (1965) 12 *NILR* 337–64.

Bostock, Chantal Marie-Jeanne, 'The international legal obligations owed to the asylum seekers on the MV *Tampa*' (2002) 14 *IJRL* 279–301.

Bothe, Michael, 'The law of neutrality' in Dieter Fleck (ed.), *The Handbook of Humanitarian Law in Armed Conflicts*, 2nd edn (Oxford University Press, 2008), pp. 571–604.

Bowett, D. W., *Self-Defence in International Law* (Manchester University Press, 1958).

Brinton, Jasper Yeates, *The Mixed Courts of Egypt*, rev. edn (New Haven: Yale University Press, 1968).

'The Egyptian Mixed Courts and foreign armed forces' (1946) 40 *AJIL* 737.

'Jurisdiction over members of Allied Forces in Egypt' (1944) 38 *AJIL* 375.

Brown, Donald L., 'Crooked straits: maritime smuggling of humans from Cuba to the United States' (2002) 33 *UMIALR* 273–93.

Brown, E. D., *The International Law of the Sea*, 2 vols. (Aldershot: Dartmouth, 1994).

Brown, Kathy-Ann, *The Shiprider Model: An Analysis of the US Proposed Agreement Concerning Maritime Counter-Drug Operations in its Wider Legal Context*, Contemporary Caribbean Legal Issues No. 1 (Bridgetown: Faculty of Law, University of the West Indies, 1997).

Brownlie, Ian, *Principles of Public International Law*, 6th edn (Oxford University Press, 2003).

International Law and the Use of Force by States (Oxford: Clarendon, 1963).

Burke, William T., *The New International Law of Fisheries: UNCLOS 1982 and Beyond* (Oxford: Clarendon, 1994).

Burnett, John S., *Dangerous Waters: Modern Piracy and Terror on the High Seas* (New York: Plume, 2003).

Byers, Michael, 'Policing the high seas: the Proliferation Security Initiative' (2004) 98 *AJIL* 526–45.

Custom, Power and the Power of Rules: International Relations and Customary International Law (Cambridge University Press, 1999).

Caddy, J.F. and L. Garibaldi, 'Apparent changes in the trophic composition of world marine harvests: the perspective from the FAO capture database' (2000) 43 *Ocean & Coastal Management* 615–55.

Cannizzaro, Enzo, 'The role of proportionality in the law of international countermeasures' (2001) 12 *EJIL* 889–916.

Canty, Rachel, 'Limits of Coast Guard authority to board foreign flag vessels on the high seas' (1998) 23 *TMLJ* 123–37.

Carroll, Will H., 'Official duty cases under status of forces agreements: modest guidelines toward a definition' (1970) 12 *United States Air Force JAG Law Review* 284–9.

Carroz, J.E. and A.G. Roche, 'The international policing of high seas fisheries' (1968) 6 *CYBIL* 61–90.

Carson, D., 'Ships, nationality and status' in R. Bernhardt (ed.), *Encyclopedia of Public International Law*, Vol. 4 (Amsterdam: North-Holland, 2000).

Cassese, Antonio, *International Criminal Law* (Oxford University Press, 2003).

Cavenagh, Jennifer (ed.), 'Australian practice in international law 2004' (2006) 25 *AYBIL* 463–696.

Cheng, Bin, 'United Nations resolutions on outer space: "instant" customary international law' (1965) 5 *Indian Journal of International Law* 23–112.

Cho, Sungjoon, 'Breaking the barrier between regionalism and multilateralism: a new perspective on trade regionalism' (2001) 42 *HILJ* 419–65.

Churchill, Robin R., 'The Barents Sea Loophole Agreement: a "coastal state" solution to a straddling stock problem' (1999) 14 *IJMCL* 467–90.

Churchill, R. R., and A. V. Lowe, *The Law of the Sea*, 3rd edn (Manchester University Press, 1999).

Colombos, C. John, *The International Law of the Sea*, 6th edn (London: Longman, 1967).

Conderman, Paul J., 'Jurisdiction' in Dieter Fleck (ed.), *The Handbook of Humanitarian Law in Armed Conflicts* (Oxford University Press, 1995), pp. 99–157.

Connolly, Christopher, '"Smoke on the water": Coast Guard authority to seize foreign vessels beyond the contiguous zone' (1980–81) 13 *NYU Journal of International Law and Policy* 249–334.

Constantinople, George R., 'Towards a new definition of piracy: the *Achille Lauro* incident' (1986) 26 *Virginia Journal of International Law* 723–53.

Crawford, James, 'International law and foreign sovereigns: distinguishing immune transactions' (1983) 54 *BYIL* 75–118.

Crawford, James and Patricia Hyndman, 'Three heresies in the application of the Refugee convention' (1989) 1 *IJRL* 155–79.

Crawford, James and Simon Olleson, 'The nature and forms of international responsibility' in M. Evans (ed.), *International Law*, 2nd edn (Oxford University Press, 2006), pp. 451–77.

Crockett, Clyde H., 'Toward a revision of the international law of piracy' (1976) 26 *DePaul Law Review* 78–100.

Cryer, Robert, 'Implementation of the International Criminal Court Statute in England and Wales' (2002) 51 *ICLQ* 733–44.

Davies, Peter G. G., 'The EC/Canadian fisheries dispute in the northwest Atlantic' (1995) 44 *ICLQ* 927–39.

Deen-Racsmány, Zsuzsanna, 'Lessons of the European arrest warrant for domestic implementation of the obligation to surrender nationals to the International Criminal Court' (2007) 20 *LJIL* 167–91.

Denza, Eileen, *Diplomatic Law: Commentary on the Vienna Convention on Diplomatic Relations*, 3rd edn (Oxford University Press, 2008).

Diamond, Jared, *Collapse: How Societies Choose to Fail or Succeed* (Harmondsworth: Penguin, 2006).

Dickinson, Edwin D., 'Is the crime of piracy obsolete?' (1924–25) 38 *Harvard Law Review* 334–60.

Doswald-Beck, Louise (ed.), *San Remo Manual on International Law Applicable to Armed Conflicts at Sea* (Cambridge University Press, 1995).

Edeson, William, 'The international plan of action on illegal unreported and unregulated fishing: the legal context of a non-legally binding instrument' (2001) 16 *IJMCL* 603–23.

Ellen, Eric, 'Contemporary piracy' (1990–91) 21 *CWILJ* 123–8.

Evans, Malcolm D., 'The law of the sea' in Malcolm Evans (ed.), *International Law*, 2nd edn (Oxford University Press, 2006), pp. 623–55.

Evensen, Jens, 'Aspects of international law relating to modern radio communications' (1965) 115(II) *Recueil des Cours* 477–583.

Fayette, Louise de la, 'The fisheries jurisdiction case (*Spain v. Canada*), Judgment on Jurisdiction of 4 December 1998' (1999) 48 *ICLQ* 664–72.

Fitzmaurice, G. G., 'Some results of the Geneva Conference on the Law of the Sea' (1959) 8 *ICLQ* 73–121.

'The law and procedure of the International Court of Justice 1951–4: treaty interpretation and other treaty points' (1957) 33 *BYIL* 203–93.

Fox, Hazel, 'Restraints on the exercise of jurisdiction by national courts' in Malcolm Evans (ed.), *International Law*, 2nd edn (Oxford University Press, 2006), pp. 361–94.

The Law of State Immunity (Oxford University Press, 2004).

Franck, Thomas M., *Recourse to Force: State Action against Threats and Armed Attacks* (Cambridge University Press, 2002).

French, Jennifer (ed.), 'Australian practice in international law 2003' (2004) 24 *AYBIL* 337–441.

Garlick, Madeline, 'The EU discussions on extraterritorial processing: solution or conundrum?' (2006) 18 *IJRL* 601–29.

Garmon, Tina, 'International law of the sea: reconciling the law of piracy and terrorism in the wake of September 11th' (2002) 27 *TMLJ* 257–75.

Garratt, Justine and Jonathan Chew (eds.), 'Australian practice in international law 2002' (2003) 23 *AYBIL* 289–395.

Garvey, Jack I., 'The international institutional imperative for countering the spread of weapons of mass destruction: assessing the Proliferation Security Initiative' (2005) 10 *JCSL* 125–47.

Giacca, Gilles, 'Clandestini: ou le problème de la politique migratoire en Italie', *New Issues In Refugee Research*, UNHCR Evaluation and Policy Analysis Unit, Working Paper No. 101, March 2004, www.unhcr.org.

Gidel, Gilbert, *Le Droit International Public de la Mer: Le Temps de Paix*, 3 vols. (Paris: Sirey, 1932).

Gil-Bazo, María-Teresa, 'The practice of Mediterranean states in the context of the European Union's justice and home affairs external dimension. The safe third country concept revisited' (2006) 18 *IJRL* 571–600.

Gilmore, William C. (ed.), *Agreement Concerning Co-operation in Suppressing Illicit Maritime and Air Trafficking in Narcotic Drugs and Psychotropic Substances in the Caribbean Area* (London: The Stationery Office, 2005).

'Narcotics interdiction at sea: the 1995 Council of Europe Agreement' (1996) 20 *Marine Policy* 3–14.

'Hot pursuit: the case of *R v. Mills and Others*' (1995) 44 *ICLQ* 949–58.

'Drug trafficking by sea: the 1988 United Nations Convention Against Illicit Traffic in Narcotic Drugs and Psychotropic Substances' (1991) 15 *Marine Policy* 183–92.

'International action against drug trafficking: trends in United Kingdom law and practice' (1990) 24 *International Lawyer* 365–92.

'Narcotics interdiction at sea: US–UK co-operation' (1989) 13 *Marine Policy* 218–30.

'Hot pursuit and constructive presence in Canadian law enforcement' (1988) 12 *Marine Policy* 105–11.

Goodwin-Gill, Guy, *The Refugee in International Law*, 2nd edn (Oxford: Clarendon, 1996).

Gray, Christine D., *International Law and the Use of Force* 2nd edn (Oxford University Press, 2004).

'The British position with regard to the Gulf Conflict (Iran–Iraq): Part 2' (1991) 40 *ICLQ* 464–73.

Grotius, Hugo, *The Freedom of the Seas or the Right which Belongs to the Dutch to Take Part in the East Indian Trade* [translation of *Mare Liberum sive de iure quod batauis competit ad indicana commerici: Dissertatio*], reproduction of 1688 edn (trans. R Magoffin) (New York: Oxford University Press, 1916).

Gualde, Vicenta, 'Suppression of the illicit traffic in narcotic drugs and psychotropic substances on the high seas: Spanish case law' (1996) 4 *SYBIL* 91–106.

Guilfoyle, Douglas, 'Interdicting vessels to enforce the common interest: maritime countermeasures and the use of force' (2007) 56 *ICLQ* 69–82.

'The Proliferation Security Initiative: interdicting vessels in international waters to prevent the spread of weapons of mass destruction?' (2005) 29 *MULR* 733–64.

Halberstam, Malvina, 'Terrorism on the high seas: the *Achille Lauro*, piracy and the IMO convention on maritime safety' (1988) 82 *AJIL* 269–310.

Hanna, Mitchell J., 'Controlling pirate broadcasting' (1977–8) 15 *SDLR* 547–72.

Harris, David, *Cases and Materials on International Law*, 6th edn (London: Sweet & Maxwell, 2004).

Havers, Michael, 'Good fences make good neighbors: a discussion of problems concerning the exercise of jurisdiction' (1983) 17 *International Lawyer* 784–795.

Hawkins, William R., 'Interdict WMD smugglers at sea', US Naval Institute Proceedings, December 2004, www.military.com/NewContent/0%2C13190%2CNI_1204_Sea-P1%2C00.html.

Hayashi, Moritaka, 'Introductory note to the regional cooperation agreement on combating piracy and armed robbery against ships in Asia' (2005) 44 *ILM* 826–8.

Heckmann, Friedrich *et al.*, 'Transatlantic workshop on human smuggling – conference report' (2001) 15 *GILJ* 167–82.

Heintschel von Heinegg, Wolff, 'The Proliferation Security Initiative: security vs freedom of navigation?' (2005) 35 *IYBHR* 181–203.

'The law of armed conflict at sea' in Dieter Fleck (ed.), *The Handbook of Humanitarian Law in Armed Conflicts* (Oxford University Press, 2008), pp. 475–569.

Helton, Arthur C., 'The United States government program of intercepting and forcibly returning Haitian boat people to Haiti: policy implications and prospects' (1992–3) 10 *New York Law School Journal of Human Rights* 325–49.

Higgins, Rosalyn, *The Development of International Law through the Political Organs of the United Nations* (London: Oxford University Press, 1963).

Hollick, Ann L., 'The origins of 200-mile offshore zones' (1977) 71 *AJIL* 494–500.

Hoyle, Mark S. W., 'The Mixed Courts of Egypt 1938–1949' (1988) 3 *Arab Law Quarterly* 83–115.

Hughes, Donna M., 'The "Natasha" trade: the transnational shadow market of trafficking in women' (2000) 53 *Journal of International Affairs* 625–51.

Hughes, Joyce A., 'Flight from Cuba' (1999) 36 *California Western Law Review* 39–75.

Hunnings, N. March, 'Pirate broadcasting in European waters' (1965) 14 *ICLQ* 410–36.

Hyndman, Patricia, 'Refugees under international law with a reference to the concept of asylum' (1986) 60 *ALJ* 148–55.

Jackson, A., 'The Convention on the Conservation and Management of Fishery Resources in the South East Atlantic Ocean, 2001: an introduction' (2002) 17 *IJMCL* 33–77.

Jennings, R. Y., 'The *Caroline* and *McLeod* Cases' (1938) 32 *AJIL* 82–99.

Jennings, Robert and Arthur Watts (eds.), *Oppenheim's International Law: Volume I, Peace*, 9th edn (Harlow: Longman, 1992).

Jiminez Kwast, P., 'Maritime interdiction of weapons of mass destruction in an international legal perspective' (2007) 38 *Netherlands Yearbook of International Law* 163–241.

Joyner, Christopher C., 'On the borderline? Canadian activism in the Grand Banks' in O. Schramm Stokke (ed.), *Governing High Seas Fisheries: The Interplay of Global and Regional Regimes* (Oxford University Press, 2001), pp. 207–33.

Joyner, Daniel H., 'Non-proliferation law and the United Nations system: Resolution 1540 and the limits of the power of the Security Council' (2007) 20 *LJIL* 489–518.

'The Proliferation Security Initiative: nonproliferation, counterproliferation and international law' (2005) 30 *YJIL* 507–48.

'The PSI and international law' (2004) 10 *The Monitor* 7–9.

Kaye, David, 'Adjudicating self-defense: discretion, perception, and the resort to force in international law' (2005-6) 44 *CJTL* 134–84.

Kaye, Stuart, 'The Proliferation Security Initiative in the maritime domain' (2005) 35 *IYBHR* 205–29.

International Fisheries Management (London: Kluwer Law International, 2001).

Keyuan, Zou, 'Enforcing the law of piracy in the South China Sea' (2000) 31 *JMLC* 107–17.

'Issues of public international law relating to the crackdown of piracy in the South China Sea and prospects for regional cooperation' (1999) 3 *SJICL* 524–44.

King, Archibald, 'Further developments concerning jurisdiction over friendly foreign armed forces' (1946) 40 *AJIL* 257–79.

'Jurisdiction over friendly foreign armed forces' (1942) 36 *AJIL* 539–67.

Klein, Natalie, 'The right of visit and the 2005 Protocol on the Suppression of Unlawful Acts against the Safety of Maritime Navigation', (2007) 35 DJILP 287–332.

'Legal limitations on ensuring Australia's maritime security' (2006) 7 *MJIL* 306–38.

Dispute Settlement in the UN Convention on the Law of the Sea (Cambridge University Press, 2005).

Koskenmaki, Riika, 'Legal implications resulting from state failure in light of the case of somalia' (2004) 73 *NJIL* 1–36.

Langewiesche, William, *The Outlaw Sea: Chaos and Crime on the World's Oceans* (London: Granta, 2004).

Lauterpacht, Elihu and Daniel Bethlehem, 'The scope and content of the principle of non-refoulement: opinion' in Erika Feller, Volker Türk and Frances Nicholson (eds.), *Refugee Protection in International Law: UNHCR's Global Consultations on International Protection* (Cambridge University Press, 2003), 87–177.

Lauterpacht, Hersch (ed.), *Oppenheim's International Law: A Treatise: Volume I, Peace*, 8th edn (London: Longman, 1958).

The Development of International Law by the International Court (London: Stevens, 1958).

'Insurrection et piraterie' (1939) 46 *RGDIP* 513.

Lavalle, Roberto, 'A novel, if awkward exercise in international law-making: Security Council Resolution 1540 (28 April 2004)' (2004) 51 *NILR* 413–37.

Lazareff, Serge, *Status of Military Forces under Current International Law* (Leyden: Sijthoff, 1971).

Legomsky, Stephen H., 'The USA and the Caribbean Interdiction Program' (2006) 18 *IJRL* 677–95.

Lenzerini, Frederico, 'Suppressing slavery under customary international law' (2000) 10 *IYBIL* 145–80.

Lepper, Steven J., '*Short v. the Kingdom of the Netherlands*: is it time to renegotiate the NATO Status of Forces Agreement?' (1991) 24 *VJTL* 867–943.

Lévy, Jean-Pierre and Gunnar G. Schram, *United Nations Conference on Straddling Fish Stocks and Highly Migratory Fish Stocks: Selected Documents* (The Hague: Martinus Nijhoff, 1996).

Lowe, Vaughan, 'Jurisdiction' in M. Evans (ed.), *International Law*, 2nd edn (Oxford University Press, 2006), pp. 335–60.

'Self-defence at sea', in W.E. Butler (ed.), *The Non-Use of Force in International Law* (Dordrecht: Martinus Nijhoff, 1989), pp. 185–202.

Lowe, Vaughan and Robin Churchill, 'The International Tribunal for the Law of the Sea: survey for 2001' (2002) 17 *IJMCL* 463–84.

Macdonald, R. St.J., 'The *Nicaragua Case*: new answers to old questions?' (1986) 24 *CYBIL* 127–60.

McDorman, Ted L., 'The role of the Commission on the Limits of the Continental Shelf: a technical body in a political world' (2002) 17 *International Journal of Marine and Coastal Law* 301–24.

McDougal, Myres S., and William T. Burke, *The Public Order of the Oceans*, reissue of 1962 edn (New Haven: New Haven Press, 1987).

McGoldrick, Dominic, 'The extra-territorial application of the International Covenant on Civil and Political Rights' in Menno T. Kamminga and Fons Coomans (eds.), *Extra-territorial Application of Human Rights Treaties* (Oxford: Intersentia, 2004), pp. 41–72.

McLaughlin, Robert, 'United Nations mandated naval interdiction operations in the territorial sea?' (2002) 51 *ICLQ* 249–78.

McNair, Arnold Duncan, *The Law of Treaties* (Oxford: Clarendon, 1961).

'United Kingdom materials on international law 1988' (1988) 59 *BYIL* 421–592.

Marston, Geoffrey (ed.), 'United Kingdom materials on international law 1990' (1990) 61 *BYIL* 464–632.

Masterson, William, *Jurisdiction in Marginal Seas with Special Reference to Smuggling* (New York: Macmillan, 1929).

Matthew, Penelope, 'Australian refugee protection in the wake of the *Tampa*' (2002) 96 *AJIL* 661–76.

Messina, Salvatore, 'Les tribunaux mixtes et les rapports interjurisdictionnels en Égypte' (1932-III) 41 *Recueil des Cours* 367–500.

Meyers, Herman, *The Nationality of Ships* (The Hague: Martinus Nijhoff, 1967).

Molenaar, Erik Jaap, 'Participation, allocation and unregulated fishing: the practice of regional fisheries management organisations' (2003) 18 *IJMCL* 457–80.

'The South Tasman Rise Arrangement of 2000 and other initiatives on management and conservation of orange roughy' (2001) 16 *IJMCL* 77–124.

'The concept of "real interest" and other aspects of co-operation through regional fisheries management mechanisms' (2000) 15 *IJMCL* 475–531.

Mukundan, Pottengal, 'Piracy and armed attacks against vessels today' (2004) 10 *JIML* 308–15.

Nash, Marian, 'Contemporary practice of the United States relating to international law' (1995) 89 *AJIL* 761–71.

Nordquist, Myron H. *et al.* (eds.), *United Nations Convention on the Law of the Sea 1982: A Commentary*, 5 vols. (The Hague: Martinus Nijhoff, 1985–95).

Noyes, John E., 'An introduction to the international law of piracy' (1990) 21 *CWILJ* 105–21.

Noyes, John E. and Brian D. Smith, 'State responsibility and the principle of joint and several liability' (1988) 13 *YJIL* 225–67.

Obokata, Tom, 'Trafficking of human beings as a crime against humanity: some implications for the international legal system' (2005) 54 *ICLQ* 445–58.

O'Connell, D. P. (ed. I. A. Shearer), *The International Law of the Sea*, 2 vols. (Oxford: Clarendon, 1984).

(1970), *International Law*, 2 vols. (London: Stevens & Sons, 1970).

Oda, Shigeru, 'The concept of the contiguous zone' (1962) 11 *ICLQ* 131–53.

Okawa, Phoebe, 'Issues of admissibility and the law on international responsibility', in M. Evans (ed.), *International Law*, 2nd edn (Oxford University Press, 2006), 479–506.

O'Keefe, Roger, 'Universal jurisdiction: clarifying the basic concept' (2004) 2 *JICJ* 735–60.

Orakhelashvili, Alexander, 'The impact of peremptory norms on the interpretation and application of United Nations Security Council resolutions' (2005) 16 *EJIL* 59–88.

Orellana, Marcos A., 'The law on highly migratory fish stocks: ITLOS jurisprudence in context' (2004) 34 *GGULR* 459–95.

Oxman, Bernard H., 'The "Tomimaru" (Japan v. Russian Federation)' (2008) 102 *AJIL* 316–22.

Pallis, Mark, 'Obligations of states towards asylum seekers at sea: interactions and conflicts between legal regimes' (2002) 14 *IJRL* 329–364.

Palmer, Gary W., 'Guarding the coast: alien migrant interdiction operations at sea' (1996–7) 29 *Connecticut Law Review* 1565–85.

Perry, Timothy C., 'Blurring the ocean zones: the effect of the Proliferation Security Initiative on the customary international law of the sea' (2006) 37 *ODIL* 33–53.

Politakis, George P., *Modern Aspects of the Laws of Naval Warfare and Maritime Neutrality* (London: Kegan Paul, 1998).

Potts, Leroy G., 'Global trafficking in human beings: assessing success of the United Nations Protocol to Prevent Trafficking in Persons' (2003) 35 *GWILR* 230–49.

Poulantzas, Nicholas M., *The Right of Hot Pursuit in International Law*, 2nd edn (The Hague: Martinus Nijhoff, 2002).

Priest-Hamilton, Kimberly C., 'Who really should have exercised jurisdiction over the military pilots implicated in the 1998 Italy gondola accident?' (1999–2000) 65 *JALC* 605–35.

Pugh, Michael, 'Europe's boat people: maritime cooperation in the Mediterranean', Institute for Security Studies, Western European Union, Chaillot Paper 41, July 2000, www.iss-eu.org/chaillot/chai41e.pdf.

Quigley, John, 'Complicity in international law: a new direction in the law of state responsibility' (1986) 57 *BYIL* 77–131.

Raab, Dominic, '"Armed attack" after the *Oil Platforms* case' (2004) 17 *LJIL* 719–35.

Randelzhofer, Albrecht, 'Article 2(4)' and 'Article 51' in B. Simma (ed.), *The Charter of the United Nations: A Commentary*, 2nd edn (Oxford University Press, 2002), I, pp. 112–36, 788–806.

Rayfuse, Rosemary, *Non-Flag State Enforcement in High Seas Fisheries* (Leiden: Martinus Nijhoff, 2004).
  'Countermeasures and high seas fisheries enforcement' (2004) 51 *NILR* 41–76.
  'The United Nations Agreement on Straddling and Highly Migratory Fish Stocks as an objective regime: a case of wishful thinking?' (1999) 20 *AYBIL* 253–78.

Reuland, Robert C. F., 'Interference with non-national ships on the high seas: peacetime exceptions to the exclusivity rule of flag state jurisdiction' (1989) 22 *VJTL* 1161–229.

Riddle, Kevin, 'Illegal, unreported, and unregulated fishing: is international cooperation contagious?' (2006) 37 *ODIL* 265–97.

Roach, J. Ashley, 'Proliferation Security Initiative (PSI): countering proliferation by sea' in M. Nordquist *et al.* (eds.), *Recent Developments in the Law of the Sea and China* (Dordrecht: Martinus Nijhoff, 2006), pp. 351–424.

Roach, J. and R. Smith, *United States Responses to Excessive Maritime Claims*, 2nd edn (The Hague: Martinus Nijhoff, 1996).

Roberts, C. M. and J. P. Hawkins, 'Extinction risk in the sea' (1999) 14 *Trends in Ecology & Evolution* 241–6.

Robertson Horace B., Jr, 'The suppression of pirate radio broadcasting: a test case of the international system for control of activities outside national territory' (1982) 45 *Law & Contemporary Problems* 71–101.

Ronzitti, N. 'The crisis of the traditional law regulating international armed conflicts at sea and the need for its revision' in Natalino Ronzitti (ed.), *The Law of Naval Warfare: A Collection of Agreements and Documents with Commentaries* (Dordrecht: Martinus Nijhoff, 1988), pp. 1–58.

Rosenberg, Lory Diana, 'The courts and interception: the United States' interdiction experience and its impact on refugees and asylum seekers' (2003) 17 *GILJ* 199–219.

Rothwell, D., 'The law of the sea and the MV *Tampa* incident: reconciling maritime principles with coastal state sovereignty' (2002) 13 *Public Law Review* 118.

Rouse, Joseph, 'The exercise of criminal jurisdiction under the NATO Status of Forces Agreement' (1957) 51 *AJIL* 29–62.

Rousseau, C., 'Chronique des faits internationaux' (1963) 67 *RGDIP* 118–86.

Rubin, Alfred P., 'Revising the law of piracy' (1990) 21 *CWILJ* 129–37.
   The Law of Piracy (Newport, Rhode Island: Naval War College Press, 1988).
   'The law of piracy' (1986–7) 15 *DJILP* 173–233.

Sartori, Maria, 'The Cuban migration dilemma: an examination of the United States' policy of temporary protection in offshore safe havens' (2001) 15 *GILJ* 319–55.

Schaffer, R. P., 'The singular plight of sea-borne refugees' (1978–80) 8 *AYBIL* 213–34.

Schloenhardt, Andreas, 'Trafficking in migrants in the Asia Pacific: national, regional and international responses' (2001) 5 *SJICL* 696–747.
   'Organised crime and the business of migrant trafficking: an economic analysis' (1999) 32 *Crime, Law and Social Change* 203–33.

Schuck, Edwin, 'Concurrent jurisdiction under the NATO Status of Forces Agreement' (1957) 57 *Columbia Law Review* 355–71.

Schwenk, E., 'Jurisdiction of the receiving state over forces of the sending state under the NATO Status of Forces Agreement' (1972) 6 *International Lawyer* 525.

Scott, Peter (ed.), 'Australian practice in international law 2001' (2002) 22 *AYBIL* 285–380.

Scovazzi, Tullio, 'La tutela della vita umana in mare, con particolare riferimento agli immigrati clandestini diretti verso l'Italia' (2005) 88 *RDI* 76–105.

Sharp, Walter, 'Proliferation Security Initiative: the legacy of Operation Socotora' (2006–7) 16 *TLCP* 991–1028.

Shaw, Malcolm N., *International Law*, 5th edn (Cambridge University Press, 2003).

Shearer, I. A., *Starke's International Law*, 11th edn (London: Butterworth, 1994). 'Problems of jurisdiction and law enforcement against delinquent vessels' (1986) 35 *ICLQ* 320–343.

Siddle, J., 'Anglo-American cooperation in the suppression of drug smuggling' (1982) 31 *ICLQ* 726–47.

Smith, Delbert D., 'Pirate broadcasting' (1967–8) 41 *SCLR* 769–815.

Snee, Joseph M. (ed.), *NATO Agreements on Status: Travaux Préparatoires*, International Law Studies 1961 (Newport, Rhode Island: Naval War College, 1966).

Sohn, Louis, 'International law of the sea and human rights issues' in T. Clingan (ed.), *The Law of the Sea: What Lies Ahead?* (Honolulu: Law of the Sea Institute, 1988), p. 51.

Song, Y.-H., 'The US-led Proliferation Security Initiative and UNCLOS: legality, implementation, and an assessment' (2007) 38 *ODIL* 101–45.

Soons, Alfred H.A., 'A "new" exception to the freedom of the high seas: the authority of the UN Security Council' in Terry D. Gill and Wybo P. Heere (eds.), *Reflections on Principles and Practice of International Law: Essays in Honour of Leo J. Bouchez* (The Hague: Martinus Nijhoff, 2000), pp. 205–21.

Spadi, Fabio, 'Bolstering the Proliferation Security Initiative at sea: a comparative analysis of ship-boarding as a bilateral and multilateral implementing mechanism' (2006) 75 *NJIL* 249–78.

Stanger, Roland J., *Criminal Jurisdiction over Visiting Armed Forces*, International Law Studies 1957–1958 (Newport, Rhode Island: Naval War College, 1965).

Stern, Brigitte, 'L'extraterritorialité revisitée' (1992) 38 *Annuaire Français de Droit International* 239–313.

Stiles, Ethan C., 'Reforming current international law to combat modern sea piracy' (2004) 27 *Suffolk Transnational Law Review* 299–326.

Sur, Serge, 'La résolution 1540 du conseil de sécurité (28 avril 2004): entre la prolifération des armes de destruction massive, le terrorisme et les acteurs non étatiques' (2004) 108 *RGDIP* 855–82.

Szaz, Paul C., 'The Security Council starts legislating' (2002) 96 *AJIL* 901–5.

Talamo, Javier, 'The Cuban Adjustment Act: a law under siege?' (2002) 8 *ILSA Journal of International and Comparative Law* 707–24.

Talmon, Stefan, 'The Security Council as world legislature' (2005) 99 *AJIL* 175–93.

Tams, Christian J., *Enforcing Obligations Erga Omnes in International Law* (Cambridge University Press, 2005).

Thomas, I, 'L'affaire du "Monica"' (2002) 106 *RGDIP* 391.

Timm, Donald A., 'Visiting forces in Korea' in Dieter Fleck (ed.), *The Handbook of Humanitarian Law in Armed Conflicts* (Oxford University Press, 1995), pp. 443–69.

Tomonori, Mizushima, 'The individual as beneficiary of state immunity: problems of the attribution of *ultra vires* conduct' (2001) 29 *DJILP* 261–87.

Treves, Tullio, 'Flags of convenience before the Law of the Sea Tribunal' (2004–5) 6 *SDILJ* 181–9.

United Nations Office on Drugs, and Crime, *Practical Guide for Competent National Authorities under Article 17 of the United Nations Convention against Illicit Traffic in Narcotic Drugs and Psychotropic Substances of 1988* (New York: UN, 2003).

Vagg, Jon, 'Rough seas? Contemporary piracy in South East Asia' (1995) 35 *British Journal of Criminology* 63–80.

Valencia, Mark J., *The Proliferation Security Initiative: Making Waves in Asia* (Oxford: Routledge, 2005).

'Piracy and politics in southeast Asia' in Derek Johnson and Mark J. Valencia, *Piracy in Southeast Asia: Status, Issues and Responses* (Singapore: Institute of Southeast Asian Studies, 2005), pp. 103–21.

Van Panhuys, H. F. and Menno J. Van Emde Boas, 'Legal aspects of pirate broadcasting: a Dutch approach' (1966) 60 *AJIL* 303–41.

Vattel, E. de, (trans. C. Fenwick), *The Law of Nations*, reproduction and translation of 1758 edn, vol. III (Washington, D.C.: Carnegie Institution, 1916).

Verdier, Pierre-Hugues, '*R v. Hape*' (2008) 102 *AJIL* 143–8.

Warner-Kramer, Deirdre, 'Control begins at home: tackling flags of convenience and IUU fishing' (2004) 34 *GGULR* 497–529.

Watkins, E., 'Facing the terrorist threat in the Malacca Strait', *Terrorism Monitor*, 6 May 2004, 8, www.jamestown.org/publications_details. php?volume_id=400&issue_id=2945&Article_id=236671.

Watts, A. D., 'The protection of merchant ships' (1957) 33 *BYIL* 52–84.

Wedgwood, R., 'The fall of Saddam Hussein: Security Council mandates and preemptive self-defense' (2003) 97 *AJIL* 576–85.

Weiss, Edith Brown, 'Invoking state responsibility in the twenty-first century' (2002) 96 *AJIL* 798–816.

Wendel, Philipp, *State Responsibility for Interferences with the Freedom of Navigation in Public International Law* (Berlin: Springer, 2007).

White, Michael, '*Tampa* incident: shipping, international and maritime legal issues' (2004) 78 *ALJ* 101–13.

'*Tampa* incident: some subsequent legal issues' (2004) 78 *ALJ* 249.

'Australian maritime law update: 2006 – Part I' (2007) 38 *JMLC* 293–308.

White, Michael and Craig Forrest, 'Australian maritime law update: 2005' (2006) 37 *JMLC* 299–329.

White, Michael and Stephen Knight, 'Illegal fishing in Australian waters: the use of UNCLOS by Australian courts' (2005) 11 *JIML* 110–25.

Whomersley, C.A., 'Some reflections on the immunity of individuals for official acts' (1992) 41 *ICLQ* 848–58.

Wickremasinghe, Chanaka, 'Immunity of officials and international organisations' in M. Evans (ed.), *International Law*, 2nd edn (Oxford University Press, 2006), pp. 395–421.

Wijewardane, D., 'Criminal jurisdiction over visiting forces with special reference to international forces' (1965–6) 41 *BYIL* 122–97.

Wilde, Ralph, 'Triggering state obligations extraterritorially: the spatial test in certain human rights treaties' (2007) 40 *Israel Law Review* 503–26.

Wolff, C., *Jus gentium methodo scientifica pertractatum*, reproduction of 1764 edn, (trans. J. Drake) vol. II (Oxford: Clarendon Press, 1934).

Woodliffe, J.C., 'Some legal aspects of pirate broadcasting in the North Sea' (1965) 12 *NILR* 365–84.

Yturriaga, José A. de, *The International Regime of Fisheries: From UNCLOS 1982 to the Presential Sea* (The Hague: Martinus Nijhoff, 1997).

Zanker, M., 'MV *Tampa*: some law of the sea aspects', paper presented to the Maritime Law Association of Australia and New Zealand, Melbourne, 4 October 2002, www.mlaanz.org/docs/Mark%20Zanker.doc.

Zhang, Sheldon and Ko-lin Chin, 'Enter the dragon: inside Chinese human smuggling organizations' (2002) 40 *Criminology* 737–68.

SELECTED NATIONAL LEGISLATION, PROCLAMATIONS AND SUBORDINATE INSTRUMENTS

Australia

Border Protection (Validation and Enforcement Powers) Act 2001 (Cth) (No. 126 of 2001).

Customs Act 1901 (Cth) (No. 6 of 1901).

Fisheries Legislation Amendment Act (No 1) 1999 (Cth) (No. 143 of 1999).

Fisheries Management Act 1991 (Cth) (No. 162 of 1991).

Interpretation Act 1901 (Cth) (No. 2 of 1901).

Migration Act 1958 (Cth) (No. 62 of 1958).

Migration Amendment (Excision from Migration Zone) Act 2001 (Cth) (No. 127 of 2001).

Migration Amendment (Excision from Migration Zone)(Consequential Provisions) Act 2001 (Cth) (No. 128 of 2001).

Wireless Telegraphy Act 1967 (Cth) (No. 59 of 1967).

Bahamas

Archipelagic Waters and Maritime Jurisdiction Act 1993 (No. 37 of 1993).

Barbados

Barbados Territorial Waters Act 1979, CAP 386.

Belize

Maritime Areas Act 1992, CAP 11.

Canada

An Act to amend the Coastal Fisheries Act, Statutes of Canada, 1994, c.14.

Grenada

Grenada Territorial Waters Act, No. 17 of 1978.

Jamaica

Maritime Drug Trafficking (Suppression) Act 1998 (Act No. 1 of 1998).

Saint Kitts and Nevis

The Maritime Areas Act (Act No. 3 of 1984).

Saint Lucia

The Maritime Areas Act (Act No. 6 of 1984).

United Kingdom

Broadcasting Act 1990 (c. 42).
The Marine &c, Broadcasting (Offences) Act 1967 (c. 41).
The Marine &c, Broadcasting (Offences) (Prescribed Areas of the High Seas)
    Order 1990 (Statutory Instruments 1990, No. 2503).
Visiting Forces Act (UK), 1952 (c 67).

United States

8 USC §§ 1185 and 1324 ('Travel control of citizens and aliens' and 'Bringing
    in and harboring certain aliens').
14 USC ('Coast Guard and Maritime Transportation Act of 2006').
16 USC §§3371–3378 ('Captive Wildlife Safety Act' and 'Lacey Act
    Amendments of 1981').
18 USC §1585 ('Seizure, detention, transportation or sale of slaves').
46 USC §2304 ('Duty to provide assistance at sea').
46 USCA §70502(c) ('Maritime Drug Law Enforcement Act', prior to 6 October
    2006 enacted as 46 App. USCA §1903(c)).
Executive Order 12,324, 46 Fed. Reg. 48,109 (1981).
Executive Order 12807 of May 23, 1992, 57 Fed. Reg. 23,133 (1992).

Presidential Proclamation 4865 of September 29, 1981 ('High Seas Interdiction of Illegal Aliens'), 46 FR 48107.

Proclamation by the President with Respect to Coastal Fisheries in Respect of Certain Areas of the High Seas (Proclamation No. 2668), (1946) 40 AJIL Supp. 46.

Proclamation by the President with Respect to the Natural Resources of the Subsoil and Sea Bed of the Continental Shelf (Proclamation No. 2667), (1946) 40 AJIL Supp. 45.

SELECT LIST OF OFFICIAL REPORTS AND PAPERS

(RFMO annual reports and UNSCR 1540 Committee reports are available on the websites below.)

Australia, Senate of Australia, *Senate Select Committee for an Inquiry into a Certain Maritime Incident: Report* (Commonwealth of Australia, Canberra, 2002), www.aph.gov.au/ senate/committee/maritime_incident_ctte/ report/report.pdf.

Australian Institute of Criminology and United Nations Interregional Crime and Justice Research Institute, 'Global Programme Against Trafficking in Human Beings – Rapid Assessment: Human Smuggling and Trafficking from the Philippines', Tenth United Nations Congress on the Prevention of Crime and the Treatment of Offenders, Vienna, Austria, 10–17 April 2000, UN Doc. A/CONF.187/CRP. 1.

International Maritime Organization, Legal Committee, 90th Session, Summary Record of Meeting, 18–29 April 2005, IMO Doc. LEG 90/15 (9 May 2005) (final preparatory work for a diplomatic conference on the revision of the SUA treaties).

United Nations Conference on the Law of the Sea, *Official Records, Vol. IV: Second Committee (High Seas: General Régime), Geneva 24 February – 27 April 1958* (Summary Records of Meetings), UN Doc. A/CONF.13/40.

United Nations Economic and Social Council, *Official Records of the United Nations Conference for the Adoption of a Convention against Illicit Traffic in Narcotic Drugs and Psychotropic Substances, Vienna, 25 November–20 December 1988*, vol. II (Summary Records of Meetings of the Committees of the Whole, Committee II), UN Doc. E/CONF.82/C.2/.

United States of America, Department of Defense, *Maritime Claims Reference Manual* (June 2005), www.dtic.mil/whs/directives/corres/html/20051m. htm.

United States of America, National Oceanic and Atmospheric Administration, 'Report of the Secretary of Commerce to the Congress of the United States Concerning US Actions Taken on Foreign Large-Scale High Seas Driftnet Fishing', 2004, 2005, 2006 and 2007 (copies on file with author).

United States of America, State Department, *Trafficking in Persons Report* (2004), www.state.gov/g/tip.

SELECT LIST OF COMMONLY REFERRED TO WEBSITES

Australasian Legal Information Institute, www.austlii.edu.au
Australian Fisheries Management Authority, www.afma.gov.au
BBC News, http://news.bbc.co.uk
Caribbean Community Secretariat, CARICOM Law, www.caricomlaw.org/
    laws.php
Chatham House (Royal Institute of International Affairs), www.chathamhouse.
    org.uk
CNN News, www.cnn.com
Commission for the Conservation of Antarctic Marine Living Resources,
    www.ccamlr.org
Conference of Parties to the Bering Sea Convention, www.afsc.noaa.gov/
    refm/cbs
Council of Europe, www.coe.int
Food and Agriculture Organization of the United Nations, www.fao.org
Frontex, www.frontex.europa.eu
International Maritime Organization, www.imo.org
International Maritime Organization, Maritime Safety Committee, Circulars
    on Acts of Piracy and Armed Robbery against Ships, www.imo.org/
    Circulars/mainframe.asp?topic_id=334
International Tribunal for the Law of the Sea, www.itlos.org
Migration News, migration.ucdavis.edu/mn
North Atlantic Fisheries Organization, www.nafo.int/fisheries/frames/
    regulations.html
North East Atlantic Fisheries Commission, www.neafc.org
North Pacific Anadromous Fish Commission, www.npafc.org
Office of the United Nations High Commissioner for Refugees, www.
    unhcr.org
South East Atlantic Fisheries Organisation, www.seafo.org
United Nations Division for Ocean Affairs and the Law of the Sea, www.
    un.org/Depts/los/index.htm
United Nations Office on Drug and Crime, www.unodc.org
United Nations Security Council, 1540 Committee, National Reports, http://
    disarmament2.un.org/Committee1540/report.html
United States of America, Central Intelligence Agency, CIA *World Factbook*,
    www.cia.gov/library/publications/index.html
United States of America, Coast Guard, Office of Law Enforcement: www.
    uscg.mil/hq/g-o/g-opl/
United States of America, The White House, www.whitehouse.gov
Western and Central Pacific Fisheries Commission, www.wcpfc.int

Index

CAMBRIDGE STUDIES IN INTERNATIONAL AND COMPARATIVE LAW

Books in the series

Unjust Enrichment: A Study of Private Law and Public Values
Hanoch Dagan

Religious Liberty and International Law in Europe
Malcolm D. Evans

Ethics and Authority in International Law
Alfred P. Rubin

Sovereignty over Natural Resources: Balancing Rights and Duties
Nico Schrijver

The Polar Regions and the Development of International Law
Donald R. Rothwell

Fragmentation and the International Relations of Micro-States: Self-determination and Statehood
Jorri Duursma

Principles of the Institutional Law of International Organizations
C. F. Amerasinghe